'As Their Natural Resources Fail'

Frank Tough

'As Their Natural Resources Fail': Native Peoples and the Economic History of Northern Manitoba, 1870-1930

UBCPress / Vancouver

ISBN 0-7748-0531-5 (hard cover)
ISBN 0-7748-0571-4 (paperback)

Canadian Cataloguing in Publication Data

Tough, Frank, 1952-
  As their natural resources fail

  Includes bibliographical references and index.
  ISBN 0-7748-0531-5 (bound)
  ISBN 0-7748-0571-4 (pbk.)

  1. Native peoples – Manitoba, Northern – Economic conditions.* 2. Native peoples – Manitoba, Northern – History.* 3. Manitoba – Economic conditions – 1870- * I. Title.

E78.M25T68 1995   330.97127'102'08997   C95-910799-1

This book has been published with the help of a grant from the Social Sciences Federation of Canada, using funds provided by the Social Sciences and Humanities Research Council of Canada.

UBC Press gratefully acknowledges the ongoing support to its publishing program from the Canada Council, the Province of British Columbia Cultural Services Branch, and the Department of Communications of the Government of Canada.

Printed in Canada by Friesens
Typeset in Stone by Irma Rodriguez
Cartographer: Eric Leinberger
Proofreader: Carolyn Bateman

Cover and frontispiece illustrations: 'At the Portage' and 'York Factory – Arrival,' wood cuts which originally appeared in Volume 1 of George Munro Grant's *Picturesque Canada: The Country as It Was and Is* (Toronto: Belden Bros. 1882).

UBC Press
University of British Columbia
6344 Memorial Road
Vancouver, BC V6T 1Z2
(604) 822-3259
Fax: 1-800-668-0821
E-mail: orders@ubcpress.ubc.ca

All considered it seems to be in the best ultimate interests of these Indians to remain in a country with which if left alone, they seem sufficiently well satisfied and to await its opening up, and then as their natural resources fail them turn to various industrial pursuits without the disadvantage of too great competition in the labour market, which will gradually be brought within their reach.

– J.D. McLean, Secretary, Department of Indian Affairs, Ottawa, 9 January 1902

It is not so much what the white man uses as what he destroys that makes the difference now.

– Chief Councillor, Berens River Band, 12 July 1890

Contents

Illustrations, Figures, and Tables

Tables

Foreword

Mary Ellen Turpel-Lafond

'As Their Natural Resources Fail' is a crucial book for anyone interested in the relationships between past and present in Aboriginal Canada. Frank Tough has written a book based on his many years of study and research of northern Manitoba society during its formative period from 1870 to 1930. This work demystifies stereotypes about Aboriginal peoples and their contribution to the development of western Canada. Tough weaves economic, political, social, cultural and legal history in a close fashion, providing the most textured and persuasive account of the transitions of the period.

From the introduction of trade with the Hudson's Bay Company and the rise of mission economies and mission life in northern Manitoba, to the transition from mercantile relations with the Company to treaty and scrip relations with the Dominion of Canada and the new province of Manitoba, the text underscores the dynamic nature of Aboriginal society in the North. It begins with the moment of great political tension – the conflict in Aboriginal communities over the surrender of the Hudson's Bay Company charter to the Dominion on very favourable terms for the Company and the ongoing struggle to assert and gain recognition for competing First Nations and Metis land rights in the northern region of Manitoba. In a sense, Tough's book is a riveting exploration of the very basic question of how the Aboriginal claim to Rupertsland was ultimately treated as less important than the Hudson Bay Company's claim, particularly when, from the outset, the Imperial and Dominion governments undertook specific legal and political responsibilities for honourable dealings with Aboriginal peoples.

The brilliance of this book lies in its economic analysis of Company-Aboriginal and Crown-Aboriginal relations, as this economic context is clearly central to any full understanding of the period. It also provides a compelling human story of this region of Canada. For example, Tough takes specific families, such as the Swanson family from Norway House, and relates the story of their scrip acquisition and how they were defrauded of this small recognition of their land interest in the North. The scrip process has always been fairly arcane and inaccessible to non-experts in the literature – or still, full of political rhetoric without any economic detail. *'As Their Natural Resources Fail'* is a solid resource in this regard, as it presents the story in well-researched, fascinating terms which will assist those in both academic and non-academic environments in understanding the grave injustices experienced by the Metis in western Canada. His analysis of treaty-making is likewise informative, richly textured, and compelling.

What this book provides better than any work I have read regarding this region is a careful picture of the diversity of northern society, economic transition, and transactions in specific communities in relation to various sectors of the changing northern economy of the period.

In a period when First Nations treaty land promises are still outstanding with the governments of Canada and Manitoba, and Metis land claims and grievances are before the courts, Tough's book is timely and valuable. It connects these current claims and conflicts to an economic history of northern Manitoba which reveals both sophistication on the part of Aboriginal participants and the continuation of grave injustice against them in their relations with government.

11 December 1995
Asimakaniseekan Askiy Reserve
Saskatchewan

Acknowledgments

I first sojourned in northern Manitoba in the summer of 1975 and since then I have expended much energy trying to figure out the relationship between past and present in that region. Although my studies have not attempted to directly connect present conditions to historical knowledge, I feel that some gaps have been filled. Prior to experiencing northern Manitoba, John Ryan, from the Department of Geography at the University of Winnipeg, encouraged an interest in economic geography. Russ Rothney's study on the fur trade provided me with an entry into this particular mercantile economy, which hitherto lacked the appeal that other parts of the world held for me.[1] Subsequently, Arthur J. Ray's *Indians in the Fur Trade* showed that the problems of mercantile underdevelopment, that is the fur trade, could be studied from the perspective of historical geography.[2]

In some respects, this present study indicates a culmination of my graduate research on northern Manitoba. My M.A. thesis, 'Manitoba Commercial Fisheries: A Study in Development,' generated no real intellectual interest at McGill University; nonetheless, it affirmed to me the usefulness of a historical geographical approach to a staple industry and indicated the important presence that Natives held in economic life. It was also clear that a focus on the economic history of Native people was both viable and needed. Although distant from northern Manitoba, I found an environment very conducive for historical geography at York University. Moreover, the encouragement I received there to test concepts empirically, rather than pursuing theory through a series of a priori assertions, was welcomed. Skip Ray, John Warkentin, Don Freeman, Conrad Heidenreich, and Hartwell Bowsfield directed course work or supervised my research. My experience at York was entirely positive.

The completion of my Ph.D. dissertation at York did not end my research on northern Manitoba. I made extensive revisions and in this present study greatly reduced the number of endnotes, quantitative data, and examples from the original dissertation. Some issues have been researched in greater detail, and the present study has benefited from a more sophisticated discussion of Aboriginal and treaty rights. Peter Goheen, Gerald Friesen, and Wayne Moodie read the manuscript with a view to its reorganization for publication. I appreciate the advice of these scholars. If more details are desired, the reader should consult my graduate research and other publications concerning northern Manitoba.[3]

The research and publication of this book received assistance. My Ph.D. was supported by a Social Science and Humanities Research Council of Canada fellowship. The Office of Research Services, University of Saskatchewan, provided a manuscript preparation and subvention grants. The two reviewers from the Social Science Federation gave very useful comments on the manuscript.

Leung Ying Ping entered the manuscript. Vivienne Beisel proofread an early version of the manuscript and Camilla Augustus created the index. The figures were drafted by Eric Leinberger, Department of Geography, University of British Columbia, and Irma Rodriguez of Artegraphica Design. The shift from manuscript to book was greatly facilitated by Laura Macleod's advice and patience, and editorial assistance from Holly Keller-Brohman.

Studies such as this are absolutely dependent upon research libraries and archives. The dedication by the staff of libraries and archives is much appreciated, especially those individuals who are willing to make an extra effort to assist a researcher. In particular, the staff of the National Archives of Canada, the Hudson's Bay Company Archives, the Public Archives of Manitoba, and the United Church of Canada Archives have been very helpful. Shirlee Anne Smith, the former Keeper of the Hudson's Bay Company Archives, was genuinely supportive of the interests of young researchers. I also found Michele Fitzgerald's academic training as an archivist and vast knowledge of the provincial government records extremely useful when dealing with the materials from the Provincial Archives of Manitoba. I feel very fortunate to have worked in archives when exchanges between archivists and researchers were still possible. Bureaucratization of archives, budget rigidities, and the 'legalization' of access to information has created an environment far less conducive to research. In one particular case, 'access' regulations are so discretionary that the tradition of availability of government records under the control of publicly funded archives has been seriously thwarted.

Along with the materials for doing research, archives provide a setting for researchers to informally share information and ideas. In particular,

Keith Ralston was a good archives companion. Numerous conversations with Mary Ellen Turpel-Lafond, Peter Usher, Victor Lywtyn, Dianne Newell, and Carl Beal have helped me understand Native history.

The Department of Native Studies at the University of Saskatchewan has encouraged the pursuit of this type of research. Colleagues, visitors, staff, instructors, and students have created a particular intellectual environment around the department. A unique and interesting dialectic exists between archival sources, upon which my research is especially reliant, and the politics of contemporary Aboriginal concerns. Past and present colleagues and students from the department – Howard Adams, F. Laurie Barron, Ron Bourgeault, Maria Campbell, Leah Dorion, Kim Fraser, Larry Gauthier, Cheryl Holst, Peter Kulchyski, Ron Laliberte, Tony Lussier, Peggy Martin-McQuire, Jennifer McKillop, Miriam McNab, Trish Monture-OKanee, Maryanne Morrison, Laurie Meijer-Drees, Kathy Nelson, Rodolfo Pino, Charlotte Ross, Jack Smith, Winona Stevenson, John Thornton, and Jim Waldram – have been a source of enlightenment and encouragement.

This book would not have been possible without the understanding and support of my wife, Amy Lam.

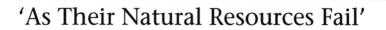

'As Their Natural Resources Fail'

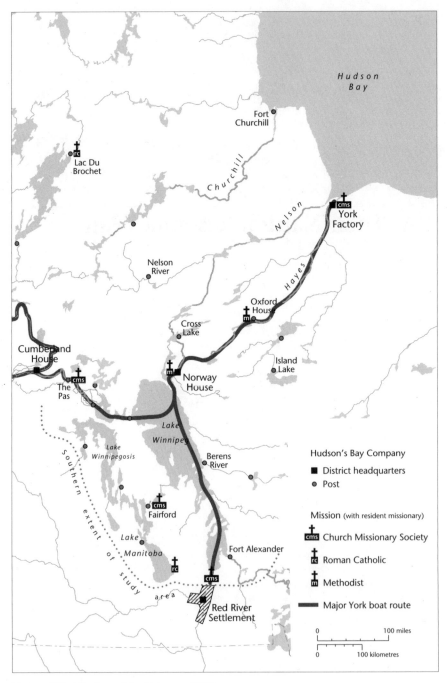

Figure I.1   Northern Manitoba, ca. 1869

Introduction

Northern Manitoba in 1870 might be best described as a diverse geography of varying cultural and physical landscapes. Resources, terrain, and historical relations combine to create a number of small regions. A brief description of the cultural geography and a survey of the resources used by Native peoples will assist the reader. Figure I.1 indicates the study region and the main communities involved. Generally, I have used place names that were in use at the time. For example, the present day location of the Cree community of Brochet, at the top end of Reindeer Lake, was once known as Lac du Brochet, a Hudson's Bay Company (HBC) post.

In the far north, the tundra and transitional forest were occupied by the Chipewyan-Dene and the Inuit. Inuit from the coast camped at Fort Churchill and the inland Caribou-Inuit made occasional visits to this post. The barren ground caribou herds also supported the *Sayisedene* (Tadoule Lake) and *Hotel-nade dene* (Lac du Brochet). This area was a particularly good source for marten, the main high-valued furs. Arctic char was the important fish. This region is drained by the Churchill and Seal rivers. Fort Churchill and Lac du Brochet (also known as Reindeer Lake and Deers Lake) were the main European posts.

West of the Nelson River, on the Churchill River system, is a region occupied by several bands of Rocky Cree or Westwoods Cree (*Ne-hiyawak*). This area had the usual resources associated with the boreal forest – fish, game, and fur-bearing animals. Beaver and mink population densities were high here. The HBC maintained posts at Pelican Narrows and Nelson River.

South and east of the Rocky Cree were the Swampy Cree. Swampy Cree bands were found along the Saskatchewan River from Cumberland House through to Lake Winnipeg and from northeastern Manitoba to York Factory. The Swampy Cree bands that traded into Norway House, Cross Lake, Oxford House, Split Lake, and York Factory and the mixed Oji-Cree bands at Island Lake and Gods Lake made use of game (woodland caribou and moose), freshwater fish (sturgeon, whitefish, lake trout, northern pike, and pickerel), and fur bearers (beaver, mink, and muskrat). On the Hudson Bay coast, waterfowl (geese, in particular) were an important resource for both Indians and traders. The Hayes River/Nelson River/Saskatchewan River was a major corridor during the fur trade. The Swampy Cree bands of Grand Rapids, Cedar Lake, Moose Lake, The Pas, and Cumberland House were able to exploit the resource-rich wetlands of the lower Saskatchewan River, where muskrat and waterfowl were normally abundant. Sturgeon could also be found in good number on this waterway.

The southern areas of this study region include the Lake Winnipeg basin and the Interlake. Most of the bands in this region are grouped together as the Lake Winnipeg Saulteaux, but those bands on the southwestern periphery of the study area (Pine Creek, Waterhen, Crane River, Ebb and Flow, and Lake Manitoba, Sandy Bay) are predominately Ojibwa that had seasonally made use of the plains to the west of the study region. For the Saulteaux in this region, Lake Winnipeg was incredibly rich in whitefish, pickerel, and sturgeon. Bands such as Poplar River, Berens River, and Fort Alexander were located at important fisheries. In the Interlake, the boreal forest gives way to mixed woods and broad-leaf forests. Moose and white-tailed deer are the main game animals here and mink, beaver, and muskrat are the main fur bearers. On the southern edge of the study region a large band of Ojibwa had settled on the banks of the Red River in the parish of St. Peters.

Indian camp at Doghead, Lake Winnipeg, 1884 (NAC, PA-38064)

The vast cultural landscape was occupied predominantly, but not exclusively, by Indians in 1870. A number of Europeans lived at posts and missions, although many resided at various places throughout Rupertsland for much of their adult lives. More numerous than the Europeans were the Natives of the land with mixed blood. At each post, Halfbreeds or Metis were an integral part of the society that had been developing for two hundred years. These Mixedblood families resided in or around the larger posts and worked in a variety of occupations. The boats that moved HBC goods and furs across Rupertsland were worked predominantly by the Metis and Halfbreeds. However, the core of the Metis nation was located just to the south of the study region, at the Red River parishes. The reassignment of HBC-contract employees, the movement of boatmen, and the retirement to Red River of Company officers and servants meant that individuals moved around Rupertsland, and a back-and-forth movement from northern posts to the Red River core of fur trade society was common. These connections continued after 1870, but with the demise of the water-based transport system, many northern communities became isolated.

These regional cultural patterns and the traditional economies had developed out of indigenous landscapes and some two hundred years of the mercantile fur trade. External forces would initiate changes and responses. The changes that occurred to the geography of northern Manitoba are the subject of this book. The pressures of mercantile domination were reflected in political discourse, especially at Red River during the upheaval of 1869-70. In February 1870, an important debate took place amongst the delegates of the Convention of Forty, the forerunner of the second provisional government that had formed to represent the interests and aspirations of the people of the Red River settlement. Some of the details of the debate provide an interesting reference point for the study of northern Manitoba after 1870. The debate accurately reflected the constraints that a mercantile economy had placed upon Native peoples, and some delegates were aware that the future of Rupertsland had been usurped by the surrender of the Hudson's Bay Company charter. Many were suspicious of the deal that had been made between the London managers of the HBC and the Canadian government. However, two contentious issues severely split the unity of the convention: the future political status of the Red River communities in the Canadian 'federation' and the advantageous terms that the HBC had received with the Deed of Surrender. On both these issues, Louis Riel's resolutions were narrowly defeated. Although the status of Manitoba in the Canadian federation has been much debated by academics, the issue of the HBC charter has not received much attention. Yet the debate about the benefits that the HBC were about to receive accurately reflected the political economy of mercantilism.

On the question of provincial or territorial status for Rupertsland, which would determine jurisdiction or control over land and resources, Metis leader Louis Riel was opposed by the country-born spokesman James Ross. Ross argued that Rupertsland should enter confederation as a territory with special rights, since the colony lacked the financial resources of the other Canadian colonies, which 'entered as full grown men and having everything' and 'we have never had the right of self-government in this Territory at all, and the bound from that to being a Territory, in the form in which we want it is very great one.'[1] Ross went on to argue that provincial status was an even greater step. Riel was better informed about the provisions of the British North America Act of 1867 and stated that 'I have ample confidence in the good sense of our people for managing all matters wisely.'[2] On this point, Riel expressed a common premise for those aspiring for self-government. Riel's brilliance was in seeing the importance of land to effective self-government, in a society in which land use was essentially based on free access and common property. He stated: 'This land question, and that of our means of raising money, constitute perhaps the principal points in the whole provincial arrangement.'[3]

Ross had a pragmatic understanding of the limitations that mercantilism had placed on political and economic development. From a contemporary view, Ross's objections to the demand for a more mature political structure were influenced by the underdevelopment that existed at Red River in 1869-70. Hence, he saw Riel's plans as a big jump – responsibility without experience. Riel was concerned about the future development of the country, and he correctly saw that land ownership was the key to the future. The gap between experience and needs created this sort of dilemma. But then, as now, many societies on the periphery of industrial capitalism would experience the anti-colonialism/neo-colonialism dilemma. Riel's assertion that land was 'our means to raise money' would seem to have been an appeal to the class interests of the convention's delegates. By anticipating land sales as a source of wealth, Riel was indicating a means to develop the Red River settlement. Thus for the Metis at Red River, the debate about the future was not a question of defending a traditional economy against commercialization, but a problem of trying to determine who would benefit from the pending changes. Perhaps Riel's vision of a Metis state financed by land sales to outsiders did not anticipate the problems of commercializing land or the fact that the finances of that state would be dependent upon more and more immigrants.

Riel pleaded with the delegates to take a position against the claim of the Hudson's Bay Company and the arrangements that had been made for surrendering Rupertsland. He believed that the Company had received too much land under the terms of the Deed of Surrender, and he argued that 'we must bear in mind that the public interest must be above those of Company.'[4] His opposition to the generous agreement was a renewal of the Metis struggle against HBC rule. Moreover he stated: 'Again, on a late occasion they tried to sell us. There never was a parallel case. A Company of strangers, living beyond the ocean, had the audacity to attempt to sell the people of the soil. Instead of being "the Honourable" Company, as they were usually termed, they ought to be stigmatized with the prefix "shameful" ... To serve their interests and purposes, they endeavoured to subvert ours.'[5] Riel connected the sale of the land with the sale of the people, and he portrayed the HBC as an absentee landlord. A fundamental antagonism existed. This demand split the convention, and since delegates voted largely on ethnic lines, he was unable to get even a bare majority of the delegates to support a resolution opposing the Deed of Surrender. The convention did not include the demand for a cancellation of the deal with the HBC as part of the list of rights.

Riel's argument was subtly challenged when the chairman of the convention, Judge John Black, reminded the delegates of the advantage of the Company's paternalistic credit system:

> I have but to ask every one of you to say from your own experience whether the Hudson's Bay Company in this country can be fairly described ... as a Company who with a father's hand have [*sic*] led and often fed you on many occasions? ... yet the Company may under the smart of such fearful experience, draw consolation from the thought, that even if it should be so, it will not be the first time in the history of the world that the best of friends have been forgotten, and the most bountiful and generous of benefactors had been abased.[6]

By creating the image of 'a father's hand,' Judge Black had conveyed the essence of HBC paternalism. Paradoxically, the dependence that the Company had created through its system of trade, based on paternalistic relations, became a reason, according to the convention's chairman, for not opposing the deal that had provided new privileges for the Company. This argument, drawn from the daily experiences of producing for a mercantile fur trade, influenced the moderate French-speaking delegates. When challenged by Riel, Charles Nolin defended his vote: 'While there are some things for which we blame the Company, there is a good deal for which we must thank them. I do not exculpate the Company altogether, but I say that in time of need we have often been indebted to them for assistance and kindness.'[7] The Company's 'kindness' and 'indebtedness' were basic to the relations between the Company and Native people. Although it is now academic vogue to argue that Natives were active participants in history and that the Company was a benign entity, an entrenched paternalism influenced the actions of the Convention of Forty. The issue of HBC compensation was not a matter of Metis resentment, but it was central to the question of the distribution of wealth for the post-1870 society that was to emerge from the transfer of Rupertsland. It is hard to imagine what effect a unified opposition to the Deed of Surrender by the delegates representing the population at Red River would have had on negotiations in Ottawa. In any event, the Deed of Surrender was protected by Section 34 of the Manitoba Act, which, in turn, became part of the Constitution through the BNA Act of 1871.

Two claims existed to Rupertsland in 1869, an Aboriginal claim, based on possession, inherent rights, and the Royal Proclamation of 1763, and a mercantile property claim based on the Hudson's Bay Company Charter of 1670. The imperial authorities were aware of these two conflicting claims.[8] The extent of the Company's control over Rupertsland could be disputed, however, since the Company's claim received higher priority, and, in truth, the Company obtained more compensation. The HBC received a sizable cash payment and a large land grant through the Deed of Surrender. Eventually, the sale of land from this grant (one-twentieth of the surveyed townships in the prairie provinces) netted profits of $96,000,000 for the Company.[9]

In Manitoba, the legal dispossession of Native lands began with the surrender of the HBC charter. The impetus for the Company to surrender its claim to Rupertsland began when the old shareholders of the Company were bought out by the International Financial Society in 1863. Banking interests and real and paper railroad companies wanted the lands of the northwest and so bought in to the age-old mercantile Company. The subsequent economic and political evolution of Manitoba was not what had been envisioned by Riel, Ross, or Nolin, and so a major issue of post-1870 Native history concerns the adequacy of compensation for the loss of possession and use of land. Given the claims to Rupertsland, were not both the HBC and Aboriginal peoples entitled to an economic future?

Significantly, the presumed autonomy of the subsistence economy, much heralded by established ethnohistorians and social scientists, was not the sort of 'economic sovereignty' that could match the power of international finance capital. Post records can be interpreted to show that Indians manipulated European traders, and this line of reasoning becomes proof of Indian economic security and sovereignty. And for many contemporary academics, the power of financial capital relative to the traditional economy is not relevant. Attempts to determine fundamental questions of dependency and autonomy by a micro-analysis of only particular types of documents (post journals) are inadequate. I think the larger organization and purpose of the fur industry and the world market are significant.[10] But instead, numerous small studies have constructed the fur trade as a racial partnership. This fallacy – the composition of the Indian and White as an historic partnership without any reference to the notion of equity – cannot explain why an Aboriginal claim to Rupertsland was worth less than the HBC claim.[11] The concept of paternalism, and not partnership, seems to capture the historic relationship between the HBC and Natives.[12] If a partnership existed during the colonial rule of the HBC, then the current problems of Native communities cannot be traced back to the fur trade era. The political outcome of the fur trade, in terms of the property interests that developed after two hundred years, is not a matter of subjective interpretation. Yet a relativist framework permits contemporary ethnohistorians to dismiss observations during the fur trade of Indian 'starvation' or 'poverty' as word meanings that cannot be applied to the relationship between Indian and White.[13] Thus, the fact that the HBC accumulated wealth while Native peoples received a marginal return for their labour associated with the production of fur has no contemporary significance. The history of the fur trade is separated from the question of property because ethnohistorical research seldom includes any economic analysis. As such, there is no apparent lead into the question of Aboriginal title from such studies. And as is too often the case, legal relations between Indians and Whites have little economic context. The method of this book involves the use of a variety of archival and published primary sources to reconstruct changes at the local and regional levels, while at the same time remaining cognizant of external political and economic forces.

The substance of the current discussion of Aboriginal self-government, which formulates in terms of amending the Constitution Act of 1982, encounters some of the same problems that faced Riel and Ross in 1870. Quite clearly, the legal and political discussions about self-government took place in an economic vacuum. This study of northern Manitoba is an effort to provide a more precise context for understanding the creation of Native communities during the transition from mercantile to industrial capitalism.

The transfer of Rupertsland entailed the buying out of the HBC claim to the territory, but, in the process, the Dominion of Canada undertook certain responsibilities for Aboriginal peoples in 1870. Several legal documents need to be examined in order to appreciate how the Canadian nation state approached Aboriginal populations at the time of the transfer. The documents that laid out the framework for transferring Rupertsland were scheduled with the Imperial Order-in-Council, which admitted Rupertsland and the Northwestern Territory into the Canadian federation (Rupertsland Order). Such an analysis provides a means for understanding the subsequent changes to law and political economy. The 1867 Address to the Queen from the Canadian parliament stated:

> That in the event of your Majesty's Government agreeing to transfer to Canada the jurisdiction and control over the said region, the Government and Parliament of Canada will be ready to provide that the legal rights of any corporation, company or individual within the same shall be respected, and placed under the protection of Courts of competent jurisdiction.
>
> And furthermore that, upon the transference of the territory in question to the Canadian Government, the claims of the Indian tribes to compensation for lands required for purposes of settlement will be considered and settled in conformity with the equitable principles which have uniformly governed the British Crown in its dealings with the aborigines.[14]

Sprague has pointed out that this address acknowledged all the entities that existed as part of Rupertsland society and that a commitment was made to protect each of them – corporate interests (HBC), individual titles (the river lots at the Red River settlement), and Aboriginal title.[15] The Aboriginal interest in land was acknowledged in the Rupertsland Order. In the Deed of Surrender, which embodied the agreement between Canada and the HBC, the memorandum of 22 March 1869 included Term 14, which stated a general recognition of Aboriginal property interests:

> Any claims of Indians to compensation for lands required for purposes of settlement shall be disposed of by the Canadian Government in communication with the Imperial Government; and the Company shall be relieved of all responsibilities in respect of them.[16]

This term also sanctioned a changing relationship between Indians and the HBC. With the surrender of its monopoly trading privileges, the Company was relieved of its traditional responsibilities towards Indian people. Canada's legal obligations to Aboriginal people, generated as a result of the transfer, were situated in the negotiations that were concerned with the type of capital that would dominate the region and the political system that would manage new economic relationships. In a request to the Queen to act upon the agreement between the HBC and the Dominion of Canada – namely, the 1869 Address to the Queen – the Canadian government re-affirmed the acknowledgment of Aboriginal interests:

> That upon the transference of the territories in question to the Canadian Government it will be our duty to make adequate provision for the protection of the Indian tribes whose interests and well-being are involved in the

transfer, and we authorize and empower the Governor in Council to arrange any details that may be necessary to carry out the terms and conditions of the above agreement.[17]

Clearly, the Crown did not assume obligations to Indians only after the conclusion of land-surrender treaties.

Following the successful negotiations for the transfer between the Canadian delegates and the HBC, Earl Granville, secretary of state for the colonies, wrote to the governor general of Canada on 10 April 1869:

> I am sure that your Government will not forget the care which is due to those who must soon be exposed to new dangers, and in the course of settlement be dispossessed of the lands which they are used to enjoy as their own, or be confined within unwontedly narrow limits.
>
> ... the old inhabitants of the Country will be treated with such forethought and consideration as may preserve them from the danger of the approaching change, and satisfy them of the friendly interest which their new Governors feel in their welfare.[18]

Similar instructions from E.A. Meredith, under-secretary of state for the provinces, to Lieutenant Governor Archibald, whose task was to establish a new political order for Manitoba and the Northwest, stated:

> You will also make a full report upon the state of the Indian Tribes now in the Territories; their numbers, wants and claims, the system heretofore pursued by the Hudson's Bay Company in dealing with them, accompanied by any suggestions you may desire to offer with references to their protection, and to the improvement of their condition.[19]

Meredith instructed Archibald to consider Indian claims but also to report on the HBC ways of dealing with Indians. Aboriginal interests were very much intertwined with the Company's surrender of its charter, and the documents that carried out the transfer, thereby establishing the Canadian nation state in what had formerly been Hudson's Bay Company territory, made reference to Aboriginal claims and affirmed an obligation to protect their interests.

This legal framework related to the polices that initiated treaties, but it is also pertinent to those areas of the former HBC territory where Indian treaties did not follow quickly after the transfer. After 1870, did the Canadian government have any obligations to Indians in the non-treaty areas of northern Manitoba? This question, which is relevant to much of subarctic Rupertsland, has not attracted much interest from lawyers or historians. In my opinion, these obligations stemmed from the withdrawal of the HBC as the sole colonial authority responsible for the well-being of Aboriginal people in Rupertsland. Both in terms of constitutional obligations (Rupertsland Order) and in terms of the continuation of imperial policy, the Canadian nation state was aware that Aboriginal interests were involved in the transfer and that obligations were undertaken as part of the transfer. These obligations were of an economic character, originating with the dispossession of land inherent in the shift of property systems. However, the obligations that the HBC had acquired in the course of the fur trade were the result of disruptions caused by trade and were not consequent upon the dispossession of property. Both the anticipated effects of settlement upon Natives and the changes caused by trade were disruptions to an economy, but with different origins. (Had settlement or capitalist development of the west not occurred for a period of time, the Canadian nations state would have still been legally and politically responsible for assisting the Aboriginal population in times of need.) The terms of the Rupertsland Order are not limited to Treaty Indians or Indians registered under the Indian Acts. The reference to 'dangers of approaching changes' for the 'old inhabitants of the Country' would certainly apply to the Metis. The Rupertsland Order is not some ancient document, but rather it provides a standard for understanding the economic history of the post-1870 era.

The organization of this study will perturb most traditional historians. The intricacies of the fur trade, Aboriginal title, and new resource industries cannot be combined into a simple narrative setting out a single blow-by-blow chronology. Chapters 1, 2, and 3 concern the fur trade and depict this industry at several levels of geographical analysis. Various local economies are described as they existed in 1870. Changes to the regional system and the HBC transport system are considered. The effects of the changing industry at York Factory are explained in detail. Chapters 4, 5, and 6 concern the question of Aboriginal title. The initial round of treaty-making (1871-6), the adhesions to Treaty Five (1908-10), and the government's approach to Metis use and occupancy of land are considered in conjunction with the theme of Aboriginal title and resources. The documentation on Aboriginal title has been looked at in detail and I argue that the central issue was the Crown's effort to contain a progressive economic agenda advanced by Indians. After the Aboriginal title material, the book reconstructs the changing economic relations that coincided with the depressed fur trade and treaty-making. Reserve settlement and agriculture, commercial fishing and state management, wage labour, and new resource industries are examined in Chapters 7 to 12. The revitalization of the fur trade after 1900 is examined in Chapter 13. Some of the changes to the regional economy that occur as a result of industrial capitalism in the 1920s and 1930s are profiled in

Chapter 14. The conclusion summarizes the findings, but more emphasis is placed on broadening the discussion. When possible, material is presented chronologically, however, thematic content and geographical information are more important than tidy chronologies. It is, of course, easier to generate general chronologies if spatial details are ignored, and this happens all too often. By examining this era at a regional and local level, I am attempting to provide more precision than is offered by general histories, but, at the same time, there is an effort to capture the effects of externally oriented structures – a feature that is so often ignored by myopic post-level studies. Only by carefully reconstructing local-level activity can misleading generalizations be avoided. The traditional angst about the need for a simple chronological narrative breaks down with a desire to appreciate changes occurring at various geographical scales. The use of maps and diagrams to present data is an important part of my argument.

It should be quite certain that Harold Innis's staple thesis is at work here.[20] A staple is the dominant commodity in any given era. Effort is directed at producing a commodity for export. The weakness of an export-oriented economy provides some cohesion in understanding Native economic history. In this sense, I have used staple to refer to commodities that are exported from northern Manitoba, although the difference between a raw material export, such as lumber, which is consumed by southern markets within the nation state, and raw materials, such as fur, which supplies international markets, can be important. The staple thesis may be a means to integrate economic history with the geography of treaty and Aboriginal rights. A legitimate approach to archival records entails focusing on the material relations of production within the ongoing evolution of a world system. However, many will object to the introduction of concepts such as labour, surplus population, exploitation, commercialization, or capital into Native history. Such concepts, along with the absence of oral history, raise the problem of an authentic voice. I leave it to those conforming to current tenets to point out that this sort of economic history is a Eurocentric metanarrative and a logocentric misrepresentation of life. While the idea of colonialism still has some standing in present academic discourse, specific empirical consideration of the origins of economic domination is lacking. Nonetheless, the implications that might flow from the information and interpretation of this economic history might not be so easily avoided in the future.

1

'To Look for Food Instead of Fur': Local Economies – Indian Bands and Company Posts

The meeting of Native peoples and the world market occurred at the local 'trade' post: where their furs, hides, and meat were traded; where their labour was needed for seasonal or temporary work; where the band formed as the family/hunting groups congregated; where emergency shelter and gratuities were made available during times of scarcity; where European goods were purchased; and where credit was entrusted in order to outfit another season of trapping. Here also, Native furs entered a commodity flow that reached from their traplines to the markets of industrial Europe. Each post was a point on the Hudson's Bay Company system.

The production and export of fur gave a common purpose to the entire subarctic and formed the basis of many traditions that identified fur trade life. Because posts were located in differing environments and performed a variety of roles in the vast HBC system, fur trade society has to be first seen from the perspective of the local economy. The local economy was composed of an Indian band of family groups living off the land and a trading post, which employed the talents of Europeans and Natives. Exchange was the reason for this integration. Many of the post's needs were met by a combination of local labour and resources, but this self-reliance was subservient to external impulses.

The Native Economy: Commercialized Hunting

Trapping, in reality commercial hunting, had been central to the Native economy for two centuries following the establishment of the Hudson's Bay Company in 1670. A commercial sector did not exist prior to the arrival of the Europeans, and, therefore, production and consumption were perfectly balanced. Trade modified production and established an economy composed of subsistence and commercial sectors. Activities designed to fulfil subsistence needs are known as 'production for use value,' while the product of labour in the commercial sector is referred to as 'production for exchange value.' The shift to production for the market, to guiding production by commercial values or prices, is an important development. In the Canadian fur industry, the exchange unit, Made Beaver (MB), guided the prices of furs, provisions, and labour for centuries. By referring to MB, the relative value of a beaver pelt, or twine for fishnets, or a month's labour were understood by all. In the fur trade, subsistence and commercial labour overlapped; a beaver provides food for the family and a pelt for exchange. For this reason, it is wrong to view bush life or time spent on subsistence activities as a dimension of a society relatively unaltered by 'white culture.'

Figure 1.1 provides a historic model for the Native economy, which recognizes the interrelationships between the two sectors. The allocation of labour time, resource inputs (game, fish, fur-bearing animals, berries, etc.), and capital and consumption goods (European goods such as guns, traps, tools, cloth, flour, etc.) are modelled to show how the Native economy operated under different conditions. The circles symbolize the relative proportion of time spent working. The inputs (resources, capital goods) and outcomes (furs, profits) are depicted by arrows. The first phase provides a reference to the harmonious economy that existed prior to the coming of the fur trade. Consumption and production are balanced. In the subarctic, local needs were met by local resources. The relative abundance of resources means that huge amounts of labour were not required to sustain society. After 1670 a commercial sector developed. Trapping, provisioning the post (hunting and fishing), and wage labour provided commercial incomes for Native peoples. The model demonstrates that even if more time is spent on subsistence activities, the commercial aspect remains paramount. Income from trapping was used to purchase equipment or the means of production, which was required and used by both the subsistence and commercial sectors. Plentiful subsistence resources reduced the cost of fur production for this mercantile industry, and an equilibrium existed between commerce and subsistence.

Nonetheless, the balance between subsistence and commercial efforts was delicate. To illustrate, the Norway House journal from December 1872 noted that two Indians had arrived bringing 'intelligence that none of the Indians on their side have any fish, which is a great draw back for hunting for they have to look for food instead of Fur.'[1] The interchangeability of the terms hunting and trapping by this journal keeper reflects the interdependence of the commercial and subsistence sectors. Figure 1.1 shows the effect of scarcity of bush food on the Native economy. Scarcity of food resources increased the amount of time required for subsistence hunting, fishing, and gathering. In the long run, the fur trade could not sustain a disproportionate amount of labour time spent on subsistence with a concomitant reduction in commercial production. To minimize this risk, flour

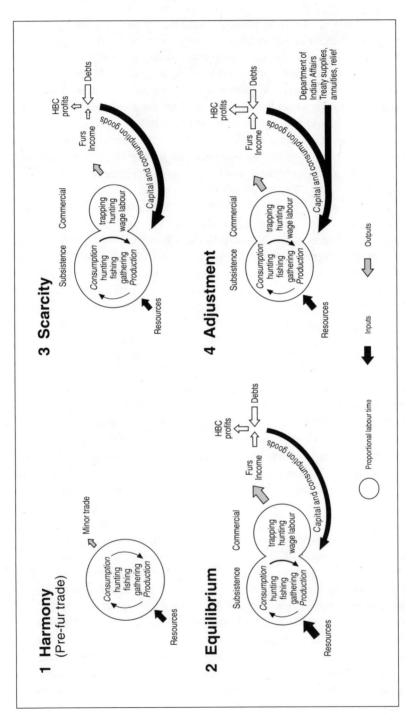

Figure 1.1 Model of the Native economy indicating historical shifts

and pork imports to the subarctic were increased, thereby reducing the risk of unpaid debts that occurred with a drop in fur production. Eventually food imports proved to be cheaper than the loss of fur production that occurred when Natives were forced to search for scarce game. The absorption by the subsistence sector of an excessive amount of labour threatened production and profitability. HBC profits and Native subsistence were intricately connected.

Initially, the HBC bore the cost of food imports, but the treaties led to Canadian government involvement in subsidizing the Native economy. Treaty supplies and relief from the Department of Indian Affairs should be seen as a policy to sustain commercial fur production. Food imports helped to alleviate distress and maintain the fur trade in areas suffering from resource depletion. The significance of imported food to the Native economy is related by an anecdote recalled by the Methodist missionary Fred G. Stevens. Shortly after a visit by an Indian agent, Stevens was at Deers Lake, where he 'asked the chief if anyone was fishing. I wanted some fresh fish. The chief replied in astonishment, "Don't you know that we have flour? The very idea of anyone fishing when we have flour!"'[2] Figure 1.1 indicates the adjustment that the Native economy made with greater food imports. Food imports permitted Natives to spend more time on commercial hunting. In terms of the relationship between subsistence and commercial sectors, it should also be pointed out that many subsistence resources were commercialized. For example, in the York Factory area, the HBC country provision needs included caribou and geese. Also, when pemmican became scarce, the HBC directed the Chipewyan to engage in the commercial hunting of caribou for venison. Although beaver pelts and other fine furs were exported, over the years many local resources were commercially harvested in order to sustain post economies.

An inherent feature of the Native economy was the outfitting of the trapper, on credit terms, with goods needed for hunting, trapping, and fishing. In the language of the fur trade, Indians were 'debted.' Credit or 'taking debt' was vital to the long-term operation of the industry. This social relationship was partly reinforced by the population cycles of fur bearers, since it made sense for the Company to carry the trapper through the lean years. HBC manager J.K. McDonald explained the need for credit in the Island Lake district:

If advances to Indians [credit] are entirely stopped at this Post the Indians will not only be unable to hunt, but they will freeze, as they have no other means of procuring the necessary clothing to enable them to hunt. If their advances are limited to the bare necessaries of life they will be unable to pay them, and if they are advanced with everything they require there is still a great chance of their being unable to pay up the whole of their advances [,] therefore Indian Balances [outstanding debts] will still appear though I will do everything possible to reduce them. The Indians of course will be very displeased at being worked different.[3]

McDonald's statement illustrates that Indian well-being, when faced with resource scarcity, was effectively determined by the amount of credit the Company made available. Credit arrangements cemented subsistence and commercial pursuits. The HBC credit terms, in turn, reflected international fur prices (see Appendix A). Production was subordinated to exchange relations. For these reasons, it is superficial to present the Native economy as a separate preserve simply because Indians hunted before and after contact. The HBC was not interested in maintaining Indians as subsistence hunters and marginal fur producers. One of the reasons that the subsistence sector persisted was because it provided a 'cheap wage' for the maintenance of the Native economy. Thus, both subsistence and commercial production were vital to the mercantile fur trade.

Some generalization can be made about the seasonal cycle of the boreal forest Indians. Soon after they were outfitted with goods in the late summer or early fall, Indians left the post for their hunting grounds. In the fall and early winter, Indians hunted, fished, and trapped. Most trappers returned to the post with their furs in late December and remained there until just after the New Year. Trapping and sturgeon fishing went on in the late winter, and some groups returned to the post for Easter. Spring was dominated by the muskrat hunt, and Indians returned to the post and settled their debts after breakup. In the early summer, some Indians planted small potato gardens,

Inside the Norway House post, 1878 (NAC, C-652)

and many families remained in the vicinity of the post by spreading out around the lake at various fish camps. Many men were engaged for the summer as boatmen on HBC brigades. While they were away, women and children supported themselves by fishing and berry picking.

The activities of Native women and children in the fur trade economy of the late nineteenth century is more difficult to document than is their participation in the earlier years. For example, the early Europeans tended to include accounts about the work of Indian women when they described Indian societies. Drawing on these observations, S. Van Kirk has made the point that Native women played a vital role in the formation of the fur trade society.[4] Van Kirk's research demonstrated that marriage between traders and Indian women not only led to the development of 'Mixed bloods,' but that Indian women provided economically advantageous kinship/trading links, generated an important demand for trade goods, acted as interpreters, and taught survival skills and languages.[5] Given the importance of the subsistence sector to the fur trade, domestic work done by women and children was vital in the late nineteenth century. In particular, women were responsible for retrieving game, except in instances when it was intended for consumption by the post; then servants would haul it. Also, women contributed to domestic food production by fishing, snaring, gathering, and gardening. Hides and pelts were prepared for exchange by women. The intermarriage of Native women and European men was an outgrowth of the integration of domestic or subsistence production and commercial exchange. Missionary records indicate that children helped to dry meat and to prepare skins. For The Pas band, Rev. Henry Budd recorded that children participated in the muskrat hunt and fished. In April of 1870, he walked over to the Carrot River and noted: 'Here the child[re]n are catching the fish enough to keep them up. What patience they must have to sit on that Ice for so many hours together.'[6] Women and children also engaged in temporary labour, especially around district headquarters, where they cleaned houses in the summer and hauled firewood. At York Factory, women plucked and salted the geese after the spring and fall hunts. They were also known to trade rabbits that they had snared. The spring muskrat hunt favoured the active participation of women and children. According to the Anglican missionary the Reverend J. Lofthouse, Chipewyan women 'carry their tents (made of deer skins) and what few things they possess, the men as "Lords" walk along with simply their guns; it [would] make British blood tingle to see a poor woman [?] along with a burden of 60 lbs or so, and often a child besides, while a big strong man walks along with his gun only.'[7] Apparently, Cree women were not in the same situation as were the Chipewyan women described by Lofthouse. York Factory's Anglican missionary, G.S. Winter, remarked that 'Many of the [Cree] Indian women expect their husbands to submit in everything.'[8] Because domestic production was essential, women continued to play an important role in the regional economy. Unfortunately, these very limited observations about bush and post life do not permit an adequate understanding of the role of women in the post-1870 Native economy.

Seasonal and Resource Aspects of Post Economies

The unique economies of a variety of posts are summarized in Figures 1.2 to 1.11. Information from HBC records, in particular post journals, along with missionary records provide frequent and regular observations on post life. Diagrams are the best means to summarize this information and to demonstrate its complexity. Daily journals provide ample information on the deployment of Company servants and temporary labourers but very little on the daily activities of Natives at their hunting grounds. Nonetheless, the presentation of a post's economic life as a seasonal cycle indicates the movements of Indian trappers. These seasonal cycle diagrams represent posts from different environmental zones and from different locations within the HBC's transportation network, thus revealing the uniqueness of each of these local economies. (Environmental differences are also indicated by the variability of species making up district fur catches. See Appendix A.)

The seasonal economy for Norway House is presented in Figures 1.2 to 1.4. As district headquarters and as a meeting place for the Northern Department Council, Norway House had administrative and transportation functions. Given its location in the transportation system, it was a logical place to build York boats. Boat building and oar making required green wood, which was rafted downriver or hauled by oxen. Oxen, in turn, needed hay (mostly wild swamp grasses), which was also brought to the post. As a local economy became more diversified and complex, more buildings were needed. This generated a further demand for labour, for building, for maintenance, and for firewood. All of these activities created a demand for more labour. The labour force had to be fed, and this was accomplished by planting several gardens, hunting a variety of game, importing some food, and by fishing throughout the year. Significantly, Norway House's food needs were not found in the immediate vicinity of the post; consequently, additional labour was required to haul food. Thus, the procurement and transportation of wild game, firewood, fish, green wood, and hay created a circular demand for labour throughout the year. However, this cumulative process was stimulated by boat building. The geographical dimensions of these resource demands are presented as a spatial model in Figure 1.2. In addition, summer freighting employed Native labourers. Diversified resource use supported a local economy that included transportation of trade goods and furs, the construction and repair of boats and buildings (requiring skilled

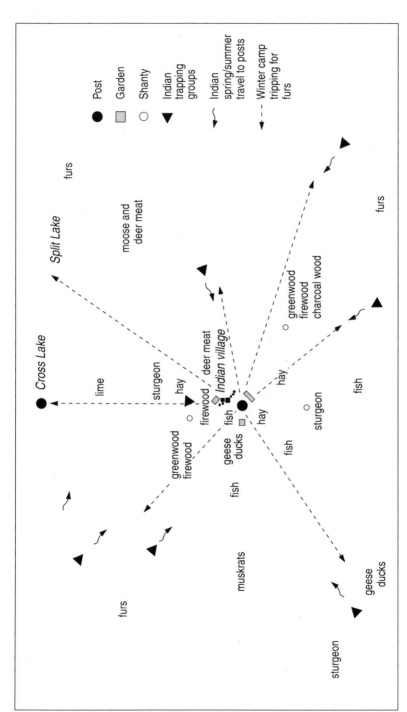

Figure 1.2 Spatial model of local resources used at Norway House, ca. 1870

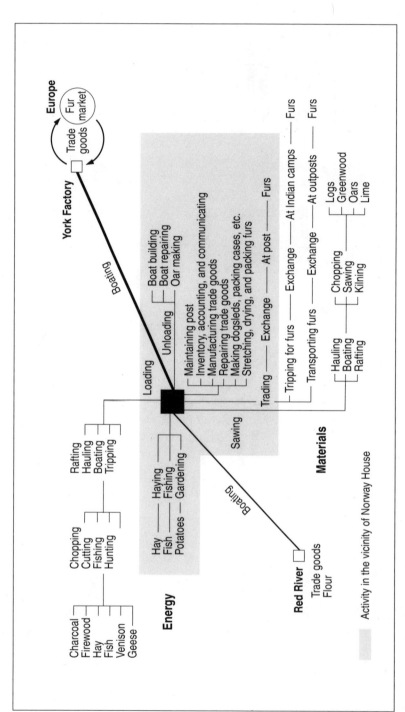

Figure 1.3 Economic activities at Norway House, ca. 1874

labour), and the procurement of a variety of country provisions. The economic role of district headquarters such as Norway House resulted in an enlarged post economy with an internal demand for labour. Figure 1.3 summarizes the types of work activities that were related to the flow of energy and materials required by Norway House.

The complexity of economic activities and the seasonal quality of life at Norway House is captured by Figure 1.4. The HBC recognized specialization amongst Norway House Natives by classifying them as 'Wood' or 'Village' Indians. Wood Indians referred to those who lived off the land most of the year and whose activities focused on trapping. Many Wood Indians were from the vicinity of Cross Lake, and they were recognized as a separate band at the treaty talks. In contrast, many of the Village Indians were Methodists and settled at the village of Rossville. The economic basis for this group stressed potato gardening, fishing, and wage labour. Year round habitation at the village was not possible, and post journals noted that starving villagers would leave for fishing places in April.[9]

The unique seasonal cycle of Fort Churchill is shown by Figure 1.5. Unlike Norway House, Churchill did not play a role in the Company's inland transportation; its outfits and returns passed through York Factory on coastal boats. Consequently, boat building was not as important at Churchill as it was at posts that served as district headquarters. Thus, the seasonal economy was simpler than that of Norway House. Sealing and whaling were part of Churchill's economy. This meant that Inuit labour was crucial to the economic viability of the post. By the 1870s, the Inuit seemed to have had a stronger presence at Churchill than the Chipewyan. At Churchill, as at all other posts, procuring and hauling wood was important. In 1869, the fuel needs amounted to 700 loads of firewood; as well, 300 loads of sawn lumber were needed. None of this wood was obtained within four miles of the post, and a good portion of the wood was obtained fifteen to twenty miles away.[10]

Churchill's resource hinterland is shown by Figure 1.6, and the evidence creates the impression that the resource needs of the fur trade were extensive. This post's trade hinterland included the distant Barrenland Chipewyan, the Caribou Eskimo, and the more closely integrated Chipewyan and Inuit 'Homeguards.' An essential part of Churchill's returns was derived from the Marble Island Inuit trade. Inuit from the Marble Island area (Chesterfield Inlet) engaged in their own middleman trade, which had the effect of extending northward Churchill's hinterland. This Inuit middleman system brought in the higher valued returns, whereas the inland trade with the Barrenland Chipewyan and Caribou Inuit tended to yield the low-value caribou parchment.

At York Factory, boat building, producing country-made goods, woodcutting, whaling, fishing, and goose and caribou hunting were major aspects

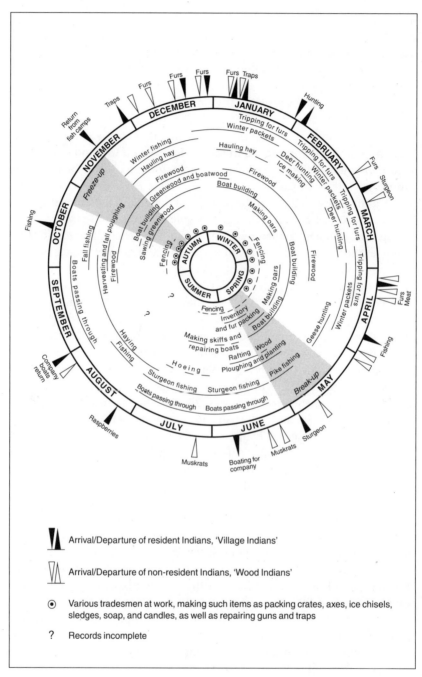

Figure 1.4 Seasonal economy of Norway House, 1873-5 (HBCA, B.154/a/70-1)

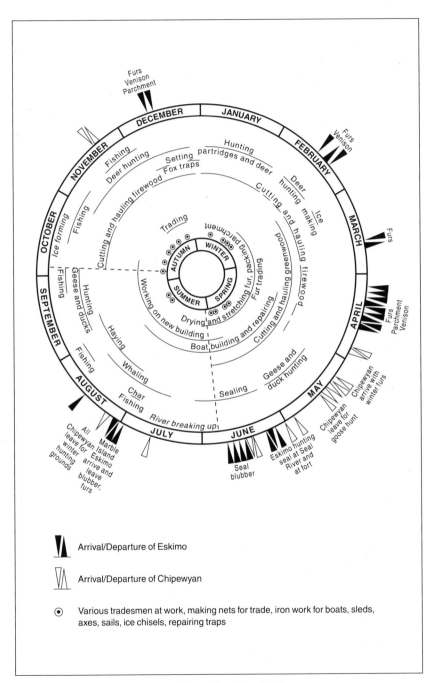

Figure 1.5 Seasonal economy of Fort Churchill, 1875
(HBCA, B.42/a/192; B.42/b/62; NAC, CMS, A.99)

of the economy (Figure 1.7). Obtaining wood was an especially labour-absorbing activity at York. Some 2,000 to 3,000 cords of firewood were taken annually from the banks of the Hayes River, and 6,000 to 7,000 planks of green wood were brought from the Nelson River. Although the wood needs appear to be extraordinary, York Factory was a large establishment, and Chief Factor J. Fortescue explained that fires were needed both winter and summer because the post was built on a swamp.[11] Fortescue argued that the Company's long occupation of the site meant that 'the immediate river banks are now entirely denuded of wood to the mouth of Hill river

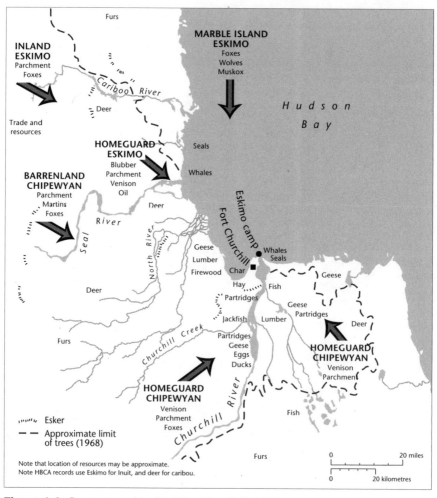

Figure 1.6 Resources and trade of Fort Churchill, 1875
(HBCA, B.42/a/192; B.42/b/62; CMS, A-99)

120 miles distant from the fort, and behind it the green woods are cut down to a depth of eight miles up the Nelson River.'[12] Therefore, considerable time was required simply to get to the cutting areas. Some twenty to thirty men were employed cutting wood, and Figure 1.7 indicates the seasonal duration of wood-related activities required by the post. Wood was rafted downriver to the post. Then it had to be moved up the twenty-seven-foot banks before wind would break up the rafts. Moving the wood from the riverbank to the wood yard was labour intensive, as Fortescue explained: 'All available force is employed for this purpose, even Indian women bearing a hand when men are scarce, the carrying alone is about three weeks work of some twenty or thirty hands, while the remainder are rafting.'[13] Generally, green wood was hauled by oxen in the winter, but the distance travelled limited hauling to one trip a day. To obtain additional green wood, more oxen would have been needed, but the available hay resources could not support more cattle. Therefore, increasingly more labour was required to raft green wood. Another environmental problem that York faced was the severe erosion under certain weather conditions of its site along the Hayes River bank. Efforts were made to slow this erosion by placing stones on the bank face, and this created work for boys.

The provisioning needs of York Factory are presented in Figure 1.8. These data clearly indicate the magnitude of the post's food needs. A comparison of 1873 and 1874 indicates that imported provisions remained constant. Therefore, if caribou were scarce, the shortfall in venison had to be made up in partridges and fish (compare 1874 to 1873). A more intensive exploitation of partridges and fish not only had implications for the occupants' diet, but it also meant that considerable effort was needed to obtain these resources. Catching 14,866 partridges or hauling 15,673 pounds of venison involved hard work and competent management. York Factory's seasonal round also included whaling. Whales were used for dog food because of the low productivity of the Hudson Bay lowland fisheries.

The seasonal cycle of Oxford House (Figure 1.9) reveals the importance of the lake fisheries. Oxford House served as headquarters for a small district, and therefore some boat building took place and its seasonal economy somewhat resembled that of Norway House (albeit on a reduced scale). Figure 1.9 shows that this economy was less complicated than the York Factory and Norway House economies. The Oxford House journals provide considerable information on the back and forth movement of Indians, indicating that the trade in furs was important.

The Pas, Moose Lake, and Berens River posts represent the seasonal round associated with a trading post type of economy. The simplicity of these economies is illustrative of the difference between a post and a district headquarters. The importance of the muskrat swamps of the lower Saskatchewan

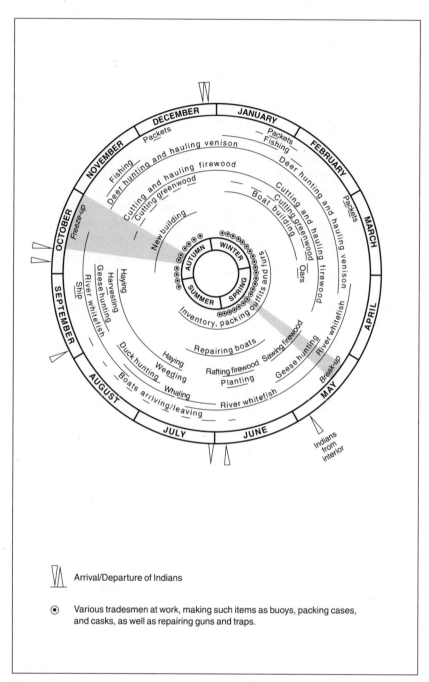

Figure 1.7 Seasonal economy of York Factory, 1875-6
(HBCA, B.239/a/182; CMS, A-100)

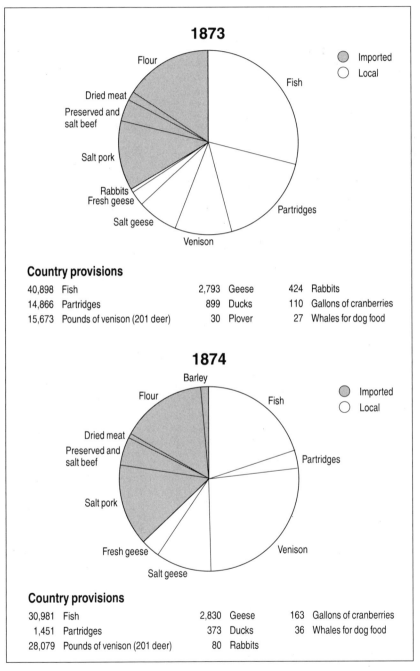

Figure 1.8   York Factory rations and country provisions, 1873-4
(HBCA, B.239/a/182)

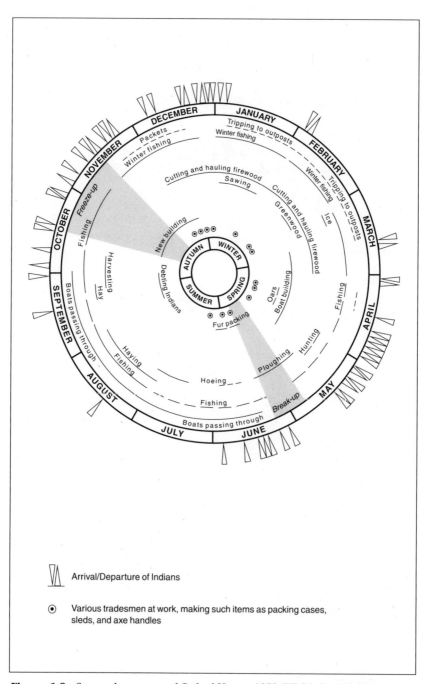

Figure 1.9 Seasonal economy of Oxford House, 1872 (HBCA, B.156/a/30)

River is apparent in the seasonal cycles of The Pas and Moose Lake (Figures 1.10 and 1.11). In the case of The Pas Indian Village, the Reverend Henry Budd's journal provides some additional insights into the Native economy. Comments on church attendance indicate Native movement in and out of the village. By the early 1870s, Natives were establishing more permanent residency patterns. This was accomplished because part of the population lived at nearby fishing lakes, and fish were brought to the village. A more settled residency pattern corresponded with gardening. In the spring of 1871, Budd recorded that he 'went out through the Village to see the people at work. Some of the people I saw were ploughing, some planting, some fencing, some hoeing the ground, and the rest hauling manure to their fields. In fact the whole Village was alive with the people; some were arriving from their planting potatoes in the Potato Island.'[14] The inclusion of gardening and cattle-raising within a commercial hunting economy necessitated change. According to Budd: 'Those who have cattle cannot all leave, the women stay at home to look after the Cattle and their husbands bring a load of fish now and again for them.'[15] Moreover, some Indians could produce fur without living in the bush for months on end. As Budd noted in November of 1871: 'Many of the men had been out hunting furs &c. but have all come home for the Sunday.'[16] The Berens River post economy is shown in Figure 1.12. The effects of good sturgeon and whitefish fisheries are apparent. This post's economic role was limited to collecting furs, thus its economy was far less intricate than the seasonal economies of Norway House or York Factory.

Economy and Place: The Landscape of the Fur Trade

An important, but usually overlooked, insight into the fur trade economy is provided by the late nineteenth-century sketch plans for the Hudson's Bay Company posts. Figures 1.13 to 1.19 are copies of sketch plans representing a variety of places in the Company's spatial system. These post plans present an image of place, where the fur trade economy was localized. Contrary to popular impressions, these plans show that the trade was not carried on from a single log cabin behind a palisade. Sketch plans and photographs not only display the complexity of fur trade society but also provide images of the cultural landscape created by the subarctic first staple economy.

The 'design' of all of these posts had some common features, in particular, the specialized functions for each building. The provisioning of the work force tended to occupy considerable space (byres or barns, fish houses, milk houses, icehouses, and provision stores). At the core of the posts stood dwelling houses, trading stores, and warehouses, while magazines, forges, blacksmith shops, byres, and oil, fish, and blubber houses were located around

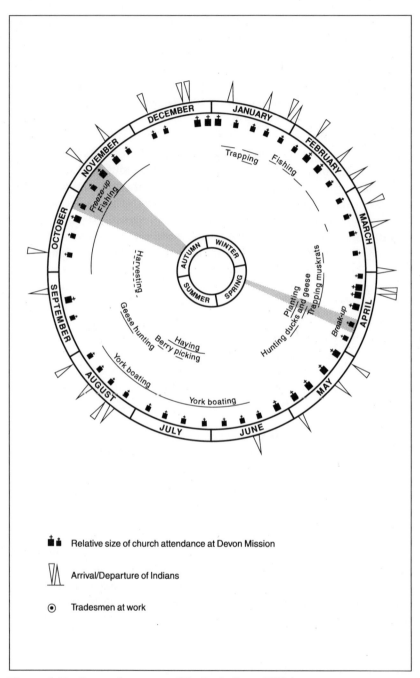

Figure 1.10 Seasonal economy of The Pas Indians, 1870-1
(CMS, A-99, A-100)

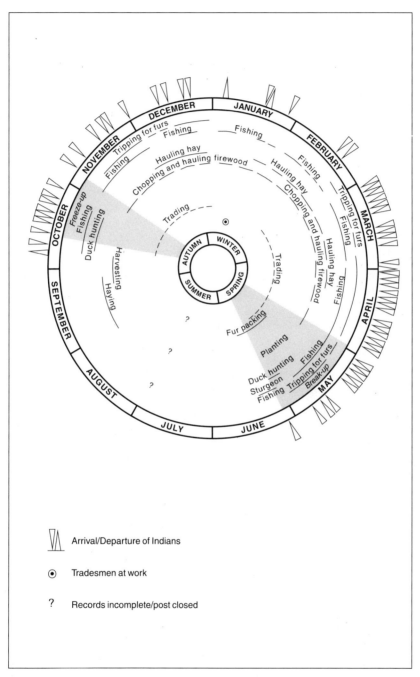

Figure 1.11   Seasonal economy of Moose Lake Post, 1875-6 (HBCA, B.318/a/1-2)

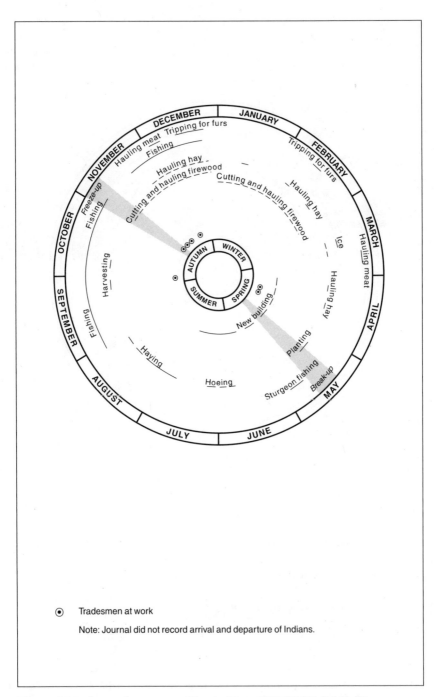

Figure 1.12   Seasonal economy of Berens River, 1874 (HBCA, B.16/a/7)

the periphery. All posts were oriented towards the waterfront, but there was no common layout.

At all posts, gardens were prominent features of the landscape. Turnips and potatoes were usually worth planting, even at York Factory. Garden plots at York Factory were built up with earth on a foundation of branches and chips. Gardens were manured. The most extensive gardening efforts undertaken in northern Manitoba were at Norway House, where several gardens were kept beyond the immediate vicinity of the post. These gardens yielded between 400 and 900 bushels of potatoes.[17] In addition, turnips, barley, peas, spinach, lettuce, radishes, mustard, carrots, and cabbages were planted. These efforts were appreciated, since the journal keeper at Norway House noted that they 'had asparagass [*sic*] at dinner today for the first time this season.'[18]

The sketch plan for York Factory portrays the complexity of a district headquarters and departmental depot (Figure 1.13). The number of buildings reflects the extent and diversity of economic functions. Domestic quarters (dwelling houses and kitchen), storage (depots, warehouses, and stores), exchange (saleshop and trading store), production (forge and shops), and

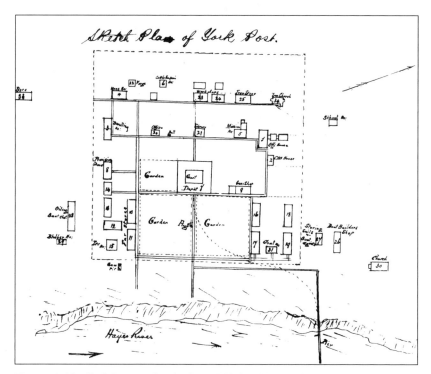

Figure 1.13   York Factory sketch plan, 1889 (HBCA, D.25/6)

administration (office) are all present. The Church Missionary Society's church and school were integrated with the HBC post. It is clear from the plan that the layout of the post was well organized. Buildings were con-

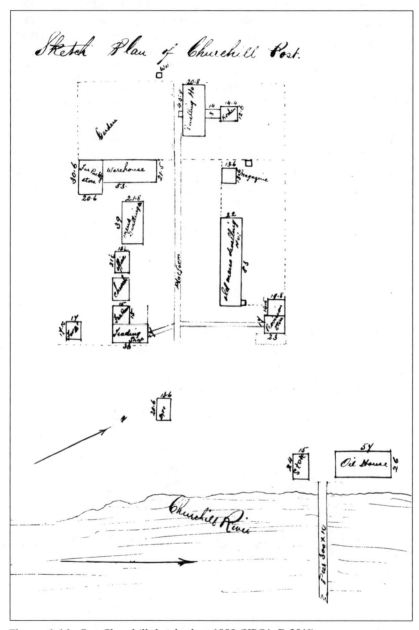

Figure 1.14 Fort Churchill sketch plan, 1889 (HBCA, D.25/6)

nected by platforms, and the post was oriented towards the waterfront. In contrast, the Fort Churchill establishment emphasized domestic quarters and storage (Figures 1.14 and 1.15), even though it was also located on the

Figure 1.15 Sketch plan of building used for whaling in Fort Churchill, 1889 (HBCA, D.25/6)

Hudson Bay Lowlands. Whaling and sealing necessitated several buildings on both sides of the Churchill River. Reflecting the fact that Churchill was not a district headquarters, it had fewer building types than York Factory. A large hinterland and the exploitation of marine resources, however, made it a fair-sized establishment.

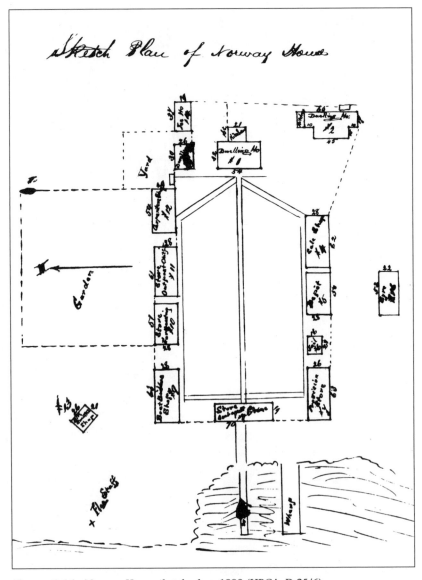

Figure 1.16   Norway House sketch plan, 1889 (HBCA, D.25/6)

The layout of the headquarters of Norway House district is shown in Figure 1.16. Norway House was a smaller establishment than York Factory, but its buildings were set up for a similar range of functions (domestic quarters, storage, exchange administration, and production). In contrast, the Methodist mission buildings were not part of the post and were located at Rossville.

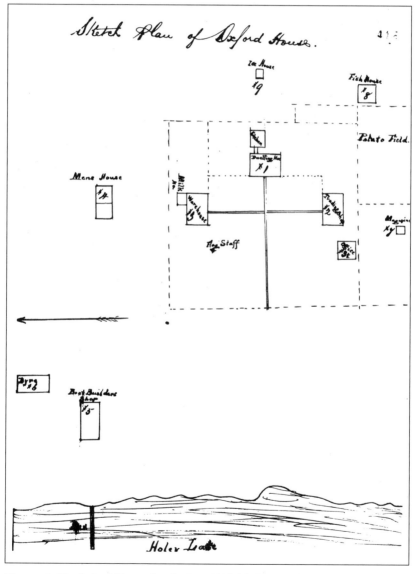

Figure 1.17 Oxford House sketch plan, 1889 (HBCA, D.25/6)

Norway House had a jail. The layout of Norway House is orderly but not overly symmetrical. Oxford House (Figure 1.17) was the headquarters for a small district, and as a post on the York Factory-Norway House route, transport was also important. Therefore, a boat builder's shop was needed. The layout of this post is relatively symmetrical.

Figures 1.18 and 1.19 show the layouts of Nelson House and Lac du Brochet trading posts. For these posts, buildings were limited to the needs of domestic arrangements and trade. The absence of a more complex economy is

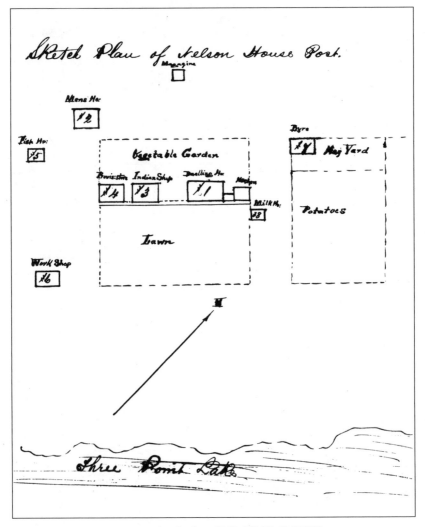

Figure 1.18   Nelson House sketch plan, 1889 (HBCA, D.25/19)

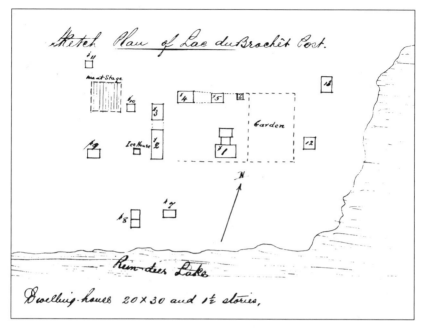

Figure 1.19   Lac du Brochet sketch plan, 1894 (HBCA, D.25/19)

apparent in the landscape. The economic role of the Lac du Brochet Chipewyan as commercial hunters for the Cumberland House district is apparent in Figure 1.19, which shows large meat stages for drying caribou venison.

The term 'trade post' is misleading; earlier references to 'factories' and 'plantations' more accurately reflect the variety of activities that occurred in and around posts. To sustain the export of fur, a lot more than trade was carried on at the posts. This staple industry was exceedingly elaborate. The local economy consisted of an Indian band composed of family groups and a post with its own round of seasonal work. While the complexity of each post reflected unique adaptations to local environments, all posts were involved in the production of fur, the distribution of European goods, and the transport of commodities. The bush – the land – sustained and reproduced the labour needed by the fur trade.

The interconnections between the post and bush economies and the interdependence between the commercial and subsistence sectors of the Native economy pertain to the concept of 'mode of production.' The economic relations of production in any society have relevance to social customs of a culture. Therefore, the effort to identify and describe the relations

Indian camp at Oxford House, 1880 (NAC, C-80063, R. Bell)

of production has a broader importance. One widely accepted approach argues that subarctic trappers worked in two separate modes of production: one commercial and European, and the other, subsistent, land-based, and distinctly Native. A capitalist and European mode 'articulating' with a non-capitalist Indian mode of production has been a favoured theoretical solution for some social scientists. The dual appearance of the traditional economy cannot be understood by creating two modes of production. Elsewhere the claim is made that Native trappers were really peasants bound to the land-owning Hudson's Bay Company – the fur trade as feudalism. The characterization of the fur trade as a variant of European feudalism seems to ignore certain political and economic facts. For example, the power of the HBC stemmed almost exclusively from advantages it created in the sphere of monopoly exchange. With respect to the Native population, the HBC lacked direct political authority, and it had little or no coercive means to assert such political power.

All this intellectual groping stems from frustrated efforts to select, from a rather short list, the appropriate category of mode of production to apply to the unique society that was evolving in Rupertsland. No one would seriously argue that peasants participated in two modes of production. These various modes of production schemes, which have come to emphasize the non-capitalist sector, tend to ignore the external market and the fact that production was subordinate to exchange relations. The presumption that these economic activities were completely separated provides no way to consider the unity of production and exchange in the fur trade. A single economy allocated labour time and applied the means of production to generate both life-sustaining subsistence and commercial income.

The idea that subsistence and exchange create a single economy is the most appropriate characterization of the Native economy at the time treaties were made. Today such descriptions inform us about the meaning of livelihood in the treaties. Bush activities defy neat classifications because often a single task could simultaneously generate commercial and subsistence returns. The fur trade had a *sui generis* quality. From place to place, and from time to time, the mix of types of activities shifted to accommodate local resource conditions and the demands of the market. Moreover, within the band, the involvement in the commercial sector varied considerably from hunting group to hunting group. Tension existed between commercial and subsistence activities. Subsistence production encouraged autonomy for Natives, while commercial production most obviously served the Company's drive for mercantile profits. Unless the unity of the economy is recognized, it is next to impossible to determine what actually happened during the turbulent days that followed the attempted annexation of Rupertsland. In the long run, the perspective that local Native economies are part of a unified, single economy provides insights into the changing relationship between Native people and external agencies.

Nonetheless, these local economies, along with an intricate transportation network and the hierarchical organization of the Hudson's Bay Company, made up a regional system that, in itself, could not remain unchanging.

2
'The Only Remedy Is the Employment of Steam': Reorganizing the Regional System

Sustaining fur yields was an environmental and economic challenge for the industry, and periodic resource crises attest to this problem. Furthermore, the production of trappers was spread out – from one end of the subarctic to the other – a geographical challenge for the Company. Trapping was an extensive activity, and much of the organization and transportation history of the trade was an effort to deal with the technical conditions that this staple demanded. But a commodity flow was created, and the wealth of the vast subarctic was efficiently channelled to a single London auction house. Transport and administration linked local economies into a regional system. The harvests of family hunting groups flowed through a hierarchical organization; and this same intricate transport system was reversed, distributing manufacturing goods back to the remote corners of Rupertsland. The labour of Native freighters held this regional system together. After fifty years, this transportation and organizational system, born out of the merging of mercantile capital in 1821, became noticeably cumbersome. Internal and external pressures necessitated change.

The Spatial Structure and Transportation System of the Hudson's Bay Company Circa 1870

The Hudson's Bay Company's district organization and spatial structure is presented in a simplified model form in Figure 2.1. This system organized the collection of furs, the distribution of trade goods, and the administration of Company business. District headquarters were linked to depot points for receiving trade goods and trans-shipping furs to the metropolis. The district headquarters had the greatest variety of economic functions; many were associated with transportation (depot, boat building, and labour pool for boatmen). Shanties were locations where seasonal labour moved from posts and headquarters to collect resources (timber, firewood, and fish). Outposts functioned as temporary points for exchange and were the responsibility of particular posts or headquarters. Other periodic exchange points were known as 'flying posts' and 'wintering posts,' although the distinction between these and outposts is unclear. The Company created these short-lived posts largely in response to opposition traders or to prevent Indians from one post trading at another HBC post. To a certain extent, the scale of posts and outposts reflected the distribution of Indian populations – larger bands traded at a post, while an outpost served smaller groups of Indians and was situated near their winter camps. If competitive pressures abated, the expense of these temporary exchange points was saved by closing the outpost, thereby passing back to the Indians the cost of transporting furs to the main post. Although most posts functioned to collect furs in exchange for goods, the permanent establishments made demands upon the local environment for a wide variety of resources. Thus, the key economic role for Indians attached to posts was as a trapper, but, depending upon the decisions of the district chief factor, post Indians might also be engaged for boat work. The district headquarters managed the district economy, communicated with central authorities, served as a depot for the district, employed most of the skilled labour, and attracted a seasonal labour pool. At the district headquarters, Natives were hired for the interdistrict transportation of country produce, country-made goods, trade goods, and furs. Very simply, before 1870 the resource demands of the trade and the need for an extensive system of exchange points necessitated the hierarchical spatial organization. These generalizations about the HBC's spatial organization (Figure 2.1) lead to an understanding of the actual post system as it existed in the early 1870s in northern Manitoba (Figure 2.2)

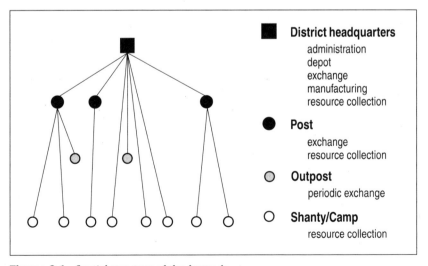

Figure 2.1 Spatial structure of the fur trade

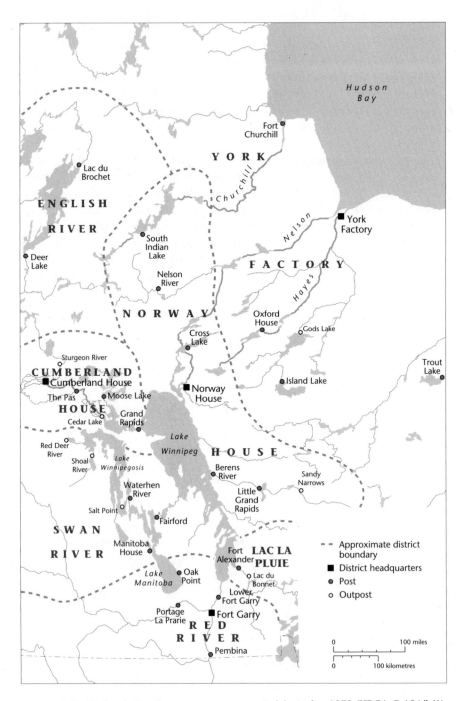

Figure 2.2   Hudson's Bay Company post system in Manitoba, 1870 (HBCA, B.154/k/1)

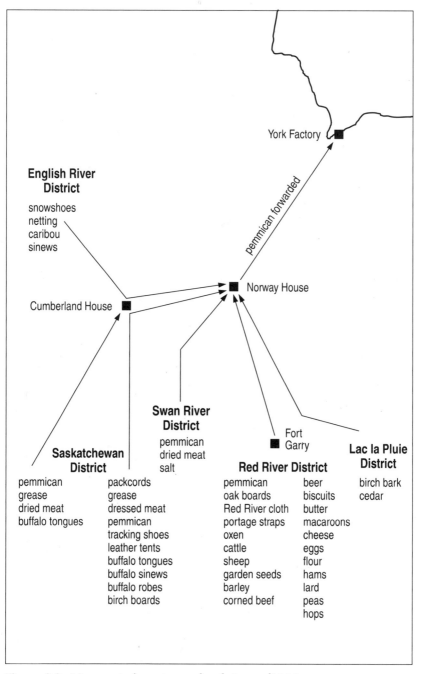

Figure 2.3   Movement of country produce between districts
in northern Manitoba, 1868 (HBCA, B.239/k/14)

The provisioning requirements of the Hudson's Bay Company were satisfied by commercial hunting and agriculture. This reinforced transportation demands, since large quantities of provisions had to be moved to subarctic districts, such as Norway House and York Factory. An indication of the regional integration made possible by the movement of country produce is portrayed in Figure 2.3. Thus, the transportation system connected the producers of the plains and the Red River Settlement with the subarctic fur districts. The nature of agricultural supplies from the Red River district reveals that fur trade life was varied. Although the trade was an export-oriented economy, it generated considerable internal exchanges because it was too expensive to import food to Rupertsland.

The organization of York boat transportation and the resulting employment effects are shown by Figure 2.4. York Factory was the depot for the Northern Department, and Norway House was an important trans-shipping centre. The outfit for the Mackenzie River district was brought inland from York Factory and was left to winter at Norway House. The Red River boat brigades would pick up the Mackenzie River outfit the next spring and take it on from Norway House to Portage la Loche. At Portage la Loche, Mackenzie River and Red River crews exchanged fur returns for outfits. The fur returns from the northwestern districts were then brought on to Norway House, and favourable conditions meant that the returns would then be taken down to York Factory. If not, the furs could be stored at Norway House over the winter. This system allowed some of the trade goods from the Northern Department's depot (York Factory) to be brought inland. In this sense, the Norway House depot functioned as a 'buffer.' Freight was situated so that it could be shipped onward shortly after the spring breakup. Using Norway House as a hub facilitated long-distance transport; the Company therefore increased the turnover of capital. The York Factory-Oxford House-Norway House axis was the most travelled corridor in the whole transportation system. Since much of the Northern Department's freight was funnelled through this part of northern Manitoba, crews hired at York Factory, Oxford House, and Norway House were employed throughout the summer. They were engaged to make two round trips between York Factory and Norway House. The Company's transportation system was therefore a vital feature of the regional economy of northern Manitoba. Norway House, Oxford House, and York Factory derived advantages from their strategic locations, but these communities were also dependent on the organization of the HBC transport for the Northern Department.

Linking Local Economies: York Boats and Native Wage Labourers
In 1870, the HBC's fur trade was based on a pre-steam power transportation system. Throughout most of the nineteenth century, the Company's freight

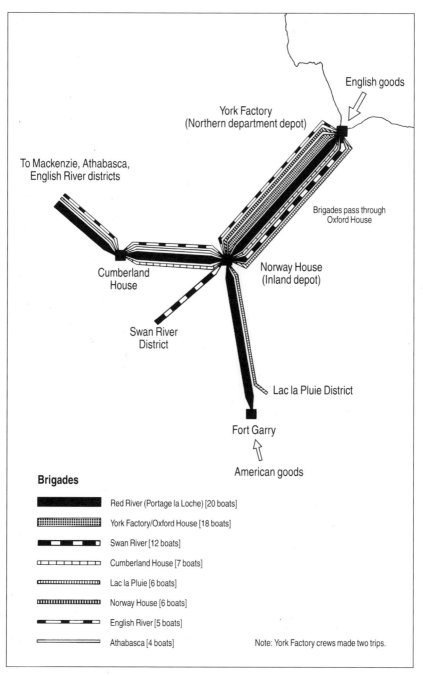

English goods

York Factory
(Northern department depot)

To Mackenzie, Athabasca,
English River districts

Brigades pass through
Oxford House

Cumberland
House

Norway House
(Inland depot)

Swan River
District

Lac la Pluie District

Fort Garry

American goods

Brigades

Red River (Portage la Loche) [20 boats]

York Factory/Oxford House [18 boats]

Swan River [12 boats]

Cumberland House [7 boats]

Lac la Pluie [6 boats]

Norway House [6 boats]

English River [5 boats]

Athabasca [4 boats]

Note: York Factory crews made two trips.

Figure 2.4 Hudson's Bay Company transportation system:
York boat brigades, 1868 (HBCA, B.239/k/14)

was moved by largely Native (Metis and Indian) York boat crews. The York boat was a unique creation of Rupertsland society, and with Native labour, local economies were connected so as to create a regional system. The major demand for labour involved the brigades that freighted fur returns and outfits between district headquarters. At the smaller posts, some Indian trappers obtained summer income by bringing furs to the district headquarters and returning with trade goods. With the exception of the Chipewyan, many Natives preferred the secure income from boating to life in the bush economy. For some Natives it was a primary occupation. Indians, even those who were primarily trappers, found that boating provided a vital seasonal component to their annual income.

Boating was a brutal form of work, and it is necessary to describe these working conditions in order to appreciate the Native role in the regional economy. Heroic images of the voyageur, the freight canoe, and the physical exertion demanded by the portage are engraved on national consciousness, part of a Canadian identity. York boat work was far more demanding than canoe freighting, and because the work was done by Natives, less appreciated. Portage work was not the only difficult aspect of York boat freighting. Willy Frog Ross, an Indian boatman on the Berens River-Little Grand Rapids route, recalled that the oars were 'so large and heavy that it took a lot of muscle and strength to pull one all day long.'[1] The number of portages on a route fluctuated with changing water levels. Generally, high water reduced portaging but it often made low-lying portages swampy and difficult to traverse. The steersman commanded the crew of seven or eight, and he

York boat steersman, ca. 1900 (PAM)

Hauling a York boat across a portage in northern Manitoba, 1915
(PAM, Bayfield, H.A., No. 24)

loaded the freight onto men for carriage across the portages. Each man usually carried 200 pounds with the help of a portage strap. York boats were hauled and dragged across portages with the aid of ropes and log rollers. Portage roads had to be cut and inadequate maintenance added to the discomfort. Given hard usage, the life of a York boat was limited to about four years, and depreciated at 25 per cent per year. At the end of the long day there was very little rest. Freight had to be readied for a quick departure, often as early as 4 A.M., and bannock, beans, and pork were prepared. Crews did not work on Sunday and, for Natives, this was one good reason for embracing Christianity. Traditionally, passengers such as missionaries travelled with the brigades and they were well treated. A crew member was responsible for setting up his tents and making his tea.

In the autumn of 1869, Rev. H. Budd of The Pas described the seasonal cycle, noting that 'it will be quite a sport for these fellows to knock down the geese after 3 months working like slaves in these heavy boats.'[2] The Methodist John Semmens critically observed:

Many a man in the North Land today had been crippled in these Portages and their families are in consequence objects of charity. Many a lonely grave evidences the severity of the work done on these Portages. One of my party after seeing the men carrying two hundred pounds across these swamps remarked that it was no wonder that so many widows were found at all the [annuity] pay stations when the husbands were compelled to work so distressingly hard.[3]

In a similar vein, Rev. E.G. Stevens described the work done on northern Manitoba portages: 'One day in camp I was concerned to see a man having a bad lung haemorrhage. Next day he was working as usual. Right there I discovered that there were worse conditions of labour than negro slavery.'[4] He also recalled the Robinson Portage: 'When carrying began the road was dry. When the work was done the way was muddy, wet with sweat dropped from the faces of the carriers.'[5] Stevens confirmed Semmens's observation, stating that 'many men were standing around doing nothing. These were pointed out to me – "They have hurt themselves carrying on the portages. Their lungs were affected. They will soon die,"' and he was told 'There are no men over fifty years of age at Island Lake.'[6] Ross provided an Indian point of view about this work: 'In those days each man had a hard task. Often sweat would be running down his face all day due to the heat and hard work. It was a hard way to make a living but many a time freighting was the only way to earn food to feed the families. Many a white man doesn't believe what a hard tough life we had in the olden days. Some think an Indian had a soft life but Ne-chee, Kesa-na-gun (Friend it was hard).'[7] Obviously, the 'original affluent society' had ceased to exist for Native hunters whose summer work depended upon York boat freighting.

Although HBC records rarely dwell on the strain of York boat work, the Cumberland House report for 1886 alluded to its difficulty and to the idea that some Indians were not conditioned to do this work. According to the report: 'The Chipewyan Indians cannot be depended on for any kind of manual labour; they will not even work in the boat between here and there [Brochet]. They are physically weak and every time we employ them as boat men some of them are sure to fall sick on the trip – in fact so many have died whilst so employed that others are frightened.'[8] Given the harshness of the working conditions, it would appear that Ross was correct in pointing out that Natives needed York boat income. When Lieutenant-Governor J.C. Patterson toured northern Manitoba, he observed that Indians 'like this kind of work [freighting], and work late and early cheerfully. They are admirable voyageurs – in fact, the finest boatmen of their kind in the world.'[9] This statement points to the valuable role Natives played in the subarctic's first transportation system. The opinion that some Natives preferred freighting to trapping does not contradict remarks about the hazardous work conditions, but it intimates that trapping was also insecure and hard.

Reorganization and Modernization of the Hudson's Bay Company's Transportation System

In the 1870s, two modifications of the HBC's transportation system were simultaneously introduced. Steam power was adopted, that is, the mode of transport was modernized; and the orientation of the system, whereby returns and outfits flowed through York Factory, was shifted to make use of a southern route. Harold Innis was inclined to stress the abruptness with which the HBC transportation system and technology changed: 'Throughout the whole of the fur-producing areas of Canada, a revolution in transportation has occurred since 1869 in which the steamboat, the railroad, and the gasoline motor have been chiefly concerned.'[10] According to Innis, transportation changes after the transfer of Rupertsland resulted in disorganization, and York Factory and Norway House became obsolete.[11] In fact, changes to the transportation system were profound, but not so encompassing as Innis claimed.

The changes in the mid-1870s reflected pressures that had been building for several decades. In the early 1850s, competitive pressures from the United States had led the Company to look seriously at a southern supply route, in historian E.E. Rich's words, the Hudson's Bay Company was 'slowly turning away from the Bay.'[12] In 1859, an American steamboat visited the Red River Settlement, and the Company responded by taking advantage of this potential competition by securing preferential freight rates. Following these developments, the Company began supplying some of its posts via the southern route, and American goods began to enter HBC inventories. In the late 1850s the inland route from York Factory was improved, but it remained expensive.[13] In the 1860s, the Portage la Loche boat brigades took part in mutinous labour actions. This raised the price of labour, thereby increasing the Company's costs and making its transportation system unreliable. Additionally, in 1871 the southern route had the advantage of a railhead at St. Paul. In the summers of 1869 and 1870, provisions for the Lac la Pluie district were imported from Canada.

By 1870, the Company's hinterland could be efficiently linked to Canada and the United States. The plan to overhaul the transportation system was forwarded to London by Donald A. Smith, an individual who played a central role in the political and economic changes that followed the transfer of Rupertsland and who also knew how to profit from such changes. The pending advantages of a southern supply route were imminent. After a meeting of the officers of the Northern Council in the summer of 1870, Smith argued: 'It appears to me very inadvisable [that] we should persevere in the use of the long, difficult and most expensive route by York Factory.'[14] Importing goods from the south would establish Fort Garry as the Northern Department's depot and would make possible the extension of steamboating. Smith noted that the old system had served the Company 'when the system was in its perfect working order; but of late years there has been an increasing spirit of mutiny among the men, which has led to the most embarrassing results.'[15] The urgency of adopting steamboats was the result of a serious mutiny in the summer of 1870: 'At the Grand Rapid[s], on the river

Saskatchewan, a general mutiny took place among the Red River people, of whom the crews of four boats left their lading behind and returned to Red River on three boats which they appropriated to their own use.'[16] In particular, Smith held the Metis responsible. Until steamboats could be introduced, he planned to hire only English Halfbreeds and Swampy Cree from Red River, and to make greater use of Norway House and Lac la Pluie for engaging crews, so that 'by these means we hope to avoid the necessity of again trusting to French Halfbreeds to perform this service.'[17] Donald A. Smith's discouraging impressions of Red River boatmen was not enhanced by the fact that they were unflinching supporters of Louis Riel's provisional government. Smith added, 'You will probably infer the necessity of a sweeping change. For all these evils the only remedy is the employment of steam.'[18] Due to the political and economic struggles of a Native working class, merchant capital was forced to innovate.

The use of steam power also relieved the HBC of its dependence on pemmican. By reducing the number of boatmen, the Company ensured that it did not need to purchase so much pemmican from the plains provisioners. This would also be an advantage for the Saskatchewan district, 'which at present conducts an unprofitable trade, [and] would be relieved from the necessity of providing vast quantities of provisions to man these mutinous brigades.'[19] These proposals reduced economic linkages, and fewer commodities flowed between regions.

The transformation of the Company's transportation system, as it had existed after the introduction of steamboating and before the completion of the Canadian Pacific Railway, is summarized by Figure 2.5. It shows the deployment of steam power and the use of a southern supply route and represents, in Rich's words, a 'shift in the geographical allegiance of the Company – away from the Bay and towards the south.'[20] A comparison of this system to the system existing at the time of the transfer (Figures 2.5 and 2.6) indicates that Grand Rapids became a break point between lake and river steamers. (Figure 2.6 reflects the investment made in warehouses and in a tramway to move goods around the rapids.) The outfits for the Norway House district were sent by steamer, but its furs were generally sent to London via York Factory. By 1873, most of the Northern Department's outfit was no longer being sent to York, but large inventories at the factory meant that goods continued to be shipped inland for a few more years. Oxford House and York Factory districts were still supplied by the Bay route under this system, but gunpowder and some country-made goods were the only freight sent inland from York Factory beyond Oxford House. Berens

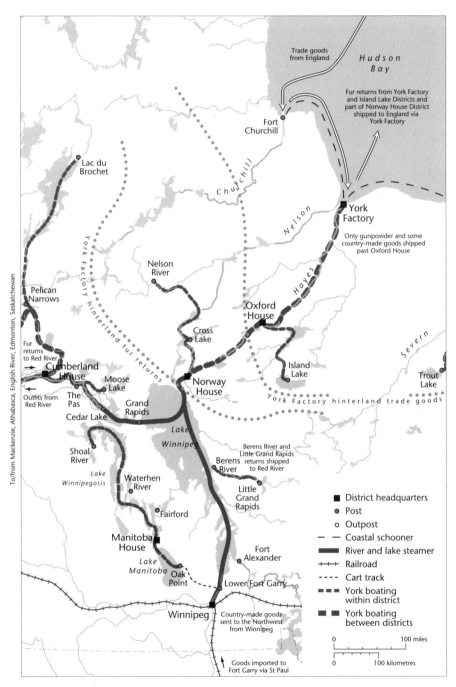

Figure 2.5 Hudson's Bay Company transportation system in Manitoba, 1875-85 (HBCA, B.239/k/14, 36; D.38/2; B.154/k/1)

River and Little Grand Rapids returns were sent out by lake steamer to Red River. Although it was also cheaper to send Norway House returns out by lake steamer, York boats needed a cargo on the trip down to York Factory. The freighting between York Factory and Norway House was generally assigned to Oxford House and York Factory crews. To further relieve the Company of a dependence on boatmen, the extension of carting between Fort Carlton and Green Lake was encouraged. In this sense, both new and old

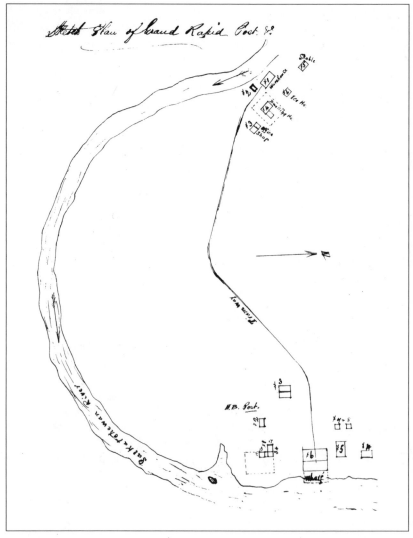

Figure 2.6 Grand Rapids sketch plan of post and portage tramway, 1893 (HBCA, D.25/19)

transport modes complemented the HBC's adjustments to the post-1870 economy that was taking shape.

The modernization of HBC transportation entailed the substitution of labour by capital. In the early 1870s, the Red River-based steamboat companies were reorganized, and the HBC secured preferential freight rates.[21] By 1880, the HBC had invested $282,000 in its steamboating operations.[22] By freighting its own outfits and returns (even with expenses and depreciation) between 1875 and 1878, the Company's steamers had generated a profit of $66,835.[23] Lake steamers shipped 760 tons to Norway House and Lake Winnipeg posts in 1880.[24] In 1876, a steamboat could move goods between Fort Garry and The Pas at a saving of 14 to 18 per cent over what a York boat could accomplish.[25]

Substituting Native labour with steam power had benefits for the Company, but a different situation developed for Norway House Natives. In 1875, Rossville's Methodist missionary J. Ruttan predicted that steamboating supplies from Winnipeg instead of boating them from York Factory, along with the end of the brigades to Portage la Loche, would mean that 'there are about 200 of these Indians thrown out of employment, the proceeds of which have been their chief support.'[26] In 1875, fur trader R. Ross noted that in 'the past five years ... [they] have witnessed the collapse of many of the old established methods of transport.'[27] He further stated that 'hitherto profitably employed in summer transport, such able-bodied men in this way earned from £15 to £20 during the season, it now becomes a serious question how the crowd of Indians collected here can earn a living for themselves and family when deprived of this principal and almost sole means of ensuring a livelihood.'[28] The actual reduction of York boats used between Norway House and York Factory is difficult to determine, since the Company tended to shift its labour supply between the district headquarters. In 1876, at least eight Norway House boats were ordered to freight furs and country produce to York. Nonetheless, the economic displacement associated with the overhauling of the Company's transportation system was one of the reasons for concluding Treaty Five at Norway House. Ironically, the treaty party arrived on the HBC steamer *Colville*, the first steamer to reach Norway House. Some Indians responded to the decline in the post's employment by migrating to Fisher River. While the effects of this new mode of transport made some Native labour redundant, a few Norway House Indians were taken south to Georges Island and Doghead to cut wood for the steamer. Since Grand Rapids was the break point between lake and river steamboating, it was here that a new demand for Native labour was concentrated.

In terms of the Company's long distance transport, the steamboat briefly occupied an interlude between the York boat and the railroad. The change to steam power was not entirely successful, and considerable capital was needed to remove boulders on the lower Saskatchewan River. In the early 1880s, the HBC became less directly involved in steamboating. To deal with a new competitor, the Company merged its steamboat interests with outside capital. As a result, it avoided the risk of competition, obtained expertise in steamboating, and, once again, secured preferential freight rates. From the point of view of Norway House management, these new arrangements were unsatisfactory since the new steamboat company unloaded upstream at Warrens Landing instead of at the post; as well, the employees were careless and unobliging.[29] Overall, it turned out that steamboats delivered neither speed nor reliability, were not particularly profitable, and lost the confidence of the public. By 1885, the HBC began shipping its western outfits by rail since it was not possible to both ship and receive in a single season.[30] Thus, after 1885, northern Manitoba would become a curious backwater. York boating continued between York Factory and Norway House as well as between posts and district headquarters. Steamboating remained a vital form of transportation on Lake Winnipeg for decades, even though this mode of transportation was obsolete elsewhere. As a result, in 1891 the post system (Figure 2.7) was not greatly different from what it was in 1870 (Figure 2.2).

In 1891, Norway House Indians were again cut from the Company's transportation system. Chief Factor H. Belanger explained why the Nelson House and Split Lake Indians had been favoured: 'Because at these places the Indians have no Treaty Money to fall back upon. This change is not so favourably regarding [sic] by some of our semi-civilized Indians here; but it has the effect of conciliating the essentially fur-hunting Indians of the lower Posts.'[31] This statement indicates that trapping incomes alone were inadequate and treaty supplements were required. From the Company's point of view, shifting freighting from the district headquarters to trading posts was a means of maintaining viable fur production. Water transportation remained important in northern Manitoba in the decades after 1870; however, around 1900, the manufactured Peterborough freight canoe began to replace the locally produced York boat.

Streamlining Company Posts

In the late nineteenth century, low fur prices put pressure on the Company to reduce its operating costs. Changes to the post system and the mode of transportation as well as the Company's rationalization schemes reduced the demand for local labour and resources. Increasingly, needs were satisfied by imports. Over time, this functioned to tear apart what had been a closely linked economy; an economy with a spatial hierarchy based on the connections provided by the York boat and a concomitant division of Native labour.

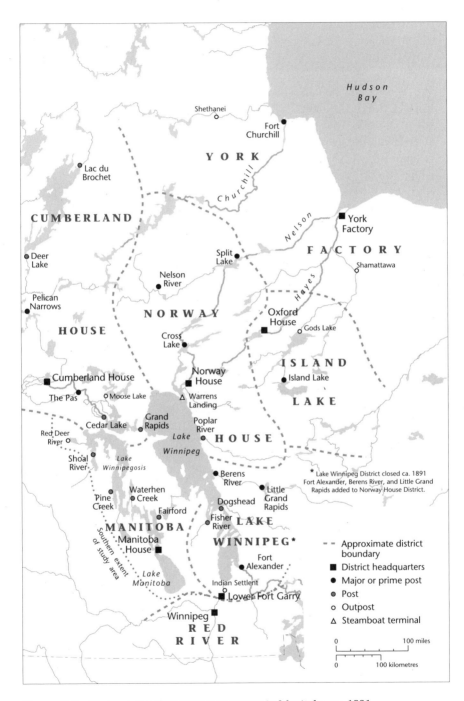

Figure 2.7 Hudson's Bay Company post system in Manitoba, ca. 1891

HBC records reveal how streamlining policies were implemented. In 1877, the Northern Council advocated closing down unremunerative stations and outposts that had been established as a response to petty competition. It was also suggested that summer employment be reduced 'to the lowest scale and of every able bodied servant being made to do boat work if required.'[32] In 1874, the HBC sought flexibility in the deployment of its work force and added the rule 'That in the Contracts of Postmasters, Interpreters, Guides and Mechanics, in addition to the Capacity appear the words "and for the General Service."'[33] Skilled and specialized labour was employed at general labour, thereby reducing the overall need for workers. In 1878, the Northern Council wanted to discharge servants whose contracts were up or those who were not useful. Permanent employees were increasingly replaced with temporary help. Ross explained in 1874 that at Norway House, 'owing to the great reduction in the complement of servants wintering at Norway House firewood and all kinds of lumber are now procured on contract by Indians, and it is found that the plan is both economical and satisfactory.'[34] Labour force reductions continued into the 1890s. Fur Trade Commissioner J. Wrigley wrote to manager H. Belanger that 'the amount of wages paid to Servants is high, but I understand you are intending to dispose with most of them and employ, when necessary, temporary [labour].'[35] The Oxford House report for the outfit of 1890 showed that district wages had been reduced by $1,666. The HBC's labour force would have been further reduced had it not been for the diffusion of a growing number of competitive fur buyers. Renewed competition meant that more outposts had to be maintained, and men were employed 'tripping for furs,' that is trading at Indian camps.

The changes to the transportation system resulted not only in unemployment for many Native boatmen but also in the reduction of the demand for York boats. That boat building had been significantly reduced during the late nineteenth century is indicated by a response from J.K. MacDonald of Norway House to a request from the Red River District:

> I cannot supply the boat you require ensuing Outfit as I am not building any boats at all in this District, nor have I any wood on hand or prepared for the purpose. I could get wood on hand or prepared for the purpose. I could get the wood out next summer and get the boat built in the winter, if that would answer your purpose. To get boat wood here we have to raft it several days journey against the Current. To get boats made here will cost you, I believe more than if you got them made in Winnipeg.[36]

Significantly, the cost of local labour and resources could no longer compete with Winnipeg prices. In 1890 at Oxford House, in order to keep labour needs at a minimum, no boat building was planned. The reduction in the demand for York boats, caused by the use of steam power, reinforced a cycle of contracting internal demand for labour and local resources.

To facilitate the streamlining of the HBC operations, inspection tours were held in the late 1880s and early 1890s. Inspecting officers reported on the means to reduce post activities and expenses. Even dogs and cattle were victims of downsizing. At Gods Lake in 1891, a 50 per cent reduction in livestock was achieved: 'The dogs were shot, as there is no market for them.'[37] Cattle were also reduced. Apparently, post economies could manage with fewer dogs and cattle, and therefore the manpower required to provide feed (fish and hay) for these animals could also be cut back. In this time period, the Company began cutting back on rations issued to the wives of HBC employees. Such a cost-cutting move suggests that the Company was no longer concerned about the 'reproduction of labour.'

The provisioning system of the HBC changed after 1870. The significant decrease in boat crews meant a decrease in the demand for pemmican. In any event, pemmican was already in short supply. Nonetheless, modernization changed the regional characteristics of the fur trade, since the pre-1870 system entailed the linking of Native pemmican producers on the plains with the demand generated in the subarctic by European and Native labourers at posts and by the boat brigades. The late nineteenth century was not a period of abundant game in the subarctic. Scarcity of game meant more time was required for hunting, and country food, therefore, became more expensive. As a result, flour and bacon replaced pemmican and local provisions.[38] By 1893, bacon and flour could be delivered more cheaply to Cumberland House than locally supplied meat.[39] This favoured the greater consumption of imported food at the expense of Native produce, and, consequently, the time available for trapping increased. Clearly, when imported foodstuffs became cheaper than locally produced food, the local economy had been 'opened up' to outside economic forces.

The late nineteenth century fur trade employed less and less skilled labour, and, as Innis noted, skilled labour was brought to Fort Garry instead of York Factory. Skilled labour became less important with the increased use of manufactured imports.[40] Oilcloths and dog chains could be imported more cheaply than those made at York Factory. In 1884, Norway House found it more convenient to import shingles and boards from Doghead than to procure local wood. It was also thought that Churchill did not need a cooper. In 1882, Fortescue recommended switching to certain American tools due to the inferiority of English tools; so even at remote York Factory, the southern influence of the American industrial system was felt.[41] Reflecting the increased use of imports and the declining use of country-made goods, the Company's apprenticeship system was abolished in 1902.[42] A journal entry in 1919 regarding the death of the Norway House blacksmith indicates how quickly the character of the HBC labour force changed: 'Magnus Budd was the Company's old blacksmith here, having received his apprenticeship at York in the old days.'[43] Since many of the tradesmen were of mixed blood, the demise of boat building and the substitution of country-made goods by southern imports had the effect of wiping out a small but skilled Native work force.

With respect to the geographical or spatial organization of the fur trade, the effects of streamlining the HBC labour force were most apparent at the district headquarters type of establishment. In 1891, J.K. MacDonald pointed out that Oxford House Natives were dependent upon wage labour: 'It also, in common with all head Posts, has not such good Fur country surrounding it, while the men are not good hunters, a very great many of them having been brought up as labourers, runners, etc.; employment of this sort, which used to be had is now all but gone, and the only resource left them is the hunt, at which many of them are not skillful.'[44] After responding to the Company's need for labour pools at important points along the transportation network, many Natives were not prepared for the unemployment that ensued from the policies adopted after 1870.

Fur trade society was based on the products of the plains, parkland, and boreal forest. A hierarchical confederation of local economies had been created after 1670. The efforts of Indians, Metis, and Europeans were structured to live off the land and to produce for an external market. Local specialization and the HBC's spatial organization created a division of labour among Native peoples. Nonetheless, fur trade society had a number of common features. Energy and movement were provided by human labour, while dogs and oxen assisted. The energy required was provided by inter-regional food imports, local game and fish, gardens, and marsh hay. In a certain sense, as long as post economies were 'closed' due to high transportation costs, local labour and resources were utilized. With these conditions, the fur trade was really an industry rather than some simple form of casual barter trade. In transportation, economic modernization, which replaced labour power with steam power, had political implications, and Treaty Five was partly a result of the loss of traditional boat work. The transition in the late nineteenth century opened up the subarctic, local resources and labour became costly, London fur prices were low, new transport modes brought in cheaper imports, and operations were streamlined. One result of the re-organization of the regional system was the reduction in skilled craft labour and a return to bush activities. In effect, the regional economy had become even more specialized at producing fur, even more trade-oriented, than it had been. And the population had become less self-reliant.

3
'Dependent on the Company's Provisions for Subsistence': The Decline of Kihchiwaskahikanihk (York Factory)

In July of 1876, the daily journal reported that a party of Severn Indians had journeyed to York Factory simply 'to have a look at the "big fort."'[1] To the Cree, York Factory was known as Kihchiwaskahikanihk, place of the great house. In 1870, this name still accurately reflected York's greatness as a centre of a vast hinterland. For the preceding two centuries, York Factory had been Europe's main entrepôt for the northwestern portion of America. But changes in the regional system during the 1870s made York Factory obsolete, and its greatness became a mere legacy. Following the Rupertsland transfer, the Company's transportation network was turned away from the Bay, which meant that York Factory was no longer situated at an intermediate place between the hinterland and the overseas metropolis. York Factory had become an expense-ridden district headquarters, and its scale of operations had to be reduced to the level of a mere trading post. This transition was made more difficult because York was plagued with environmental problems.[2] Moreover, the dreadful effects on Native people of streamlining and reorganizing the regional system were apparent. Many of the concepts and processes central to understanding the fur trade transition can be more fully appreciated through a detailed examination of the community history of York Factory. The case of York Factory illuminates the combined effects of local resource problems and changes to the regional system on Native people following the transfer of Rupertsland.

Restructuring: Replacing European Labour with Native Labour
The complex seasonal economy of York Factory came under stress in the 1870s. Inexpensive pemmican and cattle from Red River had eased the provision costs but were no longer available, and in the 1870s, the factory had to rely on caribou and geese. Although provision needs may seem extreme, food was a major means of keeping warm in a climate that required a high per capita expenditure of calories. Even the missionary G.S.

Winter was surprised when he had eaten a whole goose, and he noted that he could eat eight or ten rabbits in a single meal.[3] These demands made on the marginal environment of the coastal lowlands do not completely explain the decline of York Factory, and geographer Arthur J. Ray concluded that 'compounding these environmental problems, changes in the Hudson's Bay Company's organization of its operations had the effect of further undermining the economic viability of York Factory.'[4] As headquarters for the Northern Department and supply depot for the Northwest, York traditionally had a number of real 'bookkeeping' advantages that served to ease the pressure of an expensive environment. Before the Company's transportation system had been reorganized, new recruits and retiring servants spent part of the year at York Factory. Thus, between sixty and seventy men were available for post work, but the post did not pay the cost of this labour. With the end of York Factory's major depot function, the post lost a favourable freight structure as it had made a profit on unloading the annual ship. The end of inland shipping meant that men from all over the Northwest would no longer spend their incomes at York Factory's saleshop, which provided an important source of real revenue for the post. In addition, York Factory had lost important sources of revenue because of the demise of the old system of supply and transportation, and its expenses had increased.[5] Such changes to the Company's accounting practices and business organization were not irrelevant abstractions. Eventually, these policies affected the 'traditional' Native society since the Company would have to continue rationalizing York Factory's operations within the context of a marginal environment. In other words, the contraction of the post economy affected the bush economy.

An initial rationalization occurred in the early 1870s, and by the outfit of 1874 the staff had been reduced by one-half. Chief Factor Fortescue explained that his skilled labour could be reduced because country-made articles 'could be manufactured far cheaper nearer depots to the districts requiring the supplies than York Factory is, while the importation of Tin Plates from Canada will also save the duty[,] the wages and maintenance of several Tinsmiths.'[6] A need to reduce the size of the establishment also meant a reduction in the consumption of firewood and in the need for labour. The report on the 1873 outfit noted that a decrease in post expenses was the result of the reduction of staff, which was limited to twenty-two Europeans and ten Native servants/apprentices.[7] Fortescue pointed out that even if the expenditures of the post could be kept within the limits of the returns, a gain 'depends a good deal on the London market.'[8] Even with cost-cutting measures, the external demand for furs ultimately determined the viability of the local economy.

The reduction in the regular labour force, the loss of the 'free' labour of new recruits and retiring servants, and the loss of imported pemmican temporarily increased the demand for Native labour. This new demand for local Native labour and provisioning was evident in the settlement pattern. In 1869, York Factory had a 'settled' Indian population in about twenty tents, but two years later, Rev. W.W. Kirkby noted that the sixty or seventy settled Natives lived in houses or tents in three distinct communities.[9] When pemmican had been available, Fortescue explained that only 'two or three hunters were engaged in procuring fresh provisions for the mess and summer exigencies when the brigades were here, the results of this being that fewer Indians were taken from the winter work of fur hunting and the returns proportionately increased.'[10] However, in 1875 twelve Indians were employed during the winter hunting caribou and partridges, and they returned to the post every two weeks. Not only did the men receive employment as hunters, but their families received rations. The loss of the post's free labour generated a demand for Native labour that compensated for the decline in summer York boat freighting. For example, the York Factory journal in 1875 noted that fifty-six Indians were employed hauling firewood.[11]

In the mid-1870s, the settled community continued to expand. Furthermore, the behaviour of Indians indicated that their labour was needed. Fortescue reported in 1873 that Indians 'were adopting a rather impudent tone, only working when they pleased, and at what they pleased, generally striking at critical times, as when hay was wanted to be boated, or the schooner loaded ... and choosing such busy times to hold "land meetings" and other agitations it was felt they required a sharp lesson to bring them to their senses.'[12] Thus the initial adjustments for York Factory meant transitional employment for Natives. Longer residency near the post was encouraged. Although this residency pattern facilitated the Company's reorganization measures, it was not feasible, and in 1869, *The Proceedings of the Church Missionary Society* had predicted that 'a settled community could not exist at York Factory' since the Indians 'are compelled to separate to distant hunting-grounds during the winter months, otherwise they would starve to death. Even the few families that remain all the year round are dependent on the Company's provisions for subsistence.'[13]

Fortescue suggested that part of York's problem was the result of population growth. He noted that the low point in the Native population occurred in the mid-1830s when the population consisted of twenty-five hunters.[14] In 1880, sixty-six older men and twenty younger men took debt, and Ray suggested this meant an increase in the total population from about ninety to 250.[15] In fact, this would have been an average annual increase of 3.7 per cent per year. For the years 1874 and 1875, the mission records noted

Swampy Cree women and their handiwork in the mission house, York Factory, ca. 1910 (HBCA, 1982/17-1, R. Faries Collection)

forty-nine births and eight deaths, indicating a rapid rate of natural increase.[16] During this period, there was a significant outflow of York Indians, and only a minor inflow of Indians from the Severn area. In the 1880s, deprivation and disease led to what must have been a very high death rate; however, in 1889, Winter claimed that 'the Indians are increasing.'[17] Fortescue gave emphasis to the population pressure argument, but the real problem was that York Factory's population was too large to adjust to both the Company's cutbacks and a marginal environment. Furthermore, the hunting hinterland of York Indians was encroached upon by Indians from Oxford House and Norway House. According to Fortescue: 'Emigration is out of the question, as there is nowhere to go to, Norway House and Oxford House are themselves overpopulated, and I am under orders to discourage all movement of the Indians to the former quarter.'[18]

Protracted Scarcity and Reduction in Native Labour

In 1885, York's new manager, M. Matheson, offered his 'opinion that all the fur bearing animals are increasing in the York Factory section of this District' because trapping had not been 'prosecuted with any energy for many years.'[19] In contrast, the evidence indicates that even after 1885 the resource base was still depleted and unstable. However, by 1887, 'the conclusion has been forced upon me [Matheson] that there is in reality very little fur in the country, and that under no circumstance can the Indians be self-supporting.'[20] In 1887, caribou, partridges, and rabbits were scarce, and a greater reliance on caribou after 1870 may have induced more than periodic shortages because 'it is well understood that Deer [caribou] have become scarce in these days that instead of roaming all over the country as formerly they are reduced to bands and these keep together in one locality.'[21] After 1885, Fort Severn was unable to supply a significant amount of salted geese to York Factory and therefore more pork had to be requested. Thus by 1889, 53 per cent of rations were imported, in contrast to the situation in 1874 when only 35 per cent of rations were imported.[22]

The accounts of a depleted resource base are supported by information sent by Police Inspector J. Bégin in a 1890 report to the lieutenant-governor of Keewatin, John Schultz. Bégin stated that 'furs are very scarce and are becoming more so every year.'[23] For the winter of 1890-1 it was reported that 'a great deal of misery has as usual resulted ... on account of the entire disappearance of Deer in the Interior and of Rabbits, Partridges, and Geese along the sea-coast.'[24] Thus, as in earlier years, provisioning was 'one of the greatest drawbacks to a profitable business here.'[25] When caribou were scarce, 'the only resource for the Natives is to endeavour to reach the Factory,' and when York Factory had been a depot, their winter debts could be paid off with summer work.[26] The HBC report for 1889 outlined the interdependence between the subsistence and commercial sectors: 'Frequently the Deer do not come in our direction and starvation ensues, and to obviate this state of things I endeavoured when I came here first to get the Indians to give their attention more to hunt fur than Deer, and to enable them to do so, gave them food.'[27] There can be no doubt that York Factory's decline as a place in the HBC transportation network coincided with a crisis in the resource base of the Native economy. The enduring nature of this crisis meant that the situation was not merely a temporary low point in resource cycles.

Beginning in the early 1880s, temporary Native labour was laid off, but the streamlining of post operations continued through the 1880s and early 1890s. In 1880, Rev. G.S. Winter stated: 'On account of the poverty of their parents, many of the poor children are very thinly clad.'[28] He reported in 1882 that Indians were 'never employed, except for a few weeks in the summer ... There [sic] labour is not needed.'[29] Matheson explained his 1885 cutbacks: 'I have begun by transferring our servants to Norway House District, reducing summer Indian labour at the Factory to what is actually required (supply the remainder of Indians with the means of livelihood and sent them to the interior) allowing 2 Boat builders to Return to Europe 1 year before the expiry of those Contracts and dismissing four Indian Servants who will go to the woods this incoming winter.'[30] In 1887, it was noted that staff and expenses had been further decreased, but that more reductions were not practical.[31] In 1888, the fur purchasing tariff was reduced. These measures did not immediately balance the books, since the returns for the outfit of 1888 amounted to $6,390 while post expenses totalled $9,503.[32] By this time, the post had only seventeen servants, fifteen women, and forty-five children. The next year, another seventeen persons left York Factory. Winter commented that he had never seen such an exodus and that the establishment had been considerably reduced.[33] Between 1885 and 1889, a total of sixty-seven officers and servants had left York. In 1890, suggestions were made to reduce cattle, to confine the post's operations to one central building, and to ease expenses by limiting staff to between ten and thirteen servants. Furthermore, the 1890 report recommended that 'some of the elderly men, especially those with large families might possibly be induced to retire inland where fish and country produce can more easily be obtained.'[34] Once again it was recommended that country-made articles could be replaced with imports. Winter outlined the results of rationalizations on the character of York Factory: 'The once famous York Factory has become a small post. Many Indians [and] whitemen have left yearly [and] this summer no less than 35 are going away to seek their living elsewhere [and] when they go we shall have only 6 homes to visit [and] those will be occupied by the Company's servants.'[35] Certainly this 1891 account of York Factory is in contrast with the settled Native community that was forming around the busy place of York Factory in the late 1860s.

Restructuring: Returning to the Bush
The HBC could conveniently cut its wages by sending regular servants out of the York Factory district. However, the problem of dependent local Indians remained. A large number of them lived in a semi-settled state near York Factory. Describing this situation in the spring of 1884, Winter wrote: 'We have more Indians at the post than I have seen at this time of year. The fact is some of the poor people are afraid to go far from the fort on account of the scarcity of food: so many of them having been on the point of death.'[36] By August, it was apparent that there was no work, and Natives had to choose between starvation and returning to the bush. To deal with this problem, Matheson implemented a strategy that amounted to the spatial restructuring of the population: 'Every individual who can walk has been made to leave the Factory and go to the woods: should they do no more than earn their own livelihood it is a great benefit compared to being fed at the Company's expenses as was the case for many years with a number of them.'[37] This forced changes to the seasonal economy. Thus, one band did not come in because of lack of summer work, and some Indians remained only for a single Sabbath.

The connections between the traditional patterns of living off the land and the post economy were evident during these stressful times. In 1889, Winter recorded that the Indians 'simply come in to trade their fur, and then go roaming about the country again.'[38] Thus, the Native role in the seasonal economy was modified to meet the Company's changing priorities. Winter summarized these developments as follows: 'When we came to this station in /79 [1879] there was a large number of Indians employed by the H.B.C. ... But all except a very few have been discharged, they live in the woods ten or eleven months in the year.'[39] Certainly, the Hudson's Bay Company could not be accused of benevolence with regard to its treatment of a Native employee, as Winter's private journal reported in 1892: 'This dear old Christian had been in the employ of the H.B.Co. 40 years, & cast off in his old age to make a living as a hunter – a thing utterly impossible.'[40] Although Natives easily adapted to wage labour and a semi-settled residency pattern, the Company's economic policy forced them to return to the bush. In effect, the HBC resurrected the subsistence sector. The bush functioned as a 'safety net' when the commercial side of the fur industry (trapping incomes or wage labour) were inadequate.

Returning to the bush was not a proposition that was completely accepted by Natives. Winter recorded in 1888 that 'many semi-starving Indians remain at this post.'[41] Winter documented the adverse consequences that resulted. In 1889 he wrote:

The little boy [was] buried this afternoon. I feel very sad indeed when I think of the cause of death: for whatever others may say – he died from starvation. Doubtless the parents do not think so: but it is a fact for all that. The Indians who persist in living near the fort are in a [?] state. There is not sufficient food in the river & woods for all at close quarters & the Company are not to blame for withholding food when the people absolutely refuse to fetch it when they are able. Many are fearfully thin, and their constitutions are being undermined. Scarcely a day passes without our giving away many meals: but what is it among the many ... for it is distressing beyond description to hear and see so much poverty.[42]

Exceptions occurred, however. In 1893, Lofthouse reported that York Factory Natives were 'well off for food' because deer were more plentiful and because they had moved away from the post.[43] In spite of a Native reluctance to reorient themselves to the bush, the post was successful in shifting its social costs onto the subsistence sector. Without other sources of income (treaty annuity payments, rations, supplies), a semi-settled residency pattern was not possible at York Factory.

The Company solved its bookkeeping problems by moving the population to the bush adjacent to the post, but nothing was done to deal with the deprivation faced by York Factory Indians. In fact, York Factory had long been a region of out-migration. In 1869, before the period of economic restraint, York Factory Indians were emigrating to the south. In the late 1880s, a few of the York Factory Indians shifted towards Churchill, but the major destination for York Indians was Split Lake. The tendency to migrate was most pronounced in the late 1880s, when Winter reported that 'a good number have left the place owing to the change in the affairs here.'[44] For most, migration to new territories was a more sensible response to scarcity than a semi-starvation residency at the post or meagre subsistence in the depleted lowlands adjacent to York Factory. Thus, after the 'fearfully hard winter' of 1887-8, Winter observed that 'many of the Indians are afraid to return to their proper hunting grounds, but are going to other parts.'[45] The Norway House report of 1889 documented that York Factory Indians were 'gradually abandoning their old quarters and coming in greater numbers every year to hunt in the vicinity of Split Lake.'[46] The Company responded to these population changes. In the late 1880s, Split Lake became a 'guard post' in the Norway House district because York Factory Indians had been encouraging competitors to buy their furs. In 1891, Winter reported that some Indians had moved towards Fishing Lake north of York Factory, and that others 'are removing to the south as fast as they can; for they clearly feel that they are being starved in these parts.'[47] By 1889, only seventy-six Indians took debt at York Factory. Split Lake's population of 300 in 1900 included 250 Indians originally from York Factory. Although Fortescue had claimed that emigration was not possible, it turned out to be necessary. The Company's effort to keep surplus populations in each district was largely unsuccessful. The policy of cutting off traditional forms of assistance left the Indians no choice but to move to the Split Lake area. For those who were reluctant to return to the bush adjacent to York Factory in the mid-1880s, a move to Split Lake in the late 1880s and early 1890s offered the advantages of a better resource base, a Company post, and the prospect of higher incomes because HBC fur prices were influenced by opposition traders.

Deprivation and Adjustment
The reorganization of the regional system and the resulting turmoil to the local economy of York Factory had human 'costs.' Balancing the books by HBC officers meant deprivation for Natives. The year 1883 seemed to be stressful, and in the spring, Winter noted that there 'is in immense amount of suffering all around us.'[48] With inadequate food came disease,

and throughout this period the missionary records leave the impression that most of their efforts were directed towards visiting the sick. In 1883, the post's doctor treated some 200 Indians for laryngitis and bronchitis, and Winter buried twenty-two Indians; this was an increase in the annual mortality recorded in the 1870s. The late winter and early spring, when existence was determined by the caribou hunt, became the season of scarcity. Winter recorded in late January 1891 that 'we noticed today for the first time a few 'pinched' faces, a sure sign that the hard times have begun.'[49] In 1890, Winter recorded the effects of deprivation: 'Like many of the Indians, she is fearfully scrofulous ... Beggars still come to our house. It is dreadful.'[50] The season of food scarcity was followed by the season of disease: 'The spring epidemic of influenza has begun [and] many are being attacked.'[51] Although there may not have been a large number of cases of starvation, diet and disease were related. Malnourishment made the population more vulnerable to epidemics.

In the midst of this deprivation, Winter had to explain to the London office of the Church Missionary Society (CMS) why the mission was not self-supporting: 'I deeply regret to say that the Indians are getting poorer every year. Their poverty is more than can be imagined; and the vast majority are in debt. Such being the case it is impossible to think of them supporting their minister as you suggest.'[52] This contrasted with the situation in the late 1860s when Indians donated fur and hide to the mission. The mission journals indicate an increase in support from England, including clothing and rice.

In spite of alterations to the seasonal economy, deprivation was experienced by York Factory Natives in the 1880s and early 1890s. The report for the 1887 outfit spared the details but explained that 'no words of mine can convey any adequate idea of the suffering.'[53] Inspector Bégin found that even though Indians were given provisions, they could not pay their debts.[54] The winter of 1889-90 must have been especially difficult, since it was reported that 'numbers have eaten their starved dogs, their snow shoes, and the refuse from their dust heaps, while several died from actual starvation.'[55] In the spring of 1890, Winter documented the extent of deprivation: 'The poor people must have been starving indeed when they begged admission into the "Blubber house" to take away [and] eat the leavings of the dogs' food. They even scraped the tanks to get off the putrid meat. A woman once visited her hooks, but found no fish. She was so fearfully hungry that she took up the bait and ate. A boy ate the bait set in a fox trap.'[56] Unusable caribou portions thrown away in the fall were later eaten. The winter of 1890-1 was not a great improvement, since Winter recorded that an Indian had 'been digging up bones that were thrown away last fall [and] boiling them, so as to have something better than snow water to drink.'[57]

The suffering at York Factory was not simply due to the failure of the natural environment. The situation in the late nineteenth century reflected the inability of a 'bottom-line' mercantilism to provide security and dignity for a people who had for centuries produced fur for the 'Company of Adventurers.' In 1886, Rev. J. Lofthouse stated that 'the Company's officers here [York Factory] will do nothing to assist them, some of the old [and] sick used to get half rations every week, but all that is put a stop to since Mr. Matheson's arrival.'[58] Not surprisingly, Matheson could credit himself with reducing Indian debt balances by 2,000 Made Beaver in his first two years as manager.[59] In the same month in which Winter recorded that a family had survived for a week on three ermines, he also noted that the Company's food was only available on a barter basis.[60] In 1890, Indian debts were limited to necessities (ammunition, twine, and netting). The Canadian government did little to reduce the deprivation of the York Factory Indians. In 1890, Winter's journal noted the arrival of the North West Mounted Police, but he argued that they were not needed and that the government's interest would be better served if they would show some charity.[61] Lofthouse noted the Natives 'indirectly pay this tax [import duty] thro the Hudson's Bay Co.' and that the government does not 'know there are Indians or Eskimo on the North Western shores of the great inland sea.'[62]

In 1891, Winter indicated that the depopulation of the post would continue 'until the once famous York Factory become[s] a mere trading post, with only a post master & a few servants.'[63] Thus, in a twenty-year period, York Factory had made a difficult transition and had become, in effect, 'a mere trading post.' A prediction in 1880 that Churchill would become more important than York Factory would be borne out, but not until the twentieth century.[64] In 1885, Lofthouse had hoped that the railway to the Bay would be built soon, since 'many of these poor Indians are in a most miserable state and need something to bring them relief.'[65] But new external economic forces did not come to the rescue, and it would take several decades before the railway would influence the York Factory region. Without a settled population, the CMS withdrew from York Factory in 1894 and directed most of its efforts towards Churchill and Split Lake. With its operations rationalized to the level of a fur collecting post, York Factory's decline was arrested. For the outfit of 1892, Fur Trade Commissioner C.C. Chipman claimed: 'It is satisfactory to observe that York Factory Post itself at last shows a profit.'[66] The Indians at York Factory were considered self-supporting at the turn of the century and some Indians had returned from Split Lake.

Chief Factor Fortescue accurately described the seasonal economy of York Factory, and of all other posts, when he stated simply that 'so much does one thing depend upon another here.'[67] In other words, cutbacks to one 'thing' would have negative spread effects throughout the entire local economy. When the lieutenant-governor of Keewatin, J.C. Patterson, visited the region in 1897, he commented: 'York Factory lends itself to melancholy. It is, indeed, a deserted village. Time was, and not so long ago, when it was a very hive of industry, frequented by all the Indians in the district, and giving employment to hundreds of men.'[68] Perhaps contemporary academics can see the relationship between Natives and fur trade as shifting forms of dependency, but what happened at York Factory in the late nineteenth century cannot be construed as a partnership between the HBC and the Native population. In 1893, Lofthouse compared the Chipewyan and the Inuit: 'The Eskimo are quite as dependent on the Co. as the Indians as there are no other means of disposing of their furs etc. & getting supplies, but the Eskimo are as a race much more independent than any of the Indian tribes and were the Company to withdraw from this station they would still manage to exist, whereas the Indians would die or go to the interior.'[69] Even with respect to the Chipewyan-Dene (who are considered to be essentially independent by many twentieth-century social scientists), Lofthouse observed that they were relatively dependent on the HBC. For those Natives involved in wage labour, their dependence was even greater.

The demise of York Factory illustrates how fur trade history and Native history are intertwined. Generations of Homeguard Cree had trapped, hunted, and laboured for the Hudson's Bay Company, but with structural changes to the fur trade economy, they were left to the vagaries of the environment. When their labour became redundant, the HBC used economic coercion to drive them back to the bush. Without a perspective focusing on the interplay between the commercial and subsistence sectors of the local economy, the crises at York Factory cannot be revealed or understood. The community history of York Factory is consistent with observations that those areas in the Third World having the longest contact with metropolitan capitalism are the same areas exhibiting the most underdevelopment. York Factory experienced an obvious dissolution of its local economy, and Native peoples attached to this district headquarters bore the most extreme destitution experienced in northern Manitoba. Exceptions provide the most vital insights about history. York Factory not only illustrates the extreme changes that took place within the fur trade, but it also shows that the livelihood of the Native population was dependent upon external decision-makers. Company agents, like Matheson, were driven by the need to show a profit, and day-to-day procedures of life were shaped by accounting criteria.[70] Yet, the only effective relief from suffering came when Indians decided to leave the Hudson Bay Lowlands.

Today, York Factory is one of the forgotten places of the Canadian landscape, of interest only to the historically minded or to antiquarians. Many of the descendants of the Swampy Cree of York Factory live at Shamattawa. And now, the community of Shamattawa only receives recognition when a startling social crisis draws media attention. The many contributions of the Swampy Cree to Canada's economic development are buried under superficial images of social decay. The story of the decline of Kihchiwaskahikanihk is not so unique. If anything, York Factory merely set a pattern for many communities that came to exist in an area once known as Rupertsland. This post experienced the crisis of a single-industry town. Subsequently, community after community has had to deal with 'adjustment' and 'restructuring' when faced with resource depletion or fluctuations in the market demand for a staple. The records of the Hudson's Bay Company and, more important, the Church Missionary Society, illustrate the horror that can result from a single-minded determination to downsize.

4

'To Be Shut Up on a Small Reserve': Geographical and Economic Aspects of Indian Treaties

Thus far, land has only been considered as an essential resource for the subsistence and commercial needs of the local economy. But the use of land for the pursuit of a livelihood after 1870 takes on political and legal meanings. The demise of Native control over land illustrates that the economic history of Native people must carefully examine the imperatives of external forces. In northern Manitoba, a legal-legislative process served to dispossess Natives of land and resources. Through Indian land surrender treaties and Metis scrip, Natives lost control over resources and obtained few benefits from their original ownership. The written version of a treaty does not provide the final interpretation of treaty rights. Oral versions of the treaties and other written records of the treaties also have to be consulted. To understand treaties in a modern context requires a careful reconstruction of the treaty process. In the past, perspectives on treaties have tended to fall into two separate versions: (1) the conventional view, which relied on the exact written text and included the attendant belief that the government's Indian and treaty policy was enlightened, and (2) the general Indian view that treaties are abstract sacred agreements that recognize political sovereignty. Both views tend to ignore the economic context of treaty-making and the economic influences shaping treaty terms. An understanding of the fur trade and a variety of written records provide relevant geographical and economic insights about the origins of Euro-Canadian property rights in Manitoba.

Aboriginal Rights and Treaty Policy
The basic concept of Aboriginal rights – that by prior occupation Indians have possessory land rights or Aboriginal title and that the possession of Indian lands could not be illegally surrendered – arose out of some of the earliest experiences between Europeans and Indians. Aboriginal ownership and occupancy prior to the creation of European property relations is a

geographical fact. In Canada, the legal foundation for acknowledging Aboriginal rights is the Royal Proclamation of 1763. This document reiterates the pre-existing British policies on Aboriginal rights.[1] Indian lands in British North America were recognized as the Indian Territory, and a means for surrendering Indian title to these lands was set down. The proclamation proscribed private surrenders of Indian land and established that Indians could surrender only to the Crown. The treaty process in western Canada was an outgrowth of the Royal Proclamation.[2]

Each of the western or numbered treaties began by stressing 'the desire of Her Majesty to open up to settlement' a particular tract of country by obtaining the consent of 'her Indian subjects inhabiting the said tract' through a treaty resulting in 'peace and goodwill' between the Indians and Her Majesty since they could be assured of 'Her Majesty's bounty and benevolence.'[3] Treaties can only be understood as a process whereby both treaty commissioners and Indians attempted to define the terms for 'extinguishing' Aboriginal title. Yet, Indians expected that treaties would secure their future. The full magnitude of the pending changes in property relations could not have been evident; in many respects, Indians were really accommodating the subjects of the British Crown. The terms of surrender, however, should not be conceived merely as compensation for the displacement of a hunting economy by white settlement, a common premise of policymakers. Current policymakers see such compensation as a very restricted and limited set of items. Before the western treaties, the trapping economy was in sorry need of assistance. Indian motivation for accepting a surrender of Aboriginal title can partly be understood as a desire, by some Indians, to secure a means to become agriculturists, an economic alternative or adjunct to the fur trade. In terms of geographical scope, most of northern Manitoba falls under Treaty Five territory, but an examination of adjacent treaties is required because Treaties One and Two cover portions of the Interlake (see Figure 4.1). Moreover, the written documentation on Treaties One and Three provides a context for later treaties.

The policy framework for surrendering Indian title in western Canada was not particularly well developed. Immediately following the 1870 transfer of Rupertsland, the Canadian government looked to the HBC for information on the Native population and for advice on policy.[4] The pre-Confederation treaties in Upper Canada, especially the Robinson Treaties of 1850, influenced the process in western Canada. The deputy superintendent general of Indian affairs, William Spragge, had negotiated the Manitoulin Island Treaty in 1860. He acknowledged the purpose of the treaty approach to Aboriginal title when he pointed out that 'the inconvenience and danger of attempting to pass over the territorial rights' had been avoided.[5] These Upper Canada treaties helped set the government's basic approach to

Indian title in Rupertsland. Lieutenant-Governor Adams G. Archibald stated during Treaty One talks that the Queen 'can do for you no more than she has done for her red children in the East. If she were to do more for you that would be unjust for them.'[6] Despite the Robinson Huron/Superior treaties and the Manitoulin Island Treaty, a comprehensive approach to Aboriginal rights in western Canada had not been worked out in advance of the annexation of Rupertsland. The provisional nature of Indian policy is evident in the instructions to would-be lieutenant-governor W. McDougall (28 September 1869), who was directed to 'make a full report upon the state of the Indian tribes now in the Territories – their numbers, wants and claims; the system heretobefore pursued by the Hudson['s] Bay Company with them – accompanied by any suggestions you may desire to offer with reference to their protection, and to the improvement of their condition.'[7]

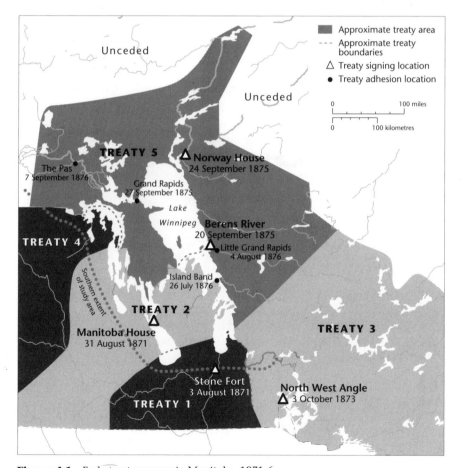

Figure 4.1 Early treaty process in Manitoba, 1871-6

The particular circumstances of Indians, their relationship to the HBC, and claims were relevant information for Ottawa policymakers. Similarly, the first lieutenant-governor of Manitoba, A.G. Archibald, had some input into the process since he was to 'ascertain and report to His Excellency the course you may think most advisable to pursue, whether by treaty or otherwise, for the removal of any obstruction that may be presented to the flow of population into the fertile lands that lie between Manitoba and the Rocky Mountains.'[8] These instructions reveal the government's concern more clearly than the wording of the treaties; the entire process was subordinated to the settlement of the West. Moreover, the government was willing to consider alternatives to treaties in order to deal with the perceived obstruction that Indians represented to expansionism.

The western Canadian treaties did not duplicate the Robinson Huron/ Superior and Manitoulin Island treaties. Some local input was solicited. Lake Superior politician S.J. Dawson advised the government on treaty matters, and his knowledge of the Fort Francis area led him to recommend the setting aside of exclusive fisheries and gardens for Indians. Vast areas were to be marked off as Indian hunting territories, and timber and mineral wealth would ensure a fund for Indian annuities.[9] Ottawa also obtained input from the Northwest Territories Council; its resolutions recommended procedures for Indian treaties. Secretary of State J. Howe pointed out to Indian Commissioner W.M. Simpson that the 'powers intrusted [sic] to you are large' and that the government was dependent 'upon the exercise of your judgment in fixing the price,' but Simpson was to secure terms favourable to the government and at a maximum cash payment of twelve dollars per family.[10] The government's policy was not well developed in 1870 and it required basic information and advice on the Indian populations of the newly acquired Rupertsland. Because of this ambiguity and because of an Indian economic agenda, the details of the terms of the treaties had to be negotiated.

The Terms of Treaties
Although the Dominion government was interested in shaping the development of the entire Northwest, its dealings with Aboriginal title were piecemeal and haphazard. As such, the terms of surrender and government responsibilities varied from treaty to treaty. In part, differences in the terms were the result of unequal negotiations. (See Appendix B for a summary of the terms of the written treaties.) With each successive treaty, different Indian bands tended to extract more concessions (for example, more annuity money or larger reserves). However, the written wording of the treaties became more specific about Indian obligations and government control over reserves. Treaty One pledged Indians to the treaty, to maintain perpetual

peace between themselves and whites, and to neither interfere with property nor molest Her Majesty's subjects. Treaty Two and all subsequent treaties added that Indians should: behave as good and loyal subjects of Her Majesty; respect, obey, and abide by the law; maintain peace and good order between themselves and other Indian tribes; not to interfere with any person passing through the said tract; and to assist officers bringing justice and punishment to any Indian offending the treaty or Her Majesty's laws. Despite concessions that increased the size of reserves (from 160 to 640 acres), the written version of each new treaty tended to reinforce government control over reserve lands and resources. Treaties One and Two, and to a limited extent Treaty Five, discussed the location of reserves with respect to specific bands, whereas subsequent treaties did not infer reserve sites but only stated that reserves would be located 'where it shall be deemed most convenient and advantageous' for Indian bands by officers of the government and that 'such selection shall be so made after conference with the Indians.'[11] The government was also given authority in the later treaties to decide about conflicting claims. These treaties also specified that reserve surrenders could occur for public works but such surrenders could not occur without Indian consent.

The issue of protecting the Native economy was dealt with in the later treaties. Treaties One and Two do not refer to hunting or fishing rights. In Treaty Three, Her Majesty agrees with the Indians that they 'shall have right to pursue their avocations of hunting and fishing throughout the track surrendered.'[12] While the written treaty acknowledges this right, it is 'subject to such regulations as may from time to time' be made by the government and excluding areas 'taken up for settlement, mining, lumbering or other purposes.'[13] Annual cash payments, relief rations, and the provision of ammunition and twine, served to sustain the Indian population in the bush and to subsidize the fur industry.

Territory and Resources: Government Priorities
The territorial dimension of treaty process was based on the government's geographical interest in particular areas and the differing priorities that Indian bands held with regard to treating with the government on land issues. The Dominion's main interest in formally treating with Indians – to clear title to land resources for agricultural settlement – is well known. However, some of the land ceded in Treaties One and Two was not prime agricultural land. The government's motivations for negotiating Treaty Five are numerous and complex. Immediately prior to the treaties, Archibald reported: 'We are all of opinion that it would be desirable to procure the extinction of Indian title, not only to the lands included with the Province, but also to so much of the timber grounds east and north of the Province, as

were required for immediate entry and use, and also of a large tract of culti-vable ground, west of the Portage, which having very few Indian inhabit-ants, might be conceded with very little additional cost.'[14] Consequently, Archibald recommended 'negotiations at the Lower Fort with the Indians of the Province, and certain adjacent timber Districts.'[15] Thus, the economic rationale for Treaties One and Two was the acquisition of agricultural land and timber resources.

The Indians immediately east of Manitoba came under Treaty Three, but the Dominion had acknowledged their rights when presents were given to them in 1870 so that Colonel Wolseley's troops could pass through their lands. A corridor between Thunder Bay and Fort Garry along with any land that could be thrown 'open to settlement' and might be 'susceptible of improvement and profitable occupation' was the government's main reason for wanting a surrender of Aboriginal title in northwestern On-tario.[16] Lieutenant-Governor Alexander Morris recalled that Treaty Three resulted in the opening up of a territory 'of great importance to Canada, embracing as it does the Pacific Railway route to the North-West Territo-ries ... and as is believed, great mineral wealth.'[17] From the beginning, gov-ernment officials knew that various forms of wealth could be obtained from Indian lands.

Treaty Five covers part of the Interlake, the lower Saskatchewan River, and the Canadian Shield country around Lake Winnipeg. In 1873, Morris rejected the idea of a treaty in this area because 'the country lying adjacent to Norway House is not adapted for agricultural purposes' and 'there is there-fore no present necessity for the negotiation of any treaty.'[18] Nonetheless, by 1874, Morris was suggesting a limited treaty around Lake Winnipeg. Ambiguity about the position of the northern boundaries of Treaties One and Two meant that the tenure for the proposed Icelandic settlement on the southwest shore of Lake Winnipeg could not be firmly established. How-ever, a geographically more limited treaty or an adhesion to the original treaty with the Berens River and Island bands would have established a complete surrender of Indian title to the lands described in Treaties One and Two.

The inclusion of bands as far west as Cumberland House and as far north as Cross Lake cannot be justified by the territorial ambiguity of the north-ern boundaries of Treaties One and Two. In 1874, Morris recommended a treaty with the Berens River Indians since 'trading, sailing of vessels and steamers will be carried on and probably settlement of the shore.'[19] The resource potential of the region permitted Morris to justify a much larger treaty, since 'the prevalence of timber suitable for fuel and building pur-poses, of lime and sandstone, of much good soil, and natural hay lands on the west shore of the Lake, together with the great abundance of white fish [*sic*], sturgeon and other fish in the Lake, will ensure, ere long, a large Settlement.'[20] Additionally, the development of steam navigation on Lake Winnipeg and the lower Saskatchewan River meant that the government was interested in securing a navigable right of way. Thus, bands between Grand Rapids and Cumberland House came under Treaty Five. Morris had foreseen that until the completion of the railroad 'the lake and Saskatchewan River are destined to become the principal thoroughfare of communication between Manitoba and the fertile prairies.'[21] The extinguishment of Indian title may have also been carried out in order to facilitate Indian reserve settlement in the Interlake. In 1875, some Norway House Indians expressed a desire to relocate and to establish an agricultural settlement on the southwest shore of Lake Winnipeg. Finally, the most comprehensive rationale for Treaty Five was provided by Morris: 'The progress of navigation by steamer on Lake Winnipeg, the establishment of Missions and of saw milling enterprises, the discovery of minerals on the shores and vicinity of the lake as well as migration of the Norway House Indians all point to the necessity of the Treaty being made without delay.'[22] Morris's reasoning clearly demonstrates that agricultural development was not the exclusive concern of the government. Even at this early date, the potential resources of the boreal forest were attracting the attention of agents of the Crown. In order to understand the role of Natives in frontier resource industries, it is necessary to identify the connections between the treaty process and resource use.

Regardless of the government's resource and location reasons for alienating tribal lands, a certain territorial ambiguity existed with respect to treaty boundaries and the particular traditional hunting grounds of many bands. Thus, some areas were surrendered by only a portion of the Indians occupying the territory described by the treaty. The resulting difficulty was resolved by adding names to band lists and then back-paying annuity arrears for the years missed. Morris was alert to the possibility that if boundaries were not properly defined, Indian title might be left unextinguished.[23] The northern boundaries of Treaties One and Two were problematic since they ran along the east coast of Lake Winnipeg and included the hunting territories of bands not properly represented at the negotiations. In 1875, the surveyor-general was not certain whether the islands around Grindstone Point on Lake Winnipeg had been surrendered.[24] The Berens River band had been invited to Treaty One negotiations and their hunting territory had been partly ceded by this treaty. A mix-up had occurred: members of the band got hungry waiting for the commissioner and this had somewhat soured their interest in negotiating a treaty.[25] Later, the Berens River band signed Treaty Five. In a similar mix-up, some Indians occupying lands just west of the Interlake in an area described by Treaty Two signed Treaty Four.

Government Approaches to Treaty Negotiations

A proclamation of 18 July 1871 called upon various Indians 'to enter into negotiations on the subject of an Indian Treaty' with the commissioner of Her Most Gracious Majesty the Queen.[26] At the end of July 1871, Indian bands gathered at the Stone Fort, but negotiations were delayed for a few days. At times, more than a thousand Indians attended. A special correspondent of the local newspaper, *The Manitoban*, provided a description of the site of the treaty on 29 July 1871, just before the talks began:

> This accession to the encampment, which immediately adjoins Lower Fort Garry, will increase the number of tents to 100 or 120, and make a very lively scene. The encampment is in the form of a semi-circle, with the chiefs' lodges – near which a handsome flag flies – in the centre. Of the followers, it must be said that they are apparently very comfortable. Most of their lodges are of birch bark, but a considerable number have good tents. Each lodge or tent has a fire in front or inside, where Indian women are ever-lasting baking bread or making tea. Any number of horses and dogs roam through the camp, and along in the afternoon one or more crowds gather near the tents.[27]

Troops were on hand, in part to prevent trade in liquor and in part because, according to Archibald, 'military display has always a great effect on savages, and the presence, even of a few troops, will have a good tendency.'[28] In a similar vein, Howe advised the privy council that the Indian commissioner 'be allowed to wear an [sic] uniform, without which they [Indians] are slow to believe that anyone, having the Queen's authority, can be sent to treat with them.'[29] An important step once the Indians had gathered was to get them to select a chief and headmen for each band so that the treaty could be negotiated. This procedure was considered essential to avoid the problem of the Selkirk Treaty (1817) since, according to Archibald, some 'Indians now deny that these men ever were Chiefs or had authority to sign the Treaty.'[30]

The written text of the treaties is only one part of the process; verbal discussions during negotiations are equally as important. A useful document that provides extrinsic evidence about treaties is titled 'Memorandum of an Address to the Indians by the Lieutenant-Governor of Manitoba.' This statement to the Indians assembled at the Treaty One talks reveals many aspects of the government's strategy. Certainly, the tone is patronizing and makes frequent use of the Queen who 'wishes her red children to be happy and content' and who as 'Your Great Mother, The Queen, wishes to do justice to all her children alike.'[31] Archibald provided additional meaning to the terms of the treaty; on the question of reserves, he stated: 'Your Great

Mother, therefore, will lay aside 'Lots' of land to be used by you and your children forever. She will not allow the white man to intrude upon these lots. She will make rules to keep them for you, so that, so long as the sun shall shine, there shall be no Indian who has not a place that he can call his home, where he can go and pitch his camp, or if he choose, build his house and till his land.'[32] Once assured that they would not be dispossessed outright, Archibald explained to the Indians what was meant by a reserve: 'These reserves will be large enough, but you must not expect them to be larger than will be enough to give a farm to each family, where farms shall be required. They will enable you to earn a living should the chase fail, and should you choose to get your living by tilling you must not expect to have included in your reserve more of hay grounds than will be reasonably sufficient for your purposes in case you adopt the habits of farmers.'[33] In his address, Archibald indicated that the effects of surrendering Aboriginal title would not be abrupt. Indians could continue to hunt. In his opening address, Morris did not state exactly what was being surrendered. The nature of Aboriginal title was never made explicit. The general impression was left that room was being made for white settlers and that Indians would not be dispossessed and that they could continue to hunt over much of the country as they always had.

During treaty negotiations, the government's position stressed that Indians would not have to make drastic changes or a sudden economic transition. Archibald stated that the Queen would only recommend adopting the security of agriculture. Consequently, Archibald indicated: 'The Queen, though she may think it good for you to adopt civilized habits, has no idea of compelling you to do so. This she leaves to your choice, and you need not live like the white man unless you can be persuaded to do so with your own free will.'[34] Archibald then drew attention to the agricultural pursuits of the St. Peters Indians. Additionally, Simpson recorded that the Indians 'are fully impressed with the idea that the amelioration of their present condition is one of the objects of Her Majesty in making these treaties.'[35] Thus, the early treaties were presented as a way of allowing Indians to adjust to changing times: very little would be given up, the Queen would be benevolent, reserves would provide security, hunting would continue, and they would be given the opportunity of pursuing agriculture.

In more specific terms, the government was not offering a mutually advantageous treaty. With the demand for large reserves, the Queen's representatives took a hard line. According to Archibald:

> In defining the limits of their reserves, so far as we could see, they wished to have about two-thirds of the Province. We heard them out, and then told them it was quite clear that they had entirely misunderstood the meaning

and intention of Reserves. We explained the object of these [Reserves] ... and then told them it was of no use for them to entertain any such ideas, which were entirely out of the question. We told them that whether they wished it or not, immigrants would come in and fill up the country; that every year from this one twice as many in number as their whole people assembled, would pour into the Province and in a little while would spread all over it, and that now was the time for them to come to an arrangement that would secure homes and annuities for themselves and their children.[36]

Threats were one approach the government used. White settlement of Indian lands, without Indian consent, was inconsistent with the Royal Proclamation of 1763. In this sense, treaty negotiations were highly unequal; Indians were not made aware of the existing legal rights of Native peoples, as recognized by the British Crown.

During more difficult talks, the government strategy became more apparent. The Treaty Three negotiations with the Ojibwa of Northwestern Ontario were extremely trying for the government officials, and at one point Morris actually broke off the talks stating: 'Then the Council is at an end.'[37] The Ojibwa would not give in and a chief had stated: 'Our Chiefs have the same opinion; they will not change their decision.'[38] However, Morris had detected a split among those gathered for Treaty Three, and rather than treat with just the bands that were willing to compromise, he then suggested that they council among themselves. At this point, certain well-known Red River Metis – James McKay, Pierre Leveillee, Charles Nolin, and Mr. Genton – were sent to attend the Indian council. The next day the Ojibwa agreed to the treaty and after the terms had been discussed, the Fort Francis chief told Morris: 'I wish you to understand you owe the Treaty much to the Half-breeds'[39] – a reference to the Red River Metis with Morris's delegation. In this instance, Morris made use of threats, exploited a split among the Indian bands, and then had the help of the Metis to bring both factions together to accept the treaty.

With experience, government negotiators developed a strategy of separating the acceptance of a treaty from the particular problems relating to the location and the size of reserves. Treaties One and Two actually indicated the locations of future Indian reserves. The references to reserves in Treaty Five came about differently. Morris explained this strategy with reference to the talks at Grand Rapids: 'We took a similar course as at "Norway House" in severing the question of terms of the treaty and Reserves, and with like satisfactory results, after a lengthy discussion the Indians agreed to accept the terms, and we then entered upon the difficult question of the Reserves.'[40] The 1876 adhesion to Treaty Five followed the same strategy since Commissioners T. Howard and J.L. Reid reported that the bands were 'anxious that the places where they are in the habit of living should be granted' as reserves and mentioned in the treaty; 'but as our instructions were positive on this point, we refused.'[41] A central aspect of the government's approach to treaties was to split the general idea of a treaty from the specific delineation of the reserves, obtaining acceptance of the treaty from Indians and then making as few commitments to the particulars of the location of reserves as possible. Such a tactic would have the effect of gaining general acceptance for a treaty by circumventing the Indian demand for large reserves. The separation of the idea of a treaty concerning Aboriginal title from the specifics of reserves was a strategy that also served to disconnect the ongoing use and occupancy of vast hunting territories from the future ownership of a small, enclosed reserve. In this manner, the government had maximum flexibility in deciding future land tenures for particular regions. The government's success with this approach to land, despite Indian opposition, indicates that the negotiations were based on unequal power.

Indian Concerns: Treaties and Aboriginal Title

It is not uncommon to hear that the reason Indians gave up their land so easily was because they did not understand the concept of land ownership. Consequently, it has been assumed that during the treaty talks, government officials were the main players and that Indians were uninformed and agreeable. The idea that Indians were culturally incapable of making a treaty is largely an ethnocentric bias, not supported by historical evidence. This problem stems from a vagueness in the use of terms describing land use and occupancy, and, consequently, the unequal meeting of two property systems has not been well understood. Nonetheless, this conventional misconception is pervasive; Duke Redbird claimed that 'the concept of "title to land" was alien to the Native consciousness except as a birthright.'[42] This notion contrasts sharply with an observation recorded by the Native clergyman James Settee shortly after Treaty One and Two were signed: 'The Indian family in general were always under the impression that the foreigners were usurpers [and] destroyers of their race and Country; that is this land belonged to them exclusively; that they had sole claim to the rock[,] ground, grass, timber[,] the fish & its water; that all these things were created for them only.'[43] Settee's observation indicates that Indians had a strong sense of exclusive resource ownership. Settee's reference to the Indian family suggests the hunting territory tenure system based on family stewardship. The written historical records indicate that Indians had a concept of Aboriginal title, that Indian chiefs were well informed about land and resources. Under very restrictive circumstances, they made the best of a bad deal.

In his address opening Treaty One talks, Archibald alluded to how Indians expressed a desire for a treaty shortly after his arrival in Manitoba. Manuscript sources substantiate this point. Shortly after Archibald's arrival in Manitoba, he received word from John Schultz that Chief Henry Prince of St. Peters was anxious to meet with the lieutenant-governor. A week later, Prince raised the issue of a treaty with Archibald, but the lieutenant-governor responded that he was too busy to treat with the Indians.[44] In the fall of 1870, Archibald corresponded about the necessity of dealing with Indian title and the disorganization at Red River; however, he was not ready to treat with Indians until he was 'in possession of information as to the occupation and rights of the different Tribes, facts which the Indians dispute among themselves, and of which the whites could not be expected to be very well informed.'[45] Chief Prince was not alone in a desire for a treaty. Correspondence from seventy Fairford Natives indicated a willingness to sell the land, but with compensation including fishing rights and a very large reserve (Figure 4.2).[46] Research by R. Daniel reported that Indians were preparing for a treaty prior to the transfer of Rupertsland; Saulteaux and Cree chiefs of Assiniboia had met in the winter of 1868-9 to establish boundaries for their specific territorial claims.[47] Pressure for a treaty was created by Portage la Prairie Indians when they denied settlers use rights to resources. In June 1871, Indians posted a notice on a church door informing settlers that 'we have not received anything for our lands, therefore they still belong to us.'[48] Archibald had succeeded in delaying a treaty in the fall of 1870, but he noted: 'As soon as the spring opened they became anxious about the Treaty. They have sent repeated messages enquiring when the Treaty was to come off, and appeared very much disappointed at the delay.'[49] Furthermore, all versions of the Lists of Rights from the provisional government at Red River (1870) called for treaties with Indians. Treaties did not catch most Indians unprepared and they played a role in initiating the process. The scope of land claims would have been narrowed had white settlement preceded the resolution of the question of Indian title.

Other sources make it clear that some Indians were thinking in terms of economic change and Aboriginal title. The prospect had been foreseen by Henry Prince's father, Chief Peguis, when he wrote to the Aborigines Protection Society (ca. 1857): 'We are not only willing, but very anxious after being paid for our lands, that the whites would come and settle among us, for we have already derived great benefits from their having done so, that is, not the traders, but the farmers. The traders have never done anything but rob us and keep us poor, but the farmers have taught us how to farm and raise cattle.'[50] Significantly, Chief Peguis wrote this long before any proposals for the western treaties. Peguis understood that the land belonged to them as property that could be paid for prior to widespread settlement.

Plan of reserve

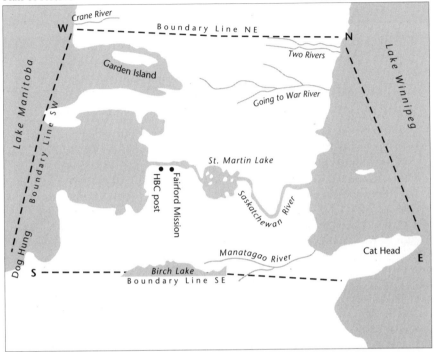

Requested reserve

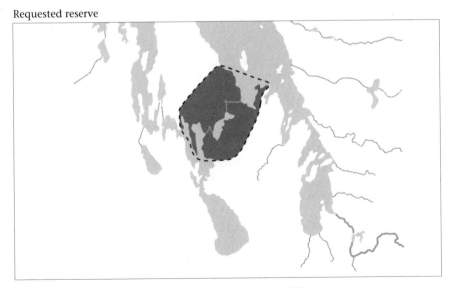

Figure 4.2 Reserve requested by Fairford Indians, ca. 1870 (adapted from PAM, Archibald Papers, Reel 1)

Apparently, some Indians were not particularly attached to the fur trade and some were willing to consider the advantages of agriculture over the economic deprivation inherent with the fur trade. Moreover, Peguis demonstrated an awareness of the dangers and prospects of white settlement well before the end of Company rule. He suggested that 'before whites will be again permitted to take possession of our lands, we wish that a fair and mutually advantageous treaty be entered into with my tribe for their lands.'[51] In fact, E.E. Rich noted that Peguis had demanded a rent in wheat from the colony's settlers.[52] Simpson recalled that 'Indians were anxiously awaiting my arrival, and were much excited on the subject of their lands being occupied, without attention first given to their claims for compensation.'[53] The political pressure Indians mounted was focused on the question of land and resources, and there was a desire to treat as soon as possible. The desire to treat quickly in the face of impending white settlement may have been based on a perception of the existence of a more favourable balance of power – when the administration was weak and not in full possession of the facts.

Statements made by Indians during treaty negotiations illustrate that they believed they had Aboriginal property rights. Treaty Three records provide important documentation on the Indian approach to the negotiations. A Treaty Three chief made the point that 'it was the Indian's country, not the white man's.'[54] Chief Ma-we-do-pe-nais stated that 'we think where we are is our property' and that he understood the context of the treaty: '*The sound of the rustling of the gold is under my feet where I stand*; we have a rich country ... where we stand upon is the Indians' property, and belongs to them.'[55] Furthermore, he made it clear to Morris that Indians would not take a passive position on the question of title, stating: 'If you grant us our requests you will not go back without making a Treaty,' however, 'The white man has robbed us of our riches, and we don't wish to give them up again without getting something in their place.'[56] During Treaty Four talks, Indians complained that certain parcels of land had been pre-empted by the HBC (due to the terms of the Deed of Surrender that transferred Rupertsland to Canada). An Indian known as 'The Gambler' stated: 'The Company have stolen our land,' and that the 'Company have no right to this earth.'[57] Similarly, Pis-qua confronted an HBC officer during Treaty Four talks stating: 'You told me you had sold your land for so much money, £300,000. We want that money.'[58] Clearly, Indians did not accept the idea that the Company, or anyone else, had possessory rights. They also objected to the terms of the Deed of Surrender. Indians obviously held a sense of tribal or collective territorial ownership, which included the idea that Indians had the right to surrender or transfer that ownership.[59] The idea that Indians considered treaties as a means towards an economic transition contrasts with the ethno-centric notion that they were culturally incapable of dealing with white treaty commissioners.

Economic situations shaped the outcome of treaty talks. Arthur J. Ray concluded that economic specialization in the fur trade and depleted resources laid the basis for treaties and therefore 'out of economic necessity, rather than intensive political and military pressure, the Indians agreed to settle on reserves with the promise that the government would look after their welfare and help them make yet another adjustment to changing economic conditions.'[60] Chief Sweet Grass explained to Archibald in 1871: 'Our country is getting ruined of fur bearing animals hitherto our sole support, and now we are poor and want help we want you to pity us. We want cattle, tools, agricultural implements, and assistance in everything when we come to settle – our country is no longer able to support us.'[61] Along with Sweet Grass's request, Ki-he-win stated that they 'wanted workmen, carpenters and farmers to assist us when we settle. I want all [that] my brother "Sweet Grass" asks.'[62] Kis-ki-on added: 'I want help to cultivate the ground for myself and my descendants. Come and see us.'[63] Simpson recalled that at Treaty One talks 'the peculiar circumstances surrounding the position of the Indians of the Province were pointed out' and 'the future of the country predicted.'[64] The difficulty in making a living at Norway House, along with the pending unemployment resulting from changes to the HBC transport system, created economic conditions conducive to a treaty. Indians were prepared to give up Aboriginal title because of the duress created by decades of the mercantile fur trade. The split among the Ojibwa at the Treaty Three talks can be understood in that context. During the 1873 negotiations, it was reported that 'the Rainy River Indians were careless about the treaty, because they could get plenty of money for cutting wood for the boats, but the northern and eastern bands were anxious for one.'[65] The northern and eastern bands were locked into the fur trade, did not have 'plenty of money,' and were interested in the support a treaty would bring for agriculture.

Furthermore, the idea that Indians considered that treaties might afford an alternative to their economic circumstances is supported by the emphasis government negotiators gave to certain terms. Simpson reported that 'the sum of three dollars does not appear to be large enough to enable an Indian to provide himself with many of his winter necessaries, but as he receives the same amount for his wife or wives, and each of his children, the aggregate sum is usually sufficient to procure many comforts for his family, which he would otherwise be compelled to deny himself.'[66] In fact, the wording of Treaties One and Two stated the value of the annuities in terms of an aggregate family income and not as a per capita figure or an individual payment. The conception of annuities as a family income figure indicates that this treaty term was part of a government's social policy. Annuity payments were not based on any sort of valuation of the land or resources. The use of annual payments and not-once-and-for-all payments permitted the winter outfitting of Indian families. Traditionally, this had been the HBC's obligation. At difficult points during the negotiations, Morris stressed the ongoing nature of the annuities. At the Treaty Four talks, he stated that the Queen would 'help you to make a living when the food is scarce.'[67] In a sense, the paternalism of pre-existing Indian-European economic relations was expanded and re-enforced by the treaties. The continuity between the paternalism of the HBC and Indian Affairs was captured when a Treaty Four Indian asked Morris 'that the debt that has been lying in the Company's store, I want that to be wiped out.'[68] Thus, treaty annuities cannot be seen as just compensation for the value of Aboriginal title, but, along with annual payments in ammunition and twine and relief rations, as a means to maintain Indian labour in a commercial hunting economy.[69] While treaties are often seen in terms of the political sovereignty of Indian bands, economic problems simmered beneath the issues raised at the talks and were the central aspect of the treaty process.

Written versions of Treaties One and Two are inadequate for presenting the Indian view, but to a certain extent their position can be gleaned from government records and newspaper accounts. Indians attempted to hold on to as much land as possible and Simpson reported that 'the quantity of land demanded for each Band amounted to about three townships per Indian, and included the greater part of the settled portions of the Province.'[70] At these talks Indians were not quick to give in, as Simpson documented: 'When their answer came it proved to contain demands of such an exorbitant nature, that much time was spent in reducing their terms to a basis upon which an arrangement could be made.'[71] Archibald's report corroborates Simpson's records on the land claims of Indians: 'Furthermore, the Indians seem to have a false idea of the meaning of a Reserve. They have been led to suppose that large tracts of ground were to be set aside for them as hunting grounds, including timber lands, of which they might sell wood as if they were proprietors of the soil.'[72] Simpson's statement demonstrates that the problem with the treaties was not that Indians did not understand their property rights, but that their need for property was not adequately recognized by policymakers. Apparently, Indians accepted the limitations of the reserves with the promise of ongoing access to common natural resources. Treaty Two did not involve lengthy negotiations because these Indians were aware of the negotiations and the terms of Treaty One.

Indian efforts to define the nature of the treaties are apparent in Treaty Three and Four documents, which record portions of their dialogue. Morris reported that the negotiation for Treaty Three 'was a very difficult and trying one, and required on the part of the Commissioners, great patience and firmness.'[73] Morris estimated that their initial demands would annually amount to $125,000. Even after a basic agreement had been worked out, Treaty Three Indians raised the following demands: an assortment of tools, free passage on the railway, mineral rights, reserves as marked out by Indians, fishing rights, and lumber. Morris reminded the Ojibwa that 'I wish you to understand we do not come here as traders, but as representing the Crown, and to do what we believe is just and right.'[74] During Treaty Four negotiations, Morris asked the Indians to 'recollect this, the Queen's High Councillor here from Ottawa, and I, her Governor, are not traders; we do not come here in the spirit of traders; we come here to tell you ... just what the Queen will do for you.'[75] Ultimately, Morris was forced to limit the scope of the negotiations by placing the treaty on the basis of some kind of trust; a belief in the Queen's good intentions. Rather than seeing Indians as culturally incapable of negotiating a treaty, decades of fur trade bargaining gave Indians considerable experience in dealing with European commercial impulses.

In contrast to the earlier treaties, Treaty Five was largely negotiated at the local band level (see Figure 4.1). Land and reserves emerged as major concerns. Treaty negotiator Howard reported on a difficulty that occurred at The Pas: 'They had heard of the terms granted the Indians of Carlton, and this acted most prejudicially at one time against the successful carrying out of my mission; but I at last made them understand the difference between their position and the Plain[s] Indians, by pointing out that the land they would surrender would be useless to the Queen, while what the Plain[s] Indians gave up would be of value to "Her" for homes for "Her white children."'[76] In particular, The Pas Indians wanted the same reserve allocation as had been agreed to in Treaty Six (640 acres per family of five). In this instance, Indians had pointed out a contradiction between the two treaties. The Crown's representative responded by suggesting that terms of a treaty could be related to the future value of the land. The proposition made by Howard, that the land was useless to the Queen, would turn out to be misleading. Moreover, the statement is illogical, since if the land was not valuable, then there should be no reason not to create large reserves.

The Land Question in the Treaty One Talks

The Winnipeg weekly newspaper, *The Manitoban*, covered the treaty talks at Stone Fort and provided verbatim or summational documentation of the dialogue between government officials and Indian chiefs.[77] The negotiations for Treaty One were spread out over nine days. The details in the reporting provided by *The Manitoban* can be reconstructed so as to establish the differing views of land and the changing bargaining positions of both sides. Basically, both the Crown and the Indians accepted the premise that a treaty was a means to deal with the question of Indian title.

Lieutenant-Governor Archibald and Indian Commissioner Simpson began the talks by very generally outlining the Crown's intentions. With respect to reserves, Simpson stated: 'The different bands will get such quantities of land as will be sufficient for their use in adopting the habits of the white man, should they choose to do so.' With respect to Indian lands with little agricultural potential, Simpson actually said: 'The Government are [sic] in fact giving them presents – not purchasing from them land of great value.'[78] The amount of 160 acres per family of five was justified on the basis of a fair policy for Indians and whites; in Archibald's words 'your Great Mother making no distinction between any of her people.'[79] The Crown's representatives supported their bargaining positions by making comparisons with the Queen's treatment of Indians in the east. The figure of 160 acres was a subdivision of land used by the Dominion Lands Survey system. Homesteads were 160 acres, but settlers had the right of pre-empting another 160 acres. The underlying reasoning for the process offered by the Crown was a fair land policy. It did not once admit that Indians had a special or unique interest in the land. On an individual basis, the Metis land grant at this time was much larger than the allocation for Indians. Homestead settlers had the means to expand their acreage. Moreover, Canada had agreed already to a huge land grant for the HBC. (Later, millions of acres would be given to railway companies.) While claiming to be equitable, in practice, the allocation of reserve lands and the subsequent allocation of Crown lands was uneven and unfair.

Nonetheless, the size of the reserve allocation was based on an agricultural use of reserve lands. Both Archibald and Simpson stated that the need for extensive hay lands could not be used as a reason for large Indian reserves. Incidentally, Simpson was very critical of the traditional use of wild grasses for haying by Red River residents. He argued that the use of large wild hay lands was the wrong approach to agriculture. To make a distinction between possible land uses and the needs Indians would have for land, Archibald stated: 'You will be free to hunt over much of the land included in the Treaty. Much of it is rocky, and unfit for cultivation; much of it that is wooded, is beyond the places where the white man will require to go, at all events, for some time to come. Till these lands are needed for use, you will be free to hunt over them, and make all the use of them which you have made in the past.'[80] Simpson also indicated that in many places Indian lands would not be encroached upon by white men for many years. Clearly, a hunting right had been acknowledged, not encumbered, by hunting regulations. Moreover, the term 'and make all the use of them which you have made in the past' would include fishing, gathering, trapping, and free access. The problem of Treaty One hunting rights illustrates the difficulty of written and oral versions of the Treaty. Treaty One, as a written and legal document, does not establish a hunting right; yet another document, a written version of Archibald's opening spoken address, affirms the right to hunt.

The initial response by Indians to the Crown's proposal for reserves did not acknowledge the restriction on size. Ka-ma-twa-ka-nas-nin conveyed that 'as for the reserves, the Indians wish it to be distinctly understood that they are to have a voice in that alone.'[81] On July 29, the chiefs laid out claim for lands that they wished to be reserved, after being assured that they could select the locations of reserves and after the method of annuity payments was explained. Despite the fact that an effort was made by the Crown's representatives to distinguish hunting territories and reserves, claims were made to vast areas. These areas probably reflected traditional areas of occupancy. Figure 4.3 depicts the claims made at the Treaty One talks based on information recorded by *The Manitoban*. The reserves claimed here have the same extensive character of that of the reserve sought by the Fairford Indians (Figure 4.2). The Reverend H. Cochrane and the Honourable James McKay, a Metis member of the Manitoba legislature, said that the claims were preposterous and urged the Indians to curtail their demands. The Crown's representatives then repeated their arguments. Archibald tried to persuade Indians of the good intentions of the Crown by arguing that Indians in the east 'were living happy and tranquil, enjoying all the rights and privileges of white men.'[82] Simpson reminded Indians that the Canadian annuity payments would not be terminated in contrast to the cash payments in the American Indian treaties. He pointed out that the per family land grant of 160 acres was twice the size of the existing family lots in the Indian parish of St. Peters. Archibald then issued an ultimatum: the Crown had laid out its propositions. At the next meeting (the fifth day of negotiations), the Crown expected to learn whether Indians would accept or reject the terms.

Yet the Indians did not give in. Ay-ee-ta-pe-pe-tung, of the Portage Indians, stated: 'But God gave me this land you are speaking to me about, and it kept me well to this day' and that 'I have turned over this matter of a treaty in my mind and cannot see anything in it to benefit my children. This is what frightens me. After I showed you what I meant to keep for a reserve you continued to make it smaller and smaller.'[83] Generally, Ay-ee-ta-pe-pe-tung held a firm position against the officials, arguing that the commissioner could take the lands if he wished, stating: 'Let the Queen's subjects go on my land if they choose. I give them liberty. Let them rob me. I will go home without treating.'[84] Commissioner Simpson then tried to undermine the Ojibwa claims by reminding them that the Cree had previously occupied Manitoba. He also argued that the time had come for the land to be cultivated. Another Portage Indian stated: 'What puzzled his band was that they were to be shut on a small reserve, and only get ten shillings each for the balance. They could not understand it.'[85]

Although the reporting by *The Manitoban* is incomplete, a number of issues were raised that indicate that the treaty had to refer to more than the final written text. Under the heading 'Providing for Posterity,' *The Manitoban* reported Chief Wa-sus-koo-koon's concern: 'I understand thoroughly that every 20 people get a mile square; but if an Indian family of five, settles

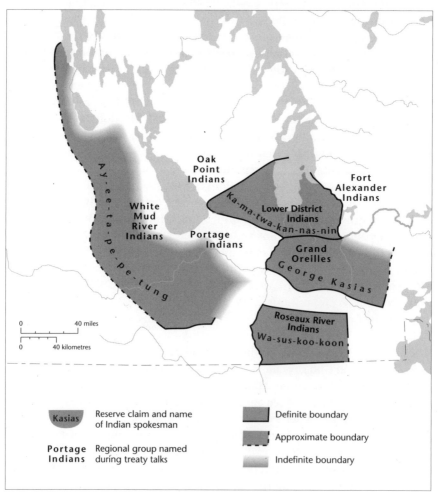

Figure 4.3 Geographical interpretation of claims made at Treaty One talks (*The Manitoban*, 12 August 1871)

down, he may have more children. Where is their land?'[86] This is a significant question because it raises the problem of future land needs. The government's response conveyed the impression that reserves could expand to meet the needs of the Indian population. According to Archibald: 'Whenever his children get more numerous than they are now, they will be provided for further West. Whenever the reserves are found too small the Government will sell the land, and give the Indians land elsewhere.'[87] The Crown's representatives clearly put forward the general principle that the future land needs of the Indian population would not be confined by the proposed reserve sizes.

Towards the close of the talks, the positions of the various Indian speakers shifted. At the end of the fifth day, Ay-ee-ta-pe-pe-tung indicated that he wanted to take a winter to think about the treaty. Subsequently, McKay 'made an eloquent speech in Indian, explaining matters,' the substance of which was not documented.[88] Ay-ee-ta-pe-pe-tung then said that he would accept the treaty for an annuity of three dollars per person. (Apparently, this was a slight increase over the offer of ten shillings.) The commissioner agreed to this demand. But this agreement was short-lived and was not generally acceptable. Again Simpson threatened to end negotiations if an agreement was not close. On the sixth day, Chief Henry Prince took a more active role and raised some objections to the treaty terms, stating: 'The land cannot speak for itself. We have to speak for it.'[89] Once it was clear that the large reserves could not be obtained, but that Indians could continue to hunt on lands, new demands were made with regard to the use of reserve lands. The Indians took advantage of the government position that the size of the reserves was defined by the needs of a family farm. Prince announced: 'The Queen wishes the Indians to cultivate the ground. They cannot scratch it – work it with their fingers. What assistance will they get if they settle down?'[90] According to *The Manitoban*: 'His Excellency entered into a lengthy statement showing that the Queen was willing to help the Indians in every way, and besides giving them land and annuities, she would give them a school and a schoolmaster for each reserve, and for those who desired to cultivate the soil ploughs and harrows would be provided on the reserves.'[91] At this point some concessions had been made.

Indians continued to make demands. Again, a property right was asserted; compensation for the Lake of the Woods road was requested. Then Prince and several other chiefs came forward and asked for clothing, houses (fully furnished), ploughs, cattle, buggies, equipment for hunting, equipment for women, and freedom from taxes on reserves. The commissioner rejected these demands by suggesting that he would be better off as an Indian. Archdeacon Cowley intervened and addressed the Indians. The Portage Indians left and it appeared that other Indians were going to leave. James McKay then requested the Indians to stay over one more night and to meet next day with the commissioner. He promised in the interval to 'try and bring the Commissioner and Indians closer together.'[92] The next day on 3 August a treaty was signed. According to *The Manitoban*, the Indians were in better humour and a cash present of three dollars, a pair of oxen for each reserve, and buggies for each chief were added. Very few details of the crucial last day of Treaty One talks have been recorded. The written versions of Treaties One and Two did ensure that certain locations would be reserved to particular bands. Figure 4.4 indicates the locations that were reserved by these treaties for the chiefs that signed the treaties. The territorial contraction of

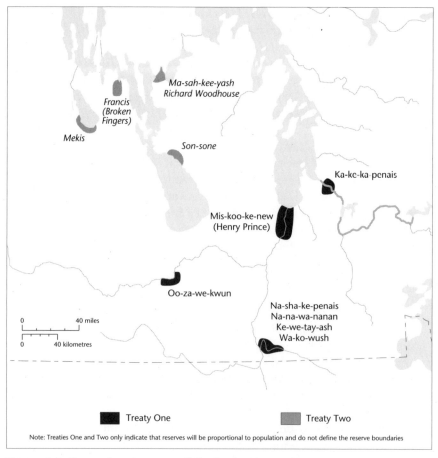

Figure 4.4 Reserve locations set aside by Treaties One and Two
(Alexander Morris, *The Treaties of Canada with the Indians* [Toronto: Coles 1971], 313-20)

Indian land claims during the treaty talks is evident in a comparison of Figures 4.2, 4.3, and 4.4.

Although demands for housing and clothing must have been viewed as excessive in the late nineteenth century, Indians were looking either to hold on to significant amounts of land or to receive economic compensation for the loss of their property. On the second day of the talks, Sheoship, a chief from Fort Alexander, addressed the Queen 'begging her to grant me where-with to make my living.'[93] In both Treaty One and Treaty Three, the Honourable James McKay played a pivotal role. Complicating any understanding of the treaties process is the fact that important negotiations occurred between the public meetings, and that these meetings were off the record.

The Outside Promises: An Economic Agenda

The controversy around the so-called Outside Promises of Treaties One and Two illustrates the problems Indians had in using treaties as a means to make an economic transition. The Outside Promises refer to specific verbal commitments made by government officials during Treaty One negotiations. There were no significant government obligations to assist Indian agriculture in either the initial draft treaty or the printed versions said to represent Treaties One and Two. However, Simpson's report on the treaty negotiations (3 September 1871) lists a number of additional terms, largely related to agriculture, which were not part of the official treaty text.[94] The *Canadian Illustrated News* reported that the terms of the treaty were liberal, and that the terms included 'to every one of the reserves set apart for each tribe some ploughs and harrows, and a pair of oxen to enable the Indians to cultivate the soil.'[95] Despite a memorandum attached to Treaty One, which listed promises outside the treaty, Ottawa officials were slow to recognize and to act on these commitments. Only some of the Outside Promises were implemented before the government formally admitted to the validity of these verbal commitments.

Discontent grew over the non-fulfilment of the verbal treaty terms, and the new Indian commissioner, J.A.N. Provencher, reported in 1873 that Indians 'accuse the representatives of Canada of obtaining their consent under false pretences.'[96] Such sentiments were verified by Indian Agent M. St. John, who reported in 1873 that they 'are not content with the terms of the Treaty, and are unanimous in the belief that they have been deceived and promised more than they have received.'[97] St. John forwarded the Indians' list of promises to the department's deputy superintendent. In a petition forwarded by John Schultz in 1873, the St. Peters Indians stated their position: 'That promises made to them at the Treaty of 1871 have not been fulfilled. And that a state of general dissatisfaction exists in consequence; that they find it quite impossible to supply their most ordinary wants with the present Annuity of three dollars; that game has become very scarce and their reservations is [*sic*] found to be small and insufficient for their use.'[98] The more favourable terms of Treaty Three reinforced the dissatisfaction among Manitoba Indians who pointed out that their prairie land was more valuable than the rock and muskeg of Treaty Three lands. In 1873, there was some difficulty in getting Indians to accept annuities. The discontent concerning the Outside Promises was eventually resolved in 1875 when the government agreed to acknowledge the terms listed on the memorandum (3 August 1871) attached to Treaty One. This revision to Treaties One and Two also increased the annuities from three to five dollars per capita, and it included an agreement to 'abandon all claims whatever against the government in connection with the so-called "Outside Promises"' apart from those terms included in the memorandum.[99] Unfortunately, Treaties One and Two were not changed so as to increase the size of reserves.

The documents around the Outside Promises issue demonstrate that Indians had made specific demands during the negotiations. Moreover, the revision to these treaties, in line with the memorandum of 3 August 1871, indicates that even the written text of a signed treaty is not the final representation of the terms of the treaties. The oral version of a treaty, aspects of which are verified by extrinsic written records, is crucial in understanding the contemporary meaning of treaty rights. Most of the Outside Promises were intended to provide the means for an agricultural economy. The historical records show that Indian political pressure – petitions, rejection of annuities, and the use of John Schultz as a political agent – succeeded at gaining some changes in the 1870s.

This chapter has considered the development of a treaty policy, especially the government's specific territorial and resource interests.[100] Indian claims to property provide a necessary prerequisite for understanding their aspirations at the treaty talks. A variety of land tenures existed amongst Indians: the St. Peters farming village was based on individual river lots, but in the commercialized trapping economy, common property and family hunting territories were standard. Indian concepts of land tenure may have differed from that of the European, but this did not prevent them from formulating a bargaining position based on ownership. Indians used the treaty negotiations to advance their own economic program, which sought to diversify their own economy. A detailed reconstruction of the talks at Treaty One serves to provide a context and to broaden the comprehension of treaties beyond the narrow legal terminology of the official treaties. These details inform us of the modern meaning of the treaties.

5
'Lands Are Getting Poor in Hunting': Treaty Adhesions in Northern Manitoba

The story of the treaty process north of the 1875 Treaty Five boundaries includes a number of interesting problems. In this part of northern Manitoba, Aboriginal title negotiations were carried out solely at the convenience of the government. The Department of Indian Affairs ignored Indian requests for a treaty for three decades. Eventually the bands of this area signed adhesions to Treaty Five, which had been negotiated in 1875. Consequently, the terms of the Treaty Five Adhesions represented minimal obligations on the part of the government to assist Indians with post-1870 conditions. The procedures followed during treaty-making were rather sloppy and irregular. As in other treaty areas, the adhesions to Treaty Five illustrate that economic circumstances shaped Indian attitudes and approaches towards treaties. Despite Indian desires for a treaty to cover area north of Treaty Five (1875), the timing of the adhesions and, consequently, the scope of the treaty talks were controlled by the government. This transparent case of a one-sided use of authority during this phase of treaty-making challenges the conviction that Indian policy was generally well-meaning and just.

Not all bands located in northern Manitoba were party to the adhesions in 1908, 1909, and 1910. Two bands living and hunting in the area described by Treaty Five Adhesions had previously signed different treaties. The Pukatawagan Band, as part of the Pelican Lake Band, was included with the 1889 adhesion to Treaty Six, although a major portion of the area where they lived and hunted was within the Treaty Five Adhesion boundaries. The Lac du Brochet (Reindeer Lake) Band of Chipewyan signed an adhesion to Treaty Ten on 19 August 1907. This treaty allowed them 'to pursue their usual vocations of hunting, trapping and fishing throughout the territory surrendered ... excepting such tracts as may be required or as may be taken up from time to time for settlement, mining, lumbering, trading or other purposes.'[1] Treaty Ten allocated reserves on the basis of 640 acres per family

Chief and councillors, Fort Churchill, after signing adhesion
to Treaty Five, 1910. Note flag and treaty medals (PAM, N8200,
A.V. Thomas Collection, No. 126)

of five. Standard annuities were included in this treaty, but presents of thirty-two dollars to each chief, twenty-two dollars to each headman and twelve dollars to each Indian were also given. At Lac du Brochet post, Commissioner T.A. Borthwick used Reverend Father Turquetit as interpreter, who 'explained to them why I was sent to meet them, and after various thoughtful questions put by the Indians bearing upon the treaty and answered by me to their satisfaction, they asked for a short recess to discuss the terms of the treaty more fully among themselves.'[2] The band then selected a chief and signed the treaty. The adhesion to Treaty Ten of the Brochet Chipewyans, whose hunting grounds straddled Treaties Five and Ten, is another instance of territorial ambiguity. However, the state had become aware of the vagueness of treaty boundaries with respect to actual band land use patterns. Thus, a general surrender clause was added, stating that 'all and any other lands wherever situated in the provinces of Saskatchewan and Alberta and the Northwest Territories or any other portion of the Dominion of Canada'[3] were also surrendered.

Lengthy negotiations, which were essential during the first treaty era (1871-7), did not occur with the adhesions to Treaty Five. Nonetheless, important issues needed to be discussed. But the government's offhand approach to Indian lands in northern Manitoba ensured that misunderstanding and problems would linger for decades.

Pressure for a Treaty

Swampy Cree from the non-ceded areas of northern Manitoba attempted to arrange a treaty with the Crown. Their reasoning for demanding a treaty is further evidence that Indians viewed treaties as a means to improve their economic conditions. After paying annuities at Norway House (1876), Commissioner R.L. Reid recorded a meeting with the Oxford House chief and councillors, 'who were anxious to know if the same bounties would be extended to them as were being extended to their brethren of Norway House and Cross Lake, and also whether they could obtain a Reserve on Lake Winnipeg, as the country in which they were living was totally unfit for cultivation, and that they had the greatest difficulty in procuring a livelihood.'[4] From this point until the Treaty Five Adhesions some thirty years later, Indians from northeastern Manitoba made requests for a treaty and aid. During this time many Natives migrated from the non-treaty area to reserves, intermarried with treaty women, and otherwise indicated a desire for a major population relocation out of the fur country. A surplus population in the fur country was indicative of a need for economic change and the assistance that came with a treaty.

Numerous requests for a treaty, sometimes involving missionaries as intermediaries, were received by the Canadian government (see Table 5.1 for a summary). In 1876, Reverend Kirkby of York Factory met with Lieutenant-Governor Alexander Morris about the suggestion for a treaty and the idea to support a movement of Indians to Lake Winnipeg. Morris suggested a written request would lead to a treaty. However, a treaty was not forthcoming.[5] Other problems had been created by the arbitrary treaty/non-treaty boundary. In 1894, the Native CMS missionary J. Settee informed Keewatin Lieutenant-Governor John Schultz concerning 'about twenty persons, who have not received annuity like their Brethren although having been residence [*sic*] previous to the Treaty' and Split Lake Indians living at Cross Lake who witnessed payments made to their friends and received nothing.[6] The original boundary of Treaty Five was arbitrary, carelessly severing kin and social affiliations. Kickee Ke Sick (York Factory) wanted a treaty 'because we are getting poorer every winter.'[7] Thus, in non-treaty areas, Indians such as J. Kitchigijik would ask: 'So I look to you for help in the way others of our people have it.'[8] In 1894, Settee reported to Schultz that the Split Lake Indians wanted a treaty because 'their lands are getting poor in hunting.'[9] Nelson River Indians used their Aboriginal title to pressure for a treaty. During the early 1880s, when a railway scheme was proposed, the annual report noted that Nelson River Indians 'do not want to see any more surveyors, explorers or white men going into their country before a Treaty is first made with them.'[10] On several occasions in the early 1890s, Lieutenant-Governor Schultz recommended the extension of treaties. Additionally, in 1897, Schultz's successor, J.C. Patterson, told Keewatin Indians that he would pass their treaty request on to the superintendent of Indian Affairs.[11] Despite repeated requests from Indians and the support of missionaries and lieutenant-governors, Indian Affairs, as an agent of the Crown, would not enter into treaty negotiations.

Table 5.1

Indications of a desire for a treaty by Indians in the non-ceded areas of northern Manitoba

July 1876	Oxford House chief and four councillors request inclusion in Treaty Five and reserve on Lake Winnipeg from Commissioner J.L. Reid.
17 July 1876	W.W. Kirkby meets A. Morris, York Factory Indians want treaty.
6 December 1877	York Factory Natives request W.W. Kirkby to write A. Morris for same privileges as Norway House Indians.
30 March 1878	Manachemin arrived at Island Lake to discuss treaty with P. Walker.
27 August 1878	Two canoes from Island Lake depart for Oxford House expecting a treaty to be made.
1 July 1880	Oxford Indians request treaty from Lieutenant Governor A. Morris.
10 September 1881	P. Walker of Oxford House inquires about treaty matters.
1884	Nelson River Indians want a treaty and consult with Norway House Indians.
1884	Chief Kichee Ke Sich of York Factory requests treaty and aid.
9 June 1885	J. Hardie of Nelson River requests a treaty.
10 July 1885	Chief Magnus Harper of Island Lake requests a treaty.

continued on next page

Table 5.1 (continued)

August 1891	Chief John Wood of Island Lake requests a treaty.
20 September 1894	Communication from J. Settee to J. Schultz: Nelson River, Split Lake, Oxford House, and Trout Lake Indians desirous of making treaty.
24 August 1897	Treaty request put to J.C. Patterson by Chief Peter Muskego of Oxford House.
Summer 1902	Chief Jeremiah Chubb of Oxford House and John Wood of Island Lake convey a desire for a treaty through J. Semmens.
20 February 1906	Split Lake Indians write requesting a treaty.
9 December 1908	Chief Charles Wastaskekoot of York Factory requests a treaty.
18 June 1909	R. Fidler of Deer Lake (formerly Sandy Lake) requests a treaty.
4 August 1909	Chief James Daliyasse of Churchill requests a treaty.

Sources: CMS, A-102; CMS, A-103; CSP, Indian Affairs, 1884, no. 4, p. 97; CSP, Indian Affairs, 1877, no. 11, p. li; CSP, Keewatin, 1898, no. 13, p. 14; HBCA, B. 93/A/8; NAC, RG 10, vol. 3677, file 11528; NAC, RG 10, vol. 3713, file 20626; NAC, RG 10, vol. 3722, file 24161; NAC, RG 10, vol. 4009, file 249462, pt. 1; PAM, Schultz papers, MG12 E1, no. 6565

Indian responses to the geographical or spatial unevenness of the treaty process are evident in subsequent migration patterns. The difficulties of making a living at hunting in northeastern Manitoba served to push, while treaty benefits functioned to pull, Indians south to the treaty region. In 1879, Indian Agent A. Mackay reported that 'a number of Indians from along the Nelson River, who formerly used to inhabit and hunt within the limits of Treaty Five, have now taken up their residence with the Norway House band' and 'Indians from the vicinity of York Factory, who have migrated to Norway House about two years ago [have claimed a right to annuities].'[12] Thus, in the 1870s and 1880s, Indians without treaty status had become integrated at Norway House and had settled on the reserve. Inspector McColl reported that 'none of those non-treaty Indians ever receive any annuity although they are always clamouring for it.'[13] At times, Indians from the non-ceded area were anxiously anticipating a treaty. Rev. E. Eves reported in 1892 that 'many more of the York Factory indians [*sic*] have moved to Split Lake and are intending to take up a piece of land that in view of being treated with before HBRR [Hudson Bay Railroad] is put through they may keep as reserve.'[14] The Ottawa civil servants responsible for Indian policy made little effort to accommodate the surplus population that was facing economic hardship in northeastern Manitoba.

Until the turn of the century, treaty requests pointed out the poverty of Indians without treaty and the somewhat higher living standards of reserve Indians. These contrasts encouraged Indians without treaty to press for inclusion. For example, in 1902, Indian Agent J. Semmens reported on a meeting with Chief Jeremiah Chubb (Oxford House) and John Wood (Island Lake) who pressed for a treaty, citing their poverty relative to treaty Indians, the higher prices for trade goods, and the need to educate their children. They were also troubled that strangers were coming into their area – timber hunters, mineral prospectors, and railroad surveyors.[15] Semmens reported that they 'believed that the country is possessed of great wealth in minerals and in fish, fur and forests, and assurance is felt that the strong hand of the King's people can bring about such changes as will materially improve the condition under which we now live.'[16] Furthermore, Chubb and Wood told Semmens that 'last of all we are tired of the old life of the woods and are ready to welcome our White Brothers and to come under the more immediate protection of Our Great Father the King.'[17] In 1907, Semmens recorded the Nelson House chief's willingness to treat:

> The Chief was very quiet in his manner, but had looked over the matter in the light of his own interests and those of his Band pretty carefully. He said that the coming of the [rail]road would interfere with the game upon which his people relied wholly. They were hunters and boatmen and knew no other employment and anything affecting seriously the fur catch would hit them hard. Surely he said the Government would consider his welfare and if his occupation were interfered with[,] would be willing to treat with him so that no misunderstanding would arise and no friction result.[18]

When outsiders encroached on their territory, Indians raised the issue of their property rights. In other words, they were aware of the pending economic changes and the wealth of the land. Some were willing to consider new economic activities and they saw a treaty as compensation for interim disruptions. Sovereignty, integration, and economic security were all interconnected as a treaty issue.

Treaty Five Adhesions: Policy and Terms
While the Indians of the non-ceded areas were willing to enter treaty, the government was reluctant to do so between 1876 and 1907. There are several reasons why the government repeatedly rejected Indian requests for a treaty. In 1880, the government did not consider treating because the land around Oxford House was neither good for agriculture nor was required for

immigration.[19] In another response in 1885, a difficult year for Indian policy, the superintendent general was 'of [the] opinion that [it] is of importance to avoid making more treaties with Indian Bands' and that 'the country occupied by these Indians ... is not wanted for settlement by Whites; and the Indians can continue to live by hunting and fishing.'[20] Thus, the government was willing to engage in the treaty process only according to its own timetable – a timetable based on an assessment of external needs and not on a concern for improving the economic conditions of Indian bands.

After three decades of agitation, the government sought extinguishment of Indian title in Keewatin (and included the names of Indians originally from the non-treaty area who had taken up residence in treaty areas to the adhesion). The Department of Indian Affairs file on the adhesions to Treaty Five begins with correspondence concerning the encroachment of commercial fishermen on the sturgeon fisheries of Split Lake Indians. Reverend Cox challenged the right of commercial fishermen to operate in non-treaty areas. This complaint revealed to the Department of Indian Affairs that the Split Lake Indians were Indians without treaty who were living in the region ceded by Treaty Five. The Department's reasoning suggested that if the hunting grounds of the Split Lake Indians were part of Treaty Five (1875), then they would be entitled to back payment of thirty years of annuities. Clearly, part of the Split Lake band territory was in Treaty Five and this illustrates the ambiguity of treaty boundaries, land use, and migrations.[21] By 1908, the intent to build a railroad to Hudson Bay had become more realistic than previous schemes; this provided the main rationale for the extension of Treaty Five. The deputy superintendent decided in 1908 that: 'In view of railway activity in that part of the country and the probable projection of the Canadian Northern to Churchill, I think it would be well to prepare the way for taking all the Indians of this district into Treaty when it becomes necessary to do so.'[22] Indians still influenced this decision since Semmens reported in 1907, 'I heard that there was a great deal of agitation at Nelson House over some surveys which were being made along the route of the Hudson Bay Railway.'[23] Thus, a number of reasons account for a treaty at this time. Along with the advantages of extending treaty benefits to Indians who had been requesting a treaty and the potential problems of commercial encroachment on Indian fisheries, the non-treaty status of the Split Lake band had to be resolved. Nevertheless, the decisive reason for treating at this time was the need to clear Aboriginal title for the railroad. Still, the department felt that it was undesirable to take all the Indians in this territory under treaty and advocated waiting until settlement pressure had increased. On the question of treaty responsibilities for the Split Lake Indians, Department Secretary J.D. McLean wrote, 'The Department does not feel disposed to hurry matters.'[24] Even after thirty years of polite requests, the department remained unconcerned about the Aboriginal rights of the Indians of northern Manitoba.

The department was uncertain about how to proceed with the extinguishment of Indian title in the unceded part of Manitoba. Options included initiating a new treaty or having Indians sign adhesions to Treaty Five or Treaty Ten. In 1907, a new treaty was considered because it would avoid the problem of back-paying annuity arrears. If established treaties were used to bring Indians outside Treaty Five under treaty, the payment of arrears to Split Lake Indians was an issue. Until the spring of 1908, it seemed that Nelson House and Split Lake would adhere to Treaty Ten, and John Semmens's appointment commissioned him to take adhesions to both Treaties Five and Ten. In fact, the Department of Indian Affairs frugal accountant, D.C. Scott, recommended Treaty Ten because the terms 'are a little more liberal than those of Treaty Five' and the Treaty Ten gratuity would be an 'additional inducement to get them to accept Treaty without arrears of annuity.'[25] Nonetheless, it appears that the department planned to avoid paying large arrears by offering only a small gratuity, and at the last moment it was decided to use an adhesion to Treaty Five for all bands.

The sites where adhesions to Treaty Five were taken are depicted in Figure 5.1. Bands were visited in the year prior to the signing in order to speed up acceptance. The discussions that occurred at these preparatory visits are not well documented. In 1907, Semmens visited Nelson House and Split Lake to discuss a treaty. Semmens took treaty at Nelson House and Split Lake and visited Oxford House, Gods Lake, and Island Lake to discuss the treaty in 1908. At the same time, he added the names of non-treaty Indians who had originally come from the newly ceded region of the adhesion to the current band lists of Cross Lake, Norway House, and Fisher River. It was necessary to secure these individual adhesions to Treaty Five since their individual entitlements would remain unsettled even though their former bands had agreed to a land surrender treaty. In 1909, Semmens treated with Oxford House, Gods Lake, and Island Lake Indians while department official W. McLean discussed a treaty with the Churchill and York Factory bands. Finally, in 1910, Semmens added Deer Lake (Ontario), Fort Churchill, and York Factory Indians to Treaty Five. Interestingly, the York Factory band, a group of Indians with the longest white contact, were the last Indians to sign a treaty in Manitoba. The inclusion of the Deer Lake band is yet another example of territorial ambiguity. Although these Indians generally traded at Island Lake, they were a separate band whose focus of activities was not located in the area described by Treaty Five. Indian Affairs' practical approach to the Indians of Keewatin was guided by recognizing and treating with 'trade post' bands.

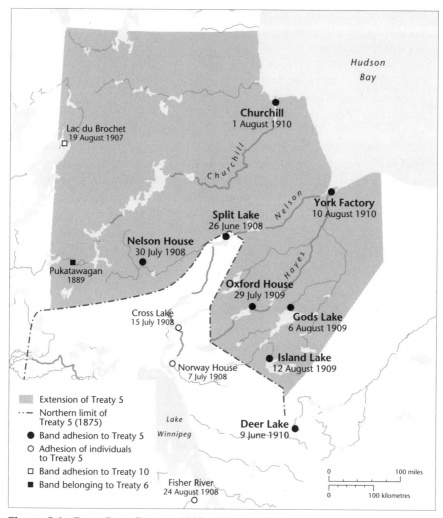

Figure 5.1   Treaty Five adhesions, 1908, 1909, and 1910

The basic text of the adhesions simply stated that the terms were not retroactive and that the Indians 'transfer, surrender and relinquish to His Majesty the King, his heirs and successors, to and for the use of the Government of Canada, all our right[s], title and privileges whatsoever, which we have or enjoy in the territory described in the said Treaty, and every part thereof, to have and to hold to the use of His Majesty the King and his heirs and successors forever.'[26] The adhesions outlined the area surrendered, included the surrender to 'all other lands wherever situated,' accepted the benefits of Treaty Five with reserves based on 160 acres per family of five, provided a proportional amount of ammunition and twine, and paid a gratuity of five dollars.[27] The Split Lake Indians were not made aware of their possible entitlement to a back payment of arrears. The decision to use Treaty Five instead of Treaty Ten was no small matter for the Indians of northern Manitoba. Treaty Ten provided for larger gratuities (thirty-two dollars for chiefs, twenty-two dollars for councillors and twelve dollars for Indians) and much larger reserves (640 acres per family of five). Treaty Ten was signed in 1906 and an adhesion in 1907 covered northeastern Saskatchewan, adjacent to northern Manitoba. Adhesions to Treaty Ten for northern Manitoba in 1908, 1909, and 1910 would have made more sense than the use of adhesions to Treaty Five, which was thirty-three years old. On the question of reserves, Semmens was told to 'be careful to make such a location as will not conflict with existing land claims in the district.'[28] While Indian claims were acknowledged by the state, the selection of reserve land and survey policies served to minimize the status of Indian claims and to harmonize their specific land needs with the existing trade and mission interests. Finally, he was cautioned that 'it is extremely important that no outside promises should be made during the negotiation of the Treaty.'[29] The reference to the Outside Promises relates back to the Treaty One talks. This caution about Outside Promises is an admission on the government's part that verbal negotiations were an important part of Indian understanding and expectations of the treaty. When the government finally decided to treat with the Indians of northern Manitoba, it selected from the existing options (a new treaty, Treaty Ten, or Treaty Five) and took the cheapest option.

Legal Problems with Treaty Five Adhesions

The written documentation on the adhesions to Treaty Five is deficient. We have a very incomplete understanding of the Indian role in the treaty-making process in this part of northern Manitoba. In 1907, the Split Lake band requested the following terms as part of the treaty: seeds and garden tools, carpentry tools, and rations during treaty payments and for the sick and destitute; farm animals, wagons, ploughs, and harrows; twine and ammunition; and hunting and fishing rights.[30] Furthermore, Chief W. Ke-che Kesik wanted 'to keep our same hunting and fishing grounds that we have had for a long time.'[31] Indian Commissioner David Laird felt that these demands were unreasonable and wondered 'if the Indians keep their hunting and fishing grounds, what do they surrender?'[32] Such an official response to these demands clearly illustrates the ongoing problem of interpreting Aboriginal title surrenders. Semmens reported in 1907 that the Split Lake Indians wanted hunting equipment and not agricultural implements, but also wanted an early survey of a reserve around the Nelson River.[33] At Churchill, during the treaty negotiations, the journalist A.V. Thomas recorded the Chipewyan concerns:

> When the Commissioner had finished, and the time for asking questions had come, some of the leading Chipewyans expressed concern for their hunting rights. If they gave up their land to the Government, would they have the right to hunt as their fathers had done before them? If they were not allowed to hunt, they would starve. They had heard about a railway being built to bring the white man to Churchill; how would that affect them? Would they have to live within the reserve which the Government would give them?[34]

According to Thomas, Semmens's answers to these and many other questions relieved their anxiety, and 'he assured the Indians that not for many years to come, probably not in the lifetime of any of them, would their hunting right be interfered with.'[35] Chipewyan compliance with the government's treaty probably stemmed from anxiety about pending disruptions, since McLean reported on a preparatory visit in 1909: 'They were afraid that changes would take place that would not be so good for them.'[36] Similar concerns were expressed by York Factory Chief C. Wastaskekoot in 1908: 'Now that the Hudson Bay Railroad is coming down our way we *hope* that the government will take us under their care. Our hunting lands will be ruined by the shriek of the Iron Horse' and 'We will be at a loss to know how to feed and clothe our little ones.'[37] At the York Factory treaty talks, Semmens reported Indian fears that government hunting regulations would 'force them into a condition of poverty.'[38] Again, he argued that 'very little of their country would be touched by the proposed railway, perhaps none at all,' and that they would be compensated for losses.[39] The issues raised during treaty talks by Indians related to their future in the regional economy. And in many respects, Indians had a better grasp of what the future held than the treaty commissioner. Semmens's oral assurances about hunting rights and compensation cannot be easily reconciled with the literal written text of the treaty adhesion, which calls for the extinguishment of all rights, title, and privileges.

Although Keewatin Indians raised issues during the treaty talks, the adhesion to the treaty were usually agreed to within a few hours. This can be understood because Indians had been requesting a treaty and because preparatory visits had been made in the preceding year. Nonetheless, Semmens alluded that at Split Lake 'the white men of the locality had prepared our way most effectively' and 'the advice given to the Indians by these men made our work very easy.'[40] The need for a treaty at Island Lake was evident from Semmens's report, which indicated that 'accompanying the illness (la Grippe) was a condition of poverty and destitution which it is impossible to describe.'[41] According to Thomas, when Semmens addressed the Indians, 'He talked to them much as a man talks to children.'[42] A standing vote was held, and in the case of York Factory, Semmens noted that 'after free discussion and quiet assurance, they declared themselves ready to vote for Treaty.'[43] This was followed by the election of chief and councillors and the signing of the treaty. At Oxford House, Indians who never handled a dollar, in Semmens's words, 'suddenly found themselves the proud possessors of the key to plenty.'[44]

The historical record indicates that despite Semmens's good intentions and naive optimism, some serious problems were created. Although Semmens had been a Cree-speaking missionary, he had requested an interpreter for the treaty party. Certainly communications with the Churchill Chipewyan were not very good. Thomas reported, 'It proved very difficult for Commissioner Semmens, upon his arrival, to make much headway with them. He could not speak to them, it is true, in their deeply guttural tongue, and the communications he received from the band through an interpreter were unsatisfactory and nebulous.'[45] These were not the circumstances required for discussing delicate concepts such as hunting rights and land ownership. Semmens erred with treaty procedures when he had the Split Lake Indians sign the wrong document. Apparently, they had signed the individual adhesions used for the non-treaty Indians residing in the treaty areas and not the adhesion intended for the Split Lake Band. J.D. McLean, the department's secretary, considered this 'a serious error' and asked Semmens 'whether in dealing with the Split Lake Indians you explained to them the contents of the Treaty which they should have signed and by which they gave up their right to 133,400 square miles of territory.' Semmens replied that the treaty had been explained, but that his clerk had passed him the wrong form.[46]

A more fundamental problem was the sequence of procedures that Semmens followed during treaty-making. The conventional treaty procedures used by lieutenant-governors Archibald and Morris began with the band selecting chiefs and councillors who articulated their concerns. In fact, Indians explained their concept of property and their expectations for compensation at the early treaties. Significantly, the procedure for Treaty Five Adhesions differed from those used by earlier treaties. The agenda included an address by Semmens, questions and discussion, a standing vote on the treaty, the election of chief and councillors, followed by signing of the treaty.[47] In general, this procedure did not enhance the authority of the chiefs before the talks and tended to relegate them to a ceremonial role (treaty signing). At Nelson House, this created a specific problem with respect to the gratuity. When 'the newly elected Chief asked that it be increased to harmonize with the payments at Split Lake,' Semmens replied that this 'was not thought to be proper as objection was not raised in time.'[48] The scope of the treaty talks during the adhesions to Treaty Five was limited by the question and answer format.

The procedures adopted by Semmens were recalled in 1940 by members of the Oxford House for an anthropologist, Leonard Mason. Mason wrote the following account:

[Semmens] was received with vigorous handshaking amidst a volley of gunshots fired by the enthusiastic Indians. All men were called into council the next morning to hear the terms of the treaty. Upon a satisfactory explanation of the various clauses a unanimous vote of approval was expressed by every Indian rising to his feet. Under the Commissioner's direction a formal election was held in the council to fill the necessary offices of chief and two councillors. Jeremiah Chubb, the first chief of the Oxford House band, and Robert Chubb and James Natawayo as councillors signed the adhesion. Either then, or at a later date upon the visit of a white 'Kitchi-okemow' (Great Chief), the three officials, who each received a medal and a uniform, were properly invested with their new rank before the assembled band. The Indian agent covered them with the Union Jack to signify their allegiance to the Crown.[49]

Handshakes and gun salutes were indicative of fur trade society and compare with the pipe ceremony used at other treaty negotiations. The oral history, as recorded by Mason, clearly indicates that Semmens's procedures deviated from the established manner of negotiating a treaty.

In the years immediately following the treaty, a number of problems arose that suggest that the treaty was not properly explained by Semmens and was therefore incompletely understood by the Indians. In 1909, W. McLean reported that Split Lake Indians would not accept treaty goods, held their own council, and then asked questions concerning hunting and trapping rights.[50] Similarly, at Nelson House, McLean answered 'various questions regarding trapping, hunting and fishing, upon which they did not appear to be intelligently informed.'[51] At the time of treaty, the concept of the reserve seems not to have been explained properly for when D. Robertson went to survey the Split Lake Reserve, he 'found that the Indians there had a very exaggerated idea of the extent of reserve to which they were entitled.'[52] A number of grievances were raised by the York Factory band between 1915 and 1918 based on a misunderstanding of the written treaty terms. For example, in 1916, E.D. Moodie of the Royal Northwest

Mounted Police (RNWMP) 'explained various other matters to them regarding the killing of game out of season etc. Nothing appears to have been
properly explained to them in the past, but now apparently they are satisfied on all points brought up at the "pow-wow."'[53] At several communities, difficulties quickly arose; these problems derived from the government's unwillingness to treat seriously with Indians or to follow the
accepted procedures.

For Indians covered by Treaty Five Adhesions, benefits deriving from surrendering Aboriginal title were largely ephemeral. The immediate impact of
the treaty at Oxford House was noted by Commissioner Semmens: 'It was
delightful to observe the transformation which took place in general appearances in the next few hours. Famine gave place to plenty. Rags were
supplanted by modern apparel. Solemnity was followed by hilarity. Every-
body was glad and it shall remains [sic] a question as to who appreciated the
situation most[,] the givers or those who received.'[54] The 'transformation'
was short-lived, and Semmens has certainly confused the givers as the
takers. In his memoirs, Semmens recalled that the adhesion to Treaty Five
'was accomplished with entire satisfaction to all parties concerned.'[55] An
all-too revelatory editorial in the *Manitoba Free Press* in 1910 warned of the
dangers of white encroachment on Native resources and argued that 'it
will be to the lasting disgrace of Canada if she allows the 6000 [?] Indians
and halfbreeds between Lake Winnipeg and Hudson Bay to be demoralized
and decimated as other Indian tribes have ... they deserve a better fate.'[56]
To the extent that the *Free Press* represented a public concern about Indian
policy, a progressive perspective was presented; but then as now, the government resists Aboriginal and non-Aboriginal efforts to define Indian/
white relations on the basis of Aboriginal rights. The department consciously
rejected the treaty process as a means to assist Indians to cope with the deprivation associated with a commercialized hunting economy. The timing
of the treaty process was based on government expediency and the needs
of a railroad company. When deciding which treaty format to implement,
the state selected the terms that offered the least to Indians. Nonetheless,
Indian people attempted to use the treaty to deal with the declining fur
trade, to protect the hunting economy from encroachment, and to participate in an anticipated commercial boom. Some of the confusion that followed the Treaty Five Adhesions was the result of Semmens's errors. The
state had gained from its experiences in the earlier treaty period, and it had
become more effective about setting the timing and terms of treaties.

A comparison between the early treaty period (1871-6) and the adhesion
period (1908-10) indicates that the treaty procedures used in Keewatin were
downgraded. Questions about the validity of the surrender of Aboriginal

title specified by the adhesions are appropriate. The problems concerning hunting rights and the confusion about the size of the reserves suggests that Semmens may not have provided an adequate explanation about the meaning of the surrender of Aboriginal title. The increasing dominant position of the government is reflected by the ease with which the adhesions were secured. The capacity of the state to serve the outside interests of capital, to open up a regional economy, and to ignore the basic needs and rights of Aboriginal peoples was increasing. In the Treaty Five Adhesions, Indians followed a strategy similar to the early treaties. Attempts were made to secure an economic base. Indians recognized disruptions originating with modernization; unfortunately the government's representatives could not anticipate the problems Indians would be facing.

6

'Terms and Conditions as May Be Deemed Expedient': Metis Aboriginal Title

A difficult historical dimension of contemporary Aboriginal rights is the so-called 'extinguishment' of the Metis claim on Indian title. In 1869-70, political activity by the Red River Metis forced the Canadian government to acknowledge that the Metis and Halfbreed populations were entitled to a share of Indian title. In order to understand Aboriginal title in northern Manitoba, a brief examination of the evolution of government policies towards the Red River and Northwest Metis is required. Metis Aboriginal title was dealt with differently than Indian Aboriginal title; distinct procedures and policies were implemented in an effort to obtain the Metis claim on Indian title. Overall, government policies concerning Metis Aboriginal title had an ad hoc quality. These convoluted policies dealing with Metis Aboriginal title are important because they define the legal relationship of individual Natives and communities to the Indian Act.

Throughout the Northwest, the government attempted to deal with Metis Aboriginal title by issuing Halfbreed scrip to individual Metis. Scrip, a coupon, redeemable for land or money, was a piece of paper issued to Metis grantees on an individual basis. Halfbreed scrip had its origins in the Manitoba Act, and, thus, an appreciation of scrip commissions in northern Manitoba requires some background discussion of the Crown's approach to Metis Aboriginal title. Whether or not Metis Aboriginal title was legally extinguished through government scrip policies is a serious question. Legally, the issue remains unresolved. Until the attempted annexation of Rupertsland, the Dominion government and preconfederation colonies had had little experience in dealing with the Metis. Economically, the terms for dealing with Metis Aboriginal title were even less appropriate than treaties as means for coping with the post-1870 conditions. Certainly, the implementation of government scrip procedures did not safeguard an Aboriginal interest in land.

This chapter will explain the story of scrip issued in northern Manitoba as a consequence of adhesions to Treaty Five. In Canadian history, Metis scrip has left a furtive image, in part because the official records of the Department of the Interior, the agency that issued land and money scrip, present such a sanitized view of the experience and because the crucial exchanges between Metis scrip grantees and scrip buyers was of no concern. Consequently, many aspects of the scrip process were not documented by the Interior department. Moreover, the mass of minutiae created by the scrip claim process has not been rigorously analyzed. By using missionary records, HBC files, and records from the Province of Manitoba, additional details have been gleaned and the story of scrip in northern Manitoba can be reconstructed.

The Manitoba Act and Manitoba Metis Lands

Until the Manitoba Act in 1870, the procedures for considering Aboriginal title did not provide for any special forms of compensation for 'Mixedbloods.' Depending upon the concurrence of the chiefs, some Metis living as 'Indians' became band members, as in the case of the Robinson-Superior Treaty of 1850. One of the political results of the 1869-70 Red River Resistance was the recognition of Metis as a distinct Aboriginal people. The provisional government's main negotiator, Father Ritchot, eventually accepted a Metis land grant in recognition of Indian title because the federal government was absolutely unwilling to accept provincial legislative control over land. This compromise resulted in an explicit acknowledgment of Metis Aboriginal title being written into the Manitoba Act. Section 31 states: 'And whereas, it is expedient, towards the extinguishment of the Indian title to the lands in the Province, to appropriate a portion of such ungranted lands, to the extent of one million four hundred thousand acres thereof, for the benefit of the families of the half-breed residents.'[1] Clearly, the Manitoba Act acknowledged Metis Aboriginal title, but it did not indicate procedures for dealing with that title consistent with the Royal Proclamation of 1763. Land was not held in trust by the Crown but was to be given out to individuals and children. Section 32 of the Manitoba Act was also important to the Metis because it protected the full range of land tenures and privileges that had developed at Red River prior to the transfer of Rupertsland. The supposition was that the Metis occupancy of the province would have been protected by these sections of the Manitoba Act.

From a geographical point of view, the Manitoba Act had the potential for enabling the Metis population to deal with post-1870 conditions because it allowed Metis families to retain their individual river lots and it provided a large land grant or land base for the future. In 1929, N.O. Coté, a long-standing senior official in the Department of the Interior, after having dealt personally with scrip for decades, reported on the government's legislative/legal framework for dealing with Metis claims. His report summarized the situation arising out of the Manitoba Act: the disposal of land and scrip (a redeemable piece of paper in lieu of real property) under Section 31 resulting in 6,034 claims of children amounting to 1,488,160 acres; 993 supplemental claims amounting to money scrip of $238,300; and 3,186 money scrips of Halfbreed heads of families worth $509,760.[2] Apparently, the terms of the Manitoba Act were more than generously carried out. However, the successes of land speculators resulted in a bitter legacy for Metis of the Red River Settlement.

The details and the outcomes of the implementation of the Manitoba Act land grants and the river lot claims have been presented by the historian Doug Sprague.[3] Sprague showed that Lieutenant-Governor Archibald's efforts to have local authority influence the implementation of Sections 31 and 32 failed. Sprague found that 'the Department of Justice superintended revisions of Sections 31 and 32 on no fewer than nine occasions between 1872 and 1880' and therefore 'unconstitutional amendments to the Manitoba Act displaced the unalterable original law.'[4] One important development was the exclusion of Metis heads of families from the 1.4 million acre grant. The adults could not be excluded completely from the grant and were given scrip, a piece of paper, worth 160 acres redeemable in land or money. The children were to get 240 acres in land (real property) from the 1.4 million acre grant. Sprague pointed out that speculators had access to the lists of claims settlement and had the means of obtaining powers of attorney. Consequently, he concluded that 'virtually all of the money scrip which was supposed to have been awarded to half-breed heads of families never reached the claimants.'[5] Metis children, although minors, experienced the illegal transfer of their ownership of real property.[6] Their interests, as minors, were not protected. Moreover, a very real dispossession of their river lots came with revisions to Section 32, which effectively meant that only those Metis with secure title under the pre-1870 land tenure system could retain their land. Sprague concluded that of all the land that should have become Metis property, they obtained less than 600,000 acres and that 'the rest of the land, perhaps as much as 2 million acres, was diverted to speculators leaving the original population land-poor in their home province.'[7]

By 31 December 1880, the claims on the Metis land grant had been 'settled,' but disputes over the river lots continued for several more years. Sprague's research contradicted government reports on the amount of money and land scrip issued as a result of Section 31. The implementation of the Manitoba Act failed to enable most Metis families to deal with post-1870 conditions. Significantly, the manner of dealing with Metis Aboriginal title in Manitoba set the terms for subsequent government approaches to the Metis of the Northwest. The government's implementation of the

Scrip speculator (left), mounted policeman, and Indians below Split Lake on the Nelson River, 1910 (PAM, N8164, A.V. Thomas Collection, No. 90)

Manitoba Act established a precedent by which Metis adults received 160 acres or dollars and their children received $240 of money scrip from scrip commissions. Later scrip commissions would issue 240 acres or dollars of scrip to both adults and children. Land scrip had the status of real property. However, money scrip, which was directed towards children, was redeemable by the bearer. Beyond issuing scrip coupons, there was no explicit recognition of Metis Aboriginal rights.[8] The government's handling of the Manitoba Metis land grant permitted the successful intervention of the private sector (land speculators) to obtain the benefits of Metis Aboriginal title. Furthermore, the Manitoba Act only dealt with Metis in the original province.

Northwest Scrip Commissions and Aboriginal Status

By 1885, the federal government had treated with Indians throughout much of the Northwest, but it had only considered the Aboriginal title as it related to the Metis of the 'postage stamp' province of Manitoba. Western lands had come under the control of the Interior department, however, Metis claims had not been considered. Until the scrip commissions of the 1880s, the only means for prairie Metis outside of Manitoba to obtain compensation for land claims was to accept Indian treaties. Such a situation not only contributed to the grievances associated with the 1885 Resistance, but it created a complex problem concerning the legal Aboriginal status of the mixed-blood population. Although the government did not reconsider Metis claims until 1885, the Dominion Lands Act of 1879 (DLA) acknowledged Metis Aboriginal title. This act provided for Halfbreed land grants 'on such terms and conditions as may be deemed expedient.'[9] Thus, the government's statutory recognition of a Metis interest in Indian title extended beyond Manitoba.

The DLA, however, provided neither means nor principles for considering Metis claims. The government did not act on the provisions of the DLA until the untimely appointment of the first scrip commission in January 1885. The satisfaction of these claims involved making declarations to travelling scrip commissions, meeting certain criteria, and accepting money or land scrip coupons. The commissions of the late 1880s essentially examined individual Metis claims to territory that had already been ceded by earlier Indian treaties. Subsequently, scrip commissions coincided with Indian treaties and treaty adhesions. Ken Hatt identified thirteen commissions that dispersed $2,885,157 worth of money scrip and 2,609,772 acres in land scrip (including the Manitoba grant).[10] During the implementation of scrip, frequent changes to scrip terms and to eligibility criteria occurred.[11] Nonetheless, both land and money scrip ownership passed from the Metis to land speculators rather quickly and generally at less than the nominal or face value.[12] Scrip buyers then converted the coupons into land. The amounts were not trivial. Scrip policies contributed to the creation of a wealthy, regional elite.

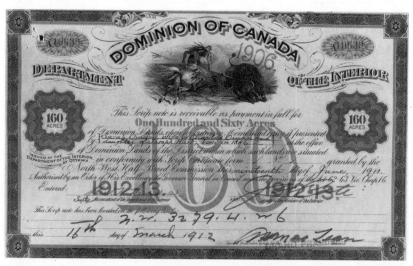

Land scrip coupon No. A10639 for 160 acres belonging to Sarah Oman, wife of Charles Oman and daughter of Joseph Hart. The scrip was located on NW 1/4 of Section 32, Township 79, Range 4, west of the 6th meridian (near Grand Prairie, Alberta), and is dated 16 March 1912. Sarah Oman lived at Fort Churchill. (NAC, C-140135)

The complex rules administering Metis claims for Halfbreed scrip became even more cumbersome for individuals that had signed onto treaty and then later wished to obtain scrip. The Indian Affairs department's procedures for dealing with Indians who withdrew from treaty in order to apply for scrip and then attempted to be readmitted to treaty are not clear. To some degree, ambiguous policies reflect the interchangeability of terms like Indian and Native during the fur trade. During the early treaty process, the Metis presented a problem for officials. As Indian Commissioner Provencher noted in 1873, many 'half-breeds live with the Indians; have the very same habits, and actually form part of the Tribe.'[13] Indian Commissioner Simpson reported in 1871 that Manitoba Halfbreeds preferred the treaty benefits instead of waiting for 'the realization of any value in their half-breed grant.'[14] An end to Indian legal status was possible for Natives through enfranchisement, a commutation of fifty dollars in lieu of annuities; and Indians with white blood were allowed to withdraw from treaty and apply for scrip. With the travelling scrip commissions of the 1880s, Natives who had joined treaty were now in a position to withdraw and claim Halfbreed scrip, and in 1886 the majority of applications were from treaty Indians.[15] In some areas, a large non-status Indian population developed as a result of scrip commissions, enfranchisements, and commutations. By 1893, some 200 non-status Indians and 993 status Indians lived in The Pas agency.[16] Halfbreed scrip and the Indian Act became fixed legal impositions on communities in which terms like Indian, Halfbreed, Metis and Native had been interchangeable. All shared a common use of the land.

The fur industry had created Halfbreed and Indian communities at trading posts. However, the Crown's legal recognition of Indian and Metis Aboriginal title was not simultaneous, and, therefore, Indian agents later faced applications for withdrawals from treaty in the late 1880s. It is often assumed that Metis with Indian status were quick to give up the long-term benefits of treaty status for some sort of windfall gain from scrip. This was not necessarily the case as scrip commissioners R. Goulet and N.O. Coté reported: 'At Norway House, Fisher River and Fort Alexander there are large settlement of half-breeds residing on Indian Reserves and in receipt of Indian annuities but who all preferred to remain members of the Indian Bands to which they belonged and to continue to enjoy as such all treaty privileges.'[17] This observation suggests that individual decisions were often based on economic concerns. Efforts were made to explain the consequences to Indians requesting withdrawal, but confusion existed with respect to the status of children. Treaty Indian children received annuity payments, whereas in the 1880s only Metis children born before 15 July 1870 could receive scrip. Inspector of Indian Agencies E. McColl travelled with the scrip commission in 1887 and explained the loss of annuities and non-eligibility of children for scrip.[18] Unlike the treaties, which provided for a land base in the form of reserves, scrip was not designed to provide a secure land base for Metis communities. In fact, withdrawing from treaty created problems, since some Metis wanted to locate their scrip on a reserve or have lots, which they had resided on prior to the treaties, removed from a reserve.[19]

The evidence indicates that the Indian Affairs department allowed Indians who had withdrawn for scrip to return to treaty status, although the terms and procedures are unclear.[20] To start with, not all Metis were allowed to withdraw and give up treaty status. Goulet and Coté explained 'that only those that satisfactorily showed that they would not need any government assistance were allowed discharge from treaty.'[21] In a certain sense, this economic qualification for scrip was consistent with assimilationist thinking behind enfranchisement. But implicitly, such a procedure is an admission that scrip did not provide adequate economic compensation or land security in exchange for Aboriginal title. In 1895, policy permitted the readmittance to treaty for some Metis who had received scrip, but they could not collect annuities.[22] The criteria for readmittance also seemed to be economically motivated. Concerning Grand Rapids Natives, McColl decided in 1893 that applications from 'able bodied Half-Breeds, whom the Hudson's Bay Company, the Fish Companies and other parties employed at good wages, in cutting cordwood, packing ice, fishing ... should not be entertained.'[23] Also Metis who sold their scrip in advance and received fair market value for their coupons could not re-enter treaty.[24] In this particular situation, temporary economic integration with the labour market meant that generations of northern Manitoba Natives would lose their legal Indian status. Wage employment was often transitory, but the implementation of scrip policies permanently denied Indian status. Treaties and the Indian Act created a legal split between Natives, which was further complicated by the scrip commissions of the 1880s. The extent to which present-day Indian reserve communities had dual origins in the pre-treaty Halfbreed and Indian populations is not generally appreciated.

Treaty Five Adhesion Scrip: Orders in Council and Middlemen
In Manitoba, north of the 1875 treaty boundaries, Metis Aboriginal title was considered during the adhesions to Treaties Five through the provision of applications for Halfbreed scrip.[25] Privy Council Order 1114 (12 May 1908) appointed John Semmens to investigate scrip claims. The Department of the Interior records concerning Treaty Five Adhesion scrip do not provide a comprehensive summary of the number of claims made or the number of claims that were allowed. Coté reported in 1929 that only 117 land and money scrip were allowed, but this is an understatement.[26] Table 6.1 is a better account of the amount and kind of scrip issued; the data indicate

that some 136 individuals received land or money scrip. Because land scrip was more valuable to scrip buyers, more land scrip than money scrip was sought by individual claimants. Orders-in-council of 29 May 1909 and 24 May 1911 authorized scrip for $240 or for 240 acres of 'any Dominion Land open for homestead entry, in the Provinces of Manitoba, Saskatchewan, Alberta or the North West Territories.'[27] Because northern Manitoba was not included in the Dominion Lands Survey, the basis of the homestead system, scrip could not be converted into real property in northern Manitoba. Thus, the grant of land symbolized by the scrip coupon had little practical value for northern Metis.

Table 6.1

Number of Treaty Five adhesion scrip claims allowed

Residence of grantee	Land scrip	Money scrip	Total
1909[1]			
Norway House	34	1	
Split Lake	2		
Cross Lake	1		
Warrens Landing	1		
Fisher River	10		
Selkirk	3		
Total	51	1	52
1910[2]			
Norway House	5		
Oxford House	2		
York Factory	37		
Fort Churchill	15	9	
Winnipeg/Selkirk	16		
Total	75	9	84
Total adhesion scrip	126	10	136

Source: NAC, RG 15, vol. 1016, file 1578625, pt. 1
1 Scrip claims granted under the authority of Order in Council, PC 1060, 29 May 1909.
2 Scrip claims granted under the authority of Order in Council, PC 1193, 24 May 1911.

Each scrip commission established criteria by which some Halfbreed claims would be accepted while others would be rejected. A good number of those individuals who received scrip were not resident in the territory covered by the adhesions to Treaty Five. Order-in-Council (PC 1060) of 29 May 1909 identified the basic categories of Natives that could have scrip claims satisfied: (1) Halfbreeds born in the area covered by the adhesion and who were resident on the date of the signing of the Split Lake adhesion; (2) Halfbreeds born in the territory covered by the adhesion but resident in territory already ceded; and (3) Halfbreeds resident in the adhesion territory on the date of the Split Lake adhesion but not born in the area covered by the adhesion. Data in Table 6.1 indicate that Metis resident at places like Winnipeg and Fisher River received scrip. Their claims were based on their birth in the territory covered by the adhesion, and a change in residency to an area already ceded (such as Winnipeg or Fisher River) did not disqualify them from making a claim and receiving scrip. Children born in the territory covered by the adhesion prior to the date of the Split Lake adhesion could have a claim satisfied, provided at least one parent had not previously received land or scrip. Reasons given for rejecting certain Treaty Five Adhesion scrip claims included: the claimants being born in unceded territory not covered by the Treaty Five Adhesion (for example, northern Ontario), the claimants being born in territory already ceded or born in Manitoba after 1870, or the claimant's parents having received land or scrip under the Manitoba Act.[28] A child born after the Split Lake adhesion (26 June 1908), but before the opportunity existed for parents to place evidence before the commissioner, say York Factory (10 August 1910), would not receive scrip. However, a mere change in residency would not allow a Metis claimant to have a claim satisfied by more than one scrip commission. Appendix C provides details on the scrip process in northern Manitoba. The paper trail created by a claim has been reconstructed from archival records.

While orders-in-council from the Department of the Interior convey the terms by which a claim for scrip can be made, scrip buyers are a central element in the scrip process. In this area, the actions of speculative scrip buyers preceded the appointment of Rev. John Semmens as treaty and scrip commissioner. The Methodist missionary at Oxford House, J.H. Lowes, presumed in February of 1908 that the government was going to treat since he wrote, 'Some sharpers have heard about it and mean to take unfair advantage of our people's ignorance and before there is any competition gobble up everything.'[29] The events associated with the Treaty Five Adhesion scrip are documented in Table 6.2. Lowes reported that HBC employees had circulated blank forms that signed scrip over to A.A. McDonald of Winnipeg. Apparently, a number of these contracts were signed. This scrip contract between Metis claimants and scrip buyers has been reproduced in Figure 6.1. The Department of the Interior became involved in northern Halfbreed Manitoba claims when J.D. McLean, Department of Indian Affairs, wrote in May of 1908 that treaty adhesions were about to be made and that 'it occurs to me that you might think it well to deal with the half breed claims in this territory at the same time.'[30] The formal decision to issue scrip came with

Table 6.2

Events associated with Treaty Five adhesion scrip

14 February 1908	J. Semmens conveys information on his summer visit to Nelson House and Split Lake regarding Treaty Five adhesion to F. Oliver, minister of the Department of the Interior.
22 February 1908	D.C. Scott is instructed to consider Metis claims with respect to the adhesions to Treaty Five.
28 February 1908	J.H. Lowes writes Indian Commissioner D. Laird about scrip buyers at Oxford House and associates C.C. Sinclair and D. Flett with Winnipeg scrip interests of A.A. McDonald.
10 April 1908	D. Laird responds to J.H. Lowes, indicating that he has no knowledge of a Native surrender.
7 May 1908	Department of Indian Affairs notifies the Department of the Interior about pending Treaty Five adhesions.
12 May 1908	Privy Council Order 1114 appoints J. Semmens as treaty and Metis claims commissioner.
26 May 1908	J. Semmens instructed about scrip.
9-10 June 1908	J. Semmens receives instructions from the minister of the Department of the Interior and deputies in Ottawa.
June 1908	J. Semmens accompanied north by C. Thompson, a scrip buyer. Semmens takes applications for scrip at Split Lake, Norway House, Cross Lake, and Fisher River. A.G. Kemp acts as Thompson's secretary.
3 September 1908	J. Semmens forwards 54 scrip applications to the Department of Indian Affairs.
September 1908	J. Semmens visits Oxford House, Gods Lake, and Island Lake in preparation for next summer's adhesion.
10 October 1908	J. Semmens reports that C.C. Sinclair and other HBC men had canvassed Oxford House in the winter of 1907-8 on behalf of C. Thompson and S.E. Richards.
March 1909	J.H. Lowes reports that A.A. McDonald's scrip buyers (Sinclair, Anderson, and Flett) had been advancing trade goods at Oxford House.
19 May 1909	A. Sutherland writes Pedley about scrip buying at Oxford House.
29 May 1909	Privy Council Order 1060 authorizes the first issue of Treaty Five adhesion scrip.
2 June 1909	Pedley responds to A. Sutherland and refuses to acknowledge the extent of the problem. He also denies responsibilities for issuing Metis scrip.

continued on next page

Table 6.2 (continued)

Summer 1909	J. Semmens takes scrip applications at Oxford House, Island Lake, Norway House, and Winnipeg/Selkirk; delivers scrip to Metis grantees. York Factory and Fort Churchill Indians informed of 1910 treaty adhesion.
Fall 1909	P.D. Tyerman and H. Halcrow form partnership.
Late Fall 1909	H. Halcrow leaves Norway House in the company of H.A. Tremayne and C.C. Sinclair to purchase York Factory and Churchill Metis scrip claims.
December 1909	C. Thompson sends F. Rousseau to York Factory to purchase scrip.
Summer 1910	P.D. Tyerman and C. Thompson enter into agreement to act together to keep scrip prices low. Some Oxford House Natives inform J. Semmens that they wish to withdraw from treaty in favour of scrip. H. Halcrow assists Churchill and York Factory Metis with scrip applications. Semmens takes scrip applications at York Factory, Fort Churchill, Norway House, Berens River, and Winnipeg/Selkirk.
1911	Fur Trade Commissioner R.H. Hall decides to purchase scrip. S.E. Richards gets Hall to join syndicate that has already advanced payments on scrip.
12 May 1911	Privy Council Order 1193 authorizes second batch of Treaty Five adhesion scrip to be issued to claimants applying in 1909 and 1910.
Summer 1911	Scrip delivered, including Fort Churchill. R.H. Hall sends H.S. Johnston to accompany S.E. Richards and C. Thompson interests. Scrip purchased.
March 1912	York Factory scrip delivered and scrip purchased.
9 December 1912	HBC (London) begins to investigate R.H. Hall's role in scrip buying.
12 December 1912	A. Nanton (HBC Canadian Committee) defends R.H. Hall.
February 1913	R.H. Hall resigns as HBC fur trade commissioner.
Fall 1913	Department of the Interior investigates Churchill and York Factory scrip located in Alberta.
December 1917	Requests to redback Treaty Five adhesion scrip begin.
1935-47	S.E. Richards negotiates with Manitoba government about scrip location and unredeemed scrip.

Sources: HBCA, A.12/FT MISC/273 and A.12/L, 13/2; NAC, RG 10, vol. 4009, file 249462, pt. 1, and 249462, pt. 1A; NAC, RG 15, vol. 1016, file 1578625, pts. 1 and 2; NAC, RG 15, vol. 1043, file 1748598; PAM, RG 17, B1, box 89, file 17.2.1; UCCA, Sutherland papers, Lowes correspondence (29 and 31 March 1909, 2 June 1909)

the appointment on 12 May 1908 of John Semmens as scrip commissioner. Indeed, for the 1908 adhesions, Semmens casually noted that 'we were accompanied by Chester Thompson[,] a very honourable gentleman of the City of Winnipeg who appeared to be connected with some Winnipeg Firm interested in the purchase of Half-breed scrip.'[31] Scrip buyers were in place when the adhesions began.

Government records documenting the procedures followed by the scrip commissioner are not extensive. Semmens received his instructions in Ottawa when he met with the minister of the interior. During the 1908 adhesion, Semmens took sixty-nine applications; most of these applications were from claimants not residing in the territory covered by the adhesion.[32] In the same year, Semmens visited northeastern Manitoba, then part of the district of Keewatin, and concluded that some of Reverend Lowes's allegations concerning the activities of scrip buyers were not supported; only two bags of flour had been advanced, and the Hudson's Bay Company was not directly involved in scrip buying.[33] During this visit to northeastern Manitoba, he identified twenty-five Halfbreeds at Oxford house.[34] In 1909 at Oxford House, Semmens explained the differences between treaty and scrip, but he dealt with the treaty first. At Oxford House only a few applications for scrip were taken. Apparently, the initial efforts at scrip buying by A.A. McDonald, associated with Chester Thompson and the Winnipeg law firm Richards, Affleck and Co., did not have much influence at communities like Oxford House. In contrast, at the 1910 adhesion (York Factory and Fort Churchill) scrip buyers were more evident. Semmens explained: 'Scrip Vendors have employed certain agitators to go through the North and assure these people that they were foolish to have taken Treaty when it can be proved that they have even a drop of white blood in their veins. These men have with very great persistence sowed discontent and expect to reap a rich harvest by these methods. The Indians are quite exercised over the situation and are much unsettled.'[35] When Semmens treated at York Factory in 1910, the influence of the agents for scrip buyers was obvious. As a result: 'Some who were Indian in appearance, habits, language and manners, and who were known only as Indians to all their friends came to apply for scrip.'[36] His advice against taking scrip was not always well received because it 'so provoked the scrip man present who promised to make things interesting for myself and the Reverend Mr. Faries.'[37] Nevertheless, a number of Indians who had recently obtained Treaty status were interested in withdrawing from treaty in favour of scrip. Both Lowes and Semmens left records indicating that scrip buyers had been actively promoting scrip claims among the Native population. The commercial success of scrip buying was related to the volume of scrip that could be obtained, this in turn was related to the number of Natives that selected a scrip claim over becoming part of the treaty.

Figure 6.1 Northern Manitoba scrip contract, ca. 1908

This Indenture made the _____ day of _____ ad 19 _____
Between _____ in this District of Keewatin (herein
after called the 'vendor') of the first part _____ and Alexander Archibald
McDonald of the City of Winnipeg in the province of Manitoba – gentleman
(hereinafter the 'Purchaser') of the second part.

The Vendor agrees to sell to the Purchaser, who agrees to buy from the
Vendor, all Land Scrip issued to him by the Government of Canada and to his
children, and all his rights and claims for any such Scrip for Two Hundred
Dollars ($200.00 for each of which, $100.00 is to be paid by the Purchaser on
the delivery of said Scrip to the Vendor, and the balance on the location of
said Scrip on land selected by the Purchaser and the due and effective conveyance of said land to the Purchaser, and all cash Scrip issued to him and his
children by the Government of Canada for the price of $50.00 each[)] to be
paid on the issue and delivery of said Scrip to the Purchaser and the Vendor
agrees with the Purchaser that he will himself and his children accept Land
Scrip or Cash Scrip as requested by the Purchaser.

And the Vendor hereby in consideration of the above agreement grants,
assigns and transfers to the Purchaser all his right title and interest to all and
every scrip Certificate or note now or hereafter issued to him by the Government of Canada, and also in the case Land Scrip should be issued to the Vendor, the land to be located with said Scrip.

And for the said consideration the Vendor hereby irrevocably nominates[,]
constitutes and appoints the Purchaser his true and lawful Attorney to receive
the said Scrip Certificate or Note from the Government of Canada and in case
Land Scrip should be issued to him to attend at any Dominion Land Office to
locate said Scrip on any land that the Purchaser may think fit and to sign any
application for location of Homestead and any other documents that may be
required in connection therewith; to sell and to absolutely dispose of any land
or lands in which such Land Scrip may be located and to convey[,] assign[,]
transfer and make over the same to any purchaser thereof, and for him and in
his name and as his act and deed to execute complete in every way and to all
such assurances acts or things as the Purchaser may see fit for all and every of
the purposes aforesaid.

The Vendor revokes all and every Power of Attorney at any time by him
heretofore made[.]

The term 'Vendor' and 'Purchaser' wherever used herein shall include respectively the executors[,] administrators and assigns of the part of the first
part and of the party of the second part as the case may be[.]

In Witness whereof the parties hereto have hereinto set there hands and
seals[.]

Signed[,] sealed and delivered in the presence of _____

After having first been read over[,] interpreted and explained[.]

continued on next page

Figure 6.1 (continued) – Copy Reverse Side

To Wit I _____ of the _____

Of _____ in the _____ of _____

make oath and say _____

1. That I was personally present and did see the within Indenture duly signed[,]
   sealed and executed by _____ one of the parties thereto[.]
2. That said Indenture was executed at _____ in
   _____[.]
3. That I know the said party and that he is of the full age of twenty-one
   years[.]
4. That I am a subscribing witness to the said Indenture which was by me
   carefully read over[,] interpreted and explained to the said part who appeared
   to perfectly understand the same and who executed the same by making his
   mark in my presence[.]

Sworn before one at _____ with Dist. of _____

This _____ day of _____ AD 19 ____

A Commissioner in and for _____

Source: UCCA, Sutherland papers, box 7, file 142, Lowes to Sutherland (31 March 1909)

Important insights into the scrip process are possible because the Hudson's Bay Company's good name became associated with the sordid business of scrip buying. In particular, Fur Trade Commissioner R.H. Hall was held responsible for scrip buying in northern Manitoba (see Table 6.2). The London Secretary of the HBC, F.C. Ingrams, wrote to Hall because 'it would appear that this scrip was obtained from them [Natives] at a price far below that market value of the land it represents, and that the Company has been brought into disrepute by this action.'[38] R.H. Hall's involvement with scrip buying in northern Manitoba was not his first encounter with Halfbreed scrip coupons. A few years earlier, Hall had been in charge of the Saskatchewan district of the HBC and had become familiar with the scrip issued at Isle-a la Crosse and Portage La Loche (Treaty Ten). At these communities, Metis claimants had been given promissory notes by scrip buyers, which, in turn, the Metis used to negotiate credit at HBC posts. Hall viewed these notes from scrip buyers as extremely insecure credit, so he actively tracked down scrip buyers and secured payment. After dealing with the Treaty Ten land scrip, Hall was well versed in Halfbreed scrip and scrip speculators.[39] When the opportunity arose to purchase scrip as a personal interest, he linked up with the very same interest that had purchased the bulk of the scrip coupons in northwestern Saskatchewan (see Table 6.2).

During the fur trade, monopoly (or more precisely, monopsony) served those that purchased from Native sellers. A similar economic relationship

developed with respect to the buying and selling of scrip issued to northern Metis. Table 6.2 shows that scrip buyers formed partnerships and then
absorbed potential competitors. The principal scrip buyers and the approaches to transacting scrip were the same for Treaty Ten and Treaty Five
adhesion scrip commissions. W.P. Fillmore had been a young law student
with Richards and Affleck and he later recalled buying scrip in northwestern Saskatchewan: 'Mr X asked me to go with Mr. Thompson to Ile-a la-
Crosse and Portage La Loche to make treaty with the Indians and issue
[scrip to] halfbreeds. I was supposed to act as an independent buyer, and
was given $5,000.00 in a canvas bag, which I carried in my hip pocket. I
assume that Thompson had the same.'[40] The appearance of acting like an
independent buyer served to mask collusion from the Metis. Fillmore recalled:

> Right at the start the scrip buyers got together and decided that it would be
> foolish to indulge in any competitive buying. It was further decided and
> agreed that [the] price to be paid for scrip would be $1.00 per acre. My
> recollection is that each scrip called for 320 acres. It was further agreed that
> [the] said lawyer and Fillmore would be the secretaries of such a syndicate,
> and that each buyer would deposit a sum of money with us. It was further
> agreed that the buyers would bring in each scrip purchased to us and would
> be refunded $320.00 out of the deposit, and when the buying ended the
> scrip purchased would be divided pro rata between them. This scheme was
> carried out, and the scrip turned in was so divided, and the deposits re-
> turned less adjustments.[41]

The Hudson's Bay Company's records confirm that in northern Manitoba
'Dr. Tyerman and Mr. Thompson entered into an agreement in the summer
of 1910 for the purpose of acting together in keeping others out of the field,
and of buying the scrips with as little expense as possible.'[42] In 1911, Hall
decided to take part in purchasing York Factory and Churchill scrip; however, his interest was absorbed by the Tyerman and Thompson syndicate
after he had been approached by S.E. Richards from the law firm Richards
and Affleck. Since advances had been made towards the purchase of scrip
by Tyerman and Thompson, a new buyer would have raised the cost of
scrip. The link between Richards and Thompson is indisputable. In 1947,
Richards provided the minister of mines and natural resources, Manitoba,
with documents indicating that Chester Thompson had willed S.E. Richards
some unredeemed Metis scrip.[43]

Horace Halcrow did much of the fieldwork for the scrip buyers, as Richards
stated:

Halcrow went for the purpose of assisting the half breeds in presenting evidence in support of their claims, and of persuading them to take scrip instead of going into treaty. It was entirely due, we are informed, to Halcrow's efforts in this matter that the half breeds did apply for scrip instead of going into treaty as Indians. The Treaty Commissioner and the Missionaries showed a strong inclination to persuade the half breeds to go into treaty. Mr. Halcrow has informed the writer that if he had not been present at the time the treaty was made, that practically all the half breeds would have gone into treaty instead of applying for scrip. Mr. Halcrow then made further advances to the half breeds to offset the moneys they would have received for treaty.[44]

This statement by an individual centrally involved with the accumulation of scrip verifies Semmens's report concerning the disruptive affects of agents for the scrip buyers. In 1946, Richards referred to Halcrow 'as agent for and on behalf of a syndicate of which I was a member.'[45] Alexander Oman, a Metis grantee from Fort Churchill, connected Horace Halcrow to Johnston, Campbell, and Alston of the HBC. According to Oman, these individuals represented scrip buying as an HBC activity (see Appendix C). While Hall was acting on his own, agents representing the syndicate sought credibility by identifying their activities with the HBC.

Converting Coupons into Land
The scrip speculators in northwestern Saskatchewan and northern Manitoba functioned as middlemen between the Metis grantees and distant land markets. They obtained land scrip from northern Metis at the lowest possible price. These coupons could only be converted to land as real property in distant southern homestead lands. The geographical distance between southern land markets and northern Metis grantees holding scrip made the direct marketing of coupons very difficult. Separation between buyers and sellers also limited Metis knowledge of land values. The Thompson/Richards/Tyerman syndicate played a middleman role. Once the syndicate had obtained scrip from the Metis grantee, the scrip could be held for speculation or converted into land by members of the syndicate, or it could be passed on to small buyers looking for eighty or 160 acres of Dominion Lands.

The conversion of Halfbreed land scrip coupons into a patent for Dominion Lands was an elaborate process (see Appendix C for details). Once a Metis grantee, of adult age, was in possession of the scrip, the grantee could locate the scrip on lands open for homestead by personally visiting a local Dominion Lands office and selecting acreage from the available lands from within the district. Only the Metis grantee could locate the scrip, in effect, apply the scrip to homestead lands. Locating the scrip had to be done in a Dominion Lands office. After the scrip had been located, the location could be assigned to another person (assignee), or the Metis grantee could apply and obtain a patent for the land he had located. The Land Patents Branch, Department of the Interior, Ottawa, approved the location and assignment and then issued the patent. In almost all cases, the patent for the land was not issued to Metis grantees but to other individuals, known as assignees.[46] These procedures, involving the Metis grantee, the local Dominion Lands office, and the Land Patents Branch in Ottawa, define the Rule of Location. A bulletin from the Department of the Interior explained the restrictions on locating, assigning, and patenting scrip:

> Land scrip cannot be assigned. Entry for land upon which it is desired to apply the scrip can only be made by the half-breed to whom it has been issued, unless special authority has been endorsed thereon (commonly designated 'red back scrip'), in which case such endorsed land scrip may be located by the holder thereof in the name of the grantee of the scrip. No assignment of right to scrip is recognized, but after the half-breed land scrip has been applied to land, the right to the land may be transferred. No transfer of such right, however, executed prior to the date of the location of the scrip on the land or executed by a person under twenty-one years of age may be recognized.[47]

The Rule of Location required the Metis grantee to visit the Dominion Lands office personally in order to initiate events that would lead to the conversion of a scrip coupon into real property. The Metis grantee could transfer or assign the location only after locating the land. The patent to the land would be issued in the name of the assignee, if the scrip had been properly located. A Metis grantee had to be twenty-one years old in order to locate scrip. Technically, this meant that a five-year-old child, issued scrip in 1911, would have to wait until 1927 in order to locate the scrip. But the requirement to locate before assigning land was neither absolute nor necessarily enforceable. As indicated by the bulletin, the Rule of Location could be legally circumvented by redbacking scrip.

At the time that scrip was delivered, scrip buyers or their agents took possession of the scrip from those grantees that had agreed to sell (see Appendix C). The coupons could pass through several interested parties before being located at a Dominion Lands office. In such circumstances, the original Metis grantee from a geographical remote northern community would not be in touch with those buyers that had taken possession of the scrip.

Scrip middlemen also took possession of minor's scrip, but they would not attempt to locate the scrip until the grantee had passed the age of twenty-one. As far as following the Rule of Location, a number of practical problems existed with respect to converting scrip. Fillmore explained the problem:

> I have always wondered how the buyer, or purchaser, of scrip from him, got title to the 320 [240] acres, which the person named in the scrip was entitled to get, by attending the Dominion Land[s] Office, and locating the scrip on a designated 320 acres. It would have been a matter of considerable difficulty to go north and find the person named in the scrip and bring him out to the Land Office. I have a hazy memory that the buyers, when purchasing the scrip, would have the vendor sign a form of Quit Claim Deed. He would sign by making his mark, and this would be witnessed by two persons, presumably other dealers.[48]

However, neither Quit Claim Deeds nor any other agreements to sell or transfer scrip interests legally allow those holding the scrip to locate the scrip in their own name.

Without the personal presence of the actual Metis grantee in the Dominion Lands office, there were only two ways to proceed with the conversion of a scrip to real property. Fillmore left a record of one means to locate scrip. He recalled:

> After my return to Winnipeg I made some inquiries, and I was told the practice was for the holder of a scrip to pick out some local Indian or half-breed and take him to the Dominion Land[s] Office and present him as the person named in the scrip. The holder of the scrip, pretending to be the agent of the half-breed, would designate the land. The patent to this land would then be issued, and the scrip holder would then have to get title. Presumably, this was done by completing and registering the Quit Claim Deed.[49]

This method of impersonating the grantee was not a legal way to proceed with obtaining a patent to Dominion Lands. Yet the proposition that Halfbreeds from York Factory and Fort Churchill travelled hundreds of miles to Dominion Lands offices in the Edmonton and Peace River districts in order to complete some paper work defies common sense. In fact, the records of the Land Patents Branch indicate that impersonations occurred with York Factory and Fort Churchill scrip locations.[50] Impersonating a Metis grantee was a convenient way for those seeking to obtain a patent based on scrip.

Fillmore's evidence suggests that Department of the Interior documents indicating that Metis grantees personally located and personally assigned scrip may be inaccurate and misleading.

The other way of circumventing the Rule of Location was to have the Land Patents Branch redback the scrip coupon. In order to redback scrip, the holder of the scrip would forward the original scrip to the Lands Patents Branch in Ottawa, accompanied by a variety of affidavits and powers of attorney purporting a satisfactory transfer of scrip interests. Requests to redback scrip usually came from major scrip middlemen. In some instances, bank managers forwarded scrip to the Land Patents Branch for redbacking. Once the scrip had been redbacked, the holder of the scrip could locate the scrip, in the name of the grantee, after which the grantee's interest in the scrip was transferred to an assignee whose assignment would be recognized by Department of the Interior officials. Redbacking was also used to locate scrip after minor grantees had become adults. In effect, redbacked scrip was a recognition that a transfer or conveyance of scrip ownership had already occurred and that the Department of the Interior agreed to allow the middleman to go ahead and locate the scrip and then assign the scrip to themselves or to another buyer. The Rule of Location could be practically bypassed by impersonation or it could be legally circumvented by the redbacking paper shuffle.

The extensive documentation effecting the transfer of scrip interests from grantees to major scrip middlemen requires a separate study. Nonetheless, most of the affidavits purporting to witness the transfer or documents executing a transfer had not been executed at the time that the scrip middlemen took possession of the scrip. This is apparent in some evidence provided by J.S. Richards, who in the years after his scrip-buying days and during a late effort to cash in on his remaining coupons, had become a judge in the Manitoba Court of Appeal. In a 1946 statutory declaration, S.E. Richards outlined the sequence of transferring scrip interests:

1. Land scrip number A10601 for 160 acres, issued by the Dominion Government to Catherine McLeod, was purchased from said Catherine McLeod by Horace Halcrow, since deceased, in his lifetime of The Pas in Manitoba, as agent for and on behalf of a syndicate of which I was a member.

2. The said land scrip was allotted to me as part of my interest in the said syndicate and became my absolute property and I became the sole owner and holder of it.

3. Subsequent to the said purchase and about the year 1919 the said Catherine McLeod made a statement in writing that she was satisfied with the said purchase price, and such statement was filed with the Department of the Interior of the Dominion of Canada, Ottawa, which

Department endorsed a memorandum on the said land scrip that it may be located by the holder thereof in the name of the grantee.[51]

Richards's declaration indicates that scrip buyers sometimes held scrip for a number of years before seeking to have the scrip redbacked and that declarations and affidavits concerning the details of the sales were drawn up many years after the actual transfers. With respect to the transfer of Catherine McLeod's scrip, assistant deputy minister of mines and natural resources J.G. Cowan noted:

> The Quit Claim Deed from Catherine McLeod is imperfect in several respects; viz., it is not dated, no seal has been affixed and although Moses Gore appears to have witnessed the signature, the affidavit, although signed by him and purporting to be sworn by Horace Halcrow, is in fact in blank and, therefore of little value.
>
> It appears obvious that the Quit Claim Deed was executed in blank and has been filled in at a later date.[52]

If the affidavits and Quit Claim Deeds were executed in blank, then dates affecting the chain of title are problematic because such affidavits do not indicate when the sale of scrip took place. Since Judge Richards regarded his scrip as his 'absolute property,' the Rule of Location was a mere formality that provided no protection to the Metis grantee.

The Rule of Location that prevented minors from locating scrip did not safeguard their scrip interests once scrip middlemen were in possession of scrip. Richards held scrip that had been issued to Jessie Campbell. In 1928, Jessie McIvor (née Campbell) wrote to the Department of the Interior asking about the scrip issued in 1911:

> I am informed that when I was a minor, my father had some dealings with a lawyer in the City of Winnipeg; this lawyer is now writing to me wanting me to give him Power of Attorney to dispose of my Scrip for the consideration of $100.00, and he to take the proceeds of the sale.
>
> I do not wish to do this as I am married and have children and I wish my children to benefit by this scrip; $100.00 would be of little use in this connection.
>
> Had my father any right to dispose of scrip (that should be mine when I came of age) when I was a minor, or had any person the legal right to purchase same[?][53]

Jessie Campbell was eleven years old when her scrip was delivered, but the questions that she raised in 1928 dispute the ownership of scrip. If Judge

Richards's title to her scrip was good, and if her interest was transferred legally, why was she offered $100 by a Winnipeg lawyer? On 25 September 1947, the Manitoba government redeemed Jessie G. Campbell's scrip coupons A10662 (160 acres) and A10167 (80 acres) from Judge Richards for $1,440.[54] Without attaining a power of attorney from Jessie Campbell, Richards might have had difficulty in redbacking her scrip coupons.

A contract in the name of A.A. McDonald indicates how members of the syndicate sought ownership of scrip (see Figure 6.1). The Methodist missionary records include a handwritten copy of a contract distributed in northern Manitoba in advance of scrip applications. This contract does not reappear in the redbacking requests, but its existence suggests the approach that scrip middlemen took to secure the sale of scrip coupons. Reverend Lowes had forwarded the scrip contract to Rev. Alexander Sutherland, general secretary of the Methodist Missionary Society in Toronto. In this indenture, the Halfbreed (vendor) transfers all rights and all his children's rights to scrip to the purchaser, A.A. McDonald. The extremely one-sided nature of the contract is revealed by an analysis of this document. The scrip buyer (A.A. McDonald) wanted land and not money scrip, a contrast with previous scrip commissions. Thus, the contract provides not only a higher price for land scrip but also obliges the Halfbreed vendor to accept whichever type of scrip requested by the purchaser. The Halfbreed vendor also appoints the purchaser as his irrevocable attorney in connection with his scrip and any land thereby obtained, thus removing any and all control from the Halfbreed grantee. The vendor is provided with absolutely no security for the payment of the purchase price. The contract effects a transfer and requires the Metis vendor to locate the property so that the paper land scrip coupon could be converted to real property. The net result could be that the purchaser could obtain land patents (ownership) without having paid the purchase price to the vendor. In this contract, the Halfbreed vendor would hold no security against the land thus obtained. The terms of the agreement are certainly improvident for the Halfbreed and his or her children, and perhaps unconscionable under the current law of contract.[55] The terms of the contract indicate how scrip buyers could use the legal system to make the scrip process work in their interests. The existence of such a contract indicates that the Crown could not or chose not to take steps to protect the entitlements of the Metis. The records of the Land Patents Branch indicate little or no concern for the terms of this contract.

Prices and Value of Scrip Coupons
Although the transfer of scrip to middlemen is understood, the price and value of scrip are practically hidden. Very few details of cash transactions

between Metis grantees and scrip middlemen are contained in the documentation of the Department of the Interior. The A.A. McDonald contract is a rare document with respect to the interactions between the Metis and speculators. Fragments of the historical record permit some consideration of the price and value of Metis scrip. The view that Metis grantees received absolutely no cash for scrip cannot be sustained by the story of Treaty Five Adhesion scrip. The anticipation that some cash would be obtained must have motivated a 1921 letter reapplying for scrip on behalf of Edith and George Gibault. The Gibault children were born after the Split Lake adhesion and their claims had been rejected in 1909.[56] Similarly in 1939, RCMP Constable J.D. Lee forwarded the claims of Jervois Anderson Spence and Eliza Mary Jane McPherson of York Factory for scrip payments.[57] These renewed efforts to claim scrip could not be satisfied by the original terms of the scrip commission and were rejected again. Both of these efforts to activate a claim, submitted years after the commission had been wrapped up, suggest that scrip had some monetary value to the grantee.

Requests to redback scrip generated documents that purported to give the prices at which scrip sold. In the Treaty Five Adhesion territory, documents associated with redbacking requests usually state that the sale price of 240 acres of land scrip was $1,000. For example, in a 24 February 1919 declaration, Horace Halcrow swore 'that the said Samuel Grey sold and assigned the said Scrip Notes to me in consideration of the sum of One Thousand Dollars ($1000.00) which said sum at the request of the said Samuel Grey I caused to be deposited to his credit with the Royal Trust Company at its office at the City of Winnipeg in Manitoba.'[58] Halcrow's declaration was supported by a letter from the Royal Trust Company in Winnipeg; the assistant manager wrote that deposits totalling $10,000 from Richards, Sweatman, Kemp, and Fillmore had been made on 24 August 1912 to the credit of Samuel Grey and others. The Royal Trust Company informed the Department of the Interior that 'we have from time to time, accounted for the monies received to the individuals referred to by forwarding to them statements of their accounts showing how the money had been invested and the revenues derived therefrom.'[59] The sale of 240 acres of land scrip for $1,000 seems odd. Table 6.3 compares the available information on the price of scrip. One thousand dollars would equal 200 years of treaty annuity payments. If buyers were actually willing to pay $1,000 for northern Manitoba scrip, there would be no reason to believe that any Natives would choose to accept treaty. If scrip sold for $1,000, it would have been improvident to accept treaty benefits; and this would run contrary to the concerns raised by Semmens and Lowes. Moreover, the sale price of $1,000 does not correspond with numerous observations that the Metis grantees did not receive equitable remuneration. Given the need for cash by Metis grantees, it seems curious that the full purchase price of York Factory scrip was deposited in a Winnipeg branch of the Royal Trust. Similarly, if most of the Metis grantees had received $1,000 for their scrip, then there would have been no reason for the Department of the Interior to abandon land scrip when it began to satisfy the Halfbreed claims in Treaty Eleven territory. Instead of land scrip, $240 in cash was issued to each successful claimant. The difference between land scrip worth $1,000 and a cash grant of $240 would have been appreciated by the Metis claimants covered by Treaty Eleven. Finally, what is the credibility of figures purporting to be the price of scrip on transfers, agreements, and affidavits that seem to have been executed in blank years later, or to cash offers for signatures in consideration of an appointment of power of attorney?

The rest of the available evidence indicates that scrip prices were much lower and that the middlemen secured most of the commercial benefits. The A.A. McDonald contract agreed to pay $200 for adult land scrip and fifty dollars for minor's cash scrip (Figure 6.1). For a family of four (two adults and two minors), this represented a gross profit for McDonald of 47.9 per cent on the presumed value of the scrip (one dollar per acre) or 60 per cent markup over the price paid to the Metis family. The McDonald contract indicates that half the money would have been paid in advance and that a final payment would occur once the scrip had been delivered. At Churchill, Alexander Oman was offered $450 for his three scrip (presumed value of $720), but he held out for $1,100 (see Appendix C).[60] His evidence shows that he had accepted an advance of $100 before the scrip had been delivered. The advanced payment made by the scrip buyers represented a claim on the claimant's scrip, but this sort of credit with a concomitant obligation was consistent with the exchange relations in the fur trade. The scrip due bills from northeastern Saskatchewan amounted to between $100 and $150. These due bills represented the amount still owing to the Metis grantee. If this amount equalled half the payment for the scrip, or if $100 had already been advanced, then the price of this scrip would be no more than $1.25 per acre. This amount is in agreement with Fillmore's recollection that scrip was sold at the rate of one dollar per acre. (See Table 6.3). Fillmore also stated: 'I do remember that the buyers seemed to be satisfied that it had been a successful and profitable venture.'[61] Semmens also provided information on the price of scrip: 'I admit that the one hundred dollars paid for this money Scrip is very little compared with the four or six hundred usually paid at Norway House for Land Scrip.'[62] One problem in determining the price of scrip is that it was bought and sold as a family set. Oman's evidence indicates that scrip buyers offered a price to the father for the entire family's scrip.

Table 6.3

Estimates of the price and value of scrip, 1906-12

Source	Dollars per acre	Estimate of the price of scrip
McDonald contract		
Adult	.83	$200 for each adult scrip
Children	.21	$50 for each children's scrip
Fillmore	1.00	
HBC scrip due bills	1.25	Most due bills were for $150
Alexander Oman	1.53	$1,100 for each family's scrip
J. Semmens		
Money scrip	.42	$100 for money scrip
Land scrip	1.67-2.50	$400 to $600 at Norway House
Redbacked affidavits	4.17	$1,000 for each 240 acres of land scrip
N.H. Bacon		
Price of scrip	2.08	$500
Value of scrip	8.33	$2,000 Winnipeg value of scrip
Value of school lands sales		
Alberta	14.38	Gross sales, 1905-30
Saskatchewan	17.27	Gross sales, 1905-30

Sources: Fillmore, 'Half-breed Scrip'; UCCA, Sutherland Papers, box 7, file 142; HBCA, B. 89/C/8; NAC, RG 15, vol. 1016, file 1578625, pt. 2; RG 15, vol. 1043, file 1748598; NAC, RG 33-51, vol. 3, exhibit 4-D

The monopoly power of the scrip-buying syndicate meant that it was impossible for the Metis grantees to receive a price for scrip that reflected an equitable share of the value of the land to which scrip could be applied. With regard to northern Manitoba, Augustus Nanton stated that 'there are very few buyers of the character of the scrip issued at these points, and therefore the half-breeds have to take practically what is offered to them.'[63] Perhaps the best indication of the real value of Treaty Five Adhesion scrip is Richards's statement that 'at the time the Agreements were entered into for the purchase of the scrip, the scrips were not worth more than one-fourth of their present value.'[64] In defense of Hall's scrip-buying activity, Richards stated:

We may say further in this connection that if the price of scrip had not risen considerably since the above mentioned scrips were purchased, that they would hardly have made any profit in the matter. You know in this connection that Messers. Thompson and Tyerman refused to consider any change in the amount to be paid at Churchill, and that it was only because the scrips had risen in value since the purchase at Churchill that they were willing to pay more at York Factory than bargained for by them.[65]

Richards's observation on the value of scrip suggests that scrip had a value or price separate from what might be actually realized as a land sale. Similarly in 1914, HBC Fur Trade Commissioner N.H. Bacon wrote HBC Secretary F.C. Ingrams about possible HBC participation in the purchasing of Mackenzie River Halfbreed scrip, noting: 'The Scrip, the value of which in Winnipeg would be about $2,000, should be bought for $500 or thereabouts.'[66]

Since homestead lands were free, and since scrip was applied to lands open for homestead, the commercial value of scrip lands is not readily apparent. Dominion Lands included a category of land known as school lands, which were undeveloped and which were sold for revenue to develop schools. This class of land would most approximate the market that sought Halfbreed land scrip. Between 1905 and 1930, the average price for Alberta school lands was $14.38 per acre.[67] Even if 240 acres of land scrip were purchased for $1,000, the scrip middlemen still secured most of the commercial benefits.[68]

A Failure of Aboriginal Policy

Almost any effort to explain Halfbreed scrip is an invitation to court confusion. The Treaty Five Adhesion Scrip Commission has been largely ignored by academics, yet the HBC and Methodist records provide a unique insight into the role of scrip middlemen. The scrip records of the Department of the Interior give an impression of orderly claims process, however, the McDonald scrip contract from the Methodists records, the HBC file on R.H. Hall's dismissal for involving the Company's name with scrip buying, and the records from the Province of Manitoba concerning Judge Richards's successful cashing in of old scrip coupons illuminate the history of scrip. Despite the confusing detail surrounding individual Metis claims and the activities of scrip middlemen, it is evident that, as an Aboriginal policy, scrip was a failure. This failure was well known by the early 1900s, and Nanton observed that with 'scrip, the halfbreeds have in every instance disposed of [it] to speculators and, in most cases, sacrificed their holdings.'[69] Nanton had also been close to major scrip buyers, his candid comments were well informed, and, therefore, he was not prone to understate the value of scrip to Metis grantees. Since York Factory and Churchill Metis were issued scrip for southern agricultural land, it appears that there was no intention to provide a community land base. After his experiences as a scrip commissioner, Semmens made some valid observations on this method of surrendering Metis title:

The claim of the Half Breeds of Keewatin is based upon Adhesions made in that territory. Why not give them land on their own soil instead of allowing them to claim valuable Alberta or Saskatchewan Lands which they will not improve. They sell to Whitemen as soon as they receive a settlement and thse [*sic*] Whitemen pay but little and gain much and grow wealthy quick on advantages intended for the Half-Breed only. If it were determined that only Keewatin Lands would be given it would dampen the ardour of Buyers and lands good enough for the Halfbreed might be given for their use in their own territory. My experience goes to show that nine tenths of these people will not settle on the land given them. They will realize as quickly as possible and then relapse into a state of semi-starvation and come back to the Indian Department for assistance in time of Scarcity or of Sickness.[70]

By following previous policies, the Treaty Five Adhesion scrip served to supply Winnipeg lawyers with a speculative investment and to leave the Keewatin Metis without a land base. A similar admission of a failure of scrip was made by N.O. Coté in a 1914 memorandum to W.J. Roche, minister of the interior. With respect to the future possibility of Halfbreed claims in the Mackenzie District, he stated: 'But when the time comes to consider these claims, it will, no doubt, be found desirable, in view of the past experiences of the Department in dealing with this class of claims, to adopt an altogether new mode of settlement.'[71] The past experiences of the department entailed a futile effort at protecting the scrip interests of Metis grantees from scrip syndicates, while ignoring the real need to protect the land use and occupancy of Metis communities.

Coté's blasé report for the Interior department noted that claims had been settled confidently and that legislation was enacted to protect improperly located scrip. In point of fact, a leak from the Winnipeg office of the Department of Indian Affairs gave scrip buyers advance notice of Treaty Five Adhesion and Metis claims. The government was aware that scrip speculators were interfering with the adhesions. When the Reverend Sutherland, Secretary of the Methodist Missionary Society, raised these problems, Commissioner of Indian Affairs Pedley replied:

As you are no doubt aware this Department does not issue the halfbreed scrip. This action is taken by the Department of the Interior, but I believe that so far as possible the interests of the halfbreed have been guarded in the regulations governing the issuing of scrip, and that the papers have to be handed to the individual who is entitled to them. After that it would be difficult, if not impossible, for the Government to interfere with the halfbreed in the disposal of the scrip.[72]

Pedley sidestepped responsibility by arguing that the Interior department issued scrip. Yet the Department of Indian Affairs was charged with the responsibility of dealing Aboriginal title and was responsible for appointing treaty and scrip commissioners. Semmens held a joint appointment as treaty and scrip commissioner. Pedley's reply to the concerns raised by Sutherland was indicative of the indifference that characterized the federal government's relationship with the Metis. His comment that the government could not interfere with the disposal of scrip inferred either that the Rule of Location was not enforceable or that it conveyed any beneficial effects. A social fraud was committed. Although Scrip Commissioner Semmens and local missionary Lowes had different interests than Fillmore or Nanton (who were intimately acquainted with the activities of scrip middlemen), all agreed that scrip coupons had little value for the Metis grantees. The federal government demonstrated little interest in protecting the land interests of the Metis. The objections of missionaries such as Sutherland and Lowes and officials like Semmens were based on moral outrage. Government policies and practices should have been challenged on the basis of Aboriginal rights, as well. Yet scrip policies succeeded in transferring millions of acres of homestead lands to scrip middlemen. Coté's report in 1929 is not about the just satisfaction of claims, rather, he documents the extent to which vast amounts of homestead lands became commercial assets. Speculators obtained this land cheaply and then disposed of it on the existing commercial land market. Metis scrip was merely a conduit through which Dominion Lands were funnelled into the market. To the extent that Metis received payment from scrip middlemen, the cost to the government of dealing with Metis Aboriginal title was borne by the private sector and not the Crown. Whether a Metis grantee received one dollar per acre or $4.17 per acre has little bearing on the validity of Metis Aboriginal title.

A comparison of scrip policies and treaty terms raises fundamental questions about the political economy of Aboriginal title. The government's policy of issuing Metis scrip without annuities raises the problem of what treaty annuities represented economically. Did annuity payments represent a commercial value for Aboriginal title or compensation for disruptions to a hunting economy? If annuities were meant as a form of compensation for pending disruption to a livelihood, then the Metis should have been entitled to annuities. Instead, the nominal value of scrip was more closely related to the price of land as defined by the homestead system. The Crown's approach to Aboriginal title clearly reflected two entirely different principles for assessing the value of Native claims. Treaty Five Adhesion scrip was designed to convert Metis Aboriginal title into an exchangeable asset – a piece of paper, a coupon – which was of greater value to land speculators than to Metis families.

The two approaches to Aboriginal title placed Native peoples under different jurisdictions. Treaty Indians came under the Indian Act and the Department of Indian Affairs. The Metis dealt with the Department of the Interior and eventually came under provincial authority, especially with the transfer of natural resources in 1930. One of the unfortunate consequences of the uncoordinated approach to Metis and Indian title was that it created a bureaucratic mess concerning status in the late 1880s. The records show that it was possible to withdraw from treaty, to accept scrip, and then later, to be readmitted to treaty, but the reasoning behind approval of any of these steps was based on protective economic criteria. Racial, kinship, or social criteria never seemed to be very useful for distinguishing between Indian and Metis. Metis Aboriginal title is not a partial claim to a racial heritage, which surely must have been a convenient colonial concept. Metis use and occupancy of land was no less than other Aboriginal people that later obtained legal Indian status. The actions of well-meaning officials and missionaries to restrict the withdrawal from treaty, or later in the case of Treaty Five Adhesions, to discourage applications for scrip, demonstrate that Metis scrip did not provide adequate compensation for the disruption associated with the loss of Aboriginal title. Like the treaties, scrip provided a mechanism for the state to secure Native lands; but unlike the treaty Indians, the Metis secured neither a land base nor ongoing compensation.

Significantly, there is nothing in the process, either in the written documents reporting on the treaty talks or in the application/declaration, which indicates that individual Metis consented to extinguish Aboriginal title. They merely applied to participate in a land grant and signed to the truthfulness of the personal information. No consent to stop using the land, to cease hunting, fishing, and trapping was ever given. No opportunity to obtain fee simple ownership of lands in northern Manitoba was offered and thus the scrip coupons were more relevant to the needs of the scrip syndicate. The state's, or the Crown's, costs for obtaining Metis Aboriginal title were minimal – both in the short and long term. The once-and-for-all costs to the Crown consisted of the transaction costs of issuing scrip coupons. The monetary costs of Metis Aboriginal title were paid by the private sector – the scrip middlemen – and only to the extent that these buyers actually paid the full purchase price. Because scrip was not converted to real property by the Metis grantees, the Crown permitted and facilitated the private purchase of Aboriginal title. Nothing in this process resembles the procedures outlined by the Royal Proclamation of 1763 or the obligations established in the Rupertsland Order of 1870.

In some respects, agents of the Crown attempted to reconcile two different property systems while ignoring the actual use of land by the Metis. The

Crown believed that Metis Aboriginal title was merely a claim to Indian title, which could be reconciled and extinguished by an individual land grant framed by the survey system and the regulations pursuant to the Dominion Lands Act. This attempt to individualize Aboriginal title did not work in the interests of the Metis.

7

'Go and Pitch His Camp': Native Settlement Patterns and Indian Agriculture

The term 'reserve' has special meaning for contemporary Native identities, but Indian reserves are a hidden part of the landscape, beyond the experiences of most Canadians. Today, most reserves appear to be located without resources, and without reason. Assumptions that reserves were strictly the dictates of government policy and that Native communities played no part in the modern history of the subarctic are common. Yet prior to the advent of formal political organizations, agitation by Indian bands centred on obtaining a reserve with a legal survey and on protecting the land from outside encroachment. The identification of particular sites as Indian property (reserves) arose out of the treaty process, but how Indian bands came to occupy particular tracts of land is not widely understood. Official reserve plans provide a useful record to illustrate reserve settlement.

Misrepresentation of the Native economy as shiftless nomadism has meant that the existence of settled Native communities prior to the treaties has not been appreciated. The mobility of the Native economy could accommodate agriculture, and with low fur prices and scarce resources, gardens provided a needed food supply. Posts, missions, family camps, and spiritual ceremonial sites combined mobility and stationary activities into a flexible land-use system. The same sites were occupied year after year. A spatial transformation of the Native economy occurred with the treaty process and transitions in the fur trade. Essentially, a settling-down process resulted. The evolution of the 'trade post' band into a 'reserve' band is shown in Figure 7.1. A shift from visiting the post to visiting the bush occurred, and the amount of time spent living in the bush could vary from year to year. The Reverend Charles Stringfellow noted: 'A large number of families are this winter to be far away from us, they having incurred large debts, necessitating their residence in the woods.'[1] In areas north of the 1875 treaty boundaries and for bands heavily involved in fur production, settling was a slow process. With the opening up of the fur trade economy, the HBC tended to import more goods and relied less on local resources. However, with competitive fur markets, the Company would visit Indian camps to obtain furs. This activity increased in the late nineteenth century and had implications for community and post life. Moreover, as Figure 7.1 suggests, legal definitions about 'Indianness' tended to create artificial social divisions. Real communities were forming around posts and missions, but the Indian Act and scrip commissions interrupted this process and communities were fractured. Nonetheless, the spatial transformation of Native life was largely the result of economic responses rather than political pressure.

The plan to settle Indians on reserves was also linked to the idea of reserve agriculture. Conventional generalizations about Indian agriculture in western Canada assume that it was the Department of Indian Affairs that first introduced agriculture to reserves and that Indians were culturally incapable of becoming successful farmers on marginal land. However, increases in gardening and stock-raising were essentially the result of Indian initiatives. A central aspect of the Indian economic program evident during the treaty talks was the Indian demand for the means (land, tools, seed, and animals) to make a transition from hunting to agriculture. For Indian agents, reserve residency and agriculture were both parts of the same process. Agricultural activities existed at pre-treaty mission settlements such as Rossville, Landsdowne (Fort Alexander), St. Peters, Devon (The Pas), and Fairford. Furthermore, Chief Peguis noted assistance from Kildonan Scots for agricultural pursuits at St. Peters.[2] The feasibility of cultivation was also demonstrated by the HBC post gardens. Moreover, Native agriculture in the study area predates missions. In 1820, Peter Fidler recorded that Ojibwa in the Interlake grew potatoes, which they sold to traders.[3] Even the Department of Indian Affairs acknowledged the existence of pre-treaty Indian agriculture since its seed corn was unsuited to the climate, whereas Indian corn had good yields.[4]

The establishment of Christian missions and increased gardening were related. Norway House's missionary E. Eves recorded parting words from 'those on the verge of the other world,' and one woman demonstrated her 'triumph of faith' by stating 'Jesus has come and brought us white food. Come and Eat.'[5] Perhaps a connection existed between the spiritual and the material. In general, subsistence agriculture developed as an important feature in the post-treaty economy until their activities provided alternate incomes. For some bands, stock-raising proved to be a successful agricultural pursuit.

Pre-Treaty Native Communities

Prior to any treaties with the Crown, a number of settled Native communities existed. This development was influenced by missionaries and fur

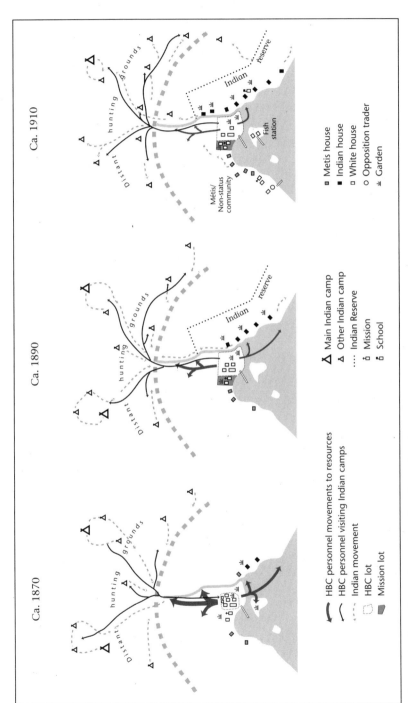

Figure 7.1 Spatial transformation of settlement and economy

traders. Major settlements existed at St. Peters, Fairford, Norway House, and The Pas. The largest and oldest Indian settlement was found in the Red River parish of St. Peters. Here Indians occupied river lots, surveyed just like the other Red River lots and parishes, and employed a land-use pattern similar to the rest of the Red River settlers (see Figure 7.2). The Pas band settled close to the Church Missionary Society's Devon Mission, which dates to the 1840s. Although this site was not an important fur trade post, it was described as one of the oldest permanent Indian settlements in the Northwest. Devon had largely been abandoned by the 1860s, but with the Reverend H. Budd's return in 1867, Indians once again built houses, planted potatoes, and fenced fields.[6] A settled population developed at the Methodist Rossville mission, which served as a labour pool for the Hudson's Bay Company's district headquarters at Norway House. Similarly, a large Native community developed at Fairford, and as early as 1851, there were ten houses near the mission. In 1871, Fort Alexander witnessed an increase in the number of houses and the amount of land under cultivation. York Factory Natives were located in three tiny communities (Ten Shilling Creek, French Creek, and Four Mile Island) close to the HBC post and CMS mission. This dispersal was necessary because of the scarcity of firewood. Evidence shows that smaller Native communities with houses and gardens were forming at the narrows of Lake Manitoba (Staggville, Dog Creek), at Shoal River, at Sandy Bar on the east shore of Lake Winnipeg, at the mouth of Little Saskatchewan River, at the Brokenhead River, and at the Grand Rapids of the Saskatchewan River. By the mid-1870s, missionaries had been encouraging settlement at Berens River, Rev. Egerton Ryerson Young explained: 'As our object has not been to centralize the Indians more rapidly than they were able to erect little houses to supplant the old, comfortable wigwams, we have only about sixty Indians as yet permanently settled at this one spot,' and that 'many others are preparing to build very soon, and to commence the tilling of the soil.'[7] In the 1860s, changes were widespread; the treaties and the reserve system complemented a spatial transformation that was already under way.

Further north, Native settlements began to form by the 1890s and prior to the adhesions to Treaty Five (1908-10). Settlement was particularly evident at Nelson House. When the reserve was surveyed, many fine gardens were in existence. Settlement was also apparent at Split Lake, Oxford House, and Gods Lake prior to the official surveys. In 1894, Gods Lake was described by Semmens: 'A number of dwellings have been erected at this point and the families of the hunters winter here supported by the fishing advantages offered by this lake, while the men of the tribe go out along the line of their traps, returning again to their homes after a brief sojourn in the forest.'[8] Settling down could be accommodated by the trapping

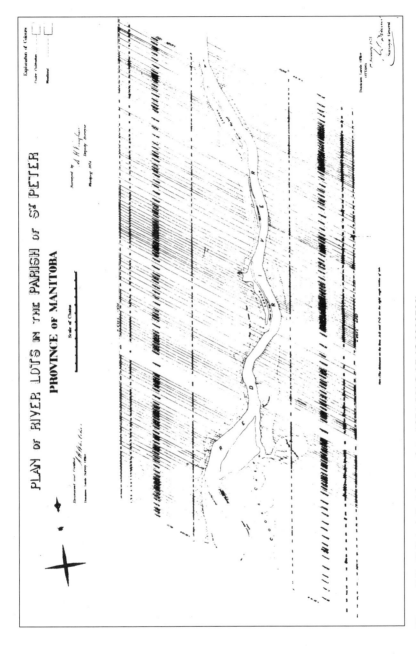

Figure 7.2 St Peter's Parish river lots, 1874 (NAC, NMC 0020709)

economy; however, this meant less participation in the production of fur by other members of the family. Nonetheless, there were many settled Native communities throughout the region prior to treaties and reserves.

The Metis and Halfbreed populations were largely concentrated in the Red River parishes prior to 1870. Some Mixedbloods from the Red River settlement moved up to Lake Manitoba (St. Laurent and Oak Point) because of fish resources and declining buffalo hunts. In the early 1870s, Mixedbloods from St. Andrews moved closer to Lake Winnipeg at Huntington. Since there were no legal definitions to separate Natives, the ethnic division of space in a community was not as distinct prior to treaties as it was afterwards. This post/mission settlement was truly Native in the sense that it was composed both of those known as Indians and Halfbreeds. In places like Norway House, some Halfbreed employees lived in the post, other Natives lived near the Rossville mission and were known as 'Village Indians,' while the main fur producers were the more mobile 'Woods Indians.' These ethnically based habitation patterns reflected different economic roles. Economic tasks were not fixed, and over time roles became flexible and interchangeable.

Clearly, pre-treaty settlement was significant, and it is incorrect to suggest that all Indians in northern Manitoba were suddenly forced by Indian agents to give up a mobile lifestyle. The settling of Native populations with support from mission agriculture was not necessarily a successful or permanent adjustment. The Reverend F.G. Stevens reflected critically on missionary efforts to get Indians to settle down: 'Over and over again, missionaries had gone and in their ignorance had persuaded the Indians to settle around the church and school and let the men make trips to the trap-line. In many places the Indians had been persuaded. They built houses and stayed at home. Trips to the trap lines were not made successfully. Debts were unpaid ... The advice given by the missionaries was not good.[9] Nonetheless, the pre-treaty settlements prepared Natives for the post-treaty economic changes.

Site and Locational Aspects of Indian Reserves

The location of reserves is an important geographical aspect of the role of Native communities in the regional economy. In northern Manitoba, Indians were generally given their choice about where they wanted to locate reserves. However, it is instructive to look at the exceptions. The Grand Rapids band wanted both sides of the Saskatchewan River, and they had already established a village with buildings and gardens on the north bank. The north side of the river, where the portage bypassed the rapids, was considered to be of strategic importance – a future townsite on the steamboat route. Therefore, the band was paid to move and to select a reserve on the south bank.[10] Another group that did not receive its first choice for reserve location was a fragment of the Norway House band, which desired the

Grassey Narrows (White Mud River/Icelandic River). Instead, this area became part of the Icelandic reserve, and the Norway House group agreed to locate at Fisher River.[11] The Sandy Bar group also wanted a reserve at the Grassey Narrows; unfortunately their homes, gardens, and graves were located on the northern fringe of what became known as the Icelandic Reserve. They were dislocated.[12] Some members of the fragmented Island band wanted a reserve on Big Island (Hecla Island), which was part of their traditional lands. The reasons for denying this request are not clear, but a number of these Indians were persuaded to settle at the Hollow Water River and to renounce any claims to Big Island.[13] Although there were not many conflicting claims for sites in such situations, Indian bands usually lost out. Most Indian bands held onto land they had developed or selected sites they wanted. Fortunately, Treaties One and Two specified reserve locations, and the selection of many reserves occurred before the commercial boom got under way. In this sense, new staple industries had to adjust to the existing settlement pattern.

The selection of reserves for some bands was conditioned by pre-treaty settlement patterns. For example, the Brokenhead band stressed that its claim was based on three generations of occupation.[14] The locational decision was sound, and surveyor J.K. McLean later noted that the river lots 'are nearly all high and dry, especially near the River. The land is of good quality with a great deal of good poplar.'[15] The partial subdivision of the Brokenhead reserve into river lots is shown in Figure 7.3. The St. Peters reserve was perhaps the best site in the region, since E. McColl explained that it was 'amply supplied with wood, water and hay lands. The soil is unsurpassed in fertility. The Red River, passing through it, is teeming with the choicest fish.'[16] The Chemawawin band selected a site on Cedar Lake because it was near a productive fishery. The concentration of Indians in the Interlake reflected the reliability of fish as a resource. The Sandy Bay and Shoal River bands loosened ties with the plains and located near fisheries. The Reverend J. Semmens described the Fisher River site selected in 1877 by the group that left Norway House:

> The land was rich and easily cultivated. The wood is abundant and varied: from the soft poplar to the hard oak from the useless elm to the lofty spruce. The natural hay lands are the finest we have ever seen in the forest land. Fish are plentiful beyond the rivers mouth among the islands ten miles distant. Fur is said to abound in the recesses of the immediate woodland. Nature seems to have provided everything necessary for the support and happiness of a thrifty people. The Indians are delighted and thankful both to the Government and to Providence that this location has fallen to their lot.[17]

Throughout the Interlake, Indians selected sites that included fisheries, high ground, hay marshes, and timber. These reserves were generally recognized as being better suited for grazing than cultivation. Finally, Indian Commissioner Provencher summarized the locational aspects of settlements: 'All these Reserves appear to have been selected with much care, and all the reports demonstrate that they possess all the requisite advantages in a triple respect, of agriculture, the chase and fishing.'[18]

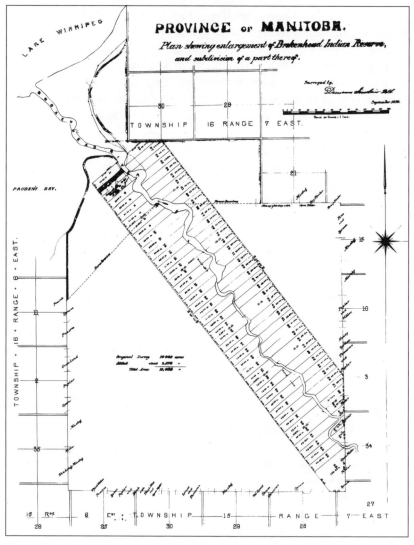

Figure 7.3 Brokenhead survey plan, 1876. Note the surveyed river lots. (NAC, NMC 0015538)

Many reserves were selected at sites close to HBC posts or outposts. In the early post-treaty period, the more mobile bands that located near HBC posts included Little Grand Rapids, Berens River, Poplar River, Chemawawin, Moose Lake, and Cross Lake. After the adhesions to Treaty Five, Treaty Commissioner Semmens reported that, with the exception of the undecided Gods Lake band, 'It is understood in every case that the location would be adjacent to the Hudson's Bay Co., Forts.'[19] The preference to locate reserves near posts demonstrates the importance of the fur trade and that economic forces shaped the distribution of Indian populations in the post-treaty period. (However, the initial establishment of inland posts in the nineteenth century took account of the locations of Indian populations.) In a certain sense, settling down on these reserves was an extension of the practice of families camping near posts during the summer. Moreover, the Company's posts were usually located near reliable fisheries. In the case of the Nelson House reserve, the band not only located close to the HBC post, but also the surveyor noted that the land selected was 'higher and better than any I have seen in this northern district, the soil being excellent.'[20] Clearly, Indians selected reserves based on their prior occupation of sites that offered a favourable combination of available resources.

Surveying Policies and Practices
During treaty negotiations, Indians requested particular sites as reserves, and their desires are evident in the wording of Treaties One and Two (see Figure 4.4). Indians also understood the need for legal protection and consequently requested prompt surveys. The need for reserve surveys was stressed by Lieutenant-Governor Morris when he wrote in 1876 that 'to prevent complications and misunderstandings it would be desirable that as *many of the Reserves* be surveyed without delay.'[21] Frequently, Indians expressed a strong desire for legal surveys to protect their improvements and resources; for instance, this was done by the Jackhead band in the early 1880s, when timber interests encroached upon its land.

Policies in the 1870s and 1880s led to a relatively prompt surveying of reserves, and because many of these sites were beyond the settlement belt a certain administrative flexibility existed. In general, when a band requested a survey and indicated a desire to settle down, the Department of Indian Affairs would contact the surveyor general. Surveyors were instructed to confer with the chief regarding specific lands to be included within the reserve; as well, waste land, marshes, and lakes were not included as part of the calculation of the total allotment.[22] When requested, surveyors laid out river lots five or ten chains wide, thereby recognizing the usefulness of the Red River land system. Large lots for the HBC were provided for by the terms that transferred Rupertsland to Canada. Both mission and Company claims were given priority when reserve boundaries were arranged. In the case of Fisher River, surveyors set out a lot for the Methodist Church, even though a mission had not been established. Surveyors' instructions were consistent with the department's economic viewpoint. Indian Affairs files recorded in 1895 that 'the Department is of opinion that too much importance cannot be attached to the inclusion of hay and arable land in Reserves for Indians situated as are those at Jack Head River in sufficient quantities to enable them, as the hunt fails, to fall back for their support on stock raising and the cultivation of the soil.'[23] Department policy also allowed individual Indians to retain use of land that they had improved prior to treaties, but such land could only be disposed of to other band members. Thus, some reserves were divided into lots, while some land remained as commons.

Survey plans for reserves provide some information on settlement patterns and site characteristics (Figures 7.4 to 7.9). The St. Peters reserve is shown by Figure 7.4. This 1885 plan of the St. Peters reserve shows that the parish boundaries remained as part of the legal description of the reserve (see Figure 7.4). The original Indian settlement of the St. Peters parish and adjacent land became the reserve of St. Peters after Treaty One. In the northwest corner of the reserve, around Netley Creek, houses and other buildings are indicated on the plan. Family names are recorded, and the headquarters of the Clandeboye agency is located. The Interlake reserve of Fisher River is displayed as Figure 7.5. The river lot system was used to subdivide land within the reserve, and the reserve boundaries were fitted to accommodate the square township system of the Dominion Lands survey. Some 166 lots were laid out at Fisher River. Lots 22 and 23 were occupied by the Methodist mission. The HBC used Lot 100, but this land was sold to the Department of Indian Affairs in 1917. The survey plan indicates that additions to the Fisher River reserve were made in 1896, 1910, and 1911.

Many northern Native communities are described as settlements spread out along shorelines. Settlement at Rossville is represented by a detail of the Norway House reserve in Figure 7.6. The Methodist mission, HBC lot, agency headquarters, boarding school, hospital, and numerous Indian houses are recorded on this 1910 plan. On this reserve, settlement spread out along the river shore, but the population tended to form three distinct communities: Rossville, Yorkville, and the upper reaches of the Jack River. Near the HBC post, lots were allocated to some of the Company's employees. Due to the adhesions, the reserve was enlarged in 1910, but 'Halfbreed settlers or other squatters were cut out of the portions to be given to the Indians.'[24] The 1883 legal plan for The Pas reserve is shown by Figure 7.7. Essentially, the reserve was laid out on the levees of the Saskatchewan and Carrot rivers.

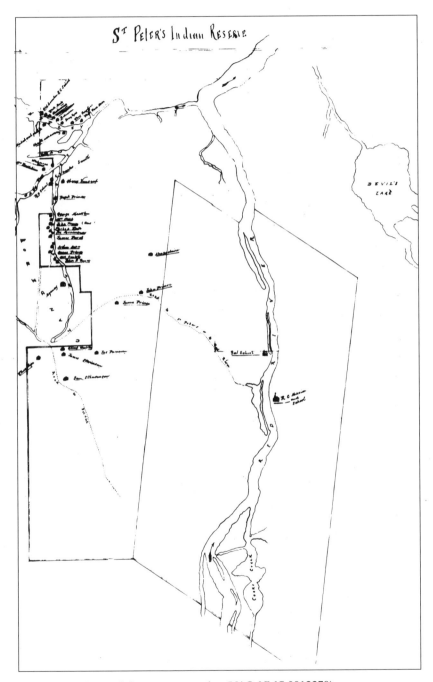

Figure 7.4 St Peter's Reserve survey plan (NAC, NMC 0012270)

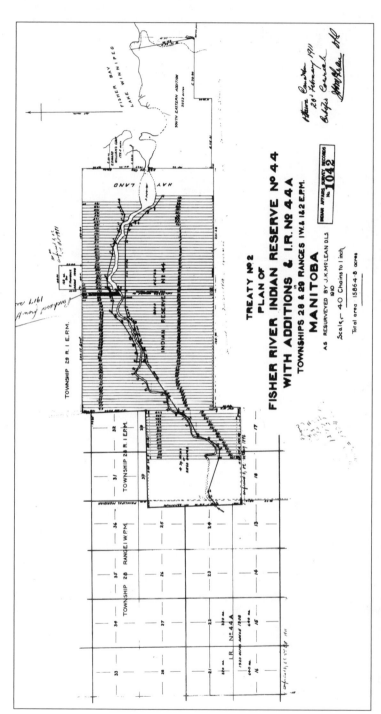

Figure 7.5 Fisher River survey plan, 1910 (NAC, NMC 0023565)

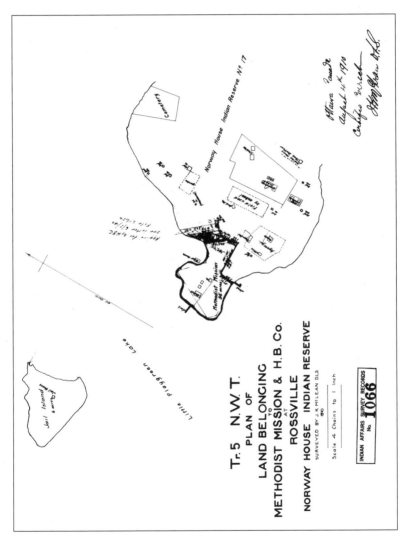

Figure 7.6 Rossville (Norway House) survey plan, 1910 (NAC, NMC 0023696)

In this plan, the surveyor, W.A. Austin, took great care in describing soil classes and vegetation cover. Figure 7.8 depicts the Nelson House plan in 1910, and this was one of the surveys that occurred as a result of the adhesions to Treaty Five (1908-10). The Roman Catholic and Methodist missions and the lots and claims of traders (HBC, Hyer, and Lamont and Davidson) were recorded. In the boreal forest, surveys at Nelson House, Split Lake, and Little Grand Rapids made some effort to restrict the size of the reserve back from the shoreline, thereby recognizing that the better land was found adjacent to the shoreline. With respect to surveying reserve land adjacent to shorelines, a comparison of The Pas and Nelson House plans indicates different configurations (see Figure 7.7 and 7.8). Reserves in the boreal forest were set out as several large blocks of land. Figure 7.8 is representative of the general configuration for surveys of more northern reserves in Manitoba.

While most bands may have received their preferred location, initial surveys did not always conform to their desires. In 1879, dissatisfaction was recorded at Norway House because the surveyor refused to include some hay lands on the Pine River. The Berens River band complained in 1881 about reserve boundaries that excluded some of the best woodlands. In the late nineteenth century, the department responded to band requests for alterations to reserve boundaries. In the Interlake area, a number of Indian reserves were surveyed and improvements were made; however, in the early 1880s, significantly higher water levels flooded portions of the reserves. Some reserves had their boundaries readjusted in an attempt to deal with the changing water levels. (For example, see Fairford, Figure 7.9.) This 1881 plan for Fairford also shows the HBC and mission lots and that several river lots had been surveyed. In some cases, lands at the back of a reserve were exchanged for better land near the shoreline. Given the marginal nature of this land and the scarcity of good land, these resurveying efforts by the department were aggravated by the fact that these Indians were allocated only 160 acres per family of five. However, band requests for strategic advantages were turned down, as in the case of the St. Martin band's desire to own both shores of a narrows, thereby controlling an important fishery.

Selection and surveying of reserves had to take account of band organization and fragmentation. Sometimes the decision to select a particular site for a reserve initiated the splitting up of a band. Indian Affairs' reluctance to grant full band status to a group was based on the extra annuity costs and not an unwillingness to grant a reserve. For instance, the closely related Moose Lake and Chemawawin Indians became more distinct when the department agreed to grant a reserve on Cedar Lake because the Chemawawin group did not want to live at Moose Lake.[25] In contrast, a split occurred with the Sandy Bay (Lake St. Martin) band over the location of a reserve, and it took years for the smaller group to get a reserve at the mouth of the Little Saskatchewan River.

During the late nineteenth century, changes in the location of reserves seem to have occurred relatively easily. The Moose Lake reserve was moved from the narrows of the lake south to the mainland adjacent to the HBC

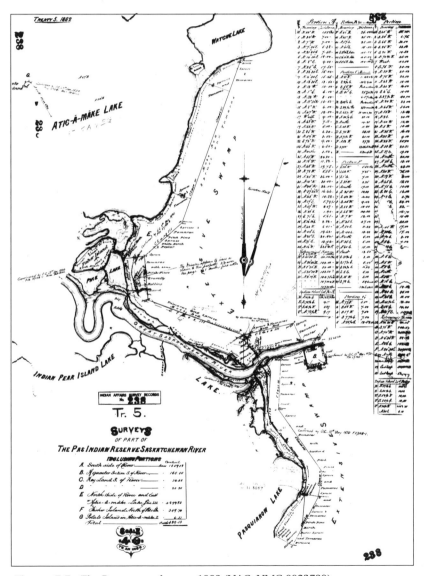

Figure 7.7   The Pas survey plan, ca. 1883 (NAC, NMC 0023790)

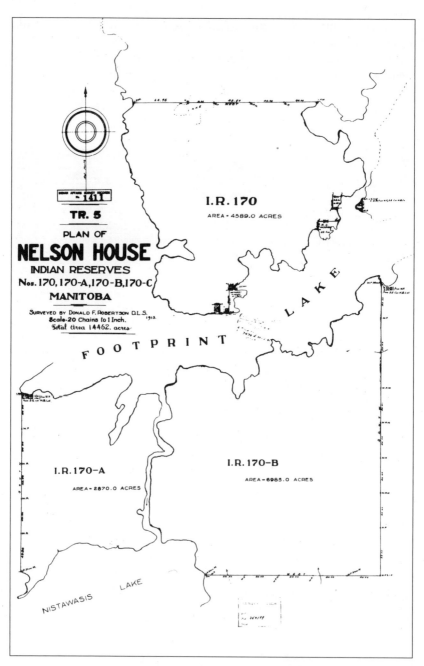

Figure 7.8 Nelson House survey plan, 1913 (NAC, NMC 0023694)

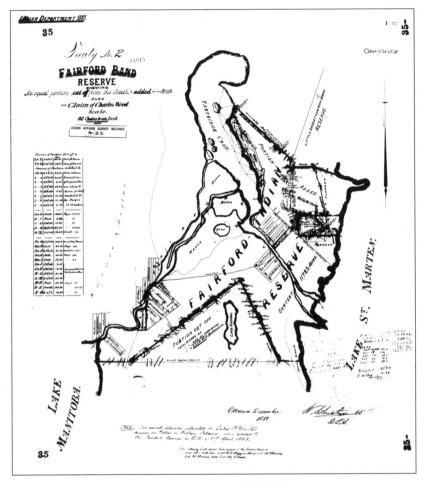

Figure 7.9 Fairford survey plan (NAC, NMC 0020708)

post and Big Island. The Pine Creek band changed the location of its reserve from Duck Bay to Pine Creek. In this case, the locational aspects of settlement were complicated by the division of the band into Indians and 'French Halfbreeds' living at separate locales. The withdrawal from treaty of the Duck Bay Metis favoured the shifting of the Indian reserve to Pine Creek.[26] Resurveying Indian reserves was more likely if the square township system of the Dominion Lands survey had not locked-up a site. In contrast to later years, the surveying and resurveying of reserves indicate a flexible approach towards Indian settlement in the late nineteenth century.

Neither official survey plans nor the department's records provide suffi-cient insights into residency patterns within Indian reserves. Legal surveys and subdivisions influenced settlement patterns. The use of river lots estab-lished a type of order on the spacing of houses and the location of gardens. Reserve boundaries did not always accommodate all pre-survey improve-ments – a problem for the Ebb and Flow and Manitoba Lake bands. For the Manitoba Lake band, settlement was generally spread out along the shore-line, but families also clustered at several points. Thus, not all the improve-ments were located within the reserve, and it was difficult to locate a school conveniently. A school location was also a problem at the upper and lower Fairford villages and for Norway House's clustered settlements. In 1879, the annual report of Indian Affairs noted that the Waterhen band had adopted a scattered residency pattern, but 'this year they are forming a kind of vil-lage in hopes of having a sufficient number of children to enable them to start a school.'[27] The extent of dispersal of homes on a reserve may have been conditioned by a desire for a school. With respect to habitation pat-terns, a report on the Norway House agency stated: 'In some places along the shores of the lakes, or on the banks of the rivers, are patches of soil. Here the Indian builds his house, and makes his garden.'[28] The dispersal pattern of Native settlements is commonly attributed to a desire for social space and the tendency for some kinship clustering, but it seems that in the late nineteenth century, settlement patterns were also influenced by the desire for a school and the need for a garden.

Progress of Reserve Settlement
The appearance of Indian reserves varied during the late nineteenth cen-tury depending upon the survey system and the size of trading and mission concerns. Some reserves remained relatively unsettled for years. By 1877, Fairford had twenty-three houses and six stables and the mission included a church, schoolhouse, two storehouses, a windmill, and a lime kiln.[29] Given that the department's policy was to settle Indians, its annual reports gave a great deal of attention to describing this progress. For example, in 1878 Fort Alexander band members were 'rapidly settling down on the Reserve, build-ing comfortable houses and turning their attention to farming, although the land along the River is wooded and a great deal of labour is required before any return can be obtained.'[30] Frequently, Indian agents recorded year-to-year improvements on a reserve, or, as in the case of Crane River, made comparative comments: 'Their improvements are unparalleled in this Superintendency.'[31] Settling down was not a consistent or even process. Among the non-Christian members of the Brokenhead band, only a small number resided on the reserve.[32] Indian Agent H. Martineau's account of

the Sandy Bay band in 1885 provides some insights into the settlement process:

> I am happy to state that the Indians of this reserve are giving up their no-madic habits.
>
> Most of them come from the Prairie tribes, and, as a consequence, were always absent from the reserve visiting their relatives and friends, or hunt-ing, only returning about the months of June or July of each year, when they came to receive their annuity money, and then they went away again for another year; so in reality the band only numbered some five or six families who remained to improve the reserve.
>
> This spring they returned earlier than usual, took up land on the reserve, hauled logs to build their houses, broke up new land and planted potatoes in it, fenced it with good new rails, and some of them sowed wheat, barley, peas, corn, beans, pumpkins, onions, carrots and turnips.
>
> The more industrious ones are building new houses, having at last de-cided to make homes for themselves on the reserve, more especially that their children may benefit by attending the school.[33]

This shift in strategy coincided with the collapse of the traditional plains economy. While Indian agents' accounts were prone to exaggerate Indian enthusiasm for settlement, their reports also differentiated the progress made by various bands. McColl reported that scarcely anyone lived on the Bloodvein River reserve in 1883 since 'the Chief ... and his followers devote the great[er] part of their time to fishing, hunting, dancing and gambling.'[34]

Changing settlement also concerns the shift from wigwams to houses. For St. Peters in 1878 it was estimated that two-thirds of the band lived in good log houses. In contrast, the subsistence-based Indians at Bloodvein only had 'five crude hovels' as late as 1899.[35] Some members of the St. Mar-tins band 'though possessing houses, they prefer their wigwams.'[36] For the Interlake bands, there was a seasonal shift in shelter – cabins in the winter with a preference for tents in the summer. Missionary accounts corresponded to Indian agent descriptions about settlement progress. The *Proceedings of the Church Missionary Society* reported in 1880 that 'there is not one family at Fairford in a wigwam. All are carefully sheltered in their neat log-houses.'[37]

Settling down on reserves did not require year-round residency. In 1902, Indians in The Pas agency resided on reserves only about four or five months of the year because economic activities required their absence.[38] Nonetheless, Martineau's description of Ebb and Flow in 1888 illustrates changes made in the early reservation-based economy period: 'Their little village is a credit to them, all the buildings are fairly neat and are all whitewashed where formerly they were only plastered over with mud. They are also improving the roads on the reserve and during the spring they erected several bridges. Their little gardens and fields are well kept, clean and free of weeds.'[39] During this period, reserve housing continued to improve as older buildings were replaced. For example, in 1901, at The Pas, Indian Agent S.R. Marlatt 'counted no less than twenty-one new dwellings in course of construction, some of them are quite pretentious in size and finish.'[40] Pre-treaty Native communities also changed. McColl analyzed the changes that had occurred at St. Peters by 1900:

> It is almost a quarter of a century since I visited these reserves, and in that time I have seen some marked changes. Twenty-five years ago St. Peter's was nothing but a string of huts and teepees scattered along the banks of the Red River. The people were living upon fish, and spent their time hunting and trapping small game. Their most pretentious vehicle was the Red River cart, whose creaking could be heard for miles crossing the silent prairie. Today there are very few if any thatched-roof houses. The buildings are shingled, well fenced, surrounded by gardens, with stables and storehouses adjoining. Twenty-five years ago the small houses had but one room in which all lived and slept regardless of relationship. Now the houses are divided into compartments.[41]

Thus in McColl's opinion, considerable material progress had been made in the form of settlement and habitation during the early reserve transition period.

Legal Indian Status and Native Settlement

Unlike the fur trade era, residency in Native communities took on legal implications with the establishment of reserve boundaries and implementation of the Indian Act. The uncoordinated manner in which Indian and Metis Aboriginal title was surrendered and the ad hoc approach to Metis Aboriginal title had serious implications for Native settlement patterns and reserve development. Indian agents frequently described band populations in terms of the existence of significant numbers with 'more or less white blood in their veins' or that there were 'a number of French, English and Scotch halfbreeds.'[42] Therefore, in the immediate post-treaty period, status Indian populations were composed of Indians with varying amounts of 'Indian blood' and other Natives whose identity went beyond 'mixed blood' and were known as 'Halfbreeds.' Those known as Metis or Halfbreeds were apparent among the Sandy Bay, Duck Bay, Ebb and Flow, Fairford, Grand Rapids, The Pas, Norway House, Fort Alexander, and St. Peters bands. With the Northwest Scrip Commissions (1885-9) some band members withdrew from treaty and applied for scrip. In 1886, Indian Agent R. Reader reported: 'The idea of leaving the treaty and receiving scrip in compensation for annuity ... took possession of some of the half-breeds in this [The Pas] agency, [and] spread almost like an epidemic.'[43] Fragmentary evidence does not explain the rate of withdrawal from treaty for scrip, or withdrawal because of enfranchisement or readmittance to treaty; but by 1893 in The Pas agency, 16.7 per cent of the Native population did not have legal Indian status.[44] The legal creation of a non-status Indian population disrupted the formation of Indian communities.

The development of a non-status Indian population proved to be a policy problem for department officials. The department's own records indicate that distinctions among Natives centred around legal status. In 1895 for The Pas area, it was recorded that 'at the different Indian settlements in this Agency there are a number of halfbreed families. These are, to all intents and purposes, Indians: they live like them and in similar houses and pursue identically the same occupations for a livelihood, but having accepted scrip (which they claim to have done under a misrepresentation), they receive no treaty money or assistance from the Government.'[45] Non-status Indians in The Pas area had been required to leave the reserve and thus they had dispersed to form several small communities. Indian Affairs policy did not know how to deal with Indians from non-ceded areas taking up residence on the Norway House reserve. Around the turn of the century, the problem of legal status manifested itself in requests for band membership and due to marriages between status Indian women and non-treaty Natives. Policy on the legal status issue was not very clear as indicated by the Berens River Indian agent who did not know how to deal with the influx of whites that developed during the commercial boom at the turn of the century: 'There is also an ever-increasing number of white men and men of mixed blood who have taken wives from the families of treaty Indians and are subsisting on the resources whence the wards of the government obtain their food supplies. This gives rise to questions as to rights and boundaries which require increasing attention from the department.'[46] Enforcement of the Indian Act would have led to the development of Native communities outside or adjacent to Indian reserves.

While the department's implementation of status and reserve residency terms may have been ambiguous, reserve development was disrupted by the status issue. Since many of the pre-treaty improved lots were occupied by Metis and had been included within reserves by survey, their withdrawal from treaty presented a problem of land ownership. One of the complications that arose as a result of scrip was that some Metis wished to use their scrip to obtain title to land they had occupied on reserves. At Fairford and Fort Alexander, Metis had occupied and improved lots, claimed ownership under the Manitoba Act, and felt that they could claim scrip while remaining on their lots within the reserve. Figure 7.10 indicates the existence of individual claims for the Fort Alexander reserve in 1891. In another situation, the pre-transfer possession of parish river lots was a major problem for the St. Peters reserve. The government's ad hoc Metis policy had presented a scrip option to some band members, and these individuals had an argument for retaining improved lots that they had worked before the treaty. However, if the government had allowed Metis leaving treaty to withdraw their lots from the reserve, some reserves would have been left with a fragmented land tenure. For the Sandy Bay and Ebb and Flow bands, a number of members withdrew from treaty but were later readmitted. Nonetheless, McColl recorded that 'during the interval the cultivation of their gardens was neglected, and therefore they retrograded instead of advancing.'[47]

The development of Metis/non-status Indian communities differed somewhat from the reserve settlement process. Metis communities developed in

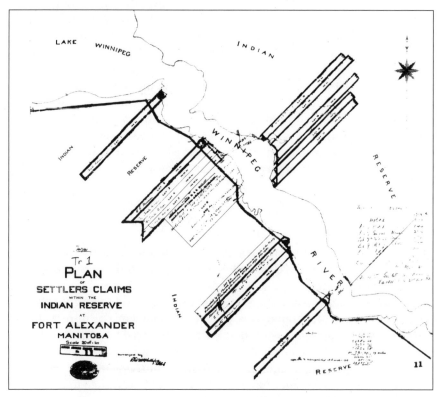

Figure 7.10   Plan of claims within the Fort Alexander Reserve, 1891
(NAC, NMC 0023595)

the post-treaty era, but by and large these communities were not based on legal surveys. Certain predominantly Metis communities grew up as a response to economic conditions: Matheson Island and Manigotan with Lake Winnipeg's commercial boom, and Wabowden and Pikwitonei with the building of the Hudson Bay Railway. Many non-status Indians and Metis located outside but adjacent to reserves. Given the failure of scrip, the location of Metis communities was largely by economic default and not the result of any coherent government-sponsored settlement program. An organized scheme could have been expected as an outcome of the state's recognition of Metis Aboriginal title.

Indian Agricultural Progress: 1870s-1880s

By the early 1870s, missionaries recorded an increased interest in agriculture. The Native clergyman J. Settee contrasted the fur trade with agriculture: 'The Indian has lost confidence of the old system and that iron yoke which ruled in his land many of them finds [it] easier to raise food out of the ground than to obtain it by the *chase* [and] in that way many of them will be brought to settle [and] form themselves into villages, as many of their relations have done.'[48] Reverend H. Budd stressed the demonstration effect at The Pas in 1872 since non-Christian Indians 'cannot but see that the Christian Indians are much better off in every respect than they are; and they see they are now beginning to have some property in the Cattle and the produce of the ground.'[49] Provencher reported in 1873 that 'one-half at least of the Bands of St. Peter[s], Pembina, Fort Alexander and Fairford are in the meantime addicted to agriculture.'[50] Commissioner Simpson felt that it would take years before Indians would be settled, but that subsistence agriculture was already providing an alternative to the insecurity of hunting.[51] By 1875, Provencher stated that Indians have 'now been made to understand the necessity of developing themselves to agricultural pursuits, since hunting and fishing can no longer supply them with sufficient means of subsistence.'[52] When Lieutenant-Governor Morris met with the hunting band at Berens River in 1876, they requested cattle, tools, and Pigeon River hay lands. In the 1870s, interest in agriculture was spurred by the acute insecurity of the hunting economy. Presumably, Indians would evaluate agriculture on economic criteria and not according to the lofty ideals of Christian civilization or the desires of Indian Affairs' officials.

Throughout the late nineteenth century, periodic reports indicated that Indians were turning to agriculture and placing less dependence upon hunting; and even as late as 1891, Inspector McColl rejoiced that 'the fast-approaching extermination of game and fur-bearing animals are accomplishing a wonderful revolution in compelling them reluctantly to abandon the unprofitable pursuits of the chase and follow the example of those enterprising settlers.'[53] The insecurity of the hunting economy was not just a problem of resource scarcity, for this was also a period of low fur prices. There were a number of problems associated with the adoption of reserve agriculture. Initially, the department found it difficult to supply tools and seed early enough in the season for planting. In the late 1870s, not enough tools were provided for each band. Nonetheless, McColl reported that Indians found their own means to cultivate: 'Numerous instances can be cited where the members of Bands with ploughs and harrows, but without cattle or horses, have actually harnessed themselves and ploughed and harrowed their fields – ingenious use of ropes and portage straps.'[54] Not all sites were suited for agriculture, and in the late 1870s members of the Island band moved from Doghead to Loon Straits where they began gardening. Progress at most of the Manitowapah agency reserves was impeded by the floods in the early 1880s; however, these people renewed their efforts. Clearly, many Indians became committed agriculturists as one response to the shortages in the hunting economy.

By the late 1870s and early 1880s, a number of reserves had either established or expanded cultivation. Indian Agent D. Young reported that non-Christian Indians who settled at Brokenhead 'took a great deal of pride in showing me over their farms this summer, the crops are clean [weeded], well cared for and fenced off from the cattle.'[55] Typical of progress was the Lake Manitoba reserve in 1877, where there were eighteen small farms composed of two acres of potatoes and Indian corn. By 1879, subsistence agriculture had taken root at Moose Lake. At Fort Alexander, wheat and potatoes were the main crops, and houses and gardens were enclosed by fences. Lake Winnipeg reserves, such as Black River, Hollow Water, Jackhead, Poplar River, Norway House, and Cross Lake all had varying sizes of potato gardens. Thus, agricultural efforts began to differentiate bands; after only a few years at Fisher River, McColl stated that they were 'the most enterprising and industrious band of Indians in this Agency. Their advancement in agriculture is most encouraging.'[56] At St. Peters, efforts included developing a drainage system to improve the land. Indian Agent R. Reader, who had been a missionary at The Pas, actively assisted these people with agriculture. By 1886, the reserve had some sixty gardens and a common field for barley. Sometimes, commitment to cultivation went beyond individual efforts; McColl reported that the Waterhen Band 'purchased a mower and a horse-rake, and fully paid for these implements out of their annuities.'[57]

Progress in this period was not simply limited to the adoption of cultivation. For bands with pre-treaty agricultural experience, techniques of cultivation changed. McColl explained in 1886: 'Instead of the small garden patches formerly cultivated by the women with only grub-hoes, extensive fields of excellent wheat, barley, and potatoes are seen on many of the reserves. The Indians are beginning to realize the advantages of utilizing the cattle and agricultural implements ... as they are enabled to raise by this improved method of farming larger crops, with less labour, than they otherwise could do.'[58] Agricultural advances in this period were paralleled by a change in the image of the Indian. In 1880, J.A. Macdonald stated: 'And the manner in which some of the bands have already settled upon their Reserves, built houses, and fenced and broken by land for cultivation, has astonished old residents of the Territories; who scarcely believed such a transformation of character in the wild Indian of the possible.'[59] Clearly, in the early reserve period subsistence agriculture was an important component of Indian livelihood. A summary of agricultural activities is presented in Figure 7.11.

Limitations to Agricultural Development
The intensity of agricultural activities varied with geography, but also Indian interest in this form of subsistence changed over time. There was not sustained progress in the agricultural sector. A variety of reasons explain changing involvement in cultivation. By the late 1880s, less St. Peters land was under cultivation; but this had happened to other Red River parishes as well. The land was worn out and a plague of Canadian thistles had forced the abandonment of fields. The Reverend E. Eves reported that Rossville's agriculture was retrogressing.[60] In general, there was a noticeable decline in cultivation by the early 1900s. Semmens reported in 1901 that around Lake Winnipeg, 'Farming is not carried on extensively or with increasing success.'[61] The most established agricultural reserve in the study region, St. Peters, also displayed a decline in cultivation. The annual report for 1903 recorded that 'in the farming line they are a long way behind their record of ten years ago; they do not raise half the grain and vegetables they did in those days.'[62]

Subsistence agriculture declined with an increase in wildlife resources. In the late 1880s and early 1890s, moose and caribou became plentiful, even at the south end of Lake Winnipeg. Muckle recorded that in a day a hunter could kill between one and three moose, whose hides were worth eight to twelve dollars each, and since flour could be purchased for a $1.50 a bag, they 'do not see the use of sowing wheat.'[63] Commercial cultivation did not progress at Brokenhead because Indians do not 'give much attention to agriculture, for the reason the moose are so plentiful that they have nearly all turned moose hunters, and what with potatoes, corn, fish, moose meat, ducks and the fur they trap they make a very good living.'[64] Moreover, Indians were not removed from the influence of the fur trade, and McColl realized that 'the fur trader is naturally averse to their adopting civilized habits which unfit them for hunting and therefore advances them traps, clothing,

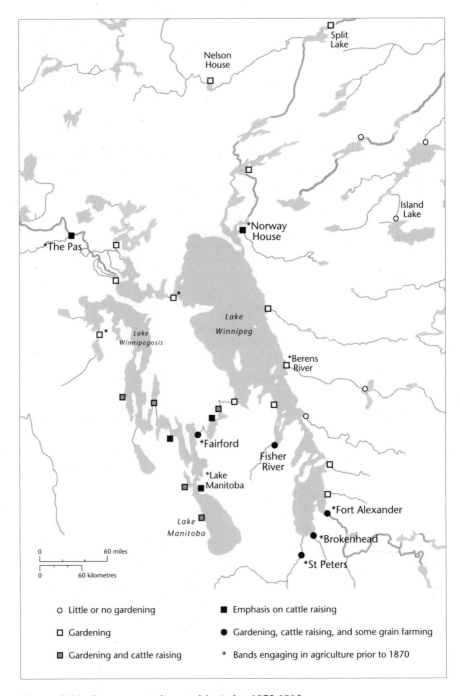

Figure 7.11 Reserve agriculture in Manitoba, 1875-1915

provisions and ammunition to induce them to leave the reserves.'[65] Commercial hunting, based on credit, could be more attractive than subsistence gardening. In particular, the conflict between fur trade and subsistence agriculture was most strongly felt during the spring muskrat hunt. The Pas post manager G. Deschambault stated the trader's view: 'And when the Indians have gone and killed a great many Rats they were ordered in to their Reserve by the Indian Agent to attend to their gardens. The Government doing little or nothing to help the Indians the whole winter, leaving it to the Company to do so. When the Spring comes they consider it their duty to order in the Indians to their miserable little patches, which they [the Indians] acknowledge never would save them from starvation during the Winter.'[66] Indian Agent Bray (The Pas) understood that the resource base did not always correspond to the department's economic priorities when he argued in 1895 that 'it appears to me to be futile to expect that these Indians, who can so easily supply their wants by fishing, shooting and trapping, should devote much attention to farming.'[67] Finally, the insecurity of the commercial hunting sector of the Native economy was reduced when fur prices increased after 1900.

The real limitation of Indian cultivation in this period was the inability to make a transition from subsistence to commercial production.[68] Department of Indian Affairs' economic policies and regulations tended to restrict commercial exchanges between Indians and the rest of the population. McColl reported in 1883 that the chief of the Pas band 'asks that liberty be granted them to sell the surplus of hay and potatoes they may have, as well as permission to sell cordwood to steamboats.'[69] The next year, McColl passed on a similar point of view from the Fisher River band: 'They want the restriction forbidding [t]heir selling the products of their gardens removed, as it shackles and cripples their progress in farming.'[70] There are indications that some bands were capable of producing a surplus; for example, the Fort Alexander band 'have about fifteen hundred bushels of potatoes to sell but they have no market. They also have some native Indian corn for sale.'[71] Some demand for agricultural products was generated by lumbering interests, and Indians responded to these markets. Commercial agricultural income was measured against other sources of income. Muckle noted that at Fort Alexander in 1893: 'Those who farm are inclined to be discouraged, as prices for farm produce have been so low that it does not pay them to ship to market, and some feel like giving it up, and becoming hunters or fishermen, or seeking employment at day's wages.'[72] Limited markets and protectionist policies hindered the development of commercial agriculture.

Another reason for a decline or stagnation of reserve cultivation is that more secure economic prospects existed for Indians. Indian Agent Martineau reported in 1887 that the Little Saskatchewan band 'make an excellent living by the sale of whitefish' and 'consequently they pay little or no attention to gardening.'[73] The commercial boom on Lake Winnipeg provided alternative incomes. In 1900, McColl argued that the 'inducements offered to other lines are perhaps, too alluring, too profitable' and that 'they prefer occupations where the returns for their labour are quicker and surer.'[74] In fact, Indians obtained employment at harvest time with white farmers and were reluctant to return to the reserve to weed gardens. In 1904, Indian Agent S. Swinford reported that at Bloodvein: 'It seems almost impossible to get these people to raise vegetables; on making inquiry as to the reason, they say it would not pay them to stay away from the work they get for the sake of raising a few potatoes.'[75] Certainly, the stagnation of reserve cultivation was not because of a lack of commercial aptitude on the part of Indians, rather the economic and geographical context of reserve agriculture did not encourage a transition from subsistence to commercial agriculture.

An understanding of Indian agriculture can be developed by looking at the case of Fisher River. The band located at Fisher River because the site seemed suitable for agriculture. Band members cleared and broke land for homes and gardens, built up cattle herds, and in 1887 harvested 2,515 bushels of potatoes and 210 tons of hay.[76] But when Reverend Stevens arrived at Fisher River in 1907, he observed that 'all cleared land was commons. Fences had been burned for firewood' and that 'not a potato was to be had.'[77] Although the department used this reserve as an example of advancing agriculture, Stevens suggested that Indians were attracted to the lumbering industry. By the early 1900s, Indian Affairs reports finally acknowledged that other sources of income were more secure for Fisher River Indians.[78] This case demonstrates that even at a site somewhat more favourable to cultivation than those reserves in the rocky shield country and with considerable experience at mission agriculture, Fisher River Indians found it more advantageous to participate in wage labour.

Stock-raising on Reserves

Although grain farming and gardening did not provide the economic base envisioned at the time of the treaties, for some bands stock-raising became a major activity during the early reserve transition period. After the introduction of Indian Affairs' cattle, some losses occurred due to inadequate care. Most bands made an effort to raise cattle. However, for the Lake Winnipeg reserves this was not a sustained activity (see Figure 7.11). Dependence on wild swamp grasses and lack of good hay lands appear to be the major limitations for the existence of large herds. In The Pas agency, water-level fluctuations in the Saskatchewan River discouraged cattle-raising, and

Indian Agent Marlatt noted that livestock was not of much consequence 'for the reason that they are too far from market to dispose of them, and as a food-supply to the owners of little value in a country where moose, bear and fish are so plentiful.'[79] He candidly admitted that Indians 'would not raise cattle at all if it were not their desire to please the department.'[80] In the Manitowapah agency, however, stock-raising became an important economic activity. Here the land was better suited to this type of agriculture. By 1892, Martineau reported that 'cattle are increasing rapidly and get very good care, evidence of which is apparent by the large stock they have on hand.'[81] In the Interlake, Indians were competent at raising cattle; Swinford noted that during a difficult time Indians had managed to save their cattle, whereas other settlers had lost stock.[82] Agriculture became the major source of income for Manitowapah bands.[83]

Indians derived a number of benefits from cattle-raising, one being that the HBC accepted cattle as payment for debt. Again, regulations affected reserve agriculture, and in 1886 a councillor wanted to know 'how many animals would they require to raise ... before they would be allowed to kill any of them.'[84] In the Clandeboye agency, Indian women milked cows and sold butter. In the Manitowapah agency, stock-raising was sustained through the early 1900s, but according to Swinford, Indians 'would do better were it not for the advice of "sharks" visiting the reserve, to kill or dispose of some of their live stock on the sly.'[85] Indian agents generally felt that Indians sold their cattle before maturity but admitted that they got good prices. Indians responded to the market, and the number of cattle and horses in the Manitowapah agency were reduced by 45 per cent between 1913 and 1915.[86] This market situation was related to the war, and Indian Agent R. Logan recorded that the reduction was 'accounted for by the way in which our home buyers, also the Americans were scouring the country for cattle, and very high prices were paid.'[87] Manitowapah Indians were successful stock-raisers because the land could support cattle and because a market existed to make cattle-raising something more than a subsistence activity.

Treaties, trade posts, and missions forever changed the landscape of northern Manitoba. In general, Indians selected places that they already occupied and sites that offered a useful combination of resources (fisheries, high ground, hay marshes, and timber). The decision by the 'surplus population' of Norway House to locate in the Interlake represented a pulling away from the fur trade. As with the smaller Interlake bands, agricultural prospects, wood, and fisheries were more important criteria than the centrality of the trade post. In the boreal forest, Indians selected reserves near well-established posts. Disorder to this settlement process was introduced when the state enforced its terms for legal Indian status, otherwise reserve development progressed within the confines of available resources and changing economic prospects. Many fish stations, steamboat landings, and sawmills, which came with the new staples economy, located on or near reserves. Thus, in the post-1870 period both Indians and frontier resource capitalists made similar locational decisions. The partial subdivision of some reserves into river lots was a logical outcome of more fixed habitation and agriculture activity, which largely predated treaties.

While reserves were convenient locales for new staple industries, pressure was brought to bear on Indian-owned land. In this region, surrenders occurred, but with less frequency than among the agricultural reserves of southern Saskatchewan. A controversial and divisive surrender happened in 1907 when the entire St. Peters reserve (some 48,000 acres) was relinquished.[88] Disputed ownership of the river lots, speculator gain, and an isolationist's rationale led to this surrender and the removal of the band to the larger, although less resource-endowed, Interlake reserve known as Peguis. The surrender of St. Peters was a fate that paralleled the Metis experience. The last of the old Red River parishes was cleared of Natives. Some 304 acres were surrendered by the Fort Alexander band in 1926 to the Manitoba Pulp and Paper Company, a site for the first pulp mill on the prairies. In this instance, the band split between those who wished to retain reserve land and those interested in employment at the mill.[89] At The Pas, 540 acres of reserve land from the south bank of the Saskatchewan River was given up in 1913.[90] This surrender provided a town site for the Hudson Bay Railway. The Pas and Fort Alexander surrenders were special cases where large permanent sites were required. Because the treaties provided access to the region's timber and fish, further surrenders of Indian land were not initiated by frontier industries. With the exception of these surrenders, the selection of reserves was permanent – even though the economy was transitional. In 1871, Lieutenant-Governor Archibald had represented the Queen at the treaty talks, promising: 'Your Great Mother, therefore, will lay aside for you lots of land, to be used by you and your children forever. She will not allow the white man to intrude upon these lots. She will make rules to keep them for you, so that as long as the Sun shall shine, there shall be no Indian who has not a place that he can call his home, where he can go and pitch his camp, or, if he chooses, build his house and till his land.'[91] These assurances were greatly overstated. Indians lost their homes when they lost legal status. Reserve acreage did not allow for future population growth. Some Indian bands lost land when surrenders occurred, although the pressure to surrender reserve land was less severe in northern Manitoba than in those treaty areas in which larger per capita reserves had been created. Reserves were merely a creation of a new category of land tenure within the European system of recognizing property. And while this category of land did afford some protection to Indians, such a category of land did not codify Indian use and occupancy of the land. The uncertainty of the treaty right to a livelihood (hunting, fishing, and trapping), along with the very small size of reserves, did not provide much compensation for the pre-treaty patterns of land use.

In terms of the policy priorities of the Department of Indian Affairs, reserve settlement progressed faster than reserve agriculture. Settlement and agriculture actually carried through from the pre-treaty era to the reserve transition period. Barriers to more intensive agriculture included marginal land subject to flooding, restriction on exchange and initiative, lack of markets, and better off-reserve employment opportunities. Nonetheless, trends in reserve agriculture were never as simple as has been implied in some academic critiques of Indian policy. For example, in 1912 the Sandy Bay band was once again attempting grain farming.[92] Among certain bands, stock-raising became a major component of the reserve economy. Cultivation satisfied subsistence needs. In 1890, Chief Berens stated: 'The missionaries and the Government taught them to get food out of the ground, and it was well for them that they were taught, or they would starve.'[93]

8
'Nothing To Make Up for the Great Loss of Winter Food': Resource Conflicts over Common-Property Fisheries

Following the treaties (1871-5), the development of a large-scale commercial fishing industry catering to an export market was the first major change in the regional economy of northern Manitoba.[1] Fur bearers had long been commercialized by 1870. Fisheries, a very reliable resource, were brought more firmly under the sphere of exchange relations in the 1880s. This development altered Native resource use and redefined the role of the Native in the regional economy. An account of the commercialization of fisheries provides many additional insights into the impact of the market on the Native economy. This change in resource use can be understood by contrasting local and export-oriented fisheries. To fully appreciate the significance of fish prior to the industry that developed in the 1880s, it is useful to examine Native common property fisheries. Commercial companies seriously threatened Native livelihood. Consequently, a major campaign aimed at restricting commercial fishing was conducted by Natives and others.

Aboriginal Fisheries as a Common Property Resource
Fisheries were a source of great affluence for Indians, and this resource remained as a common property – even with the advent of the fur trade. The regularity of fish runs, the fact that various species of fish spawned during different seasons, and the relative ease with which fish were harvested during a spawning season made fisheries one of the most reliable Native food sources. For instance, there are indications that Indians fished under the ice and that sturgeon could be caught during the winter at open rapids. Regarding the impact of contact on Native fishing, it is not always possible to distinguish Aboriginal and early fur trade fish technology; but it seems that Indians fished with spears, hooks, hoop nets, gill nets, and weirs.[2] The lake whitefish and lake sturgeon were the two most important species exploited among a variety of larger freshwater species. The large concentration of spawning whitefish during the cool fall season meant that the whitefish

could easily be preserved for the winter by freezing them. Sturgeon held special significance – one of the Ojibwa totems was the sturgeon. Sturgeon are large fish ranging from ten to eighty pounds, and Peter Fidler recorded that one 'as large as a small Indian canoe' was found in Lake Winnipeg.[3] Not only did the sturgeon provide an abundant supply of food (flesh and eggs), it also had multipurpose uses and in this sense it resembled the buffalo. This fish provided a substantial amount of oil, its bladder was used as glue, and its skin was made into a jar.[4] Another advantage of the sturgeon was that it could be kept alive in a holding pond as a convenient future source of fresh food. While it is difficult to present all aspects of Aboriginal fisheries, fish were a very important resource.

During the fur trade, life in subarctic posts was dominated by fisheries. Tending nets and hauling fish absorbed the labour time of many post employees. Daily diet, and even survival, was often dependent upon freshwater fisheries. John Richardson observed during the winter of 1819-20 that whitefish is 'a most delicious food, and at many posts it is the sole article of diet for years.'[5] European traders introduced gill nets made of twine and metal ice chisels to subarctic fisheries. Traders organized fisheries so that large quantities of fish were taken and stored at posts. The inland penetration by the Hudson's Bay Company of the boreal forest was strongly conditioned by the location of fisheries. For instance, Cumberland House, the first of the Company's inland posts, was located near a fishery. Even after the organization of a system of provision distribution drawing heavily on the prairies for pemmican, fish remained critically significant. The Company's winter transportation depended on sled dogs, which were sustained by fish. An examination of Norway House journals between 1872 and 1876 reveals that there was a distinct fishing cycle: jackfish were sought in the early spring; in the early summer the focus shifted to sturgeon; more fishing went on in the late summer; the crucial fall fishery centred on whitefish; and whitefish were again intensively exploited after freeze-up. Posts also purchased sizeable quantities of sturgeon from Indians in the late winter. In this sense, Indians engaged in fishing for commercial exchange prior to the treaties. Not all the fish obtained was used to feed HBC employees. Since fish was stored at Company posts, during times of scarcity Indians would visit posts and receive fish as an item of relief. Inexpensive fish helped to keep the costs of the HBC's paternalistic economy low. Furthermore, abundant fisheries easily satisfied Native subsistence needs and more time could be spent on trapping. This inexpensive food made it possible to conduct a profitable fur trade in many areas. Although fisheries were an important adjunct of the fur trade, this resource remained a common property for Native people as well.

Initially, federal government policy on western fisheries recognized the importance of this resource to Native people. In an 1869 report to the Privy Council, the minister of the Department of Marine and Fisheries explained pending resource conflicts:

> Exclusive control should be jealously preserved as well on our own behalf as for the sake of the Indian population. The forest hunting grounds of the Indian tribes cannot coexist with agricultural and lumbering enterprises, and the game of the plains will here, as it has done everywhere else, disappear as the country becomes settled. But the waters may be fished without sensibly diminishing their supplies so long as kept under our own control, and the Indians can always rely on them for fish-food when the chase shall no longer afford them the means of subsistence to which they are accustomed.[6]

Even before the federal government established its control over the Northwest, officials understood that effective management of fisheries was needed to avoid a crisis and to ensure Indian subsistence. In 1872, the first Fisheries Department report on Manitoba noted 'that the white fish [sic] forms a staple article of food with the Indians and half-breeds.'[7] Local Fisheries official W.T. Urquhart reported that the whitefish, 'as an Indians hunter said to me "Is to us [the Indians] in the water what the buffalo is on the land."'[8] As the depletion of buffalo herds became more pronounced throughout the Northwest, a contrast with the more diversified economy of the Interlake Indians was noted by the Indian Affairs Department in 1878: 'Those whose reserves are in the vicinity of Lake Manitoba, will not be seriously affected by the disappearance of the buffalo, inasmuch as they depend principally upon fish and game, together with root crops, for their subsistence.'[9] The stability of the situation in Manitoba, in comparison to the rest of the prairie-parkland, was the result of the concentration of Indian populations on the shores of lakes Winnipeg, Manitoba, Winnipegosis, and St. Martin close to important fisheries. The stability that fisheries afforded is evident in Indian Agent A. Mackay's comment on the Moose Lake reserve: 'This is a very good reserve for the Indians (apart from farming purposes), as there is hardly ever a want for something to eat. The lake is full of good whitefish, which are caught both winter and summer, and the Indians live well here, while others are starving.'[10] The development of reserves did not prevent Indians from travelling greater distances to exploit better fisheries. For instance, the St. Peters band fished on Lake Winnipeg in the fall. In the first few years after the signing of treaties, Indians successfully adapted to game scarcity by exploiting fisheries more intensively.

Commercialization and Export Markets

In the 1860s and the 1870s, the Red River Settlement had a market for freshwater fish; however, the thrust for expanded commercial development came in the early 1880s when rail connections put this resource within reach of American markets and capital. In the 1870s, prices existed for fish at the settlement. In 1872, an effort failed to create a larger scale fishery, but Urquhart reported that a large number of whitefish were 'brought down from the lake, for sale at Winnipeg' and that the price of whitefish was sixteen shillings per 100 at the fishery.[11] The fisheries reports for 1876 and 1877 recorded yields, itemized gear, noted price increases, and documented that hundreds of men were involved in fishing lakes Winnipeg and Manitoba and the Red and Assiniboine rivers.[12] Thus, the existence of both a lake price and a Winnipeg market price, and the large number of fisheries in the mid-1870s clearly indicate that a local Winnipeg market provided adequate demand to encourage a gradual shift from a local fishery to a small-scale commercial fishery.

In the 1880s, the emerging small-scale local market-oriented fishing industry was displaced by export-oriented companies. This development was led by Reid and Clarke, two fish traders who, in 1881, formed the first export-oriented commercial company. Their operation was based on the fishery off the Little Saskatchewan River (Dauphin River). Initially, the production of fish oil was the major concern, and, according to Inspector of Indian Agencies E. McColl, Indians participated in the 'reckless and improvident destruction of fish ... during spawning season, more especially for the manufacture of oil for traffic.'[13] Clearly, Indians were involved in commercial fishing from the very start. On Lake Winnipeg, fish companies such as Reid and Clarke and C.W. Gauthier carried on their own fishing operations and traded fish from Indians and other fishermen 'whose catch is small, and who part with their fish either in the local market or sell them to larger dealers who export them to the United States.'[14] On Lake Manitoba, large fish traders were active by the mid-1880s. The export of fish to the American market and the corresponding emergence of commercial fishing companies on Lake Winnipeg (the major fishery in the province) resulted in substantially increased production. In fact, the production figures for the 1880s indicate that fish exports expanded rapidly from 127,117 pounds in 1883 to 2,063,107 pounds in 1888.[15] In 1885, Reid and Clarke shipped to the United States 280,000 pounds of their total catch of 334,000 pounds of fresh whitefish (i.e., 83 per cent.)[16] The connection between commercial operators and the American market was well known as a teacher from Lake St. Martin remarked in 1889 that 'the great Fish Companys [*sic*] – who for years ... have been catering to a foreign market from New York to St.

Louis.'[17] The labour force included Canadians from Ontario, Icelanders, and Native people. In 1887, the two largest companies (Reid and Clarke; and C.W. Gauthier) employed 80 white men, 40 half breeds, and 185 Indians.[18] However, Captain William Robinson employed 150 men, all from Ontario, except for ten Icelanders.[19] Indian involvement with commercial fishing was most pronounced at the Little Saskatchewan River and Grand Rapids. Figure 8.1 depicts the Lake Winnipeg fishing industry in the 1880s and clearly demonstrates the rapid development of the industry after Reid and Clarke's first visit to the Little Saskatchewan River in 1881.

Native Participation in Commercial Fishing

One of the consequences of the development of commercial fishing in the 1880s was a decline in Indian fishing for immediate needs. From the start, Indians opposed the expansion of commercial fishing. In 1882, McColl reported that the Little Saskatchewan band made 'loud complaints against David Clarke for wholesale traffic in fish.'[20] The Indian agent at Berens River stated in 1884: 'They represent [*sic*] that their fisheries are encroached upon by parties from Winnipeg, who, if allowed to continue the destruction of the whitefish and sturgeon at the present rate, will eventually exhaust the supply and deprive them of their principal source of subsistence.'[21] Similarly, Indian Agent H. Martineau for the Lake St. Martin area reported in 1886: 'Fear is entertained by some [Indians] that whitefish will become scarce in consequence of the increasing fishing operations carried on by white traders' and that 'the Indians express a desire that some check on them should be instituted by the Government for the preservation of this valuable fish which is the Indian's main support.'[22] Clearly, Indians recognized the importance of fish, and they believed that the resource was theirs, or at least believed that they had a special claim to this resource.

In 1886, Indian Agent Mackay lamented that 'during the winter many of the Indians caught great numbers of whitefish, which they sold to traders, thus helping to destroy the fisheries and means of subsistence.'[23] The fact that many Indians appeared to oppose commercial fishing by white men at the same time that others reverted to selling fish to these same traders appears contradictory. The acquisition of goods promoted participation in the fish trade. In 1886, Fisheries Inspector A. McQueen described this trade: 'There were upwards of one hundred Indians engaged [in] fishing, who traded their fish for flour, bacon, tea, tobacco, twine, clothing &c., supplied from two stores doing a thriving trade in this locality.'[24] Similarly, it was reported that at Sandy Bay on Lake Manitoba 'in the winter time they get a ready sale at good prices for all whitefish and pike that they take.'[25] For Brokenhead at the southern end of Lake Winnipeg in 1884 trade was vigorous 'as the

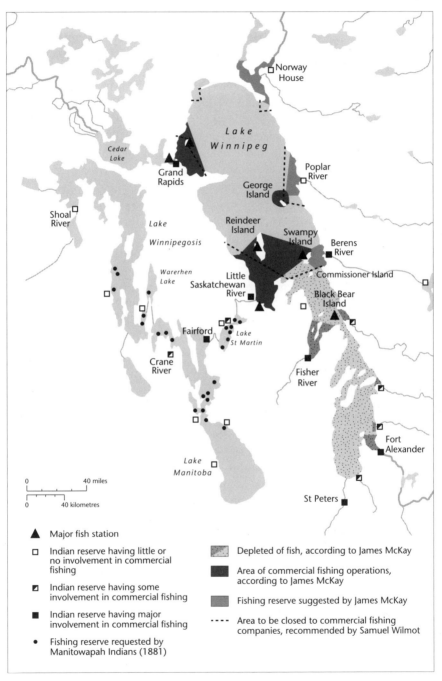

Figure 8.1 Manitoba commercial fisheries, ca. 1889

fishing was good, men from Winnipeg came and bought the fish from them at their doors, giving fair prices, they were therefore comparatively comfortable throughout the year.'[26] Unlike involvement in the domestic economy, participation in the fishing industry was not universal. In 1890, a chief from the Interlake noted that fall and winter fishing were unsuccessful and emphasized that 'some young Indians want to work for freezer men to get money and spend it; don't know what way, but old Indians, squaws and children get no good, no work, no fish.'[27] This chief recognized that 'young men and boy Indian get some good' but the others 'get nothing to make up for great loss of winter food, which came up river very plenty old time before.'[28] The switch from largely subsistence to subsistence/commercial exploitation of fish had different impacts on the same band of Indians. Participation in export-oriented commercial fishing by Indians may have been motivated partly by a desire to influence the rate of harvesting and a realization that with or without Indian labour, commercialization of fisheries would continue.

The development of commercial fishing, even when it provided remunerative seasonal income, disrupted the Native economy. The 1888 annual report for Indian Affairs recorded that 'to the north of Beren's River the Indians were able to catch a good number of fish, but that south of that locality very few whitefish were captured, and that in fact the portion of Lake Winnipeg extending south of Rabbit Point has been almost depleted of whitefish.'[29] Indian agents also pointed out that Indians were able to 'obtain other smaller fish at all the reserves.'[30] Commercial fishing was largely species specific (whitefish and, to a much lesser degree, sturgeon), and the fact that other types of fish could still be obtained indicates that overfishing, and not some other intervening factor, was likely responsible for declining whitefish yields. In 1890, it was reported that fishing was poor at Lake St. Martin, Fairford, the Little Saskatchewan River, and Lake Winnipeg south of Berens River.[31] By the late 1880s, the Indians and Indian agents were reporting serious declines in whitefish catches at many reserves and a growing concern by Indians.

Declining productivity led to a breakdown in Native fisheries that had reached crisis proportions in the late 1880s. The Department of Indian Affairs noted other ill effects created by commercial fishing. McColl reported in 1889:

> Instead of the Indians being benefited by the fisheries, I find the very opposite to be invariably the case, for not only is the supply of fish, upon which they principally depend for subsistence becoming rapidly exhausted, but also the general condition of the Indians within this agency is getting apparently worse every year. Since the commencement of those fisheries their

reserves are not properly cultivated, their gardens are frequently neglected and their houses often deserted. At the approach of winter, when the fishing season is over, they return to their homes empty-handed and heavy-hearted, to wander about in search of food to keep themselves and families from starving.[32]

Thus, those members of the Little Saskatchewan who left the reserve and gravitated to the fisheries made 'an excellent living by the sale of whitefish'; in contrast, 'those who reside on the reserve do not live in such abundance but their means of livelihood are certainly more certain.'[33] Ultimately, the penetration of large-scale commercial fishing into what had been previously a stable Native subsistence fishery brought relative instability and long-term insecurity to Indians.

Incomes from commercial fishing were attractive enough to draw Natives out of the fur trade. However, the payment of wages in the form of trade goods rather than cash had the effect of reducing Native incomes. In 1889, J. Butler, the missionary at Berens River, observed that Indians employed at C.W. Gauthier's sturgeon fishery received $1.25 per day, but that the actual cash value of a day's work, as represented in goods, only amounted to fifty cents.[34] Additionally, it was reported that the traders realized fifty times more for the fish than what they had paid the Indians.[35] Unequal trade existed, as indicated by the markup after the exchange between the trader and Indian. Indians were no longer resource owners: they were confined in economic roles as producers and wage labourers in those areas where commercial fishing was established.

Struggle for Subsistence

During the 1880s, an opposition to commercial fishing (which centred on a concern to maintain subsistence fisheries for Natives) developed into a major political struggle. Considerable government attention was devoted towards assessing the impact of fish companies on the resource base. Reports on the state of fisheries made by Indian agents may have been regarded sceptically by some officials, since the Indian Affairs Department was responsible for the welfare of the Indians. In 1888, Lieutenant-Governor Schultz became aware of the situation on Lake Winnipeg because R. Phair emphasized: 'The time will come when the subject will force itself upon the attention of the government, and the cries of perishing Indians unanimously appeal for a solution to this great problem.'[36] Schultz sought a complete account of the situation and sent G.I. McVicar (1888) and J. Cornish (1889) to investigate and report on the fisheries. Both McVicar and Cornish expressed concerns about the fishery and noted that fish were wasted when nets were not lifted on Sundays, and that all fish, apart from whitefish, trout, and sturgeon were thrown away. They also reported that those directly concerned with commercial fishing did not anticipate any danger of overfishing.[37] Similarly, C. Inkster accompanied McColl's inspection tour of 1889, and the information he reported to Schultz corroborated previous reports by Indian agents regarding the failure of Indian fisheries. He also reported that Indians believed the failure was due to 'the White Men with their big nets.'[38] Schultz also solicited the perspectives of some lakeshore residents. George Bruce, a missionary at Fairford for more than thirty years, confirmed that bands adjacent to Lake St. Martin experienced a failure of the 1889 fall fishery to an extent that he had not previously witnessed.[39] R. La Touche Tupper confirmed the existence of a problem with wasted fish: 'Over 10,000 spoiled whitefish were thrown in the lake from one net off the Little Saskatchewan.'[40] He also noted that optimistic arguments regarding the potential of the fishery were based on the size of Lake Winnipeg and overlooked the fact that the lake was very shallow.

Schultz can be credited with taking the initiative to investigate the conflict between Indian and commercial fisheries. The evidence collected by Schultz verified the reports of Indian agents and implied that a serious crisis was impending. Indians were not apathetic about the situation that commercial companies had created. Phair reported that 'one is not surprised to learn of the Indians meeting from time to time in council to deliberate [about] what they shall do "when the white man takes all the fish away."'[41] Phair recorded a statement by an old and unnamed Indian that summed up an Indian perspective on commercial fishing:

We have waited long for our guardians to do something for us. They must know surely that our food is being carried away to the States. The fish are becoming fewer and fewer and more difficult to catch especially in our ways of taking them. Our little canoes and handful of net toiling along the shore in shallow water are but a drop in the lake compared with these companies with their steamers and enormous nets enclosing fish of all kinds. This state of things can only go on for a little while. Just as the traders left us, stores and all, when the furs were gone and it did not pay them to stay, so the fishermen will go, but with this difference: in the former case we did all the catching and received an equivalent for our furs; but here these men catch all the fish, and we get nothing, and when they leave the mischief is done.[42]

This Indian Elder indicated a concern for the subsistence use of fish over an export market and the inequality in the scale of exploitation. The comparison with the fur trade focused on the economic role of the Native and the consequence of resource depletion. Many of the problems still common to

Canada's staple economies – the disruption of the resource base and the unavoidable departure of the outsiders once money can no longer be made – are accurately identified by this Elder. With the pending encroachment on the Poplar River band's fishery, their headman stated: 'My people do not want them to come because the fish is all we have to look to for a living.'[43] Butler informed Schultz that the Hudson's Bay Company man 'believes there will be trouble, if the fishing Co. fish sturgeon in those waters next summer.'[44] In 1890, the Norway House band petitioned, in Cree syllabics, for the protection of the whitefish. The chief and councillors informed Schultz that 'we dread the approach of these white fishermen, we have heard from relatives at Poplar River, the Great Saskatchewan how quickly their fishing affects the supply of the small nets of the Indians' and they hoped that 'at least this River [the Nelson] will be saved from these white fishermen.'[45] Thus by 1890, Lake Winnipeg Indians were demanding an end to the commercial encroachment on their fisheries.

At Berens River in the summer of 1890, the chief asked the fishing company to remove its nets; as well, some members of the band had planned to cut the company's sturgeon nets. Schultz responded to this political crisis by visiting Berens River where he met Indians from Berens River, Poplar River, and Black River. Apparently, the threat by the Indian agent to take the Indians to Fort Garry 'in irons' had prevented the Indians from acting; they nonetheless informed Schultz that 'the young men were determined to go and cut the nets adrift to give a chance for a few fish to come inside the mouth of the river where we could catch them.'[46] Schultz, after listening to their concerns, informed the Indians that they had no right to cut the nets, that the Indian agent should have prevented them from doing so and furthermore that should they break the law 'the arm of the law is long enough and strong enough to reach you here if necessary or in your winter hunting grounds.'[47] The Indians suggested that the large fishing companies should fish the deeper parts of the lake and could not understand why the well-equipped white fishermen 'come to spread his nets just at our foot, and take away the food from our children's mouths?'[48] Thus, the continued encroachment of commercial companies on Native nearshore fisheries caused the Indians to consider firm action in order to protect their subsistence rights. The meeting came to a conclusion when Schultz assured the Indians that he would report exactly what they had said and that 'the Government at Ottawa will give all reasonable complaints their fullest consideration.'[49]

Investigating Resource Conflicts

In the summer of 1890 Samuel Wilmot, Fisheries Department, investigated the fishing conditions on Lake Winnipeg. The decision to hold this investigation was a result of considerable pressure from both Indians and their agents. Moreover, some 'leading citizens' of the province were concerned about the fishery and believed that 'means should be instituted to stay this too rapid destruction of fish by judicious regulations, which whilst protecting the fish, will not too seriously interfere with the fishing industries of the country.'[50] The arguments of the fishing companies rested largely on a simplistic comparison between the fishing potential of Lake Winnipeg and the rate of exploitation of the Great Lakes. The fishing companies, the Winnipeg Board of Trade, and the local officials of the Fisheries Department expressed common ambitions and opposed regulation. Fisheries Inspector McQueen rejected the claim that the decline of fish populations in the south end of Lake Winnipeg was related to commercial companies, arguing that the companies never really fished there. McQueen also argued that commercial fishing provided an important source of employment.[51] Wilmot viewed over-exploitation as a problem limited to areas where whitefish congregated prior to spawning, but he basically agreed with the Indians that 'a gradual but steady depletion of the whitefish product of Lake Winnipeg [is] going on, from the effects of the present system of fishing in certain parts of the Lake.'[52] Apparently, the fish companies began the season fishing the north end of the lake and then, at the end of August, moved their nets to the entrance of the Little Saskatchewan River. This, of course, prevented the passage of whitefish to the spawning grounds of Lake St. Martin. Hence, Wilmot recommended closing off Sturgeon Bay (at the mouth of Little Saskatchewan River) and other parts of the lake to commercial fishing (see Figure 8.1). Wilmot stated in no uncertain terms that 'commercial fishing of any description should be wholly excluded from this bay [Sturgeon Bay].'[53]

The state employed a pluralistic harmonizing approach to resolve the resource conflict between Indians and the large companies. Wilmot outlined this strategy whereby 'the Government should meet this subject in the spirit of reciprocity; as between the requirements of the Indian, the settler and the fish trader each have their rights and are entitled to full consideration.'[54] This mistaken notion suggests that a variety of 'resource-users' have similar claims to the fishery. Wilmot was agreeable to providing the Indians with exclusive fishing grounds – a suggestion that did not become policy. However, when asked to report on the advisability of providing the Indians bands with more capital to fish, he commented: 'It would be undesirable that Indians should be supplied with large boats and longer nets in order to fish in open or deeper parts of the lake. If the Indians desire to fish in waters outside their reserves, or other waters set apart for them, they place themselves in competition with other fishermen, and should therefore make their own provision for such outside fishing.'[55] This argument overlooked the unfairness of the existing competition between

American-financed companies and Native subsistence rights. Wilmot's rejection of the idea of capitalizing Native fishermen stemmed from an 'evenhanded' approach to resource conflicts. Eventually, control over capital would determine who would control the fisheries; Indian Affairs did not provide Indians with enough capital to challenge the large companies. (Net twine, provided as a treaty right, was intended to support a small-scale fishery.)

The extent to which commercial companies were solely responsible for resource depletion is not easily quantified. However, Wilmot concluded that 'if the improvident system of commercial fishing practised by fishing and trading corporations be allowed to prevail, as at present, the whitefish wealth of the lakes of the North-West will soon become exhausted.'[56] Extinction of the whitefish was not the immediate problem. The capital-intensive fishing companies were not facing this prospect. In contrast, Indians had limited access to and ownership of technology (capital) and as such could not afford to move to new fishing grounds. Their first desire was to maintain the subsistence nearshore fishery close to their reserves. The companies, equipped with steam-powered tugs, could move to new fishing grounds further out on Lake Winnipeg and to the north end of the lake. Declining production had economic and social effects since the available Indian technology failed to yield fish in the same quantities as during the earlier period of subsistence-based fisheries.

The prospect of depletion in the late 1880s contrasts with Fisheries official W.T. Urquhart's impression some twenty years earlier: 'Yet nowhere, not even in those waters where the white fish [*sic*] are most largely taken is there any sensible diminution in the supply. In some places in Lake Winnipeg, indeed, which have been fished year after year it has been found that the white fish have shifted their spawning grounds; but in no lake or river of the North West do I hear that they are becoming scarce, or that they are more difficult to obtain than they were years ago.'[57] Urquhart had not anticipated the development of an export-oriented industry. During the decades that followed the treaties, subsistence rights were at the centre of a major political struggle for Indians. The government attempted to accommodate all of the various interests during a period marked by the dominance of commercial use of fish over subsistence use; but in the end, the state provided inadequate protection for Indian fisheries. Some of the suggestions made by Samuel Wilmot of the Fisheries Department became regulations, such as a commercial and domestic licensing system and some confinement of where companies could operate. The government could have redressed the imbalance in the regional economy by providing Indians with sufficient capital to engage in commercial fishing. In this sense the opportunity for Natives to benefit from a commercial fishery was lost. Although Wilmot attempted to regulate the fishing industry, he could not stop the process of the expanding commercialization of this resource.

The consequence of the extension of the market and the alienation of Aboriginal title resulted in a loss of control over a regional fishery. The rapid commercialization of fisheries – through a type of privatization of common property – not only threatened subsistence rights and the domestic economy, but also diverted labour to commodity production. As in the fur trade, Natives became primary producers.

9
'A Great Future Awaits This Section of Northern Manitoba': Economic Boom and Native Labour

In October of 1888, a Winnipeg newspaper, the *Manitoba Daily Press*, announced: 'Trade On Lake Winnipeg Export Will Be Close Upon $300,000.'[1] Some 1,000 railway cars of freight had been shipped from Lake Winnipeg's Selkirk terminal; included were 40,000 railway ties, fish, and lumber worth $90,000.[2] The paper reported that 'In fish, lumber, ties and cord wood, the export trade from Lake Winnipeg at the close of the present season will exceed $300,000' and went on to boost the region: 'Considering the infancy of the lumber and fish trade a great future awaits this northern section of Manitoba.'[3] In pre-wheat boom Manitoba, the northward movement of a commercial fish and lumber frontier was a major economic boom for the province. The employment effects of these industries were not left unnoticed: 'It is estimated that in the lumber, fisheries and in the boats six hundred men, white people and Indians have found employment this year.'[4] A rail link to Selkirk encouraged lumber and fish production, and the year 1888 marked the crossing of a commercial threshold. The development of these industries, closely related to the expansion of steamboating, transformed the regional economy. The organization of capital in steamboating, fisheries, and lumbering was closely interrelated since these industries were complementary economic activities.

As reported by this newspaper article, Natives were a part of this new staple economy. A staple is an economic term that denotes the export of raw materials from a region. The focus on the production, transport, and export of staples has been an important concept in Canadian economic history. Native people participated in a labour pool for an economy based on resources that only two decades previously had been exclusively their property. These new staple industries also represented a diversification of incomes, and thus Natives were no longer solely dependent upon the fur trade. During this period, the experience of Indians in the Interlake contrasts sharply with our image of the Plains Indians as a destitute and marginalized people. For this reason, it is necessary to reconstruct the economy during the reserve transition period. The mistaken notion that Native people have not made important contributions to Canada's economic development is similar to the idea that no Native would alter tradition by participating in the white man's economy, because both viewpoints are contradicted by the historical record.

Transportation and Staples

In the subarctic, transportation innovations were closely related to the demand for staples by metropolitan markets. Steamboating on Lake Winnipeg and the Saskatchewan River originated with the Hudson's Bay Company's effort to reduce costs. In 1880, the Company distanced itself from directly operating steamboats when it linked up with financing from Scotland, Montreal, and Winnipeg to form the North West Navigation Co. (NWN Co. operated on Lake Winnipeg) and the Winnipeg and Western Transportation Co. (WWT Co. operated on the Saskatchewan River). The HBC came to this advantageous arrangement by exchanging its steamers for equity and a freight rate rebate; but it also co-opted a potential rival.[5] With the completion of the railway in 1885, steamboats were less vital to the movement of furs and goods, and the Company's interest in steamboats waned. In contrast, Captain Peter McArthur and Captain William Robinson, who had been involved in the NWN Co., made steamboating a dynamic feature of the regional economy of the Manitoba Interlake.[6] Numerous vessels were launched after 1885 because the region was essentially a transportation backwater. Railways did not compete with steamboats; instead new staples were brought by steam vessels to railheads at Selkirk, Winnipegosis, and The Pas.

Steamboat *Grand Rapids* at Black River, Lake Winnipeg, 1929 (PAM)

The tendency for rail development to displace steamboats to new frontiers did not occur here, and steamboats operated well into the 1930s. Terminals, harbours, and fuelling stations associated with steamboating are displayed by Figure 9.1. Clearly, post-1885 steamboating was not based on long-distance freight but was part of a system geared to extracting resources. The HBC allowed small capitalists like McArthur and Robinson to take over steamboating, but in the long run its own position within the regional economy was eroded. Steamboat ownership facilitated the production of fisheries and lumber, and in commercial terms these new staples dwarfed fur returns.[7] Furthermore, these new staple industries competed with the HBC for Native labour.

William Robinson, after losing on investments in Selkirk real estate in the 1870s, built up a significant commercial empire based on Lake Winnipeg's natural wealth. By 1885, he had secured control over the North West Navigation Company. Robinson's relationship with Booth Fisheries rejuvenated his Selkirk boat yards. R. Barris described his progress: 'Methodically, William Robinson worked his way up both lakeshores buying out the independent fish interests and establishing a steamboat freighter system to relay fresh fish to new freezing plants at Selkirk. Similarly, the Robinson Lumber Company bought out weaker timber business adjacent to Lake Winnipeg, and initiated a lucrative market steamboating lumber south to railway contractors hungry for building planks, piling, and ties.'[8] Robinson operated fish stations and sawmills on Lake Winnipeg, and his Selkirk establishment included planing mills, a department store, icehouses and freezers, and a large fleet of lake boats. Barris concluded that Robinson's 'business sense had thrust deep into the richest resources of central Manitoba' and that he exploited every opportunity: 'Robinson had milked Lake Winnipeg of its fish, its lumber, its freight transport, and its cheap labour. He had muscled out the minor lumber operations around the lake; he commanded the majority of the lake's boatmen; he managed Booth fish interests as his own; and he had wrested control of North West Navigation from his partner, Peter McArthur. Robinson had jostled and schemed for a monopoly on Manitoba waterways, and won.'[9]

Robinson's diverse economic concerns were paralleled by a variety of economic strategies. His connection with the NWN Co. was a link to the old fur trade, and Native labour at Grand Rapids was managed for him by the HBC. As with other staple capitalists, he saw the need to extend his economic activities backward – and so his boat yards built the vessels used by his other operations. His fishermen and lumberjacks spent their incomes in his stores. His lumber was consumed by a provincial market, but as a comprador, an intermediary, Robinson's fish production was exported to the American market. And he remained loyal to his patrons, the Booth

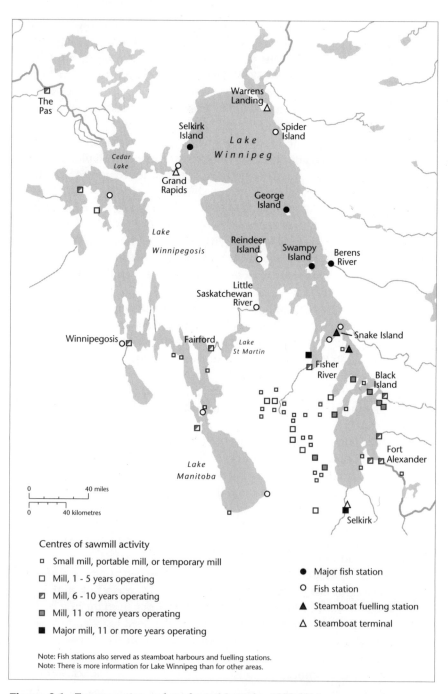

Figure 9.1 Transportation and staples in Manitoba, 1870-1915

Fisheries Co. Robinson's importance and social stature could be measured against the likes of the HBC commissioner C.C. Chipman.

If Lake Winnipeg was Robinson's preserve, lakes Manitoba and Winnipegosis provided a similar base for Peter McArthur. In this area, the resources did not provide the same scale of operations as Lake Winnipeg. McArthur's sawmilling and freighting operations on Lake Manitoba commenced in the 1870s. In the late 1890s, he shifted his activities to Lake Winnipegosis. The opening up of Lake Winnipegosis country to lumbering coincided with the surge in commercial fishing. McArthur left the fisheries to the Armstrong/Booth interests and built up his Standard Lumber Company at Winnipegosis.[10] This extended lumbering to the north shore of Lake Winnipegosis. The completion of a spur line to Winnipegosis facilitated exports because it was not feasible for steamboats to move between lakes Winnipegosis and Manitoba.

Although the Saskatchewan River had provided a route to move freight by steamboats to the Northwest since 1870s, it was not until the early twentieth century that steam vessels were used to seriously export local resources. At this time, a lumbering industry began at The Pas. About 1908, Captain Horatio Ross established Ross Navigation at The Pas, and growth in the resource economy supported an expansion of his fleet. Barris described the influence of steam vessels: 'At Ross Navigation warehouses and offices, clerks juggled the industrial future of the north country on paper; all money, men

Fishing station at Matheson Island, 1924 (PAM)

and machines in the North seemed to lead to Ross Navigation ledgers.'[11] Steamboats facilitated the initial development of a mining industry. Ross Navigation vessels brought ore from Mandy Mine (Flin Flon) to railhead. The expansion of steamboating came late at The Pas, but it served to open up the country for exporting staples.

The HBC introduced steampower in order to reduce its dependence on Native labour. This new mode of transport did not completely displace Native workers, and an increase in the volume of freight and the need for fuel stimulated a demand for some additional labour. The historical record indicates that there was a Native presence in steamboating. Observers recorded that Natives were skilled at steamboat work. In 1915, H.A. Bayfield noted that on the Nelson River 'the half breed skipper of the tug showed remarkable skill in handling his boat in this intricate waterway.'[12] The vagaries of the Saskatchewan River made navigation extremely difficult, and Natives from Cumberland House were known as skilled pilots. On Lake Winnipeg, one Indian held the rank of a master on a large steamer, and another Indian held the same position on a smaller steamer.[13] Barris noted that on the Saskatchewan River, a Metis in charge of the boat was a first mate, his son was the navigator, and the crew included twenty Metis. Many deck crews included Natives.[14] Ross Navigation employed Natives, and Indian crews built some of his vessels. The expansion of steamboating after 1885 resulted in several employment opportunities for Natives: both as skilled labour (piloting, boat building) and general labour (deck hands, wharf and warehouse workers, and woodcutters).

When Norway House Indians were sent to Georges Island and Doghead to cut steamer cordwood in 1875, it marked the beginning of a commercialization of a common property resource. Natives engaged in the exploitation of forests in a variety of ways; cutting logs for sawmills was a major change to the economic landscape. They also worked in bush camps or on an individual basis to provide ties for railways as well as cordwood for steamers and urban markets. The earliest instance of lumbering came in 1876, when logs were cut on Black Island for a sawmill at Bad Throat (Manigotogan) River. Native participation in this new resource industry was a viable economic adjustment in the post-1870 period.

Sawmill operations in northern Manitoba were limited to Lake Manitoba, Lake Winnipegosis, and the southern portion of Lake Winnipeg (see Figure 9.1). A southern demand for lumber increased as settlers improved their houses and as Winnipeg grew. Railways and branch lines generated a strong demand for bush work. In 1895, lumber from Lake Winnipeg amounted to 43 per cent of Manitoba production but satisfied only 8 per cent of demand.[15] Lumbering, especially on Lake Winnipeg, exhibited a high degree of instability in terms of ownership and duration of operations. Sawmills frequently changed owners, went into bank receivership, or suspended operations. The use of portable sawmills was another approach to Lake Winnipeg forests. Even this mobile capital was not necessarily cost effective; the records of Indian Affairs noted in 1917 that portable sawmills are usually a business failure in Manitoba.[16]

Lumbering created a demand for labour largely met by Natives. Reserves such as Fort Alexander, Hollow Water, and Fisher River had a long attachment to the forestry industry. In 1882, the firm Drake and Rutherford wanted 'to build our mill on the Indian Reserve ... they [the Indians] are very anxious that we would build there [Fisher River] as it would be a great benefit to their giving employment to any number that would work both winter and summer.'[17] In 1883, Inspector McColl stated: 'From fifty to seventy-five Indians are employed at the three saw-mills in the vicinity of the reserve, and receive from $25 to $30 a month.'[18] Indian Agent MacKay noted that the economic impact at Fisher River was not simply the result of bushwork:

> The success of the band is, however, in a measure due to their having three lumbering mills in the vicinity of their reserve, where they are able to get work as lumber men, sawyer, &c., at which I am told they are very good, and if required of them, they could run the mills themselves, without the aid of white men. These lumbering companies have rendered great assistance to the band, they pay them good wages, sell them lumber and goods cheap, and often teach and aid them with their gardens. The majority of the men are able to do carpenter work, such as building houses and boats, making furniture, &c.[19]

Methodist minister Fred Stevens recorded that, with the appearance of a lumbering industry at Fisher River, the Indians 'soon adapted themselves to this kind of work and became expert lumberjacks,' and he indicated that Robinson had said: 'I have employed Scots from Glengarry, French Canadians from Quebec, Swedes from Sweden and all kins [kinds?] of lumberjacks, but the Fisher River Indians are better than any others.'[20]

Fisher River was not the only reserve that provided a labour pool for lumbering. Reverend Young visited Fort Alexander in 1882 and 'found a considerable number of tents there occupied by the families of Indians working at the mill.'[21] Young noted that the mill was worked day and night, that only three Canadians were working at the mill, and that the 'Indians were engaged in the most intricate portions of the work, feeding the saws, working with machine like quickness and precision.'[22] Incomes from lumbering were attractive. The annual report for Indian Affairs in 1882 indicated that not all the annuities were paid to the Hollow Water band since those 'employed at the reserve in Mr. Dick's sawmill, refused to go after theirs [annuities], stating that the amount received was not worth the time lost in going after it.'[23] In 1884, Indian Agent S.J. Jackson stated that among the Hollow Water band 'a number of the younger men work in the logging camps during the winter months. They are valued by the lumber companies and are in great demand.'[24] When Bayfield visited Bad Throat River, he noted that 'a large gang of half breeds and Indians were working' at the mill.[25] Bush work may not have split the male from the family since Jackson stated: 'In the winter a few go into the camps where the logging is done, as a rule taking their families with them.'[26] In 1909, when a mill had been established at Black River, Inspector J. Semmens reported that 'these people, who have long looked for employment, have found themselves in the midst of plenty and comfort.'[27] Indian involvement in lumbering was not confined to Lake Winnipeg. Sawmills at Fairford and Winnipegosis often employed Natives. The reports of travellers, missionaries, and Indian agents all observed that Natives provided skilled and general labour for the lumbering industry.

Native income from woodcutting included earnings from making cordwood and railway ties. In 1883, the Fort Alexander and Brokenhead bands worked at taking out ties and demand was strong: 'The men had plenty of work all winter and most of the summer at good wages, taking out railway ties up the Broken Head river [sic].'[28] In 1892, two to three dollars a day could be earned cutting cordwood in the Clandeboye agency. Indian Agent Jackson described how woodcutting influenced the spatial dimension of the Native economy: 'A number of families from this band [Jackhead] are at the present time cutting cord-wood on an island (Snake) about thirty miles southeast of the reserve; they are cutting at so much the cord, for a firm that contracts to supply wood to the different steamboat companies which navigate Lake Winnipeg. The man in charge at the island informs me that they give work for the year round to a large number of the Indians who live on the adjacent reserves.'[29] The expansion of the fishing sector necessitated an increased demand for steamer cordwood. Snake or Matheson Island was an important fuelling station and a gathering point for Native labour. Jackson's report indicates that labour was paid by the amount produced rather than on a time basis. Even as late as 1914, cordwood and railway tie work was still important to Clandeboye agency Indians.

Historical records show that instability in the lumbering industry adversely affected Natives. In 1884, the removal of a mill from the mouth of the Winnipeg River was 'a great loss to this place [Fort Alexander], and the Indians only now realize the benefit they derive from it in the way of work and wages.'[30] In 1889, HBC records for Fort Alexander indicated that Natives could not pay their bills because the mills had been shut down. Similarly, for Hollow Water, the department records stated that 'the Indians got considerable employment in connection with that Mill. The Mill has, however, been moved away and Indians deprived of that source of employment.'[31] In 1886, the annual report explained that 'since lumbering has been abandoned on the reserve' the Hollow Water band 'are compelled to resort largely to their former occupation of fishing and hunting for their subsistence.'[32] Reversion to the old economy was not the only available response to a mill closing. Seasonal movements to places where other work was available occurred in this period, thus migration was another response to mill shutdowns. In 1890, Indian Agent A. MacKay explained that the closing of the Fisher River mill meant that 'Indians cannot get so much work to do as formerly, and have to go a considerable distance to find employment.'[33] With this observation on the Black River band, Jackson revealed a major weakness in the regional economy in 1904: 'The men work in the bush during the winter at the lumber camps, and make quite a lot of money in this way. This cannot be called an employment that is likely to be permanent, as the timber is being cut so fast that the work will be done in a very few years in this particular locality.'[34] When the focus of lumbering operations shifted northward, southern reserves such as St. Peters, Brokenhead, and Fort Alexander still engaged in woodcutting by collecting deadwood or cutting cordwood on reserve land for the home-fuel market. In 1914, Indian Agent Colcleugh recorded: 'Brokenhead Indians request to cut 1000 cords. This is the only way these Indians have of making a living during the winter.'[35]

The reserve settlement pattern suited the needs of the Interlake lumbering industry. Reserves provided sites for mills, reserve timber supplemented Crown timber berths, and settled Indians formed a nearby labour pool. There are no indications that Native incomes in this industry were especially low; this small-scale and unstable frontier industry could probably not afford the additional costs of bringing in non-resident workers. The lumbering industry that developed at The Pas did not follow the pattern established on Lake Winnipeg. There is no evidence that Natives were excluded from employment with the Finger and The Pas lumber companies; however, these firms developed in association with railway and mining development, which attracted a non-resident labour force.[36]

New Staples and the Changing Economic Landscape

The cultural landscape of the Interlake changed with economic development in the post-1870 period. With the exploitation of new staples, the appearance of settlement was no longer defined by just fur post and mission. Furthermore, the existing arrangement of posts and reserves did not meet all of the requirements of the new industries. Thus, Matheson Island

Staple industries at Black River, Lake Winnipeg, 1929. Note fish plant, cord wood, gill-net racks, sailboats, and lumber. (PAM)

was settled as a response to the needs of steamboating and commercial fishing. Nonetheless, reserves provided sites for many sawmills and fish stations, and places such as Grand Rapids and St. Peters became major labour pools for lake industries.

New settlements, steamboat harbours, and fish stations tended to locate on islands. In 1899, Bayfield described Selkirk Island: 'This Hamlet consists of about a dozen large fish freezers, as many rough shacks for the men to sleep in, three or four boarding houses ... and about a dozen tepees and a poplar dock.'[37] Selkirk Island, George Island, Moose Island, and Spider Island became resource hamlets, largely occupied during the summer fishing season. Native families moved to these locales, and Bayfield estimated that 200 Indians and whites stayed on Selkirk Island. In 1900, the lieutenant-governor of Keewatin, J.C. Patterson, toured Lake Winnipeg fish stations and was 'surprised to find extensive and commodious docks built, with stores, dwellings, large freezers, and everything which would indicate a prospect of permanency for the industry,' and at Selkirk Island 'there is a large establishment, in fact quite a village.'[38] Most of these island fish stations remained seasonal resource hamlets. On Lake Winnipegosis, however, lumbering, fishing, and a spur line made Winnipegosis a more settled hamlet. Here a sawmill and fishermen's shacks were joined by a railway station house, a new HBC post, stores, warehouses, hotels, and churches.

A fishing industry resulted in the spread of small stations, and steamboating needed fuelling stations (Snake Island and Bullshead) and break-in-bulk points (Grand Rapids and Warrens Landing). In addition to terminals and fishing facilities, Warrens Landing included a guest house, along with Indian houses and tents. For a while, Grand Rapids became a very important location in the new staple economy, whereas under the fur trade regime it had been a minor post. Indian Agent Reader explained its unique economic role: 'Situated at the mouth of the Saskatchewan, where the arrival of steamers in summer and the cutting of cordwood and ice in winter afford the Indians ample means of supporting themselves, this is perhaps one of the most important places in the district. Consequently daily labour is gradually superseding the hunting pursuits.'[39] Native clergyman J. Sinclair stated that no other place on the lower Saskatchewan 'has so many advantages as Grand Rapids, a man can earn a dollar every day all the year round.'[40] Native labour was required in the winter for 5,000 tons of ice and 400 cords of wood, and summer employment entailed fishing and working on steamboats and wharves. Ice was cut up and then stored in an icehouse for the summer fish season. When the focus of the fishing industry shifted northeast from Selkirk Island, Grand Rapids ceased to be so significant and the demand for labour declined. Cordwood and ice were still needed, and Poplar River Indians became part of an employment scheme previously experienced by the Grand Rapids Natives. Indian Agent C.C. Calverley reported in 1909 that 'at least $5,000 can be made by this band in cutting wood, putting up ice and fishing for the fish companies.'[41] At this time, settlement now included docks for steamboats and two masted yawls, racks for drying fishnets, stacks of cordwood and lumber, and large icehouses. The cultural landscape of this part of Manitoba does not conform to our images of a prairie province. This difference is reinforced by the observations of visitors to the region who never failed to note the active role played by Natives in the staple economy.

In terms of the provincial economy, fishing and lumbering were dynamic new industries that represented a push northward by southern economic forces. In contrast to the promises and assurances made by the Crown's treaty negotiators, the frontier closed in fast. The economic landscape of the fur and mission era was modified by steamboat harbours, fish stations, and sawmills. Steamboats suited the economic needs of the region, and the population of Lake Winnipeg gained a mobility that did not exist with the HBC's York boat system. Native peoples played an important and active role in sustaining the economic growth vital to the provincial economy. During this economic boom, local labour, not non-resident whites, was the main source of workers for frontier resource capitalists. The ease with which Native peoples moved back and forth between subsistence and available seasonal wage labour in the new staple industries worked to the advantage of both Natives and capitalists. Modern social overhead costs associated with capitalist industries were not borne by the likes of Robinson and McCarthy. These industries did not incur the expense of bringing in an alien, non-resident labour force. Subsistence resources and support from the Department of Indian Affairs (treaty supplies and annuities) reduced the expenses usually associated with a wage economy. The development of transport, commercial fishing, and lumbering also served to diversify the economy of the northern Interlake and Lake Winnipeg region.

10

'They Make a Comfortable Living': Economic Change and Incomes

Diversified economies provided relative economic security for a number of Indian bands during the early reserve transition era (1870-1914). For several decades, Indians from around lakes Winnipeg, Manitoba, St. Martin, and Winnipegosis were active participants in a rapidly changing economy – an economy quite different from the fur trade regime. Wage labour and a wide variety of subsistence and commercial resources combined to create remarkably flexible and innovative approaches to providing for family needs. Specialization developed among bands within the region and between members of the same band. Indian participation in commercial fishing, lumbering, and wage labour was not welcomed by the Hudson's Bay Company since its monopoly over Indian labour power was eroded. Similarly, the Department of Indian Affairs was ambivalent about Indian involvement in the booming regional economy. Although diversified incomes meant that the department was spared the expense of rations and relief, policies tended to stress isolation of Indians and reserve agriculture.

Diversification of Native Economic Activities

In the post-1870 period, involvement in commercial fishing, lumbering, and reserve agriculture were not the only changes in the Native economy. A variety of other activities (farm labour, commercialized gathering, and wage labour) represented a further diversification of the Native economy. Indian Agent Swinford described the diversity and security in the Manitowapah agency:

A lot of money is earned by the Indians of all the reserves at fishing during the winter, there is also a good deal earned at hunting, trapping, digging seneca root, picking berries and working as boatmen on the lakes. Many of them work for settlers during haying, harvest and threshing time; others work at the sawmill at Winnipegosis, and in the lumber woods, and this year a number have been working at the big government canal at Fairford River. A few are still skilled at building boats and birch bark canoes, and make money at it; others are good at making snow-shoes, light sleighs (jumpers), flat sleighs and such like; but there is one thing they can all do the year round, so that they never want for food, and that is catch fish.[1]

Clearly, Indians from this agency were economically active in the early reserve transition era. For Sandy Bay in 1896, Martineau added that among women 'butter making is ... developing into an occupation.'[2] In 1898, McColl recorded that many Clandeboye Indians were 'employed as voyageurs, guides to tourists, at fisheries, lumber camps and sawmills, cutting cordwood, hunting &c., while others are farming, stock-raising and hay-cutting, from all of which they make a comfortable living.'[3] McColl drew special attention to the St. Peters reserve, which adjoined the town of Selkirk and which was at 'the head of navigation of Lake Winnipeg, where the Indians can find employment not only at the mills, but at loading and unloading barges and steamers.'[4] On Lake Winnipeg, lumbering was more important at the south end, while commercial fishing was based at the north end. By 1900, commercial fishing had reached Norway House, but bands north of this point, especially in the unceded territory, were generally confined to a fur trade economy. Figure 10.1 displays a classification of local Native economies at the turn of the century. Clearly, Indian economic adjustments by 1900 had interacted with external forces to create highly differentiated local economies. Indians from bands in the ceded territories had more ways to earn incomes than the Indians north of the 1875 Treaty Five boundaries. Bands in the ceded territory had more diversified and more complex economies. The numerous accounts recording the demand for Native labour are summed up by Semmens's report in 1905: 'The fish companies, the mill-owners, travellers and explorers and steamboat-owners, all seek for help from our native population.'[5]

In Clandeboye and Manitowapah agencies, gathering for the market was added to the reserve economy. Deadwood, hay, seneca root, wild fruit, and berries were the main products of commercialized gathering. Brokenhead Indians in 1882 responded to new demands created by staple industries: 'The hay along the lake is good, and they have put up three times as much as they require. Last winter they sold about twenty-five tons to lumbermen and received a good price for it, which has the effect of causing them to make more this summer.'[6] Indian Agent Muckle reported in 1885 that the St. Peters Indians 'who put up hay for sale got a good price for it (from three to six dollars a ton), and as the making of hay in this part of the country costs something under a dollar a ton, they were well paid for their work.'[7] The gathering of seneca root for a market dates back to the 1880s as Muckle

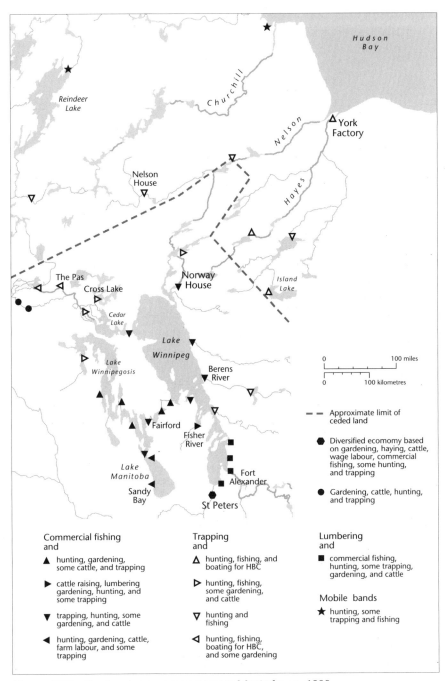

Figure 10.1 Band and reserve economies in Manitoba, ca. 1900
(CSP, 1899-1900, 'Indian Affairs')

reported that the Indians of Clandeboye 'sold between $1,000 and $5,000 worth of Seneca snake root (Wene-se-kase, the Indians call it) this summer, and made from $1 to $3 a day in trade, digging it.'[8] The demand for seneca root (needed for medical purposes), and the skill required to identify and to dig the root, would maintain this type of commercialized gathering as a Native economic activity for decades. In 1886, Muckle noted that St. Peters Indians had expanded their gathering activities: 'The people here have a new industry, which brings them cash at the expense of neglecting their homes, that is berry picking. They go out in boat loads, to Elk Island and other places along the shores of Lake Winnipeg, picking blueberries, cran-berries and plums. One man in one week, picked an ox-load of plums; he took them to Winnipeg, and sold them for $40.'[9] The combined gathering of different products had important income effects. In 1892, the annual report on St. Peters stated: 'Permits were given to sell dead or fallen timber, of which they sold nearly seven hundred cords, and were paid for the same, in good substantial clothing and provisions. By this, and the sale of about one thousand tons of hay, the farmers of the band passed a fairly good winter, and managed to supply themselves with seed grain and potatoes.'[10] Gathering went on regularly, and McColl reported in 1899 that Indians 'gather tons of huckleberries, raspberries, Saskatoon berries, cranberries and strawberries, which are in constant demand in the market' and that 'thou-sands of cords of wood are annually sold at Selkirk, and a large quantity of hay is also disposed of to dealers, which nets them a handsome amount.'[11] For reserves on the southern periphery of the study area proximate to a market, Indians responded quickly to demands for deadwood, hay, seneca root, and wild fruit.

For some bands, off-reserve farm labour became an important compo-nent of the post-1870 economy. Indian Commissioner Simpson reported in 1871 that 'in the Province of Manitoba, where labour is scarce, Indians give great assistance in gathering in the crops' and 'I found many farmers whose employes [sic] were nearly all Indians.'[12] In particular, Indians from Manitowapah and Clandeboye agencies provided labour for white farmers. Typically, the annual reports noted Indian participation in off-reserve farm labour, such as the example of Sandy Bay at the turn of the century: 'The greater part of the adult male portion of the band come down to work in the Manitoba grain fields during harvest and threshing.'[13] This was seen as distracting from reserve development; Indian Agent Jackson argued that the Ebb and Flow band 'go out to work with the farmers a good deal and neglect their own places.'[14] Similarly, Swinford recorded that Indians 'can get such steady work at good wages with the settlers that it is difficult to keep them on their reserves long enough to look after their own little farms in a proper manner.'[15] In this sense, farm wage labour conflicted with reserve gardening and the policy priorities of the Department of Indian Affairs.

Prior to the opening of the Mandy Mine, mining did not have a big impact on the larger regional economy. Nonetheless, when mining activities appeared, Natives were drawn into this new industry. In the case of gypsum, the 1901 annual report for the Interior Department recorded that 'the Manitoba Union Mining Company, composed of Canadian and American capitalists, have staked out a large area of land valuable for this commodity and purpose developing the claims at an early date.'[16] By 1902, Indians from the Interlake were working at Gypsumville; with reference to the Fairford band in 1904, Swinford noted: 'The gypsum mine and mill are a regular Ophir to the Indians there, as they can get all the work they want winter and summer at good wages.'[17] The historical record does not establish the duration of Indian employment in this sector; however, reports on the Fairford, Little Saskatchewan, and St. Martin bands indicated that Indians were an important labour pool for the initial development of gypsum. Although prospecting activity actually preceded the extension of the Hudson Bay Railway, metal mining in the region began with the gold strike in 1911 in the area east of Lake Winnipeg. Not surprisingly, Indian Agent Colcleugh reported in 1916 that 'during the past winter quite a number of the Black River and Hollow Water River Indians have been working at the mines in the Rice Lake mining district.'[18] While mining was not as significant as lumbering and commercial fishing prior to 1915, Indian reserves again provided a convenient labour pool for this emerging sector of northern Manitoba's economy.

Native labour was also instrumental in the completion of infrastructure projects. Indian Agent McLean reported that Indians from the Peguis reserve worked out of the rail terminus of Arborg and 'are able to make good wages.'[19] In 1914, Indians in the Clandeboye agency were working on railway construction, and Fort Alexander Indians worked on power line construction. Most employment related to rail construction was provided by the Hudson Bay Railway. Some of The Pas band members were employed cutting out the right of way at the turn of the century. Natives were involved in the building of the railway to The Pas, a project that was completed in 1908. In 1907, Indian Agent Fischer recorded that 'a number earned a good deal of money during the past summer in connection with the railway construction and surveys.'[20] Inspector of Indian Agencies Jackson described the employment situation in 1912: 'Owing to the construction of the Hudson Bay railway, work will be plentiful for all the younger men of the band [The Pas] for the next two years of three, on the survey work as well as the construction, more especially in clearing the right of way and transporting supplies for the contractors.'[21] The Moose Lake band was close to the railway and thus: 'For the past two years the young men have been able to get all the work they wanted on that road, and have earned some money in that way.'[22] Fischer noted that construction-related employment meant that 'wages paid for labour have been high. A good many had potatoes for sale over and above their own needs, for which good prices were paid.'[23] Once again, Indians increased their agricultural efforts in response to the available market. As railway construction progressed, it incorporated Native labour from Norway House, Cross Lake, and Split Lake just as The Pas and Moose Lake Indians had experienced the frontier economy.[24] Apparently, for the railway construction, the strongest demand for Natives was for survey work and freighting goods. Most of this labour was boom related; however, Natives settled at railway towns (Wabowden, Thicket Portage, Pikwitonei, and Gillam). Natives played a vital, if forgotten, role in the building of this railway that shaped the future industrial economy of northern Manitoba.

The post-1870 regional economy had pronounced seasonal and spatial characteristics that were quite different from the fur trade regime. The settling of Indians on reserves represented a spatial change from the pre-treaty period. Unlike on the prairies, where the pass system was a form of social control to regulate Indian off-reserve movements, seasonal migrations to resources and for employment or wage incomes were the norm in the Interlake and northern Manitoba. Those bands still under a fur trade economy, largely in the non-ceded area, continued well established seasonal movements. Those Natives involved with the new resource industries made seasonal and spatial accommodations that represented important adjustments.

In a certain sense, the obvious diffusion or investment of frontier resource capital and the creation of wage incomes suggest the 'modernization' of the regional economy. Nonetheless, economic life was still heavily influenced by natural forces. In terms of labour time, subsistence activities did not necessarily conflict with wage labour since these activities could go on side-by-side (commercial and subsistence fishing). And when wage labour was not in demand, the labour force could find some of its sustenance from subsistence activities. The situation in 1881, as recorded by the annual report, demonstrated how natural forces could have negative effects on a seasonal economy:

> The Indians of Manitoba and of a large portion of the district of Keewatin, suffered considerably during the last winter, owing to a combination of causes, among which be mentioned, as respects the Indians of Lake Winnipeg, the partial failure in most places, and total failure in many, of the fisheries; the scarcity of muskrats, which form a large portion of their means

of subsistence; the paucity of fur bearing animals generally; the early flight of the wild fowl, owing to the unusually early setting in of winter; the flooding during the open season, by an unprecedented rising of the lake, of many of their planting grounds, and the consequent destruction of the most of their crops; and an early frost which blighted the crops that were not destroyed by the high water.[25]

This observation was made prior to the establishment of a more diversified economy. Clearly, a seasonal wage would at times provide protection over the failure of subsistence resources. The new staple industries provided complementary demands for labour. As Indian Agent T.H. Carter reported, among the Fisher River band 'some are employed by the fish companies on Lake Winnipeg during the summer and in the lumber camps in the winter.'[26] For some, lumbering with winter bush work and summer sawmilling represented the greatest continuity of employment among the various sectors of the regional economy.

The diversified economy in the post-1870 period required seasonal movement. Figure 10.2 shows some of the movements for seasonal employment between 1890 and 1915. Farm labour, steamboating, lumbering, commercial fishing, and railway construction required Natives to migrate. Such migration patterns were not the same as the mobility demanded by the trapping economy. Prior to the railway, The Pas band scattered over a 300 square mile area from October to May in family hunting/trapping groups. In 1914, Jackson stated: 'A large number of the younger men of this band [The Pas] are away a greater part of their time, both summer and winter, with survey and prospecting parties, and in this way earn a large amount of money during the year.'[27] Thus, a specific portion of the population (young males) left the band, did not gather with the band in accordance with tradition through the spring/summer season, and earned money instead of paying off HBC credit.

Clearly, participation in wage labour required adjustments. In 1887, Indian Agent Muckle described Fort Alexander Indians starting for fall fishing: 'It was quite a scene to see boat after boat with all sails set (loaded with men, women and children) running away before the wind for the lake, all happy looking and comfortable. The majority will return just before the ice sets in, but some few families will remain at some favoured spot for fishing and hunting during the winter.'[28] In this instance, entire families moved for commercial income; however, not all band members followed an identical resource strategy during the winter. Later there was a tendency for seasonal movements to separate family members. In the Manitowapah agency in 1905, Indian Agent Marlatt explained that 'formerly, it was the custom for an Indian when going away to hunt or labour to take his family with him,

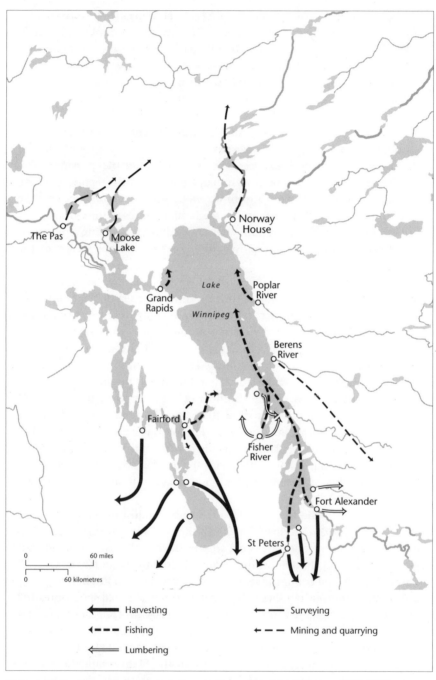

Figure 10.2   Seasonal movements for employment in Manitoba, ca. 1890-1915

this is gradually dying out and the family is left at home to go to school, and attend to the cattle and gardens.'[29] After treaty payments, the Berens River band scattered: some of the members engaged in subsistence hunting while others were attracted to the commercial fisheries. The St. Peters band were a particularly mobile group of workers. Semmens leaves no doubt as to their importance to the Lake Winnipeg economy:

> As soon as the waters flow free, all the young men of the tribe are in demand as boatmen. Steamers, schooners, fishing smacks and tugs must all be manned and for the most part from St. Peter's. This draws so heavily on the vim and muscle of the reserve that only the infirm are left to care of the women and children and carry on farm work. This continues until October. At this time comes the winter draft of men to the shanties and lumber mills, where they are employed from November until April.[30]

In 1915, H.A. Bayfield, while travelling on the Northern Fish Company's 'Wolverine,' observed that many Natives got on at Selkirk and started out for work at the George Island fish station.[31] As the commercial fishing industry expanded into the north end of Lake Winnipeg, Native labour followed in the wake of this resource frontier. Similarly, when sawmills relocated, Indians migrated to where work was available. Thus, the new staple industries promoted seasonal employment that often required Natives to migrate. The transformation of the natural resources of Lake Winnipeg into commercial wealth created a strong demand for Native labour.

The records of the Hudson's Bay Company verify the observations made by Indian agents and others that Natives played an important role in the regional economy. The redirection of labour from the production of fur to frontier resource industries could not have gone on without comment in the HBC business records. Chief Factor R. Ross alerted the Company to the developing problem as early as 1883: 'A new disturbing element is now beginning to be felt in this business of this district through the establishment of saw mills and lumbering operations as far North as Dog Head and Fisher River ... a good many of ... [the] Indians are giving up hunting and are going to work in the lumber camps.'[32] The impact was serious enough for Ross to suggest that the 'situation unquestionably demanded a remodeling of our system of business without further delay.'[33] The HBC Inspection Report for 1887 noted that 'the Indians at St. Peters are spoken of as being amongst the best off and most prosperous in the country' and that Lake Winnipeg Indians 'appear also to be well off; in addition to hunting, there being employment at the Lumber Camps[,] Saw mills and at Fishing.'[34] Similarly, in 1889, it was recorded that the Berens River Indians 'appear to be comparatively well off. Many of them are employed by the fishing cos. on

Swampy Island and other points in the neighborhood. Are lazy as hunt-ers.'[35] Spatial and economic changes at Manitoba House were recorded in this report: 'The Indian hunt at this place is not much at its best as the greater part of the Furs are caught by half-breeds; the Indians are getting lazy and indolent, in fact those on the Reserves are useless; there are only one or two families that follow the old style of hunting that is camping out and moving from one place to another.'[36]

Apparently, reserve settlement and development did not complement fur production. Often the HBC had to rely on Metis as commercial trappers, whose economic options were more restricted than treaty Indians. Refer-ences to laziness and indolence do not reflect an Indian work ethic at all but demonstrate that Indian commitment to producing furs for the HBC was on the decline. The term indolent appears in HBC records when Natives are no longer dependent upon the Company for economic security. Obviously, the terms indolence and laziness are contradicted by other HBC observa-tions regarding the energetic and active involvement of Indians in the wage economy. Again, the HBC Inspection Report in 1891 on Fairford provided insights into post-1870 developments that challenged the Company's posi-tion in the regional economy: 'All Treaty Indians owing to furs being scarce a large portion of their time is devoted to fishing, for the produce of which a good market is provided by dealers in the settlement and to other points along the lake – not industrious.'[37] Significantly in the post-1870 period, fur scarcity did not lead to deprivation or to increased dependence upon the HBC because other incomes could be earned. According to HBC sources, Indian participation in the staple economy went on unabated. In 1905, the Fort Alexander Inspection Report stated that 'the Indians are taking them-selves more and more to lumbering, fishing and other such work in prefer-ence to hunting.'[38] Fur prices were low until 1900. Natives were not held to the fur trade, despite the cultural appropriateness of the traditional economy. Economic forces pulled their labour and energies away from the traditional economy and towards the new staple industries.

Fur scarcity, low fur prices, more settled habitation patterns, and alter-nate incomes promoted the withdrawal of Native labour from HBC service in the Interlake and Lake Winnipeg region. However, at Grand Rapids, the Company was able to accommodate the changing regional economy. In 1887, Chief Factor Belanger noted that fishing employment provided se-cure incomes and that Natives would not hunt since 'very few of them would risk the uncertainty and undertake the fatigue of hunting expedi-tions without which very few furs are to be obtained as fur-bearing ani-mals are very scarce.'[39] Fish companies also competed with the HBC by selling goods to Indians. By 1891, however, the HBC made an arrange-ment with William Robinson's fish and steamboating interests to contract

Native labour. This also permitted the post manager to balance outside wage labour with the needs of fur collection. A. McLean wrote in 1891 that he did his 'utmost to keep my best hunters at their traps, only giving them a days work or so at the ice to enable them to procure provisions.'[40] By 1893, the Company's revenue at Grand Rapids was derived from a variety of sources: fur trade, 17 per cent; fish oil, 18 per cent; treaty advances, 24 per cent; and labour for ice and cordwood, 41 per cent.[41] Thus, 83 per cent of the post's revenue was derived from new industries and treaty annuities, a clear indication that this region's economy was no longer centred on the mono-economy of fur. The situation at Grand Rapids was unique since old mercantile and new staple interests came together to make use of Native labour. In general, however, the Hudson's Bay Company records show that Natives withdrew from the fur trade and participated in the changing regional economy. New resources industries provided more favourable employment than the old paternalistic mercantile economy.

Incomes and Class Formation

Native participation in the regional economy can be understood by examining incomes and by considering the possible effects of economic growth on Native social structures. Figure 10.3 shows sources of income by Indian agency for 1900. At the turn of the century, the types of incomes varied considerably between agencies (regions). The lack of alternate activities made The Pas agency Indians (with the exception of Grand Rapids) dependent upon the muskrat swamps. In the Berens River agency, Lake Winnipeg commercial fishing and wages accounted for most of the income. The most varied income structure was supported by the resources of the Manitowapah agency. For Clandeboye Indians, hunting was a relatively insignificant source of income. In this region, farming and wages made up a major portion of income. Presumably, other income would include commercialized gathering or sales of moccasins and leathercraft.[42] The diversity of the regional economy is reflected in the variety of income structures at the agency level (See Figures 10.1 and 10.3).

The annual reports of Indian agents provide some insights into wage levels. In 1899, McColl estimated that 'Captain Robinson pays annually upwards of $40,000 to the Indians in my inspectorate for lumbering, cutting cord-wood, making ties, working on steamboats and at the fisheries.'[43] In 1901, Semmens stated that income from commercial fishing on Lake Winnipeg totalled $80,000.[44] Occasionally, an export industry like commercial fishing would result in advantageous linkages; Indian Affairs records noted that a sturgeon fisherman paid $1,100 for sturgeon nets knitted by Brokenhead women.[45] Although there is not a great deal of information on wages, the rates quoted by Indian agents suggest that Native labourers were

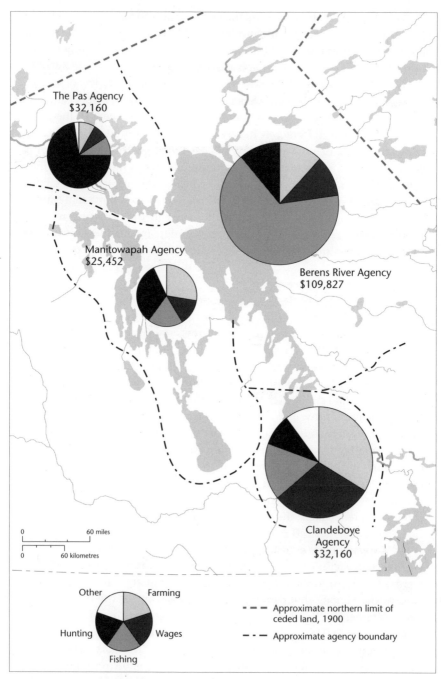

Figure 10.3 Sources of income by Indian agency, 1900 (CSP, 1901, no. 27, 'Indian Affairs')

not paid on the basis of their race. In 1882, Indians from Sandy Bay earned as much as two dollars per day for farm labour; in 1893, Natives at Grand Rapids earned $1.50 per day. In 1901, Indian Agent Swinford reported: 'More money is being earned every year at haying, harvesting, threshing, &.; and this year some of the Indians have their teams and wagons working at threshing, &c., earning three and four dollars per day. In this kind of progress one can use to advantage the slang expression "money talks."'[46] In 1903, five to six dollars per day could be earned at fishing. Certainly this contrasted to the Company's wages for York boat work, which, in 1910, amounted to between fifty cents to $1.50 per day in trade goods.[47]

Payment for Native labour took a variety of forms. It seems that Natives were generally paid on the basis of how much they produced, but frequent references to daily wage rates may also indicate time-based wages were a method of paying for labour. Furthermore, Natives were often paid in money, and cash was an important feature of the regional economy. In 1903, Semmens stated that 'most of the people have ample chances to earn money almost every season of the year.'[48] Marlatt noted that the 'money thus earned [through fishing, lumbering, and farm labour] will be largely expended in procuring the winter's supply of provisions and clothing.'[49] In the early post-1870 period, Natives were also paid in kind or in trade. In 1886, Muckle stated that digging seneca root earned '$1 to $3 a day, in trade ... in fact the whole business with Indians is in trade; when they have anything to sell they take flour, dry goods and groceries for it and very seldom receive any cash.'[50] The existence of such a mercantile bias is understandable given the absence of a system of commercial distribution not connected to the old fur trade or the new fish and lumber interests. Thus, the new staple companies – commercial fishing and lumbering – imitated the HBC by operating their own stores.

Although there is not enough information to provide a more precise analysis of incomes and forms of payment, Indian agents commented on living standards. In 1889, The Pas agency Indians, who were still beyond the influence of wage labour, were issued extra relief supplies because the muskrat and fisheries failed. The security of Grand Rapids labourers was easily contrasted with the rest of The Pas Indians. In 1893, Muckle's comment, couched within the department's economic policy framework, stated that the 'St. Peter's Band are getting more independent every year; they are more inclined to look after themselves, and at present are almost if not entirely self-sustaining.'[51] McColl recorded the effect of the spread of the labour market on the Poplar River band in 1900: 'Judging from their appearance, their present condition is better than in former years, for they were destitute of any employment whatever except a little hunting until the fisheries were established at Little Black River, where they are receiving good wages for their labour.'[52] Similarly, in 1901, the effects of a boom and the extent of employment for the Berens River agency was noted. McColl stated: 'I found the Indians in better condition than they have been at any time during my twenty-four years among them. This was owing to the prosperous condition of the fishing industry and the extensive lumber interests of Captain Robinson, of Selkirk, with either of which industries nearly every Indian is more or less intimately connected, and from which he draws an ever-increasing yearly revenue.'[53] At about the same time, Swinford attributed 'the better health of the [Manitowapah] Indians to the supply of work there was to be had outside the reserves last winter, at the gypsum mines, lumber camps, saw-mills and cord-wood camps. They had their winter fishing to attend to, and a good spring hunt brought them through the winter in good health, well clothed, and in better condition generally than I have seen them before.'[54] By the turn of the century, Native participation in the changing regional economy had brought a measure of material prosperity.

Since Natives were participating in a buoyant regional economy, it would be reasonable to expect some changes with respect to Indian personal property. At St. Peters in 1884, Muckle noticed 'five sewing machines, all of which were paid for, two reapers, thirteen mowers, and one threshing machine, which cost over $300, a number of buggies, light driving waggons, and lumber waggons, which are replacing the old Red River carts.'[55] Similarly, Indians purchased sailboats from the Dominion Fish Company. During this period, Indian agents measured progress in terms of the accumulation of property. McColl's statement provides an illustration of this ethnocentric viewpoint: 'The Indians of St. Peter's are far in advance of those of the other two [Clandeboye] reserves in the acquirement and possession of personal property.'[56] For St. Peters, positive comments on 'progress' came as early as 1885: 'In fact, the people of this band who have settled down will compare favourably with most of the old settlements along the Red and Assiniboine Rivers in their agricultural pursuits, in their houses, in their clothing, in the number of their cattle and agricultural implements, and are more prosperous and make more money in a year than thousands of people in the older Province.'[57] Changes to Native material culture were consistent with Native participation in the regional economy, which was no longer defined solely by the traditional fur trade.

The spread of the market, the growth in new staple industries, and the creation of family or local wealth imply that changes to the social structure were occurring. In 1904, the lieutenant-governor of Keewatin, D.H. McMillan, recommended that

the time is rapidly approaching when some other machinery will have to be established for the administration of justice in this district. Trade is extending over the district and property is being accumulated. The probating of wills and the administration of the estates of intestates is a subject that seems not to be provided for, and I am informed that a number of instances have recently arisen where no machinery could be discovered by which the estate of a deceased person could be administered in the district.[58]

The need for a means to deal with the legal problem of inheritance indicates that some family incomes were greater than the bare needs of sustenance. Not surprisingly then, the enhanced commercialization of the regional economy brought the accumulation of prosperity, which was followed by the perceived need for the importation of property law to deal with the administration of estates. Observations by Indian agents allude to occupational specialization, if not to an evolving class system within the bands. In 1901, while at the St. Peters reserve, McColl found 'that one of the machine companies had one of the Indians, W.D. Harper, acting as agent, selling mowers, rakes, wagons' and that 'he had been very successful and there was no difficulty in regard to the payment for them.'[59] Even with traditional pursuits, commercial gain on the part of the individual was now possible. The 1896 annual report for Fort Alexander recorded: 'John Robert Bunn and Duncan Two Hearts are the kings amongst the hunters; they some winters get from three hundred to six hundred dollars' worth of fur. Bunn put thirty dollars and Duncan ten dollars in the post office savings bank last year as a beginning.'[60] In 1900, McColl learned that Two Hearts had earned enough 'by hunting last year to buy a large sail-boat worth over $700' and that he 'has money deposited in the bank in Winnipeg.'[61] Similarly, a Mrs. Flett used her sewing machine to make tents and sails and earned a cash income on the Brokenhead reserve. Indian Agent Taylor recorded that, in The Pas agency, 'Several of the Indians are trading for themselves, and are doing fairly well. Some of the younger educated ones are clerking for merchants in The Pas.'[62] For Natives in Northern Manitoba, class formation (small-scale accumulation of wealth) during the early reserve transition era was a change from the old social structure of fur trade society.

Sweeping statements about the failure of Indian Affairs agriculture polices overlook the fact that a few individuals found an appropriate economic strategy in the pursuit of agriculture. Although agriculture did not become the exclusive base for the reserve economy, some individuals specialized in farming. Marlatt reported on a Fairford Indian's success in 1902: 'Councillor Storr of this band, has eleven head of fine three-year-old steers for market this fall. This man is milking eighteen cows this summer, has a cream-separator, in fact almost everything usually found around a well-appointed farmhouse.'[63] In 1905, Storr had a herd of ninety-five cattle, and there appears to be a pattern where a few Indians had sizeable herds 'and those who do not take an interest in their stock and are only keeping a few head of cattle just to oblige the government.'[64] In 1896, Indian Agent Muckle described a Fort Alexander farmer: 'Councillor Joseph Kent, a pure Indian, has a fine farm of about ten acres, raises all kinds of vegetables, with some wheat, barley and oats' and 'has ten head of cattle, two horses, and some pigs and chickens. He also fishes and hunts a little.'[65] A Brokenhead councillor known as En-in-go (the Ant) had a reputation for being a hard worker, and he actively promoted agricultural pursuits among the band. En-in-go may serve as an example of an Indian who promoted Indian Affairs' economic policies in order to respond to the post-treaty times. Finally, some agricultural success was possible on marginal land. The annual report for the Norway House band in 1903 drew attention to 'One treaty Indian, Willie Moore (if he was seen on the streets of Winnipeg he would be taken for a Scotchman) had over two hundred bushels of potatoes last fall.'[66]

One of the most exemplary Native entrepreneurs in this period came from Fort Alexander. In 1887, Muckle recorded: 'Robert Henderson, one of the councillors of this band, who is a trader, bought a new yacht this summer of about ten tons burden, paying cash for it, he is now the owner of two schooners, and does a trading business of thousands of dollars with the Indians and others about Lake Winnipeg.'[67] His economic role was somewhat similar to the Metis traders based at Red River prior to 1870, however, previously such a dynamic social force had not been based on the Lake Winnipeg economy. Henderson's accumulation was not temporary, since Muckle reported in 1896: 'Robert Henderson has cattle, a good little farm, a fine schooner of twelve tons burden with which he freights all over the lake and brings in railroad ties or cordwood. He is a busy man, never idle: fishing in winter, boating in summer, and, as he states, has three good meals a day, but I know that he always has a little over.'[68] Indian agents' observations about the economic pursuits of individual Indians only provide glimpses into the social structure; firm explanations about the process or extent of social class formation are not forthcoming.

Diversity characterized the Native economies in the reserve transition era because bands became economically specialized (Figure 10.1) and because within bands Indians pursued different occupations. In particular, young men tended to specialize in wage labour. In 1883, the report on St. Peters noted that 'a great number of young men in this band get work at good wages on the steamboats, loading barges and cars with lumber and cord wood.'[69] The situation was similar at Fisher River, as Jackson stated: 'Nearly all the younger members of this band are working out with the numerous fish and lumber companies.'[70] This age difference in economic activities was apparent in Jackson's 1905 report on Poplar River: 'In the winter a number of the older men do a lot of hunting and get a considerable amount of fur, the younger men going into the logging camps at good wages.'[71] The pursuit of different incomes by different age groups may have been a successful short-term economic strategy, but in the long term, wage labour may have adversely affected the accumulation of knowledge associated with the traditional economy.

Within bands, economic specialization was not limited to particular age groups. In 1888, Martineau described the Fairford band: 'The band is divided into three classes, viz. hunters, fishermen and farmers; the hunters and fishermen farm but very little ... as to the fishermen as long as they can take fish they will do nothing else. The portion who follow farming are certainly doing well.'[72] At this time, Clandeboye Indians were divided into fishermen, hunters, and labourers. By 1903, Jackson stated that 'the Indians of this reserve [St. Peters] are almost altogether occupied in working for wages and being employed by outside parties.'[73] After 1900, Indians from southern reserves were more often than not identified as labourers or as a labouring class. Indian Agent J.O. Lewis described the nature of St. Peters wage labour in 1907: 'Some of the families have a wide connection in the settlements outside of the reserve. They do not make good farmers, but are much sought after as labourers. Many of them are now engaged in railway construction. In the winter season many are found in the wood camps at Molson, Lac du Bonnet and adjacent places. In the summer a large number go out to Lake Winnipeg as fishermen, sailors or labourers for fish companies. A few are in Winnipeg, making good wages as mechanics.'[74] For the southern reserves, in particular, Indians were involved in a transition to wage labour.

Chief George Barker's memoirs, *Forty Years A Chief,* recalled aspects of the Lake Winnipeg economy; his experiences are consistent with observations from other sources. Around 1912, Barker and several young friends travelled around the south end of Lake Winnipeg searching for work. Only casual work was available since the quarries were closed. Later, Barker found employment on a steamboat as a fireman and second engineer. He recalled that 'my years on the boats gave me a chance to meet many people. I was very well treated by all those with whom I worked, both white and Indians.'[75] He also worked at the Bisset mines. Later on, Barker's memoirs stress trapping, suggesting that wage labour had been more important in his younger years.

Wage labour became a preferred form of income among many Natives. Even in areas where the fur trade regime was dominant, wage labour was desired; for example, with respect to The Pas Indians, Indian Agent Reader noted in 1885: 'Men and boys loaf around the various forts playing at the chess or cards; not because they do not like to work for the Hudson['s] Bay Company or for any one else, but because there is not sufficient work for all, and they prefer seeing wages for their work.'[76] In 1907, Lewis provided some insights by explaining the importance of wage labour to St. Peters Indians:

> Very few of them take an interest in agriculture. They prefer to be employed where there are large gangs of men. Many are now working on railway construction. Employers of labour from Winnipeg and other places are often on the reserve drumming up men. The freedom from the restraint of the reserve, the association of numbers, and the ready money received in wages, are inducements that easily entice them away. The families are well supported and all well dressed. The interiors of their houses are fairly well furnished as compared with the same class everywhere. In many of their homes are sewing machines and organs.[77]

Especially for the St. Peters Indians, post-1870 adjustment meant integration with a capitalist labour market and not assimilation through agriculture or isolation on the reserves as envisioned by the Department of Indian Affairs. Nonetheless, security was conditional, for as Jackson stated in 1904: 'There is no scarcity of work, and as long as the fish and lumber lasts, this band [Fisher River] will have no trouble in making a living.'[78] Native participation in the regional economy did not preclude subsistence pursuits; and Indian Agent C.H. Carter noted that Fisher River Indians were 'more energetic in hunting than in other occupations.'[79] The continuation of subsistence activities made good economic sense.

While the Native economy in the Interlake was diversified in the post-1870 period, it was essentially dependent upon the decisions of outside agencies. Thus, the production of new staples and economic linkages to the regional transportation system resembled the fur trade, in so far as economic efforts were directed towards exporting commodities. As such, Natives were dependent upon the capitalist business cycle. The Reverend F. Stevens explained why traditional employers (missionaries and the HBC) were unable to afford Native labour in the Norway House area in 1913, when the labour market had shifted northward: 'In the North there was a boom on ... The Hudson's [sic] Bay Railway was under construction. Survey parties were working. Prospectors were seeking gold. All the Indians were earning high wages. Some Indians were lighting their pipes with one dollar bills. Gramophones and jam were everywhere. Missionary stipends remained the usual starvation rates. They [missionaries] could not compete in the labour market.'[80] Lewis explained the impact of the business cycle on St. Peters in 1909: 'During the period of industrial activity of a few years ago the Indians found plenty of work and were well paid. During the last two years they have not been so steadily employed nor at so fair remuneration.

The standard of living among the Indians has been higher, and in a measure kept pace with that of their white neighbours.'[81] Game and fishing regulations also restricted access to resources. At this time, hay and wood prices were low. In the Interlake, Indian agents reported that vacant land was being settled and that game and fur resources were being depleted.[82] The situation of the St. Peters Indians was exacerbated, according to Lewis, by the demand for skilled labour and because Indians had not acquired skills; however, he added: 'There is also a prejudice against him [the Indian] among other mechanics. I doubt whether he would be allowed to join a union.'[83] Although St. Peters Indians made a transition to wage labour, they did not become skilled workers; this possibility was precluded when the reserve was surrendered and the band was moved northward into the Interlake. Any discussion about Natives and the labour market must be disciplined by facts associated with place and time. About the same time that demand for St. Peters labourers was diminishing, a buoyant labour market developed north of Norway House. In this sense, the new resource economy had a frontier quality.

Hunting, fishing, trapping, and gardening are terms that adequately sum up Native economies at the time of treaty talks (1871-75), but by 1900 this was no longer true. The strategies that Natives employed in the post-1870 period served to diversify local economies. Natives played a necessary role in the economic development of this part of the province. Moreover, migrant Indian labour from the Interlake was important to the province's grain economy. In the pre-mechanized agricultural economy of western Canada, Native labour was needed for harvesting and threshing. Many family farms benefitted from the availability of this affordable 'factor of production,' although this aspect of prairie history remains an untold story. The new economy that emerged in the Interlake and Lake Winnipeg region was not factory capitalism. No simple or pure mode of production adequately describes the economic relations that developed. As resource-based frontier industries quickly superseded the centuries-old mercantile fur trade, economic relations became complicated. Independent commodity production, contracted production, and wage labour were remunerated through credit, payment in kind, and money. Work routines remained seasonal or temporary; for example, McColl described dock work as 'an occupation that the Indian is, by temperament, well adapted for, as the work is done in large gangs under hurried excitement, and is paid for as soon as done.'[84] Treaty rights, or access to subsistence resources and annuities, meant that Indians could not be readily coerced into participating in the staple industries. Modernization in this era did not need a landless industrial proletariat in order to pursue new sources of wealth. In all these activities, the work was hard. But the seasonal nature of the work and emphasis on physical productivity and not time differentiated this working life from the drudgery of a closed, monotonous factory environment.

The move out of a 'hunting' economy, or in reality the demise of the paternalism of the HBC, was not the consequence of massive disruptions of industrialism. Rather Native people were attracted to the income security of frontier industries. If hunting and trapping are today classified as having a stronger cultural component than working in a sawmill, then Indian participation in the new regional economy must have been prompted by economic concerns. Traditional culture did not serve as a barrier to the spread of frontier resource capitalism.

Involvement in the labour market had cultural implications. Specialization, division of labour, and family accumulation of wealth influenced band society. New incomes not only improved access to basic goods but also increased the range of commodities consumed by Natives. In 1886, Indian Agent Muckle commented on Indian appearances in the early reserve period: 'The greater number of them wore their blankets, feathers, leggings, paint and long plaited hair, now they dress as whites do, and it is a difficult matter for a stranger to distinguish them from settlers.'[85] Contemporary explanations of cultural change that focus on the missionaries, the Department of Indian Affairs, and boarding schools as sole agents of disruption are incomplete and inadequate. While it can be shown that economic security increased during the early reserve transition era, written records are really quite silent about social and cultural disruptions associated with economic change. E.P. Thompson commented on this problem in historical writing by noting that just because there was a measure of economic prosperity does not mean that people were not 'less happy or less free at the same time,' meaning that 'From standard-of-life we pass to way-of-life. But the two are not the same.'[86]

11
'Wait until Advancing Civilization Has So Interfered with Their Natural Resources': Surplus Labour, Migrations, and Stagnation

During the post-1870 era, two distinct regions were created in northern Manitoba. Government policy had established ceded and non-ceded areas. Because Aboriginal title had been dealt with in the treaty areas, resource capitalists were free to invest, employ Native labour, and create wealth by exploiting the natural resources of areas ceded by treaties. In general, the diversified economy of the Interlake and Lake Winnipeg region is separated from the stagnant mercantile economy of northeastern Manitoba by the northern boundary of Treaty Five (1875). In addition to subsistence resources, commodity exchanges, and wages, treaty Indian incomes were augmented by annuities, supplies, and relief. However, in the region north of the 1875 boundaries of Treaty Five, Natives were trapped in a traditional economy and suffered serious periodic shortages, low prices for furs, and diminished wage employment. Moreover, the experiences of the York Factory band indicate that the Company cut socially necessary expenditures – the paternalistic economy had become less benevolent. In economic terms, a surplus population existed in the fur country that was still under the control of the HBC. Given these contrasting economic landscapes, migration pressures were inescapable. The movements and intended movements of Native peoples are important indications of their responses to a changing regional economy. Population movements reflected the relative availability of resources and incomes.

Post-1870 Migrations
Migrations in the post-1870 period were an essential aspect of Native adjustments to changing regional economies. Generally, migrations were a response to a stagnant fur trade and a locally depleted resource base. In the post-treaty era, Department of Indian Affairs shaped migrations. This was an important change from the population movements that occurred in the

fur trade era. Figure 11.1 summarizes major migrations and relocations. Some of the bands with a plains orientation, and who gravitated to the Interlake, are also shown. The Interlake was an attractive area for settlement as evident from the reserve settlement process. In contrast, James Settee, in the wake of the 1885 Resistance, reported on the failure of the settlement process in Saskatchewan: 'I am at the same time trying to get the Government to take an interest into the welfare of these poor Indians living in the Great Plains' and that 'Great number of them are perishing away from the face of the earth through starvation.'[1] He added: 'I am working with all my might to get a certain portion of the water on Lake Winnipeg where there is an abundance of fish where the Government might plant them and keep them alive a few years.'[2] Settee's plan did not receive approval from the Department of Indian Affairs.

The movement by a portion of the Norway House band to Fisher River provides an example of how the interplay of forces – Indians, the HBC, missionaries, and the Department of Indian Affairs – influenced migrations. As a district headquarters, Norway House needed a labour pool. Since the 1840s, Methodist missionaries had encouraged Indians to settle and garden. According to HBC Chief Factor Ross, the problem in 1875 was 'the overcrowding of Indians in the vicinity of Norway House Post, resulting from the policy of forming them into a christian [sic] community of some civilized householders, and which naturally results in much misery and starvation.'[3] However, a surplus labour pool at district headquarters was a logical outcome of the commodification of Native labour. At Treaty Five negotiations, the chief stressed that steamboats would put an end to freighting and that they wanted to migrate to Lake Winnipeg to live by fishing and farming. The missionaries had encouraged and supported the migration plan in the spring of 1875 even before treaty negotiations. Ross was not impressed by this approach to the surplus resident population: 'Beyond encouraging all the miserable halfbreed families who were settled here to move to their own country I certainly could not approve of the scheme that once initiated and sanctioned by the Government would speedily depopulate the whole low country from Churchill to Lake Winnipeg.'[4] As senior HBC manager, Ross was aware that the free movement of Natives could wreck the fur industry in northern Manitoba. After 1880, socially contrived scarcity and environmental problems were very acute for the York Factory Swampy Cree. The material circumstances of trappers could have not been very good if a bit of land and the prospects of potato gardening could 'speedily depopulate the whole low country.' Rather than relocating surplus labour to more advantageous sites, Ross recommended redistributing the Native population in the immediate country: 'The interests of the trade as well as those of the Indians are involved there can be no doubt, and I would

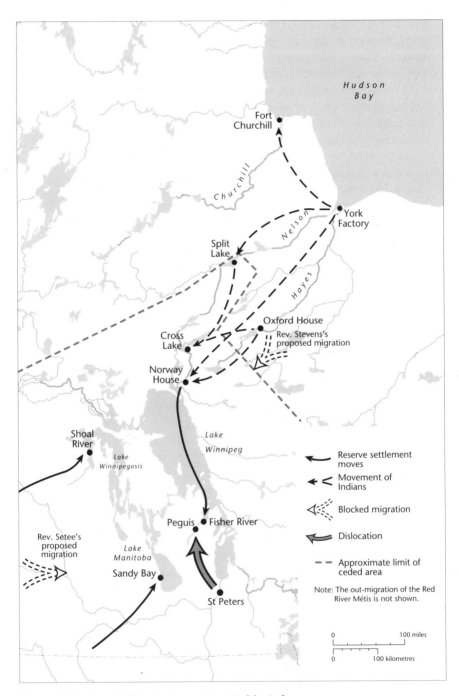

Figure 11.1 Post-1870 migration patterns in Manitoba

strongly urge the immediate establishment of one or two wintering stations further in the interior' and 'I have good reason to believe that many of the village Indians would in that case follow with their families and so benefit themselves and the business alike.'[5] From the point of view of the paternalistic Company, a surplus population was required, but it preferred to shift this population from a residency near the post to territory still within the Norway House district. This was more advantageous than the continued expenditure of Company paternalism or the movement of Natives to a new region. Spatially, Ross's recommendations were similar to the efforts to shift the surplus population of York Factory from the post to the bush. Local patterns of residency and movement have implications for the ability of the colonial economy to channel Native labour into the commodity flows that define the world system. The commercial capitalist nature of the fur trade necessitated a surplus population.

In the case of Norway House's surplus population, various interests were accommodated. In 1877, a considerable flotilla (three York boats, ten fishing skiffs, and twelve canoes) made up, according to Reverend Semmens, 'the most wonderful migration Lake Winnipeg had ever known.'[6] While these Norway House Indians did not get Grassey Narrows as a location for their reserve, they had extracted during the treaty talks assistance to relocate to the Interlake. The Hudson's Bay Company earned $1,000 in revenue by assisting with the move to Fisher River. Some 180 Indians made the move in 1877 and 1878. Thus in 1880, Ross could report: 'The village of Rossville being now relieved of its surplus population, is no longer in a chronic state of starvation, and can manage to subsist without much assistance from this Post.'[7] In the case of the Fisher River move, the HBC benefitted from the migration. The move to Fisher River also provided, as Settee's 1885 scheme illustrates, the possibility of a region that offered a favourable economic base.

The next major migration pressure came from the Swampy Cree of the Hudson Bay Lowlands who had been attached to York Factory. About 1885, a few Cree families moved northward and began trading at Churchill. The majority of the destitute York Factory Natives shifted to the Split Lake area. In the late 1880s and early 1890s, a steady stream of reports documented this inland move.

Travellers passing through Oxford House to York Factory noted that the more favourable environment of the former meant a higher living standard than that of the coastal Swampy Cree. In the 1890s, harsh conditions would induce Indians of northeastern Manitoba to move to the Norway House area. In 1890, J.K. McDonald recorded semi-starvation at Oxford House: 'Such a want of these [fur bearing animals] as has seldom if ever before been known.'⁸ In 1895, W.J. McLean informed Lieutenant-Governor J. Schultz about migration pressures in northeastern Manitoba:

> The general condition of the non-Treaty Indians of the District, I was informed, is poor. Large game, as well as fur bearing animals, are becoming scarce; and as therefore the Indians have to subsist chiefly upon fish, which is hard to procure during the severe winters of the far north, and often with inadequate means, cases of much suffering for want of food ... and their knowledge of the fact that so many of their brethren to the south of them are now recipients of Treaty money and other assistance from the Government, and with good soil and a more genial climate favourable to the successful growing of grain and vegetables for their support, produces a strong incentive for their desire to come further south and within the limits of Treaties.⁹

Depleted resources, stagnant fur prices, declining post labour, and lack of alternatives tended to push Indians out of northeastern Manitoba.

Since the government had repeatedly ignored requests for a treaty from Indians trapped in this region, Indians were pulled to the Norway House/ Cross Lake area. However, simply moving from the non-treaty area and taking up residence in a treaty area did not qualify these Indians for treaty rights. When the rest of northern Manitoba adhered to Treaty Five (1908-10), the former residents of this area could take scrip or have their names added to the Norway House, Cross Lake, or Fisher River band lists. Figures 11.2 and 11.3 are based on information on the previous residences of individuals who acquired treaty rights in 1908, and they show migration patterns from the non-ceded to the ceded area. Most of the migrants were from Oxford House and York Factory. Both of these places were district headquarters attempting to cut costs and balance the books. A surplus population had been created around district headquarters because the HBC had reorganized post economies to reduce employment. In contrast, few Indians left the prime fur posts (Nelson House, Trout Lake, and Island Lake). A number of the new members of the Cross Lake and Norway House bands came from Split Lake. Thus for some York Factory Indians, Split Lake was a step on their migration to the south. With the expansion of commercial fishing to Playgreen Lake, the annual report for the fur trade reported that 'employment in the neighborhood of Norway House Post is so abundant that several families of Indians have come up from Interior Posts to settle.'¹⁰ Very simply then, between 1885 and 1908, Indians were pushed away from the old mercantile economy of northeastern Manitoba and were pulled towards the treaty area with its fisheries and more buoyant demand for

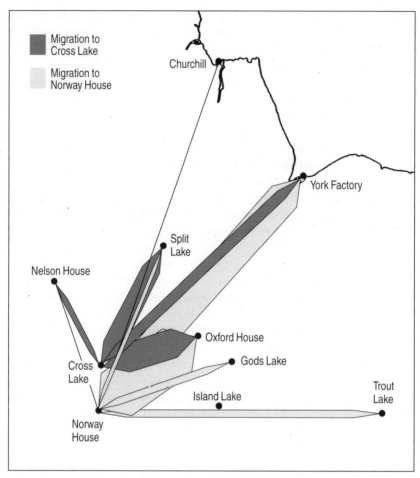

Figure 11.2   Indications of migration in Manitoba prior to 1908
(Department of Indian and Northern Affairs Canada, Annuity Paylists, 1908)

labour. A surplus population had left Norway House for Fisher River in the 1870s, only to be replaced a few years later by a movement of York Factory and Oxford House Natives.

Another Methodist Migration Scheme
In 1897, a somewhat unconventional Methodist missionary, Reverend Fred G. Stevens, who was not known for his deference to the church hierarchy, proposed that Indians from northeastern Manitoba be encouraged to move to the Interlake. This was not the first time such a proposal had been considered. In 1890, Inspector Bégin suggested to Schultz that 'it seems a pity

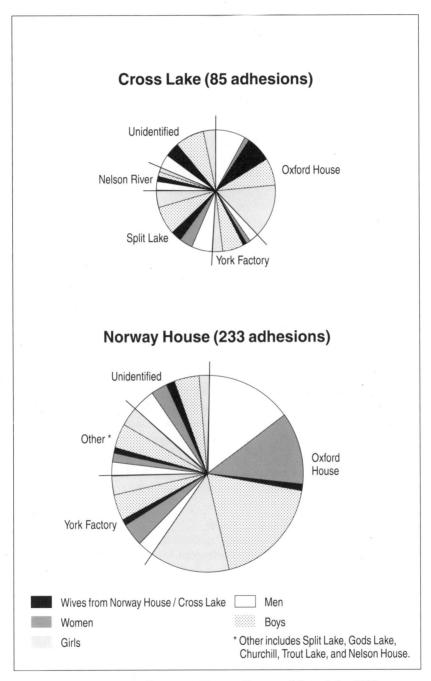

Figure 11.3 Individual adhesions to Norway House and Cross Lake, 1908 (Department of Indian and Northern Affairs, Annuity Paylists, 1908)

that they could not be assisted to a Reservation far enough south where they can procure fish, and to at least raise potatoes.'[11] Although Stevens's plan had been accepted by the Methodist convention in 1897, this migration was never more than a scheme. His failure to implement a plan illustrates the thinking of those 'responsible' for Indians – the church, the Company, and the state.

In 1897, Stevens notified Indian Affairs that Indians from Oxford House, Gods Lake, Island Lake, and Nelson River wanted to establish an agricultural colony near Fisher River. Stevens recalled that 'starvation stared the Indians in their faces. One of these cycles of scarcity was closing in upon the Northland. The Secretary of the Board of Missions wrote me commanding me to, at once, desist from my plans.'[12] According to Stevens, his 1897 plan had been undermined: 'When Dr. McDougall [Methodist clergy] reached Winnipeg, a bargain was made between the Department of Indian Affairs, the Hudson's Bay Company and the Methodist Church. The HBC was to feed any destitut[e] Indian, the Department of Indian Affairs was to foot the bill, and the Methodist Church was to remove F.G. Stevens from the district.[13] Stevens's plan was only temporarily thwarted; and as he had feared, Indians in that area experienced extreme destitution. Although reports about destitution at Sandy Lake (east of Island Lake) in the winter of 1899-1900 were denigrated by officials, he eventually established that starvation had occurred and that deaths had resulted. Consequently, the migration issue was raised again, and Stevens claimed that Indian Commissioner D. Laird had granted permission to bring Indians out of the district. Stevens also reported that Captain Robinson would assist with transport on Lake Winnipeg and provide employment for the incoming Indians. Nonetheless, the move did not occur. Stevens was unable to communicate with the Indians since the HBC 'kept my letters and destroyed my migration scheme.'[14]

Indians' desires and intentions were not independently documented, but it is probable that a number were interested in Stevens's migration scheme. For example, in 1893, W.J. McLean wrote to Schultz stating that Indians from northeastern Manitoba wanted to move south. Figure 11.1 shows that many Indians were migrating from their traditional areas at this time. Stevens claimed that some 200 people from Oxford House and Gods Lake wanted to move: 'I had a conference with some of the chiefs of the tribes and they said they would willingly leave the country if the governors would take them out and give them land farther to the south.'[15] Since the government had repeatedly refused to arrange a treaty with these Indians, Stevens's plan was their only alternative to remaining in this stagnating region. Interestingly, those opposed to the move never suggested that Indians were unwilling to migrate. Nonetheless, Stevens faced an institutional rigidity that was unwilling to seriously consider the advantages of the Interlake over stagnating northeastern Manitoba.

A variety of reasons were offered to counter Stevens's scheme and to maintain isolation. The Department of Indian Affairs' files reveal that members of the Methodist hierarchy, McDougall and Semmens, influenced decision-making with respect to Stevens's effort to deal with deteriorating economic conditions. They claimed that the situation in northeastern Manitoba was not really so bad, that their lands had not been encroached upon, and that a single season of starvation was not abnormal.[16] Moreover, a move to the Interlake was not accepted as a valid solution to the problems facing the Indians of northeastern Manitoba. McDougall and Semmens noted that after years of government assistance, Fisher River was not an agricultural success, and that Indians still lived by hunting and fishing. Furthermore, they argued that conditions would not improve with a move, since there was no longer a strong demand for labour on Lake Winnipeg. In fact, migrants could unsettle the existing labour market; they would be restricted by game and fish laws, the fish supply would be overtaxed, and there was not a great demand for cordwood. Semmens noted that the government would have to feed and take care of these Indians and that such a migration could establish an unwanted precedent.[17] Any number of excuses were offered to prevent Indians from moving from the non-ceded to the ceded area.

Opposition to this move by Semmens and McDougall was supported by the general legal and economic policy expounded by the Ottawa office of the Department of Indian Affairs. J.D. McLean stated: 'It has never been any part of the Department's policy to take Indians from unceded territory and bring them into premature contact with civilization, but rather to follow the natural order of events and wait until advancing civilization has so interfered with their natural resources as to convince them of the absolute necessity for turning for their maintenance to industrial pursuits, with which they have in the meantime become more or less familiar.'[18] Moreover, McLean opposed an out-migration from 'the low country' and hinted at long-term policy objectives: 'All considered it seems to be in the best ultimate interests of these Indians to remain in a country with which if left alone, they seem sufficiently well satisfied and to await its opening up, and then *as their natural resources fail* them turn to various industrial pursuits without the disadvantage of too great competition in the labour market, which will gradually be brought within their reach.'[19] Indian policy was formulated so that Indians were conceived of in terms of their relationship to land and their role in labour markets. In other words, policy was not simply formulated by abstract legal obligations concerning Aboriginal title. Cultural assimilation was not merely, as it is often argued, the consequence of a belief in racial

superiority on the part of Ottawa bureaucrats. Semmens conveyed the opinion that the migration scheme 'would be unjust to the Hudson's Bay Company and a serious disadvantage to the fur trade.'[20] As in the case of the
move to Fisher River, the HBC feared that Indians could not be held to the
fur trade, especially in a region that provided favourable economic alternatives. The HBC believed that it needed to hold a resident Native population
in the country, some Methodist officials argued that the Interlake was not
an advantage, and senior officials of the Department of Indian Affairs were
unwilling to fulfil responsibilities for Indians from the unceded territory. In
Rupertsland and the Northwestern Territory, treaties were not the sole source
of Canada's obligations to Aboriginal peoples. In the post-1870 period, and
without any clear legal basis, department policy served to restrict the spatial
or geographical options of Indians in the non-ceded area. This had the effect of maintaining surplus labour for the fur trade. Finally, the deliberate
policy of allowing economic forces ('advancing civilization') to dislocate
Indians from their resources stacked the treaty negotiations in the government's favour.

Regardless of arguments about the potential of the Interlake to absorb a
few hundred Indians from the northeast, the lame excuses advanced between 1897 and 1901 to prevent a population move were largely based on
convenience. Later decisions by the department demonstrate that there was
no sincere desire to enhance the economic security of Indian bands. In 1907,
the St. Peters reserve was surrendered, and by 1920, more than 900 Indians
had been moved to the Interlake (see Figure 11.1).[21] The new reserve, Peguis,
was located adjacent to Fisher River. The economic dimensions of this coerced move were not lost on Indian Agent J. Watson: 'These people in the
past have worked mostly as, sailors, and wood-cutters, but now that they
are moving on to their new reserve, they are preparing to go more into
farming.'[22] This is a bit of curious logic from Indian Affairs – Indians were
being moved away from an area of good agricultural potential so they could
'go more into farming.' The officials of Indian Affairs were never comfortable with the fact that many St. Peters Indians preferred wage labour to
yeoman farming. The department steadfastly prevented a few hundred Indians from leaving a stagnant region with a surplus population but later
removed a much larger band, which had been residing on excellent land,
from a good labour market. With respect to Aboriginal title, the obvious
contradictions in the treatment of Indians from St. Peters and northeastern
Manitoba demonstrate that the Department of Indian Affairs understood
how to use external economic forces to undermine Indian communities.

Stagnation and the Problems of Transition
After Treaty Commissioner Rev. J. Semmens had concluded the last adhesion

to Treaty Five at York Factory, he described the economic problems facing Indians in the newly ceded territory. Semmens met up with Governor General Grey, who was on a canoe trip in northeastern Manitoba. Grey was interested in the situation concerning Indians he had seen in Keewatin and asked Semmens for his views. Semmens recommended a uniform system of wages 'so that Indians rendering services to the Company should be properly paid,' since they suffered under the variable wage rate.[23] Semmens's judgment was that a daily wage of $1.50 was needed 'in order to give workmen a chance to support their families properly.'[24] Wages had been compressed in this region. He stated: 'No men that I know work so hard [and] live so poorly, and serve such long hours as the Indians of our North Land. I think it very desirable that their remuneration be placed on an improved basis.'[25] His observation that Native men in the North 'work so hard [and] live so poorly' undercuts social science romanticism that portrays the Native economy as a happy mix of cash and subsistence incomes. Furthermore, old mercantile biases remained in the form of payment. Except at Norway House, wages were 'paid in trade at the stores of the Company and the Indians are somewhat dissatisfied with this arrangement. It would be of very great advantage to them if the balance of wages due could be paid in cash.'[26] Payment of wages in cash would have encouraged competition, which in turn would have reduced the HBC markup on goods. Working conditions had deteriorated. With the loss of pemmican, a poorer diet (bacon and flour) resulted. Portages were not maintained, and this meant more physical exertion was required to move freight and York boats. The real deprivation consequent upon this mercantile system can only be appreciated when it is pointed out that the highest Native incomes in the newly ceded area were earned by those fortunate enough to supplement winter trapping income with summer boat work. Apparently, even the traditional economy was in need of serious labour reform.

Several observations indicate the limitations of the preceding mercantile development. Semmens was concerned with 'the question of utilizing and turning to good account the abilities of the people whose greatest curse is that they have nothing to do.'[27] To remedy the situation, he wanted 'to see a market established for all that the Indian people can produce: needle work, basket making, fruit gathering, fish curing and many other lines of industry could be fostered to a greater extent than at the present time.'[28] No doubt, this concept of cottage industries had merit; however, it was not a natural outgrowth for an economy accustomed to using imported manufactured goods. In retrospect, Semmens's opposition to Stevens's migration plan did not result in a more viable economic strategy for northeastern Manitoba. Thus in 1915, the annual report on York Factory and Churchill noted that they 'live exclusively by hunting and fishing, and live under conditions that are not capable of much development.'[29.] The destitution in northeastern Manitoba was a result of a failure in Indian Affairs policy to recognize the stagnant fur trade and to attempt to alleviate suffering through migration or a treaty. The lieutenant-governor of Keewatin, J.C. Patterson, provided some insights on this abnegation of responsibility: 'The natives of the district of Keewatin have given the Government of Canada no trouble; they have been ... patient under privation, and obedient to the authority of the Hudson's Bay Company ... Had they been a turbulent, quarrelsome people, costing the country a few millions, in order to bring them to reason, probably they would have been dealt with more liberally.'[30] Although a legal argument could be made that the Crown had no treaty obligations in unceded territories, the Canadian government had acquired responsibilities for the Aboriginal population with the transfer of Rupertsland in 1870.[31]

Although Natives were the main source of labour, certain observations suggest that their role in the resource economy could be eroded. In 1896, Reader reported that Grand Rapids Indians 'are not doing as well as they were some time ago, owing to the influx of Icelanders to work for the fishing companies.'[32] Natives were never completely displaced from the lake fishery, but McMillan noted that by 1903 the whitefish fishery 'is now largely in the hands of the Icelandic setters.'[33]

While Natives participated in the new resource economy, control over the economy rested with external agencies. Specifically, external markets set prices and determined production. For example, in 1915, Lake Winnipegosis fish buyers brought an end to the season when the price for pickerel dropped 50 per cent. With the First World War, Indian agents reported that even with low prices, the HBC would not purchase furs. Thus, Native incomes were dependent upon the buoyancy of external markets. McColl noted that 'it is evident that as long as these industries last, most of the Indians in my inspectorate will, along with their other pursuits, be enabled to obtain a comfortable livelihood.'[34] There was little in the structure of the resource economy that was designed to provide long-term security for Natives. Another dimension of post-1870 change was recorded in 1906 by Indian Agent J.O. Lewis: 'The Indian of St. Peters has become the hewer of wood and drawer of water to the white man.'[35] Indeed, as the treaty process had dispossessed Indians of their resources, they really were left with no option but to sell their labour as hewers of wood and drawers of water.

The early reserve transition period (1870-1914) was a period of change, and I have shown that neither the creation of reserves nor the decline in the fur trade put an end to an active economic role for Natives. From the description of economies at the band level, it is apparent that two economic regions emerged in northern Manitoba (see Figure 10.1). The treaty process separated northern Manitoba into ceded and non-ceded territory. This legal partition tended to correspond to an economic division of northern Manitoba. Bands in one area suffered under the mono-economy of the fur trade, while to the south, many communities were incorporated with new resource industries. During this period, the Hudson's Bay Company's influence was eroded by capitalist resource firms such as Robinson, McArthur, and Armstrong/Booth fishing companies. This competition was serious enough for the Company to consider buying out Armstrong's fourteen trading posts and seventeen fish stations. In 1913, Armstrong's assets were valued at $550,000 and paid 10 per cent on stock. Furthermore, his company had fish sales of $580,000 and merchandise sales of $575,000, and $60,000 worth of furs were purchased.[36] This pattern of revenue indicates the degree to which resource capitalists were diversified. The high ratio of merchandise sales to the value of fish and fur indicates the importance of local incomes. Moreover, the linking of production (fish and furs) and distribution (merchandise) in the same business organization meant that much of the money paid as wages was 'recovered' by the trading posts.

The economic changes in the Interlake and Lake Winnipeg region were reflected in population movements. Faced with low fur prices, the HBC had restricted the fur economy. But in the process, a surplus population was created. A portion of the Norway House band responded to these new economic conditions by moving south to Fisher River. This relieved the Norway House district of a surplus population for a few years. The 'space' created by the Fisher River group was quickly filled by Natives from York Factory and Oxford House. In the Hudson Bay Lowlands, the capacity to earn an income was even worse than when the Norway House district had been 'over populated.' Out-migrations from York Factory, Oxford House, and Norway House were part of a legacy of demographic changes ushered in by the fur trade. The northwestward movement of the Ojibwa, the southwestward drift of the Swampy Cree, and the concentration of the Metis as a surplus population at Red River following the merger of the Hudson's Bay Company and the North West Company in 1821 illustrate the interrelationship between economic and demographic changes.

In the post-1870 era, Native migration patterns became more complex. New resource industries permitted Natives to leave the fur trade. Additionally, the Department of Indian Affairs, through treaty and reserve policies, could control migrations. Efforts to relocate Plains Treaty Indians or Natives from northeastern Manitoba to economically more prosperous economic regions were blocked by Indian Affairs. Similarly, the department had the authority to force relocations. The St. Peters band was politically and economically coerced into moving to a new reserve on the Fisher River. Underlying all the false rationalizations that prevented Natives from northeastern Manitoba from moving south was an isolationist policy. And the surrender of the prosperous St. Peters reserve was also justified, in part, by isolationist thinking. In 1908, Indian Agent Lewis argued: 'It is generally conceded, however, that the removal of this band to a reserve somewhat more remote from immediate contact with civilization will promote their moral welfare. It will take another period of moral training in the wilderness to enable them to resist the enticing allurements of civilization.'[37] The surrender of the St. Peters reserve was an indication that economic development was less important to the department than 'moral welfare.' Modernization and progress were rife with contradictions between the political will of the Department of Indian Affairs and the transformation that was predicted by capitalism.

The cynical rationalizations of the Department of Indian Affairs were evident when the records on non-ceded areas of Manitoba and the St. Peters surrender are compared. A rationale was improvised to prevent Reverend Stevens from moving Natives from a stagnant area to a more promising region, but the same rationalization was quickly discarded when the department came to the aid of Selkirk area land speculators. Over 900 Indians were moved to Peguis a few years after Stevens had failed to bring destitute Indians out of the fur country. Missionaries influenced the economic dimensions of department policy, and Semmens was more concerned with the economic prospects of the Hudson's Bay Company than the well-being of Indians of the low country.

All too often, Indian Affairs policy is studied in isolation or evaluated in terms of the legality of Aboriginal title. In the case of the plan to move Indians out of northeastern Manitoba, mercantile interests were very relevant. Policymakers like McLean viewed the question of Indian title in terms of waiting for advancing civilization to interfere with natural resources and make industrial pursuits an absolute necessity. Aboriginal title was bound up in land and labour markets. A poor and surplus population strengthened the government's position when it came time for the adhesions to Treaty Five. In effect, the Natives of northeastern Manitoba were stuck in a legal and economic vacuum. With the surrender of its charter and the transfer of Rupertsland, the Company sought to be relieved of its responsibilities for Aboriginal populations. This meant cutting back on its paternalistic expenditures (debts, gratuities, and sick and destitute costs). Because the Department of Indian Affairs had rejected Indian requests for a treaty until 1908, Indians in this non-ceded territory obtained little assistance from the Canadian government. In fact, the Department of Indian Affairs used the resulting deprivation as a lever.

When the rest of Manitoba was brought under treaty (1908-10), the spatial mobility of Indians was nearly frozen by the Department of Indian Affairs; except for transferring individuals band memberships between reserves, very little regional movement occurred. However, once a surplus population increased beyond the capacity of the traditional economy, policies and programs were designed to entice Natives to leave their communities.

12

'The Fish and Waters Should Be Ours': The Demise of Native Fisheries – Regulation and Capitalization

The more regulated fishing industry that followed Samuel Wilmot's 1890 investigation was the result of actions taken by Indians. Indians pressed for conservation and regulation measures in order to maintain subsistence use of the resource. Nonetheless, the application of regulations adversely affected Native fisheries in so far as new fisheries regulations restricted Native access to this resource. Moreover, the Fisheries Department rejected requests to use regulatory means to protect Indian fisheries effectively. Indian attitudes towards fisheries regulations stemmed from the ambiguity of implementing the treaties. After 1890, the commercial fishing industry became even more capitalized and concentrated. This reorganization of the industry affected the livelihood of both Native and white fishermen. In this period, fish stocks were over-exploited and commercial sturgeon fisheries were depleted. Both government regulations and a capitalist fishery served to further alienate Indians from resources and to diminished their influence over the future of the regional economy.

Fisheries Regulations and Native People
The development of large scale commercial fishing represented the transition from production almost solely for use value (domestic or subsistence purposes) to production for exchange and use value. The previous conventions that managed this common access resource were not adequate to maintain fish populations under the pressure of the efficient and capital intensive commercial industry. Wilmot's investigation, which had been initiated after the protests of Indians, resulted in a revision of fisheries regulations, and it marked the first of a series of efforts to manage the fisheries. Historical records, however, suggest that Indian attitudes towards regulations and their participation in domestic and commercial fisheries were complex. Similarly, interpretations of the legal basis for the regulation of what had been an Indian resource prior to the treaties are not straight-

forward. The written version of Treaties One and Two, including the amended versions, do not mention hunting and fishing rights. Treaty Five, however, states:

> Her Majesty further agrees with her said Indians that they, the said Indians shall have right to pursue their avocations of hunting and fishing through-out the tract surrendered as hereinbefore described, subject to such regula-tions as may from time to time be made by Her Government of Her Domin-ion of Canada, and saving and excepting such tracts as may from time to time be required or taken up for settlement, mining, lumbering or other purposes by her said Government of the Dominion of Canada, or by any of the subjects thereof duly authorized therefor [*sic*] by the said Government.[1]

The written text of Treaty Five gives the right to the government to regulate the Indian hunting and fishing, but it does not explain for whose benefit the fisheries should be regulated. Fisheries regulations also explicitly claimed a jurisdiction over Indian fisheries. Section 16 of the 1894 version of 'Regu-lation Relating to Fishing in Manitoba and the North-West Territories' stipu-lated that: 'These regulations shall apply to Indians and halfbreeds, as well as to settlers and all other persons.'[2] In contrast to this legal basis for fisher-ies regulations, an Indian chief at Berens River argued in 1890 that 'when we made this Treaty, it was given us to understand that although we sold the Government these lands, yet we might still hunt in the woods as before, and the fish and the waters should be ours as it was in our grandfathers' time.'[3] The ownership of water and fish is not clearly stated in Treaty Five, and the only significant reference to water simply stated: 'But reserving the free navigation of the said Lake Winnipeg and river [Berens River], and free access to the shores and waters thereof for Her Majesty and all her sub-jects.'[4] An Indian interpretation, which simply acknowledged giving up the land and not water resources, could easily be supported because the word-ing of the written treaty only stated that Indians gave up 'forever, all their rights, titles and privileges whatsoever to the lands.'[5]

One of the first regulations to affect Indian fishing was a two dollar com-mercial fishing licence fee. Indians considered the fee a form of taxation and a violation of treaty rights. Although Treaties One and Two did not refer to resource rights, Indians did not accept the licence fee. Indeed, as Indian Agent Muckle reported in 1888: 'They consider it an injustice to them, as they were promised free fishing to make a living by at the time of the treating they say. This I believe is a fact as I have spoken to a number of outsiders who were present at the making of the treaties and they all say such a promise was given by the commissioners.'[6] In terms of contempo-rary understandings of treaties, this evidence is vital because an Indian agent has recorded the observations of whites who witnessed Treaty One. This testimony supports an important aspect of the Indian oral version of the treaty. A petition from members of the Fort Alexander band argued that they could not afford to pay the fee and that the sale of pickerel in the winter was an important source of income.[7] In 1889, the chief of the Brokenhead band reacted to the licence fee by stating: 'When we made the Treaty with the Government we sold our lands of course, but we did not sell our fish, this commodity we reserved for our own exclusive benefit. The fish then being clearly our own we can sell it to whomever we choose without paying licence.'[8] From an Indian perspective, access to resources was not extinguished by a treaty with the Crown. Officials from the Department of Fisheries felt that Indians earned good wages and could afford the licence; and at any rate, the traders usually paid the licences for them. Indian agents were unable to get fisheries officials to change their position on the commercial licence fee for Indians.[9]

The practice of exploiting whitefish spawning areas and the waste of these fish as a result of the trade in fish oil made the regulated closed season another major concern for Indians. Indian Agent Martineau reported in 1881 that Indians complained about the members of the St. Martin and Little Saskatchewan River bands' wilful destruction of whitefish during the spawning season and then leaving 'them in quantities spoiling on the beach.'[10] In the early 1880s, Indian agents believed that the trade in fish oil threatened the subsistence use of this resource and that it encouraged Indians to violate the closed season. In 1882, Martineau reported that he had an agreement with the Indians on the closed season but that white men had persuaded Indians to fish for commercial purposes. In the same year, Martineau attempted to enforce fishing regulations by seizing whitefish caught by traders on the spawning grounds of the Little Saskatchewan River. However, McColl reported that the confiscated fish were 'released by the Superintendent of Fisheries in Winnipeg, who gave authority to this party to engage in fishing there this year again.'[11] The chief of the Fairford band complained about 'restrictions prohibiting the Indians from fishing on the Little Saskatchewan River, whereas speculators from Winnipeg had been scooping and dragging whitefish by thousands daily during the fall.'[12] Consequently, Indian agents found it difficult to get Indians to adhere to regulations. Conservation regulations were being used against Indians, and non-Indians were benefiting from a natural resource that had been alienated from Indian control.

Reverend J. Butler observed that Native fall fishing occurred when the spawn was ready to be deposited; that some spawn was deposited when the fish struggled in the nets; and that the spawn ran from the fish when the nets were lifted. He also claimed that Indians fishing during the spawning season did not affect the supply of whitefish any more than 'the supply of chickens is affected by the consumption of Easter eggs.'[13] Furthermore, Butler argued that the spawn of whitefish caught by the companies before the start of the closed season was not ripe and therefore was destroyed. La Touche Tupper noted that those dependent upon fish – Indians, Metis, and whites – are limited to 'fishing the outer edges of the feeding grounds' and consequently 'only took the surplus from the edges.'[14] A councillor from the Berens River band corroborated Butler's observation when he argued in his own words that 'when an Indian puts his little net near shore in the water when the white fish [sic] come there to spawn he is there just in time to spawn and when he struggles in the net he drops that spawn, and our Indian's [sic] are always careful when they take him out of the net to pass their hand down so as to let everything run out.'[15] Indians would not accept the allegation that they were responsible for the depletion of lake fisheries. A councillor from Berens River recalled that English and French Halfbreed buffalo hunters had fished the lake and asked: 'How was it that white fish [sic] were not scarce then?'[16] This councillor also felt that catching whitefish before the spawning season was responsible for the change in fish populations.

Nonetheless, the fishing regulations permitted some discretion since the minister of marine and fisheries had the power to 'grant to Indians or their bands, free licenses to fish during the closed seasons, for themselves or their bands, for the purposes of providing food for themselves, but not for the purpose of sale, barter or traffic.'[17] Preventing Indians from obtaining fish during the closed season meant relief would be required from the Department of Indian Affairs. In the early 1890s, Indians were permitted to fish during the closed season, although it was reported that some fish caught by Indians at that time would later be sold in the open season. Subsistence fishing during closed seasons seems to have ended by 1895, and by 1897, the Indians were reported to be observing the closed season. The establishment of a closed season was a major development in the regulation of Manitoba fisheries, and it was a necessary condition for a fishery that produced for a market. Traditional Indian resource harvesting strategies were affected by these policies in the late nineteenth century.

The demand for exclusive areas for Indian fishing was one response to the expansion of commercial fishing. Anticipating the effects of settlement on fisheries, the Department of Indian Affairs in Ottawa requested, in 1881, information on Indian fisheries. The Manitoba superintendent was asked to report on what rivers, lakes, and streams should be reserved for the exclusive fishing rights of Indians (see Figure 8.1) after which an 'application may be made to the Department of Marine and Fisheries.'[18] A former Treaty Three commissioner, S. Dawson, acknowledged in 1895 that they had not anticipated the encroachment on Indian fisheries and stated that 'otherwise the [treaty] clause in favour, of the Indians would have been made stronger.'[19] Phair outlined a cogent argument on the government's inconsistent Indian policy:

> The independence and elevation of the native races have a direct connection with the land and water, and the Government has rightly judged that as regards the former but little advantage could be gained without protection; hence, the white man is prohibited using or appropriating anything on the land assigned the Indians by the Gov't. But why should this prohibition be confined to the land? The water is just as much a means of support to the Indian as the land; why should he not have some protection against those who come to his very door and take the fish from his children.[20]

The lack of legal protection for Native fisheries was an obvious weakness in government policy.

Numerous appeals were made for exclusive fishing areas, such as the request in 1892 by The Pas Indians to reserve Clearwater and other lakes. The Pas Indians had learned that 'the small fishermen at Grand Rapids are not killing as many fish near the shore, as they used to, and it is the big fishermen that have done this.'[21] In fact, The Pas Indians were more concerned about class than ethnic exclusion when their chief stated: 'We do not want to bar any breed [Metis] or poor whiteman from fishing these lakes to make a living, we only wish to exclude the Grand Rapids [commercial] fishermen and those like them.'[22] Indians were willing to share, but they also wanted to maintain local control over a resource by excluding external operators. Apparently, there is only one case of a successful effort to create an exclusive fishing reserve. In 1898, the Indians of Berens River were granted some sort of a reserve by the Department of Marine and Fisheries since Pigeon and Paterson bays were closed to all fishermen except band members and white settlers living in the vicinity. Various reasons were offered as an explanation for the Fisheries Department's reluctance to exclude commercial fishing from Native fisheries. The Department of Marine and Fisheries suggested that exclusive Indian fishing privileges would provoke conflict between Indians and white fishermen. In 1905, it was argued by the deputy minister of the Department of Marine and Fisheries that Indian fishing reserves could not be set up in areas already opened up to white settlement. Neither of these reasons constitute a valid defence of Fisheries Department policy, since requests for fishing reserves came long before white settlement and because Indians were primarily concerned with excluding large fishing companies and not small-scale white fishermen. The Fisheries Department did not respond to demands for exclusive Indian reserves by using the regulatory process to further Indian economic security.

Expanded Production: 1890-1915[23]

After 1890, fish harvests increased, and the industry expanded northward as new fisheries were brought into production. By 1904, the Lake Winnipeg fishery produced 7.5 million pounds of whitefish, a dramatic increase over the 2.5 million pounds marketed in 1890. The overall trend until 1905, except for a drop in the late 1890s, was towards expanding yields. The success of the industry allowed Fisheries Inspector McQueen to predict: 'It is safe to say that fishing will in a few years be second only to farming in Manitoba,' although he cautioned that the industry might be 'hampered too much by unnecessary restrictions.'[24]

Indicators demonstrate that McQueen's pronouncement was wrong, and that the existing regulations did not protect certain species from overharvesting. After 1905, whitefish yields declined significantly. During this era, pickerel yields increased relative to whitefish yields; an indication that the exclusive exploitation of whitefish in the 1890s had upset the balance between the populations of these two species. Moreover, declining whitefish catches necessitated the commercial exploitation of pickerel. In the late 1890s, after some of the Lake Winnipeg fisheries had been overfished, the Lake Winnipegosis whitefish fishery was brought into production. Additionally, official figures for the early years of commercial fishing understate whitefish yields. Waste was central to the manner in which the industry developed. At the north end of the lake, as much as 60 per cent of the fish were not marketed.[25] Captain William Robinson admitted: 'Oh yes, the first fifteen years of fishing was a tremendous slaughter.'[26] Much of this waste can be explained by the industry's exclusive desire for whitefish, which meant that other species caught in gill nets were thrown away. The industry's inability to preserve fish for market meant that fish were wasted.

This period of establishment and consolidation of commercial fishing witnessed both the spread of commercialized sturgeon fishing and the demise of sturgeon fisheries. The geographical expansion of sturgeon operations was an effort to counteract the effects of localized depletion. In the 1880s, sturgeon fishing for the market began at Grand Marais and Pigeon River, but the pursuit of sturgeon resulted in the introduction of commercial fishing to the lower Saskatchewan River and the Nelson River. Figure 12.1 shows the production of sturgeon for the Lake Winnipeg fishery (including tributaries), and there can be no doubt that the collapse of this commercial fishery occurred. Overfishing caused the decline of this fishery. The sturgeon's biological characteristics make it a species that cannot easily

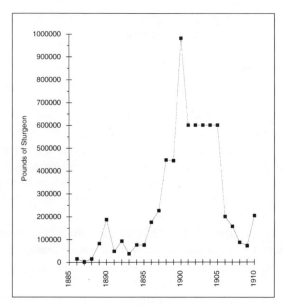

Figure 12.1   Lake Winnipeg sturgeon production, 1886-1910 (CSP, 1887-1912, 'Fisheries')

survive the effects of an intensive fishery. The sturgeon is a slow-growing fish that takes a number of years to reach sexual maturity. In the Nelson River, males take fifteen to twenty years and females twenty-five to thirty-three years to reach maturity. At the time of first spawning, males are thirty to forty inches in length and females are thirty-three to forty-seven inches in length. Sturgeon reach the reproductive stage long after they are large enough to be easily caught. Additionally, sturgeon are not frequent spawners. Estimates suggest that the males spawn once every two to seven years, and females only spawn every four to nine years.[27] Slow growth and infrequent spawning make the sturgeon unable to respond to aggressive fishing.

While sturgeon fishing had been carried on in the 1880s, a more important fishery emerged in the late 1890s, and by the turn of the century, sturgeon fishing had expanded into the Saskatchewan and Nelson rivers. This expansion was partly induced by a change in market conditions. In 1897, the value of sturgeon and its products had doubled and even tripled, while the price of whitefish had decreased. In the same year, La Touche Tupper noted that 'there was a large increase of sturgeon fishing,' and that 'the industry is gradually creeping up the east shore' of Lake Winnipeg.[28] In 1898, sturgeon and caviar production began on the drainage of the lower Saskatchewan River. In 1900, the Poplar River, Norway House, and Cross

Lake bands began to engage in sturgeon fishing. The Department of Fisheries adopted a policy of favouring local residents for sturgeon fishing. Of the 180 sturgeon licenses issued for the Nelson River in 1903, all but four went to Indian and Metis fishermen.[29] Similarly, only residents of the lower Saskatchewan River were granted licenses in 1903. Native participation in sturgeon fishing at the turn of the century contrasted sharply with their opposition to commercial fishing in the 1880s. Fisheries Inspector La Touche Tupper explained how support for commercial operations developed: 'I only licensed residents, and near the Indian reserves at Berens River, Bloodvein, I only issued to Indians of the reserve, much to their benefit and satisfaction. They all took out licenses and strictly observe the law. The Berens River chief personally sees that all the nets are taken up Saturday; all offal disposed of, and only the proper number of yards of twine used.'[30] Initially, the residents of the lower Saskatchewan River responded to commercial sturgeon fishing by petitioning for the closing of the fishery, 'fearing the intrusion of outside men.' But according to Fisheries Inspector E. Miller, Indians and Metis later became 'anxious to avail themselves to the fullest degree of the opportunity for a profitable industry so offered.'[31] However, opposition to sturgeon fishing occurred when extremely efficient pound nets were used by commercial fishermen. The use of pound nets at the Saskatchewan River fishery was defended by Miller because they 'formed the necessary nucleus for the opening up of a valuable industry,' and because fish 'would remain an unrealizable asset if fishing by outsiders was entirely prohibited.'[32]

The dynamics of the geographical spread of commercial sturgeon fishing were outlined by Miller, noting that 'the great demand for this fish has caused the fish companies to push their operations' into the lower Saskatchewan River, and that sturgeon was 'the only fish, which under existing conditions of transportation, could be profitably marketed from the lower Saskatchewan and Nelson river districts.'[33] By 1904, sturgeon fishing had pressed beyond Cedar Lake to Cumberland Lake. In the same year, winter fishing of whitefish had begun on Moose Lake, whereas the year before, Miller had reported that 'no attempt was made to take out whitefish or less valuable fish.'[34] This set a pattern: the introduction of commercial fishing to remote lakes and rapid-ridden rivers of the north began with the exclusive fishing for high-priced sturgeon. The firm of Ewing and Fryer found sturgeon fishing on the Nelson River profitable enough to develop a transportation system employing York boats, a gasoline boat, and a steam tug to trans-ship over rapids and downstream from Sipiwesk Lake to the station at Spider Island. In the 1920s, sturgeon fishing proceeded up the Churchill, Fox, and Hayes rivers.

The decline of sturgeon as a resource was the most serious debasement of the Native economy in the post-1870 period and an illustration of complete failure of state resource management regulations. Those charged with fisheries management were aware of the importance of sturgeon to Indians and the legacy of depleted sturgeon fisheries in Canada.[35] Figure 12.1 implies that there was a boom in this industry's development, and a corresponding increase in commercialized income for Indians. The annual report for Indian Affairs recorded that the Indians from Moose and Cedar lakes made 'a good deal of money from sturgeon-fishing and the sale of caviare.'[36] Reports indicate that Indians were paid a dollar per fish. So, in 1902, 5,200 sturgeon averaging twenty-six pounds generated $5,200 of income for the Indians at the Nelson River fishery (the average value of twenty-six pounds of sturgeon was $1.56). Thus, 5,500 pounds of caviar valued at one dollar per pound meant a loss of income of $5,500, since fish were purchased in the round.[37] Clearly, companies derived more benefits from the commercialization of sturgeon fisheries than did Indians. The boom was followed by a collapse (see Figure 12.1), and, not surprisingly, one of the major sturgeon exporters, Ewing and Fryer, ceased its operations. This decline in sturgeon production was apparent on the Nelson River; in 1902, 135,200 pounds were harvested, while by 1907, only 7,000 pounds were landed.[38] Initially, Indians opposed commercial fishing, but as with the fur trade, they became incorporated into the market and began producing for export. On account of the sturgeon's biological characteristics, and the lack of regulations capable of dealing with a strong commercial demand, Indian benefits from this depleted fishery were short-term.

Fisheries Inspector Miller's optimism in 1904 was not an adequate basis for fisheries management: 'A feeling exists in some quarters that allowing fish to be sold from these waters [Nelson River] will endanger the food supply of the Indians, but the extent of water is so great and the resident population so small, that this fear is groundless, and from a material point of view, the existence of a market for fish cannot fail to be of great benefit to the Indians and encourage industry among them.'[39] There are indications that fisheries officials were unable to detect stress on sturgeon populations. In 1904, it was reported that the Winnipeg River was 'teeming with young sturgeon,' suggesting that overfishing had changed the age distribution of the sturgeon population.[40] In 1910, the overseer of the Winnipeg River was naively delighted that very little caviar had been manufactured out of the 173,800 pounds of sturgeon, because this 'would go to show that the fish were not parent fish.'[41] The absence of older sturgeon or the breeding stock indicates that overfishing was well under way. The future propagation of the species was at risk because only young sturgeon were being caught. In order to maintain overall yields as the average weight of the species declined, even more fish had to be caught. In 1898, Inspector of Fisheries E. Miller had suggested that 'the development of the fishery at this point [Cedar Lake] for export purposes is considered to be prejudicial to the interests of the resident population.'[42] Although Miller changed his perspective and approved commercial fishing, the case of Lake Winnipeg sturgeon is a clear example of how unregulated market forces were detrimental to the long-term interests of the resident population.

Capitalization and Depletion

Major capital investments by commercial fishing companies constituted one of the earliest changes in the Interlake's economic infrastructure following the fur trade. Expanded production after 1890 was achieved by a similarly rapid capitalization process. In 1890, the Lake Winnipeg fishery investments were valued at $79,460; but by 1905, the industry was worth $501,740.[43] After 1893, the investment in steam tugs and shore stations (wharves, icehouses, freezers) increased over sailboats and nets. The trend towards greater and greater investments in vessels and plants indicated the increasingly capitalistic nature of the industry. To a certain extent, such demands for capital on Lake Winnipeg were the result of the distances that had to be travelled to bring the fish to market. Furthermore, the exporting of fresh fish created the need for more cold storage facilities.

On Lake Winnipeg, an expanding, capital-intensive mode of production coincided with the reorganization of the fishery. In 1898, Captain Robinson formed the Dominion Fish Company through a forced merger of the other major fishing companies. At the same time, in Chicago, the A. Booth Packing Company was reorganized and became the largest fish firm in the United States. The A. Booth Packing Company owned Robinson's Dominion Fish Company. According to F.W. Colcleugh, the fisheries inspector for Manitoba, the smaller firms were forced to sell their business to a syndicate.[44] The reorganization of the fish companies, both in Manitoba and in the United States, under the direction of Booth interests was not unusual; it was part of the prevailing movement at the centres of financial power towards trusts and combines. The effects of this merger, however, were felt in the 'remote' fisheries of Lake Winnipeg.

During this decade of rapid centralization of capital, the relationship with the U.S. market and the American ownership of fish operations became apparent. In the 1890s, records of the Department of Fisheries indicate that, despite frequent denials by the companies in Manitoba, their operations were owned and controlled by Americans. For example, the Manitoba Fish Company issued 1,003 shares, of which only three were held by residents of Canada. In 1893, Captain Robinson elucidated the relationship between American capital and Manitoba fish in an interview with federal fisheries officials: 'That is the way all business is done there. When a firm starts business as a rule they go to some firm in the United States, as there is no market in this country, and they make arrangements, probably in the beginning, to get a certain amount of money, and as to the price of fish.'[45] Early Manitoba resource capitalists required U.S. financing and obtained benefits from the association. Production for the external market generated a dependence of Manitoba firms on American buyers.

For the fishermen, both Native and white, the consequences of the combining of commercial firms was a drop in the prices paid for fish and essentially a compression of their incomes. Their reaction to this merger was to petition the federal government and to form the Fishermen's Protection Union. Their 1900 petition read:

> The said American company practically exercise a monopoly of the whitefish business on the said lake; thereby injuring us to an immense extent not only by the rapid depletion ... but also in many other ways incident to a monopoly, as by greatly and unjustly depressing the wages, prices and profits obtainable by us as such fishermen as aforesaid, and by practically excluding many bona fide Manitoba companies from Selkirk and Winnipeg, etc., which would otherwise form and engage in the said fishing industry.[46]

In particular, the fishermen demanded a reduction in the yardage of nets employed on the lake. This petition was supported by Icelandic and Native communities.

The increase in fish yields after 1900 occurred because of an expansion in the capital employed. These trends, however, were preceded by the formation of a monopoly under the Dominion Fish Company. On Lake Winnipeg, the development of the north end of the lake continued. When whitefish yields from Lake Winnipeg dropped in 1901, the exploitation of whitefish and sturgeon was pushed into the drainage of the lower Saskatchewan River. Not surprisingly, in 1908, a Native missionary from Cumberland House would complain that 'an American can be allowed to deplete our waters of fish' and go on to protest the 'wholesale slaughter of our fish.'[47] The merging of capital, incorporation of new areas into commercial fishing, and the expansion of investment suggest that certain production problems existed that are not demonstrated by the total harvest figures. Figure 12.2 is a crude representation of a catch/effort ratio for the Lake Winnipeg whitefish fishery. Changes in annual yields are indicated as pounds of fish per foot of gill net. These data show a decline in catch relative to effort. The

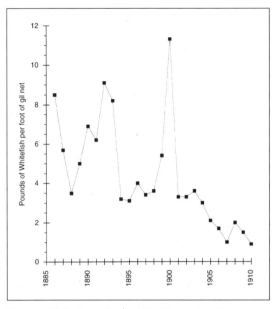

Figure 12.2   Pounds of whitefish produced per foot of gill net in Lake Winnipeg, 1886-1910 (CSP, 1887-1911, 'Fisheries')

industry responded by investing more capital. Despite fluctuating yields, the industry appears to have been caught in a depletion/profitability bind. This explains the buying up of smaller companies by the Dominion Fish Company, expanded investment, and the lowering of incomes. After 1905, the total production levels dropped, and this trend continued until 1907, when fishermen demanded an investigation.

Consolidation of a Commercial Fishing Industry

The declining yields after the 1904 peak and the financial crisis of 1907 created a juncture that necessitated another government investigation. The protest of fishermen in 1899, 1900, and 1907 eventually resulted in an investigation of inland fisheries by a federal Royal Commission (Dominion Fisheries Commission for Manitoba and the North West 1909-10).[48] Evidence of abusive exploitation of the province's fish resources came from local fish merchants. More evidence of declining fish stocks was presented. All Winnipeg fish merchants maintained that the subsidiaries of U.S. interests stifled the local market. Fish merchants argued that the best fish was shipped out of the country and that only poorer quality fish was marketed in Winnipeg. One fish merchant who encountered difficulties in getting whitefish from Lake Winnipeg stated: 'It seems to me we are catering to the United States, foreign market' and that 'Canadian people in this neighbourhood should be allowed this privilege, why should we let the best fish leave the country and we have to pay such exorbitant prices.'[49] Thus, resource development was oriented towards foreign interests, and local merchants and consumers did not have access to the fish. Moreover, pressure on fish stocks was all too apparent. Prior to commercial fishing, whitefish averaged four pounds. During Wilmot's investigation, the weight had dropped to an average of three to three-and-a-half pounds. During the sittings of the Royal Commission of 1910, considerable testimony was provided to indicate that the weight of whitefish had declined to between two pounds and two-and-a-half pounds. This drop in the average size of whitefish meant that production could only be stabilized or increased if proportionately more fish were caught to compensate for the decline in average size. Under the prevailing economic structure, the resource was being depleted and the people of Manitoba had very limited access to its consumption.

The most cogent testimony before the royal commission was provided by Johann Solmundson, an Icelandic clergyman and secretary of the fishermen's union. Solmundson believed that the problem was between capital and labour, and he maintained that there 'have been American interests here, and this very fact is the key to the whole situation.'[50] He also described the supply problem facing the industry:

> The story of the white fish [sic] is identical with the story of buffalo. The lake was filled with whitefish when the white man came here first, and it is through the white man's work that it is gone ... evidence goes to show that these interests are rich enough to maintain that hold and to keep going on after them, and possibly to chase them into the last spot in the north end of the lake. And it is shewn that from the beginning, when the immigrant settler could catch enough fish for his family on a small scale, which it was then, until now, when it takes a good-sized steamboat to catch anything worth the investment, and this has all come about in thirty short years.[51]

Although Solmundson drew an analogy between the buffalo and the whitefish and suggested that a tragedy similar to the wiping out of the buffalo was occurring, he did not explain the conflict in purely racial terms. Instead, he argued that a capital-intensive fishery had caused the demise of the means of survival for both Natives and settlers. Finally, he provided an analysis of dependency relations in 1910: 'Gradually three interests were formed. The corporate interest, of which the Booth Company has been the holding company. Secondly, the labour interests on the lake, and 3ly., [*sic*] and last, a sort of go-between-interest in the Icelandic local merchants, and those three are so intertwined that it will take superhuman wisdom to prescribe a remedy for the malady.'[52] A capitalist fishery, employing local middlemen as intermediaries between producers and the external market, had consolidated control over the resource to such an extent that it was difficult to conceive of alternatives.

After several sittings of the royal commission, an interim report was issued. The commissioners stated: 'We have reached the conclusion that all the lakes of Manitoba have been over-fished, and that some of the more valuable species such as the whitefish and yellow pickerel have decreased very seriously in size and in abundance, and that the sturgeon, the most valuable fish found in these waters, is on the point of extinction.'[53] They agreed with the testimony concerning declining fish populations: 'We have abundant evidence that the Manitoba fisheries have been unduly controlled by foreign fish operators, who have indicated the prices of fish and have secured the major portion of the profits. The people of Manitoba have benefited little from these Great Lake fisheries.'[54] On the question of the local market, the interim report noted: 'Moreover, inferior grades of fish have been sold in the Canadian market, while the better grades including the larger size fish, have been exported to the United States markets.'[55]

These 'facts' did not withstand the political process. The correspondence of the Department of Fisheries documented that considerable political pressure was put on the commission. The final report was delayed for two years, and it reversed most of the findings of the interim report, merely recommending better management of the resource. In fact, the final report went so far as to deny the foreign ownership of the industry![56] If they had consulted *Moody's Manual of Railroads and Corporation Securities*, they would have learned that the entire capital stock of the Dominion Fish Company (along with other Manitoba operators), was owned by the American Booth Fisheries Company.[57]

Native fisheries that fell under the influence of the external market did not remain 'traditional.' Many Natives sold fish or worked as wage labourers. Some scholars will undoubtedly see parallels between the fish industry and the fur trade. Claims could be made that Native peoples entered into a partnership with the Booth Fish Company and that both had mutual interests and were interdependent. In point of fact, fishermen, especially Native fishermen, had no equity in the system that exploited the natural wealth of the fisheries. Their benefits were short-term.

As the industry developed, Native subsistence fisheries declined. By the time the royal commission issued its report in 1912, fishermen were in a marginal position; their labour, regardless of race, was subordinated to American capital. During the boom, abundant fisheries and labour combined to produce wealth. But, like the fur trade, most of the commercial value was quickly transferred out of the region.[58] Because the economic surplus from this industry was controlled by American companies, the region lost control over its economic future. The reorientation of Native fisheries to the external market resulted in the loss of the resource and a decline in their traditional system of management.

Government regulations were misplaced and therefore largely ineffective. The commercialization of fisheries necessitated government regulations. Initially, regulations sought to balance commercial and subsistence resource uses. Restricting subsistence fishing during the closed season undermined Indian access to resources that had been theirs as a birthright and which they thought had been protected by treaties with the Crown. Sturgeon, a vital pre-commercial component of the Ojibwa economy, was depleted. The government did not assist Indians; they were neither provided with capital to produce for the market on their own nor were they allowed to own exclusive fishing areas. Government regulations were more concerned with stamping out subsistence fishing during the closed season than with the rapid and reckless commercialization of Manitoba fisheries. American capital and ineffective government regulations resulted in an erosion of Native benefits from lake fisheries. The problems of the industry – low incomes, threatened fish stocks, foreign ownership, and truncated local markets – were outlined by a royal commission. The federal government chose to ignore these findings and to capitulated to foreign capital. Given that the state was not concerned with protecting national interests, the Department of Fisheries could not be expected to guide the development of the region's fisheries in a manner that would promote Native economic security. In effect, the spirit and intent of the treaties was disregarded. Government policy could have been designed to convert the natural wealth of these fisheries into a tangible asset for Native communities.

13

'Civilizing the Wilderness Will Affect Us': The Demise of the Hudson's Bay Company and the Re-Emergence of Competition

Changes in the regional economy and the mobilization of land and labour altered the mercantile landscape. The fur industry itself was not static or unchanging in this era. In advance of industrial capital, a renewed struggle for the fur country occurred after 1900. New markets and rising prices resulted in a reorganization of the industry. Innis maintained that the post-1870 period showed a decline in monopoly that was accompanied by numerous changes:

> The period after 1869 has been one of the most interesting periods in the history of the trade ... The trade has gone through a period of remarkable transportation and communication changes. These changes, beginning with the disappearance of Hudson's Bay Company control, have gained momentum after 1900 and especially after 1914. The increased demand for furs following improvements in manufacturing and the importance of new fur-bearing animals like the white fox have been of pronounced importance.[1]

The post-1870 changes can be understood by considering the spatial diffusion of new fur buyers, the forms of organization of competitive fur buyers, and the role of new markets in restructuring the fur trade. The establishment of competitive fur buyers in this period was a spatially uneven process. The decline of the Hudson's Bay Company's monopoly and the Company's adaptation to a variety of competitive fur buyers is an essential theme of the economic history of northern Manitoba. After 1900, the subarctic fur trade was revitalized because of the dynamic external imperatives of the North American fur market. The development of this new market effectively challenged the Hudson's Bay Company's dominance.

In 1873, the replacement of English sterling with Canadian currency in the HBC accounts foreshadowed impending changes that were not simply bookkeeping procedures. The pull of the south was being felt. In the 1880s, with respect to the Keewatin District, there are references to the old system of trade, abolition of the Made Beaver, and resistance to change on the part of post officers.[2] Traders may have been less adaptable to change than Natives, as this explanation for the resignation of a Fort Alexander officer in 1891 seemed to indicate: 'That while still active he passed nearly half a century in the Company's Service and, thoroughly impressed with old ideas, he found it difficult to adapt himself to the altered conditions of the present day.'[3] The theme of change and survival of the HBC dominates this period; the district annual report for 1919 finally recognized that 'in years gone by the Fur Trade was as the Company made it, but I regret to state that the time has come when we will have to adapt ourselves to the trade as it now is.'[4] In terms of the concepts of change and stability, it is the Company that resisted modernization of its economic relationship with Natives. Indian responses to competitive fur buyers initiated change.

After 1870, the HBC's dominance of the fur industry in northern Manitoba declined significantly. With the re-emergence of competition after 1870, both Natives and fur buyers practised trade in a manner that resembled the trade of the 1790-1821 competitive period. The monopoly that existed after 1821 lost influence. Although the HBC reorganized its transport system and reduced the overhead expenses of its posts after 1870, responses to competitive fur buyers called for changes to patterns of exchange.

Spread of Competition
The Company had an acute sense of the spatial aspects of profitability. The initial proposal to build a railway to Hudson Bay in the 1880s generated this observation by the missionary Lofthouse: 'the Co. are [sic] greatly opposed to Churchill being occupied because there is a great stir in Canada now concerning the Hudson Bay Route for exploration, and the Company desire [sic] to keep this part of the country closed on a/c of the fur trade.'[5] In 1889, the Nelson River post was considered to be a location that produced a fair profit margin because fur prices were lower and goods prices higher than at other posts.[6] This condition existed because of an absence of competition. The annual report for 1895 noted that the 'only Post at which pure Fur-trading is carried on is Little Grand Rapids, and this is still a profitable place, which it would be well to maintain.'[7] The use of the term 'pure fur trade' implies the archaic trade, prior to the influences of competitive cash buyers. Similarly, in 1896, the Keewatin District, along with those districts close to Hudson Bay, were described as purely fur trading districts with profitable results.[8] Thus, those areas that today have been carelessly labelled as isolated and remote, produced the most wealth.

Certain generalizations about the diffusion of competition are possible. Figure 13.1 reconstructs the diffusion of competition. With the expansion of fishing companies, furs became a sideline. For the Manitoba district in 1888 it was recorded: 'Certainly the party that purchases fish from the Indians will get fur also. This we have already seen at Fairford.'[9] Commercial fishing spread northward on lakes Manitoba, Winnipegosis, and Winnipeg, and by 1899, the Company's trade was suffering at Norway House due to the arrival of commercial fishing. In the Manitoba District, fish merchants seriously undermined the Company's supply of fur. Although the Company engaged in the fish business in the Manitoba District, it did not seriously develop this resource. The same mistake was not made when commercial fishing reached the lower Saskatchewan River. For The Pas area, the Company realized that 'To retain the trade it will be necessary to deal in fish as well as furs,'[10] and for a number of years the Company engaged in the fishing industry. Lumbering on the lakes meant a similar leakage of furs for the Company. While new resource industries focused on the exploitation of fisheries and forest, these commercial interests were a means for spreading competitive challenges to the HBC. Old mercantile patterns of life were altered.

Merchants from places such as Selkirk and Prince Albert, and free traders from Duck Bay, put pressure on the periphery of the Company's Keewatin district (see Figure 13.1). The activities of Prince Albert merchants brought a west-east diffusion of competition to the Cumberland district and the western side of Keewatin. Revillon Frères was well established in the Cumberland district by 1904, and its influence was felt in the western side of the Keewatin District. Although Revillon Frères competed with the HBC throughout much of the subarctic, this firm was never established within the Company's historic core of the York Factory-Norway House axis. Revillon Frères closed its post at The Pas in 1923.

One free trader who competed in the Keewatin district was a Norwegian by the name of Hyer. Figure 13.1 shows Hyer's area of operations. HBC records noted Hyer's presence in 1875, and his operations spread throughout the Keewatin District. Hyer provided enduring competition to the HBC until the early years of the depression, when the Campbell brothers usurped his place. But Hyer failed to establish a presence in the muskrat swamps of Cumberland District. Although, Hyer affected York Factory's hinterland, he did not establish residence on the Bay.

On the coast, only the occasional resident trader became established. For example, Revillon Frères was reported to have had a representative at Churchill in 1908. During the sporadic construction of the railway to the coast (1910-29), free traders were in a position to challenge the HBC at its old

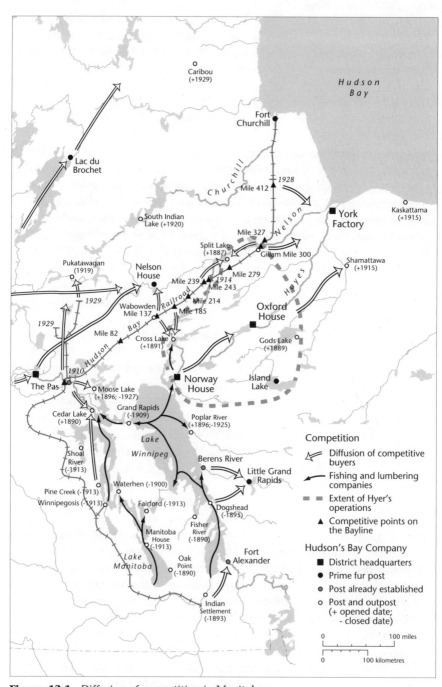

Figure 13.1 Diffusion of competition in Manitoba

centre at York Factory. During the First World War, two free traders, Ray and MacDonald, operated in the immediate vicinity of York Factory but were bought out by the HBC in 1920.

The Company, in its desire for monopoly, often feared the encroachment of 'civilization' (competitive pressures from settlements such as Portage la Prairie, Westbourne, and Gladstone). Consequently, for the outfit of 1906: 'The Fur Trade in this [Manitoba] District continues to gradually give way to the inroads of civilization.'[11] Railways represented civilization's rapid encroachment on the Company's monopoly. In 1897, the HBC anticipated the eventual arrival of the railway in the Cumberland District: 'This comparatively near approach of Railway communication will undoubtedly affect the trade of the District, and the changes in Tariffs and the abolition of Indian Debts will be needed in order to render it possible to make a profit upon the altered trade.'[12] A railway to Winnipegosis was held responsible for the weak results of the Pine Creek post, and the Company responded by building a post at Winnipegosis. The completion of the railway to The Pas increased competition because it made cash buying feasible. The Inspection Report for 1909 anticipated the general commercial changes that would occur: 'The trade at the [*sic*] Pas henceforth will be of a mixed character, requiring a more modern Store and a stock not wholly confined to the requirements of the Indian Trade.'[13]

One of the strengths of the HBC was its transportation system, which could regularly move goods and furs across the subarctic. However, railways offered an alternate transportation system for the small-scale fur buyer. Therefore, those traders associated with auction houses or small partnerships operating at a few locations, had trade goods and furs shipped without the responsibility for the overhead cost of an entire transportation system. Additionally, railways promoted commercial fishing, lumbering, and mineral exploration. Not only did these activities siphon off Native labour and their furs, but these new organizations also established competing merchandising operations. Not surprisingly, The Pas was transformed by 1911: 'The Pas is already an incorporated town with a number of traders and shop keepers besides the Company, all dealinh [*sic*] in fur, while some of the Winnipeg Fur Houses keep resident buyers there. For the time, the commercial facilities are much in excess of the young town's requirements, and we cannot expect a profitable trade there until conditions adjust themselves.'[14] As with other large mercantile companies, transportation was key to the survival of a profitable monopoly; once that advantage gave way, the economic landscape was quickly transformed. The Hudson Bay Railway advanced in stages, but by 1919 the Bay line, according to district manager C. Harding, 'appears to be a breeding ground for the Opposition, and as they thrive they generally spread to other vicinities.'[15] Important fur trade posts – Nelson River, Split Lake, and Cross Lake – came under steady competitive pressures. The Company responded by purchasing an opposition post on the Bay line and by operating posts at Wabowden/Setting Lake and Gillam. With a rail centre at The Pas, traders were in a position to push northward to Pukatawagan. On the rail line, the Company specifically purchased fur on a cash basis. With the completion of the railway to Churchill came white trappers and competitive fur buyers. However, the Company had already moved the focus of the Chipewyan trade to the new Caribou post. A further indication of the importance of the railway was that the district headquarters moved from York Factory to Churchill with the completion of the railway.

Corresponding to the development of the Bay line was an interest in mineral exploration. In 1927, the annual report for the fur trade recorded that: 'With the opening up of the country by the Hudson Bay Railway, and the present mining activities going on all over northern Manitoba, we may look for an increase, rather than a decrease opposition of this class [small trader].'[16] For example, the Campbell brothers were described by the HBC as a 'concern, who ostensibly went into the country for the mining and prospecting trade [but who] branched out into the fur trade at each point where they are established.'[17] As in the case of lumbering and commercial fishing interests, the early phase of mining development included a minor interest in furs. Thus, in the post-1870 period, the Hudson's Bay Company was faced with the diffusion of both new economic organizations that engaged in a petty trade and new fur trading companies.

Spatial Responses to Competition

In order to understand the changing fur industry, an understanding of the Hudson's Bay Company's spatial responses to competition is vital. The Company's reaction to opposition fur buyers was not limited to just prices, and officers had a keen sense of the spatial dimensions of competition. The annual fur trade report indicated in 1918 that 'it will be remembered that Norway House is the Gateway into this District, and the fact that the Company do [sic] not compete as keenly as possible tends to invite the opposition to that point, ultimately further into the District.'[18] Again, the Company saw the Hudson Bay Railway as a breeding ground for the opposition; thus Mile 412, the end of steel, was 'the rendezvous of every trader in that section.'[19] To counter this opposition, the HBC's spatial responses included sending men to Indian camps, opening outposts and posts to contain the opposition, and directing Natives to different trapping territories where they would be less likely to encounter competitors.

Norway House Company men were sent to Indian camps in the Cross Lake Indians area to oppose free traders in 1868. In 1927, competition at Island Lake became greater than it had been at any previous time, and the Company's officer responded with more men, dogs, and 'tripping.' Competition not only altered the terms of trade, but extra expenses were incurred. For example, in 1885 it was reported that the Company had 'heavy expenses in keeping men and dogs employed running to the hunting camps to collect skins, which is unavoidable when opposition is in the vicinity.'[20] Natives were employed as runners and camp traders, and in the 1920s, separate accounts on the 'camp trade' were incorporated into the post balances. Tripping also occurred because many Indians did not own dogs. Because competitive buying forced frequent visits to Indian camps, the cost of trapping was reduced, and Natives were saved the expense of transporting a good portion of their production. The missionary J. Hines recorded the intensity of rivalry associated with 'tripping' for furs:

> The Company in this district [Cumberland House] have [*sic*] ceased to use York boats for the transaction of their business, they have neither regular brigades, nor appointed times for visiting outposts. The reason for this is, there are many opposition traders in the country, and to visit the outposts at stated times, would be like giving their trade into the hands of their opponents, as they would visit the Indians a few days before the Company's men and so collect up most of the fur. Therefore when the Cos' [*sic*] men go, it is generally at an unexpected time, and invariably they start in the night. No one knows anything about their going, until after they have gone.[21]

In the period after 1870, post locations and the opening of guard or outposts were an important part of the Hudson's Bay Company's strategy to counter the opposition. Poplar River was an outpost that opened and closed according to competitive pressures. In 1865, it was established as a flying post because of opposition; but it was re-established as an outpost in 1874. In 1887, the Company learned that the opposition intended to expand northward in the Cumberland District. Consequently, a guard post (Deer Lake) was set up at the south end of Reindeer Lake to protect Brochet. Similarly, with possible encroachment on York Factory in the late 1880s, an outpost was built at Shamattawa. At the same time, Gods Lake was upgraded to a permanent post. With the building of the railway to The Pas, the HBC post there became a 'guard post.' Many outposts were opened after the outfit of 1919 and throughout the period of high fur prices in the 1920s. To protect the profitable prime fur post Little Grand Rapids from illicit whisky traders from the east shore of Lake Winnipeg, an outpost was established seventy miles to the south. With the northward push of the Hudson Bay Railway, the archaic system of long distance travel by Chipewyans was forced to change. The annual report for 1927 recorded: 'Civilizing the wilderness will affect us in more ways than one, and in order to protect the Native from the vices of civilization, we intend to establish this Fall an inland post for the Chipewyan Indians. This post is located approximately 120 miles North West of Fort Churchill, located in the centre of their hunting grounds.'[22] One of the insidious 'vices of civilization' was the decline of the Company's monopoly. In this instance the Company had to respond to the completion of the railway and did so by moving Chipewyan trade activities out of Churchill. The shifting back and forth of Company posts affected the Native economy; a post journal for 1895 recorded: 'While at Poplar River, I informed the Indians that the Post was to be closed. They were astounded, and could say nothing.'[23]

In addition to tripping for furs and building new posts, the Company also responded to competition by directing trappers to territories where there was less likelihood of encountering competitors. In 1878, Nelson House Indians were directed towards the rich fur grounds of Southern Indian Lake, and this 'effectively checkmated the opposition.'[24] In 1888, the factor at Churchill wanted a fishery at the South Lakes but was concerned that Indians might come into contact with competitors. In 1887, Matheson outlined a strategy to deal with encroachment on York Factory: 'To the North in the country adjacent to Split Lake I usually send several Indians; these however I [have] this winter kept on the Coast between the Nelson and Churchill Rivers; ostensibly to hunt Foxes, which I trust they will as it used to be a splendid country for them, but my principal object is to prevent them meeting the opposition who sent in large supplies from Norway House as far as Split Lake.'[25] Matheson not only provided evidence that the Company attempted to isolate Indians from competitors, but his tactics also raise questions about the autonomy of the 'traditional economy.' For some trappers, the post manager was not merely buying furs but also influencing decisions about production. The ability of the Company to direct Indian activities away from competitors was generally most successful in the non-treaty region and in areas where competitors were not securely established.

Hudson's Bay Company Relations with Competitors

The relationship between the Hudson's Bay Company and the opposition fur buyers was not always based on dog-eat-dog competition, but the Company always feared strong and reckless opposition. Failure to make profits was explained by such opposition. From the Hudson's Bay Company's viewpoint, inexperienced opponents often conducted reckless trade practices.

For example, in 1933, the annual report noted the appearance of new competitors who 'traded with Norway House Indians and their lack of experience was, in a large measure, instrumental in causing them to pay extremely high prices for any furs purchased.'[26] This observation, like many made throughout the post-1870 trade, counters the argument that presupposes that Indians were incapable of dealing with whites on economic terms. Nevertheless, the Company found it difficult to deal with mobile free traders who, rather than carry over goods, would dispose of trade items very cheaply and who would, at the same time, buy furs above the value. In such instances, the Company did not oppose these traders by altering prices. There also existed a preferred category of opponent, like Hyer, whose 'tactics are not such as to give rise to disorganization of the trade and his opposition is therefore preferable to that of mere reckless competition.'[27]

One means of dealing with competitors was to purchase their furs, although at times instructions not to purchase traders' furs were sent out. There are a number of instances of buying opponents' furs, and this was particularly the case for muskrats in the Cumberland House district. In 1909, Cedar Lake muskrats were purchased from an opponent with a narrow profit margin. Similarly, furs from petty trade, such as purchases made by commercial fishermen, found their way to the Hudson's Bay Company.

At times, the Company and other fur buyers cooperated to minimize the losses that might ensue from reckless competition. In 1891, Chief Factor Belanger 'adopted the course of arranging a reasonable Fur purchasing Tariff with Mr. Hyer, which is strictly adhered to by both parties.'[28] Similarly, in 1907, an opposition trader at Cedar Lake agreed to follow the Company's tariff. More important, in the mid-1920s, the HBC and Revillon Fréres, a large competitor, took steps 'to put a stop to this cut-throat competition.'[29] Consequently, it was reported in 1926 that 'Revillon Freres conducted their opposition as usual in a sane and business like manner, and the arrangement recently entered into ... should have very beneficial results.'[30] An arrangement with a trader at Gods Lake in 1927 did not result in lower prices, but he followed the HBC in controlling of debt. In 1931, it was recorded that the main opponent at Norway House, Hyer, was amenable to cooperation and was not 'instrumental in raising prices in any way.'[31] The depression fur markets should have encouraged cooperation between fur buyers. Given the ability of Native trappers to alter to the terms of trade, firms with long-term interests realized that collusion enhanced survival. On such occasions, only the appearance of competition, and not the theory of a 'perfect market,' characterized trade relations in this era.

A seldom-used approach to competition was for the Company to take over its opponent's business. In 1889, the Hudson's Bay Company bought out Carscaden and Peck. It was anticipated that the removal of this powerful firm would 'largely decrease our expenses and proportionately increase our fur receipts' in the Norway House and Island Lake districts.[32] The Company did not usually purchase troubled competitors since 'as a rule, it is bad policy to buy out competition.'[33] For example, it was reported that at York Factory in 1920: 'There was also considerable dissatisfaction amonst [*sic*] the Indians owing to the elimination of the opposition.'[34] Trappers were sensitive to monopoly; agreements covering credit and price were preferable to the elimination of other firms.

Structural Changes to the Organization of the Industry

During the 1783-1821 period, the fur trade was organized around two large companies, each with separate systems of transportation and posts. Although the Hudson's Bay Company and the North West Company differed in organization and financial structure, both these companies were essentially large economic organizations with operations throughout the subarctic. In contrast, the post-1870 period witnessed the HBC challenged by small, petty traders with limited capital. Over time, small regional companies with established trading posts developed. Prior to 1900, there was a constant ebbing and flowing of competitive firms such as Hyer; Stobart and Eden; Carscaden and Peck; and Shanon and Hartman. Throughout most of the subarctic, Revillon Frères was the Company's most extensive opponent, but it was not a serious threat in Manitoba. After 1900, the demand for fine furs – a marked shift in the utility of furs – along with changes in transportation and communications, forced changes to the structure of fur buying. These developments permitted a line of credit between middlemen and small regional trading companies and white trader/trappers. Figure 13.2 indicates the locations and variety of competitive buyers in 1924.

A major change after 1900 was the expansion of the number of fur auction centres. St. Louis and New York developed as important fur markets. For example, the Funsten Brothers and Company of St. Louis originated as commission merchants in 1881, but by 1915, public auction sales were the preferred means to dispose of furs. The Canadian Fur Auction Sales Company was established in 1910, and in 1922 a fur exchange was founded in Edmonton. Winnipeg acquired an important middle position in the development of the North American fine fur industry. The HBC began to purchase furs outside its system of fur posts when it established a commission sales office. When the entire Manitoba district was shut down in 1913, furs from this area were purchased through the Company's Winnipeg office. Innis noted another important change in this period: 'A striking evidence of this change in the fur-trade came with the announcement in June, 1921, by the Hudson's Bay Company that it would purchase furs on consignment for sale at its London auctions.'[35] The development of primary markets in

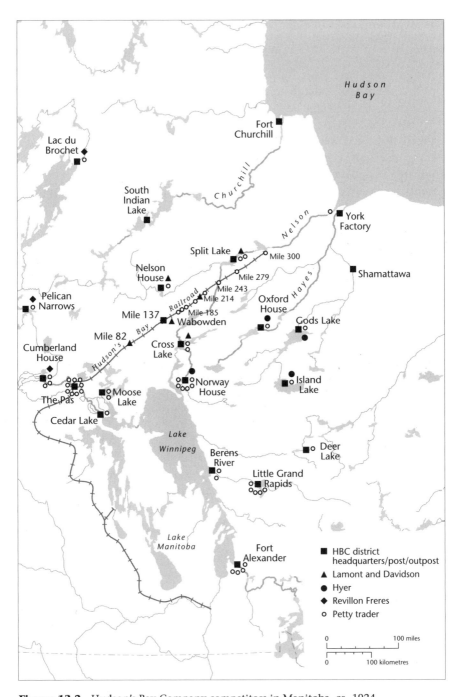

Figure 13.2   Hudson's Bay Company competitors in Manitoba, ca. 1924

the fur country was an outgrowth of a more diverse structure for marketing furs in the metropolis.

The Company's records noted the development of competitive fur buying organizations connected to Winnipeg wholesale houses. The connection between wholesalers who provided credit to opposition fur traders presented serious problems for the Company. The HBC annual report on the fur trade for 1923 argued that 'generally speaking the various Opposition firms to be contended with throughout this District [Keewatin] are troublesome, in respect that the great majority of them have little or no capital, but are able to obtain credit with comparative ease from the different Wholesalers. Such Opposition appears to be contented if able to make a substantial payment to their Wholesalers and at the same time obtain a living.'[36] In order to sustain this credit relationship, the petty trader was required to make a substantial payment; spring furs were purchased from trappers at the full or even more than the market value. Consequently, the majority of small traders 'do not make any more out of their trading than do our Post Managers, and that is their wages and keep.'[37] In 1924, the HBC noted an additional strength of the Winnipeg Fur Auction Company due to 'frequent sales of the Auction Company ... traders are enabled to compete successfully for the trade at a minimum of risk on account of the quick turnover.'[38] The Company demonstrated additional concern when auction sales and local fur buyers became too closely integrated. In the case of the Northern Trading Company, the annual report for 1924 noted that this 'firm has been taken over by a number of Jews who are closely connected with the Winnipeg Fur Auction Sales Company who also finance a number of small traders.'[39] However, by 1925 the Company felt that cash sales in Winnipeg helped to contain the auction sales/northern trader combination.[40] Although auction sales provided opposition to the HBC and developed a system of grading furs, Innis argued that 'the commission house which rests between the upper and lower mill stones of the fur-buyer and the trapper will probably protect itself at the expense of the trapper.'[41] In a study conducted for the Manitoba government, J. Melven described the structure of the fur trade in the 1930s: 'To take a typical example, a trapper of the north may sell his catch to a northern fur trader, the trader ships it to a fur auction in Winnipeg, the fur auction sells it to a Winnipeg broker, the broker having a customer in view, ships it to New York.'[42] Although an alternate market structure made a protracted challenge to the Hudson's Bay Company, the unstable structure that evolved was riddled with middlemen operating between producers and consumers.

An important structural change to the industry began with the appearance of white trappers in the north. This marked the onset of white labour in the actual production of fur. This development was yet another example of the industry's ability to survive by restructuring the racial groups that made up the labour force. Although white trappers contributed to a declining resource base and competed with Natives for these resources, white trappers also reinforced competitive fur buying. Numerous white men played the dual role of trapper and small trader. The annual report for outfit 1902 recorded that 'a man professing to be a white trapper has taken up quarters about Cross Lake Post' and that 'he is paying cash more or less freely for furs.'[43] The market situation served to pull whites into the Far North as trappers. The HBC journal for Churchill indicated the importance of white trappers in 1929 – one of these independent trappers outfitted by the HBC at Churchill operated as far north as the Eskimo Point.[44] Furthermore, Innis argued that white trappers hastened changes, demanding cash for furs and fur grading.[45] The white trappers' preference for cash often meant that incomes were not spent in the region.[46] Much of their earnings represented a further draining of wealth from the area.

One peculiarity of the economic structure at this time was the involvement of missionaries as traders. For example, H. Hutley, a minister for sixteen years, changed vocations and engaged in the fur trade at Nelson River. At Brochet, missionaries traded against the Company. The report on Brochet for 1900 stated:

Both the Bishop and the Priest have given me, at great length, their version of how they became associated with an opposition trade at this Post. There is probably some truth in their statements in regard to unfair treatment, provocation etc., but the main fact[s] I think are that without some opposition to force the Company to a fairly liberal treatment of the Indians, the usefulness of the Mission would cease as the Chipewyans would go and trade at more competitive points in Athabasca and the Esquimaux to Churchill.[47]

This candid comment also indicates that, out of necessity, missionaries had economic interests. Again, major decisions about Native livelihood took account of prices and commercial incomes.

The Hudson's Bay Company could not always come to terms with the wide variety of problems posed by competition. Even before the coming of rail, some competitors had access to cheap transport. The use of schooners by Carscaden and Peck meant a saving of 30 to 40 per cent over the transportation costs of the Company.[48] Similarly, in 1898 for the Manitoba District, the Company's average tariff valuation was thirty-three and a third per cent below the prices of the competition; however, the Company's collection was of better quality.[49] The Company records also argued that trappers supplied Indians with whisky, 'taking furs in payment.'[50] By 1930,

Pukatawagan and Cedar Lake were identified as areas where an illicit trade in liquor was carried on by the Company's opponents. In 1930, the manager at Brochet felt that he was at a disadvantage when he pointed out that 'it is hard to understand why it is not good business for us to buy fur for goods at the same price as he [opposition trader] does for cash.'[51] The response to this concern noted the advantages of the free traders: 'First, they do not have to pay rail and ocean freight on the long journey to England, and possibly, also, do not carry insurance on their furs; secondly invariably sell their furs to a dealer and not in the open market and are consequently saved brokerage charges or selling commission. We pay rail and ocean charges and insurance ... and 6% deducted for warehouse charges.'[52] Additionally, the opposition incorporated some Natives into their trading operations, such as 'the poorer type of half-breed and who operated these Posts on the maxim of "get the fur at any price."'[53] Some opponents were alert to Native social organization. Lamont and Davidson were described as a principal competitor of the trader-trapper variety. They financed traders/trappers who were 'married to Native women, and gathered around them their relations and friends, and go off and form camps by themselves, the Indian relatives are advanced by these men and a close watch is kept on all the fur they catch, and [the] same is taken from the Indian just as soon as he returns from his trap line.'[54] Thus, in this period, the structure of the industry evolved to include a variety of competitive organizations; and once again, kinship proved to be a useful adjunct to trade.

The records of independent traders like Arthur J. Jan or written memoirs of Indians such as Tom Boulanger provide useful insights about the breaking down of monopoly. There is some evidence that free traders made good profits, as Boulanger stated: 'Old John Hire [Hyer] was worth one hundred thousand dollars.'[55] Similarly, Boulanger recalled that, after Billy Kneel, an employee of Hyer, had died, 'John Hyer found his books and his money, twenty-five thousands dollars.'[56] Boulanger's perception that these traders were well-off is very important; however, he did not provide any critical reflections concerning the source of this wealth.

At times, the Company was overly optimistic about the eventual demise of free traders. The annual report for the Cumberland district reported on Jan's operations, stating 'that another real bad year would clean him out.'[57] Jan, however, was not 'wiped out' in the early 1920s, and he reflected on his trading experiences: 'It took me a couple of years before I could grade furs I made a few poor buys before I learned. From then on I was reasonably accurate and my grade would practically always agree with the Winnipeg grade. In the early days the trading was all barter and there was no cash at all. There was a profit on the merchandise so that a trader could be slightly out on the grade and still not lose. Later there was more cash used.'[58] As with the HBC, this free trader looked to merchandise for profit. Jan also noted that it took time to 'catch on' to Native tricks, such as putting one or two frozen arctic hare among white fox or placing sand in the castor (gland extract) to increase its weight when distant market prices soared during a shortage.[59] More important, Jan recalled his relationship with a Winnipeg auction house: 'George [Soudack] helped me in many ways. One in particular was that if he received a shipment of my fur and the market was not right and he considered prices offered were too low, he would hold the shipment and advance me enough cash to carry on until he could sell in order to show me a profit. This was done several times.'[60] With a crash in prices after the First World War, Jan noted that he had lost because he bought furs at four dollars per pelt that would not sell for fifty cents. However, Soudack had facilities to store Jan's furs and paid him a small advance even though it took two years to clear the furs.[61] Similarly, Soudack had participated in Jan's closed-bid sales at The Pas. Clearly, the link between trader-trapper and auction house was a vital aspect of the post-1870 competition.

External Markets and Structural Changes
The role of external markets is central to any account of the industry in the post-1870 period. A close financial relationship between fur purchasers (who were linked to consumer markets) and traders in producing regions usurped the HBC-styled mercantilism. Consequently, price changes were rapidly transmitted between consumers and producers, partly because of changes in the nature of the demand for fine furs and partly because of technological changes in communications and transportation. Thus, Innis noted that 'the organization of the manufacture and sale of fur goods has changed materially ... especially since 1900, and in a revolutionary fashion since 1914.'[62] Until 1900, consumer markets did not seem to generate price instability within the same season, and the HBC continued to set tariff prices for an entire trading year. Prior to 1900, price changes occurred in producing areas when trappers broke away from the monopoly. With the entrenchment of competitive alternatives to the Company and the development of North American fur markets, variability in consumer fur markets became crucial in setting fur prices in northern Manitoba. The changes that characterized the period after 1900 (the entrenchment of competition, the decline of the HBC monopoly, and erosion of the London market) are related to the development of a North American fur market. A general increase in prices, price changes within the trapping season, and extreme variability in prices from year to year coincided with the decline in monopoly. These notable market events are important aspects of Native economic history. This was a period of economic change – not stability.

In 1938, a former HBC employee, J. Melven, reflected upon changes to the industry as a consequence of the First World War: 'Thus, in the Northern part of the province the fur trade for a long period of years, and indeed until 1914, remained in status quo, largely the preserve of the Hudson's Bay Company whose supremacy in the trade was not seriously questioned until the Great War upset many other things beside the fur markets of the world. On the whole, the trade in the North was very profitable. Fur markets were steady and the violent fluctuations of recent years were unknown.'[63] He outlined a number of trends that occurred as a consequence of the market upheaval:

> Prior to 1914 ... fur values were more or less steady, any fluctuations taking place being easily explained by change of fashion or temporary lack of supply. But as soon as the War started, the large fur markets panicked and the winter of 1914-15 saw values decline to a point never before reached. The trade sank into insignificance but as the War went on from year to year the Trade recovered and shared fully in the tide of prosperity caused by War expenditure here and in Great Britain and the States. Values rose steadily until the climax was reached in the 1919-20 season when almost unbelievable prices were realized for furs. This prosperity attracted large numbers of men to the northern part of the province, numerous trading companies were formed and the old time trader and Indian found competitors everywhere.[64]

In terms of fur prices, the war had a great impact; and the changes that followed constituted a significant reorganization.

Melven's account of the effects of the First World War is substantiated by the Company's records. On 2 August 1914, a telegram from London explained the disappearance of the London fur market and called for no new fur purchases.[65] The London and Leipzig markets were related, and hostilities disrupted commercial relations. The war affected the prices for the returns of the 1913 outfit, and the instruction not to purchase furs made it difficult for the Company officers to pursue the fur trade in northern Canada. Their records indicate what adjustments were made:

> As it was necessary for the Company to endeavour to make some purchases, in order to retain their connection in the interior, a nominal purchasing tariff was compiled on the basis of 83% below the prices realized at the March Sale of 1914, and issued to the District for use during the winter of 1914/15. The consensus of opinion, however, amongst the district Managers was that the tariff being so low would prove hardly any incentive to the Indians to hunt, while it was anticipated that independent Fur Traders would

be willing to take greater risks than the Company, and would not allow them to purchase skins at tariff price. As a matter of fact this turned out to be the case. The Company were [*sic*] hampered on all sides by independent traders, taking advantage of the definite instructions necessarily given our Post Managers not to buy above the authorized purchasing tariff.[66]

This strategy produced poor results for outfit 1914 since 'the price paid was generally too low with the consequence that the bulk of the Canadian catch was secured by the Company's competitors.'[67] While acknowledging the severe erosion of the position of the HBC, the Company records also noted the increased American demand for Canadian furs. The Company indicated that competition between the London and North American markets had increased and demonstrated a concern that buyers in the primary markets would increase competition.[68] The annual report for 1916, reflecting the perspective of the Company's management in Canada, suggested:

> The most direct method of combating this opposition, or at least of regulat-
> ing it, would appear to be the release of Furs by the Company on this side
> on such occasion as when a strong demand forces a big advance in price,
> otherwise the practice of meeting competition under these circumstances
> further enhances the speculative opposition of the Company under the
> present selling policy and affords the opposition all the facilities for re-
> munerative business, incidentally filling a demand which is usually satis-
> fied before the Company['s] returns come to London market.[69]

Such a strategy would have provided an outlet for Company furs in North America at a time when markets were weak in Europe. This strategy would also have had the advantage of slowing down rapid price increases, which tended to disrupt the Company's trade in the fur country. Instead, the Company chose to entrench colonial relations and would not allow the London market to temporarily relinquish its position, even though a more effective containment of competition would have resulted from direct sales in North America. London ordered that furs be shipped for sale on the London market.[70]

Canadian managers could neither compete effectively in the primary markets nor flood the North American markets. London's ambivalence towards confronting the North American market also served to reinforce the transportation cost advantages of its opponents. The annual report for 1915 stressed the 'violent fluctuations in the fur market'[71] and at this time, the Company adjusted its trading balance to account for fur inventories.

Large quantities of unsold furs now had to be recognized in the account books. For outfit 1916, it was noted that prices had never been higher.[72]

During the buoyant wartime markets, Revillon Frères directly competed with twelve of the Company's sixteen posts in the Cumberland District. In this period, high profits on furs permitted the opposition to thrive. The Company also prospered during this period because of a high markup on the stock on hand (costed at pre-war-inflated prices). Hence, the Company profited from wartime inflation. Not all of the problems that the Company experienced at this time were the consequence of the London Committee's colonial attitudes. When N.H. Bacon became fur trade commissioner in 1913, he charged that the fur trade department was disorganized and lacked control.[73] Nonetheless, at a very crucial time in the development of the fine fur markets, control from London undermined the ability of Canadian management to respond. This was not the first instance in the history of mercantilism when political control was incapable of recognizing economic gain.

The strong demand and high prices during the war did not last. Melven explained the consequences:

When the inevitable fall in values came, it came rapidly and without warning and was complete. All were caught in the avalanche – trappers, traders, dealers, brokers and manufacturers. The trade had to be readjusted from top to bottom. The companies and traders, whose only experience of the trade was gained in a short period of unnatural prosperity, disappeared and many more or less destitute trappers were left stranded in the north. A sharp lesson on the danger of booms had been given to one of the oldest trades in the world but like many other lessons it has been forgotten and the lesson has had to be learned again several times since, age being no criterion of wisdom.[74]

The collapse experienced during the outfit of 1920 affected Native incomes, and the annual report stressed that it 'was the hardest year I know of to handle Indians, even the best of them. They had been accustomed for the last few years of high prices, to getting practically anything they wanted, paying their debt later without any trouble and having a balance due them in cash or barter. It was hard to convince them that their era of prosperity was ended. They are now confronted with the proposition of paying for goods at top notch prices with furs at half price or less.'[75] For Natives, buoyant markets had brought short-term prosperity and a false sense of economic security. They had experienced the downside of the market most directly, and this occurred after consumption had increased. This situation presented problems for the HBC since the Native trappers would turn to the competition if the Company did not provide the 'necessary outfit for his hunt without question.'[76] The drop in prices reduced the number of small companies, and Revillon Fréres men sought employment with the HBC. The slump in the market in the spring of 1920 was characteristic of the turbulent markets of the 1920s. In 1923, the London fur market experienced a drop in values.

Jan's memoirs supplement HBC records as a source of information on the market during the post-First World War period. According to Jan:

> One of the most trying years I had in the fur business was shortly after the war. That year, Funston [sic] Brothers of St. Louis tried to corner the fur market. They were a large company with many agents. Prices were forced up and in many instances, double the price ever reached before. It was a good hunt in my district and up to March I had shown an excellent profit. In March I was in The Pas for a short visit and took in a small lot of furs. Prices realized were out of sight. Muskrats were selling at four dollars and fifty cents to five dollars per pelt. In previous years they sold at one dollar, it was considered an excellent price.[77]

The Native trapper in northern Manitoba was linked to the market, and the market had evolved to the point where price changes occurred very quickly. During the spring breakup, Jan had no communication with the outside world for over a month. He was not aware that shortly after he had left The Pas, 'the break came and the corner in the furs failed.'[78] Later, Jan learned that Funsten Brothers had gone bankrupt.[79] Jan, a trapper-trader in the remote border area of northwest Manitoba, was aware of changes occurring in the metropolis. Nonetheless, the volatility of prices in the metropolis caught some traders short in the hinterland.

Again, in 1923, a crash in fur values occurred, followed by reorganization of the firms in the subarctic. The Northern Trading Company required assistance from the Canadian Fur Auction Company when it went into debt to Nesbitt Liquidators. This reorganization concerned the Company as 'a number of Jews immediately connected with the Winnipeg Fur Auction Company will endeavour to take it over.'[80] In this instance, the market worked towards a merging of fur buyers (in the primary market) with auction sales. Similarly, Revillon Fréres was diminished by the drop in 1923.

The world depression affected fur markets as well as the producing regions. An anxious telegram from the London governor wanted to know on what basis the Company was purchasing furs, and it indicated that circumstances did not warrant further purchases.[81] The value of furs at the HBC purchase tariff, a good indication of trapping incomes, declined between 1930 and 1933. Trapping incomes declined 24 per cent (1930-1), 23 per cent (1931-2), and 20 per cent (1932-3).[82] Although the gross profits for the fur trade department did not represent high dollar aggregates, the

Company was able to recover in the early years of the depression. Between 1930 and 1931, profits declined 345 per cent and the HBC lost money; however, in the two succeeding years, profits increased 48 and 147 per cent respectively.[83] Overall, trapping incomes declined 53 per cent between 1930 and 1933. Melven provided a variety of reasons for the instability in the fur markets, one being the international depression: 'It [the fur market] is the first to react to international unrest. It is at the mercy of feminine fashion which knows no law and very little sense and the manufacturing end being mainly in alien hands, labour troubles are frequent and often prolonged. In short it produces a luxury product which is dependent on the material prosperity of the few and until the long hoped for general economic betterment of the masses arrives, the fur market will bend to the caprice of the rich.'[84] The depression of the 1930s represented instability and, clearly, Native trappers were not isolated from the international market. One characteristic of the post-1870 competitive fur trade was the evolution of a more direct influence of external markets upon fur-producing regions. For Native trappers, this meant greater instability in commercial incomes.

The Cycle of Exchange, Profits, and Competition

During the 200 years of the mercantile fur trade, the Hudson's Bay Company devised a system that allowed it to issue credit to individual trappers and the means to track profitability on an annual basis. The use of the Made Beaver (MB) standard to value trade goods and Native produce (furs, hides, and provisions) permitted the Company to apply exchange value to a barter system. The use of MB allowed the HBC to modernize barter in such a manner that it could account for the effects of European fur markets and identify profitability. The granting of credit (debting) to Natives in the form of trade goods for continued fur production was an essential element in the seasonal cycle. During intense competition, 'trippers' would visit Indian camps with goods and flour to forestall free traders from collecting furs. The issuing of goods on credit – or 'debting Indians,' as the traders expressed it – was central to the whole economic relationship between Indians and the Hudson's Bay Company.

Under monopoly conditions, the Company could 'whipsaw' the Indian trapper by reducing the buying price of furs and increasing the selling price of trade goods. Innis pointed out that the HBC could protect itself from a fall in fur price because 'the Company must take a wide margin on the price of the goods.' Thus, the Indian was 'whipsawed' on credit, and a 75 per cent recovery of debts under competitive conditions was considered favourable. Consequently, high prices meant that 'the good hunter is forced to pay the poor hunter's debts.'[85] Thus, in 1877, the attention of the northern district managers was drawn 'to the necessity of reducing the Indians Tariffs to a minimum as far as can be done without injury to the trade. This step is rendered absolutely necessary in consequence of the heavy decline in the value of Furs.'[86] The concept of profit was purely mercantile: reduce the buying price of furs, advance the price of merchandise, and then deduct operating costs. Goods were marked up over the cost landed price (the cost of the trade good plus the cost of transportation to land at a particular post). Debt bondage alone could not sustain such a system; elements of paternalism continued to permeate the Company's operations. Standing Rule 33 defined the relationship between trappers and the Company:

> That the Indian be treated with kindness and indulgence, and mild and conciliatory means resorted to, in order to encourage industry, repress vice, and inculcate morality: that the Indians be liberally supplied with the requisite necessaries, particularly with articles of ammunition whether they have the means of paying for it, or not, and that no Officers in charge of District or Post be at liberty to alter or vary the standard of usual made of Trade with the Indians except by special permission of Chief Comm. [Commissioner].[87]

Regardless of productivity, or the ability to pay for goods, Indians were to be provided with the necessities required to continue hunting. Credit and gratuities represented a form of company paternalism that committed the HBC to supporting a subsistence wage. Innis's point that the good hunters supported the poor hunters is apparent in this economic relationship. However, with an increase in competition, the issuing of credit as part of a subsistence wage was not so tenable. In 1872, the Northern Department's Minutes of Council recorded: 'As a Rule, the old system of indiscriminate advances to Indians or others [should] be discontinued.'[88] By 1878, the Minutes of the Northern Department Council stressed the need to confine credit to reliable Indians and only 'to a limited extent to enable them to hunt.'[89]

The HBC's practice of assuming the overhead or social costs of fur production was essential in order to maintain a labour force in the face of fluctuations in the resource base and the uncertainty of hunting. Company paternalism did not mean that the trade was not profitable or that exploitation did not occur. In 1868, the Reverend H. Budd of The Pas noted: 'They are making good hunts, most of them, and the H.B. Company will reap all the benefits.'[90] In 1886, the Reverend Lofthouse noted that Company welfarism had been suspended because 'the only thing the present officer in charge here thinks of is getting fur, and for this purpose to make the poor Indians really and truly a slave, the poor things are obliged to submit to any treatment as there is no other possible outlet for their fur.'[91] Similarly, the

Reverend J. Hines reported in 1890 that, in The Pas area, abundance benefitted the Company: 'Fur here this year is plentiful, but the "Honble" H.B. Co. knows how to arrange the prices both of their goods, and the furs so that the poor Indians may not be benefitted by the abundance – I am told on good authority that here 6 rat skins will only bring 2 lbs. of flour. *What extortion!'*[92] Under monopoly conditions, unequal trade was a persistent feature of the fur industry.

Native Responses to Competitive Markets

Indians understood price concepts and made special efforts to improve their incomes. Native incomes improved as the HBC monopoly gave way to more competitive fur-buying markets. Cumberland House records noted in 1875 that Indians who used to trade with the Company took their furs to Red River and returned with goods to trade.[93] For Norway House in 1873, it was recorded that a council of Indians was interested in doing all they could for a free trader 'by giving their Fur & a few Fish from each man and also to induce other traders to come out.'[94] Similarly, because of the crisis associated with the disintegration of York Factory's local economy, Indians who migrated to Split Lake were within range of competitors and they held out every encouragement for traders to establish themselves among them. Messengers were even 'dispatched to invite other traders to come into their neighborhood.'[95]

The economic behaviour of Indians indicated an appreciation of value and prices because they encouraged competition between fur buyers and, as well, exploited differences among Hudson's Bay Company posts. Variability in Company post tariffs was generally the result of competition. The report on the fur trade for 1901 alleged: 'By the division of control which formerly existed, and which the Natives very well understood and aimed to profit by, there was a certain amount of competition between Posts which was a source of loss to the Company. Indians were inclined to play fast and loose with more Posts than one, obtaining advances at one and then barking furs at another before their desertion from the first Post would be reported.'[96] Similarly, different bands traded to circumvent some of the rigidities of the Company's trade system. Churchill Indians traded with Norway House Indians for goods they could not get at Churchill. Chipewyan would trade selectively; at Fort Churchill they traded meat, deer skins, and secondhand snowshoes while they traded their furs at Brochet (due to a more favourable tariff). The environment of the Churchill band favoured marten over beaver, and therefore, the HBC tariff was set to reflect the scarcity of beaver. In the Norway House area, marten were more scarce than beaver. The Churchill Chipewyan, however, were known to trade their marten to the Nelson River Cree for beaver. While the Company's purchase prices worked against

Chipewyan Indians at Brochet with furs, 1924. Note the importance of fox pelts. (NAC, PA-19679)

the 'comparative advantage' of the local environments, Chipewyan and Cree found a way to work around this system. Such economic behaviour could only be based on an understanding of prices. The influence of competition was more strongly felt at Brochet than Churchill, therefore the Company's tariffs were more favourable to trappers at Brochet. This situation resulted in a long-standing intra-company post rivalry in which the factor at Fort Churchill attempted to restrict Brochet's trade, noting that the original purpose of the post was to provide provisions (caribou venison).

Frequent references were made in the late 1860s, early 1870s, late 1880s, and early 1890s to the Fort Churchill Indians trading at Brochet. The Fort Churchill inspection report explained that 'owing to the low prices paid for Furs most of the Chipewyans have gone to Lac du Brochet where much higher prices are paid and there is opposition.'[97] To complicate matters for the Fort Churchill trade, the Chipewyan were encouraged to trade at Brochet by the Roman Catholic priest with the story that the Company was going to abandon Churchill. Indians also responded to the selection of goods offered. For example, Churchill Chipewyan went to Brochet to obtain rifles. Additionally, Chipewyan trade was intercepted by the Nelson River post and Norway House Indians. Even inland Eskimo (Inuit) shifted to Brochet. At great expense, the factor even responded to a request from the Chipewyan to build an outpost at Shethnanei Lake. The strain between two HBC posts illustrates that the effects of competition were felt well beyond the immediate locales of resident 'opposition.' While Brochet and Churchill are considered by some as isolated places, and the Chipewyan have been labelled Aboriginal in the pure pre-contact sense of the term, their economic history demonstrates an understanding of commercial values and the ability to manipulate the procedures of the Hudson's Bay Company.[98]

The preference for Brochet over Churchill indicates that Natives made spatial responses within the HBC trade system. The example of Cumberland House Natives travelling to Red River to trade, when the district was overrun by free traders, is another instance of a spatial response to the problem of value for producers. At times the Hudson's Bay Company's transportation system worked against the Company. Chief Factor Fortescue recalled that 'about the same time free traders began to appear at Norway House [1873] the York tripmen began to take their fur, silver fox and marten there, not paying their debts here, and on one occasion went so far as to give them all [to] the free traders, though offered the same price by our own officers there.'[99] Although the Company matched prices, Indians preferred to sell to the free traders, thereby ensuring a continuation of viable competition. The transportation system was reorganized to isolate York Factory tripmen, but as late as 1891, these boatmen were still bringing out the more valuable furs to trade with the opposition.

Another spatial response by Indians was to move towards areas where opposition existed. Shamattawa Indians were drawn off by free trader opposition at Oxford House. Similarly, in the mid-1880s, Nelson River and Norway House Indians were drawn off by the better prices at Pelican Narrows. In 1901, it was noted that if Grand Rapid Indians 'are not paid full prices they take their furs to a competitive point.'[100] As a result of the railway, the 1922 district report documented that 'there are also a considerable number of Traders who visit their vicinity from the Hudson's [sic] Bay Railway. Since the opening up of the Hudson's Bay Railway, the Indians from Cross Lake now hunt in the vicinity closer to various points on the Hudson's Bay Railway than to Cross Lake and at which points there are stores run by opposition firms.'[101] Thus, spatial responses included changing trapping areas. Indians would not go to the rail line if the prices were higher in the interior.[102] For Fort Alexander during the Great Depression, the spatial responses to the Company's very small markup on the cost-landed price of trade goods meant 'the Indians preferring to walk six miles to Pine Falls if they can save money thereby.'[103] Overwhelming evidence indicates that competition induced a variety of economically rational responses from Natives.

There was no complete or straightforward transition from Company monopoly to a 'pure' price system. Fortescue argued that at York Factory in the late nineteenth century, the costs of trade were increasing, but as 'the MB tariff is inelastic and Indians do not understand variable prices of goods and

[with] London prices declining the valuation allowed us was reduced which was cutting into the profit at both ends.'[104] There are no reasons to indicate why Indians would have the information needed to understand the London fur market, but it is not difficult to appreciate why Indians would resist price increases for trade goods because the Company felt that its profits were under pressure. There is some evidence of the continuation of an eighteenth-century observation about an Indian backward sloping supply curve (an increase in price causes a decrease in supply). In 1920, it was reported that 'the high prices recently paid for Fur instead of acting as an incentive for the Indian to hunt, was the means of making them lazy.'[105] Observations are not consistent with regard to the effect of price as an incentive for production, since in the same year it was reported that in the Saskatchewan District: 'Beaver and Musquash collection both increased. This I attribute to the high price obtainable for them in the early part of the season, causing them to be vigorously hunted.'[106] In fact, by 1937, Natives may have become extremely sensitive to market prices, as the Norway House records noted: 'Rats coming in very slow, Natives must be hanging on to them expecting that they may go higher.'[107]

At times the Company seemed incapable of understanding Indian economic behaviour. In 1874, Fortescue suggested: 'The Fur tariff at York is low, being still at the old scale, and the temptation to take part of their hunts where they may obtain more favourable prices is too strong for Indians to resist.'[108] After the extreme destitution on the Hudson Bay Lowlands, the Norway House factor H. Belanger was sorry to learn that 'Indians coming from the Coast prefer dealing with the opposition, and they are not well disposed towards the Company.'[109] The suspension of gratuities and rations could not have endeared York Factory Indians to the Company. Changes in 'attitude' were common, as the Oxford House report for 1889 recorded that Indians were getting 'very awkward and dishonest, and cannot be trusted; our opponents stuff them with all sorts of nonsense, prejudicing their minds against the Company.'[110] Similarly, the Berens River journal noted in 1888 that the Indians were bold and troublesome.[111] Clearly, Native responses to the development of competitive markets encouraged changes in the fur trade. While Indians may not have felt bound to a partnership or alliance with the HBC when other prospects existed, the Company's personnel seemed to have expected reciprocity from Native trappers.

Competitive Markets and Debt Peonage
Under monopoly conditions, the debting system of the Hudson's Bay Company outfitted trappers to produce furs. The debting system provided a form of stability to an unstable economy – an economy that experienced constant fluctuations in animal populations and market prices. Competition

affected the credit system of the HBC: first because debt repayments were based on obligations that could only be enforced by monopoly; and second, because competition undermined the ability of the Company to profit on both trade goods and furs and, therefore, to absorb losses on bad debts. In the post-1870 period, the HBC expanded its advances to include 'treaty debts' and 'scrip debts.' Debts were carefully tracked. For example, at Oxford House in 1891, each trapper was advanced $16.86, which at the fur tariff amounted to $30.58.[112] With the increase in competition, debting Natives became less financially feasible, and the Company gave serious consideration to abolishing advances. Nonetheless, this proved to be more difficult since the removal of credit out of a fear of non-repayment cancelled any obligations on the part of Indians to the Hudson's Bay Company. Trappers suffered under debt peonage but, in turn, expected long-term obligations from the Company. The removal of any debt obligation meant that the supply of furs to any particular buyer would, largely, be determined by price. The new market was defying the older social obligations of fur trade society.

Even under competitive conditions, arguments were made for continuing the debt system. In 1889, debting was defended at the Nelson River post: 'At this place we cannot abandon the principle of giving debt to the Indians. They must be equipped with certain necessary supplies in the Fall, to enable them to hunt successfully, as they do not remain hanging round the Fort.'[113] Again, missionaries provided insights into debt bondage. In 1893, Reverend Hines of The Pas noted: 'Their policy [HBC] is to keep the Indian in debt, in order to have him in their power hence it is they who order him away from the Mission and tell him when he is to come back.'[114] At York Factory, Reverend Winter found it strange that Indians did not 'consider it a sin to be in debt'; yet, five years later, he realized that in spite of the problems of credit, 'it seems that the system cannot be discontinued.'[115]

Without credit, fur production was impossible; but it was difficult to administer debts under competitive conditions. Out of necessity, Company credit policies were volatile. The extent of change in the credit system depended upon the place and the time. Records suggest that sometimes the Company actually stopped issuing credit. Thus, in December of 1882, the Norway House post stopped all advances to Indians and traded on a cash basis. Correspondence from Norway House in 1885 emphasized an attempt to 'end the old but ruinous system of trade.'[116] At Fairford in 1891, it was noted that 'the Indians at this place are a bad lot, so therefore advances have been put a stop to entirely, there are so many traders it is not safe to trust them.'[117] By 1890, the policy was generalized so that 'no credit should be given to any Indian not faithful to the Company.'[118] This policy continued and in 1893 the manager of Cumberland House district expressed 'the opinion that the time had arrived when debts could no longer be continued in the Company's interest.'[119] Again debts were abolished for Cumberland House in 1899, and no debts were issued in 1900 at Berens River and Cedar Lake.

The system of production was such that the outfitting function of the fur buyer could never be completely abolished. Nonetheless, competition had the effect of increasing the amount of unpaid debts. When possible, the Company preferred a more selective issuing of advances. Thus, in 1885, Norway House post issued credit only to good hunters and limited the amount to necessities. A similar policy was adopted at Oxford House in 1890. Advances were limited 'to necessary equipment to enable Indians to start on their hunts.'[120] In some years, debts increased at Churchill, even though only advances necessary for hunting were issued. Competitive markets did not necessarily mean that Indians reneged on their debts, as 'most of them did their utmost to pay' in 1887-8 at Norway House.[121]

The debt question was complicated by advances on the value of treaty and scrip. In the cases of treaty debts, goods were advanced so that Indians could consume against their treaty annuities. In 1889, advances were abolished at Cross Lake because treaty debts had not been paid. Pressure to pay had various results, and it was reported for Poplar River in 1888 that 'every Indian paid his treaty advances and that with the greatest good will'; but in 1891 Indians paid only half their treaty debts.[122] Competitive situations and alternate economic activities complicated the collection of debts. The debt situation at Berens River was documented in 1900: 'A meeting of the Natives was held today (Chief and Councillor in attendance) where I addressed them regarding the course I intended pursuing in my work, laying great [s]tress on the abandonment of "Treaty Debts" in future, and on touching on "Fur Debts." The Company making a distinction between Hunter and Fishermen. So it was decided that if one did not get it, the other would not accept it. So at present no debts are to be given and which relieves me of considerable risk.'[123] But Indians could not maintain this collective stand. Another council meeting decided to pay some debt and it was reported that Indians were 'paying debts exceedingly well.'[124] Debt peonage was such an inherent feature of the fur trade that even the development of a competitive market had little effect.

The consequences of restricting credit varied. In 1891, it was reported at York Factory that 'the discontinuance of Indians Debts has had no prejudicial effect upon the trade.'[125] However, at Norway House, 'the stoppage of debt is looked upon as an injury that calls for the retaliation of trading with others instead of with us as usual.'[126] With the temporary collapse of the fur markets in 1914, the HBC severely restricted credit and reduced the purchase tariff. The result was that many of the best hunters were 'lost.' To avoid such a recurrence, it was noted in 1918 that 'the majority of such opposition advance the Indians to quite an extent, and in order to retain the best hunters, it is necessary for the Company to advance such Indians to the extent which will enable them to get out to their hunting grounds.'[127] However, in the Saskatchewan district in 1922, neither the HBC nor the opposition advanced Indians. At other times, the Company's strategy was based on an ability to outmanoeuvre its opponents. Post managers would cut credit, hope that opposition would advance outfits, and then 'extend every effort towards securing the furs from hunters that have had advances from our opponents.'[128] Indeed, 'The Honorable company' was known to collect competitor's furs, as when 300 MB was obtained from Poplar River because the HBC got to the fur just before a trader from Doghead had arrived to collect debts.[129] The issuing of debts was, therefore, an ongoing problem during the post-1870 fur trade, and in 1929, debts were still being issued to Chipewyan Indians. As late as 1937, the Company at Norway House faced a traditional situation: 'The time has now arrived as far as this place is concerned that we have only about ten men who can be relied on to pony over when given an advance. In fact no debt whatever would be good order.'[130] The credit system was central to Company/Native relations and to the development of a competitive market; other pursuits disrupted, but did not completely alter, this relationship.

Competitive Pricing Strategies and Trade Goods

Alterations to the Hudson's Bay Company's method of exchanging goods for furs were the result of the re-emergence of competition and the spread of money. Thus by 1889, Fort Alexander's business was based on bartering for furs on a cash basis. Although annuity payments in hard cash opened the way for a monetarization of the regional economy, the lack of independent merchandisers meant that fur buyers would compete on the basis of trade goods. While free traders obtained furs from trappers, the Company often purchased these furs from fur traders with hard cash. Early on in the transition, Company account books switched from English sterling to Dominion currency, but the centuries-old Made Beaver was used at Norway House for prompt trade until July of 1901. Thus, it took three decades before currency units completely replaced the MB valuation. To understand the fur purchasing and the Native role in shaping the market, it is necessary to closely examine the Company's price strategy.

During monopoly conditions, the Company could profit on both sides (furs and goods) of this exchange. Quite understandably, Indians would resist HBC attempts to increase the MB prices of goods so that the Company could maintain its profit position when the value of furs was declining. During the period between 1885 and 1930, fur prices initially declined, and opposition traders practised variable pricing of both trade goods and furs. Thus, under the specific market conditions prior to 1900, the Company's profits were 'whipsawed.' To respond to opposition, the Cumberland House district report of 1875 argued that district managers should have the ability to change prices and that traders were needed who could deal on a cash basis.[131] Prices were changed, and with the spread of more rapid communication, price variability increased. Clearly, some of the Company's opponents had better knowledge of the market price of furs. In 1886, competitors in the Cumberland district were 'kept regularly informed of the price of furs in the European and American markets, and last season as soon as they knew the increased value they at once raised their tariff for all fur, in some cases double what we were paying.'[132] The Company did not stick to rigid standards of trade, and communications between its posts tended to propel the price system, pushing up prices. Sometimes separate markets existed between Indian camps and HBC posts. Although the HBC argued that trade goods prices were inelastic due to a lack of Indian familiarity with the London fur market, alternate fur markets and the spread of price information undermined the mercantile profit based on the separation of consumers and producers.

With competitive pressures, the HBC altered its purchasing prices as a result of Indian economic behaviour. In 1877, the factor at Fort Churchill raised the tariff on mink and marten to satisfy Chipewyan demands and to prevent them from going to the Lac du Brochet post. Similarly, Fortescue was forced to improve the prices of marten and fine fox at York Factory in 1875 simply because of the opposition bordering on his district. In January of 1881, the Norway House tariff for mink was increased from one-half to one MB because Indians did not think it was worth trapping; however, by December of 1881, the tariff was cut back to one-half MB, and it was noted that there was not much opposition. In 1885, the tariff for lynx and bear was raised, and a large beaver was increased to two MB because Norway House Indians were going to Pelican Narrows. Nevertheless, at this time, post prices were raised as high as possible; but even a markup of 50 per cent on cost landed goods would not pay working expenses.[133]

The Hudson's Bay Company had very definite policies in response to price competition. The HBC was a price taker and not a price setter. In a certain sense, this practice advanced the credibility of competitors. The district annual report of the fur trade for outfit 1917 acknowledged that the Company 'never advance a price until force[d] to by competition, and such traders claim (with telling effect in some places) that as credit is due them for the advances they should get the Furs.'[134] The idea of raising the fur tariff and lowering the goods tariff was considered to be a bad policy; consequently, a markup of 25 per cent on heavy goods was too small for Oxford House.[135]

The Company's records explained this policy: 'In purely fur trade districts ... it has always been considered best not to alter the prices for goods but to confine the changes to the fur tariff alone, as, if the goods tariff is once reduced it is almost impossible to return to the original prices without creating great discontent.'[136] Moreover, the strategy was to use the goods' markup to offset losses on the fur tariff. Thus for 1914: 'The best method to adopt would be to meet the prices being paid by our competitors for furs, and wherever possible, raise the price of our goods to offset the amount paid in excess of our tariff.'[137] During the period of intense wartime competition, the HBC pursued a strategy of purchasing as much fur as possible, with little or no profit, while attempting to profit on merchandise. Additionally, new trade goods presented opportunities to secure profits. In 1877, the attention of northern district managers was drawn to 'the necessity of framing as heigh [sic] a Tariff as possible in valuing for sale any supplies which have recently been imported for the first time into their Districts, such as fancy Goods and other articles of a similar description.'[138] The HBC did not always meet the opposition on the price of furs, as this incident in 1919 at Norway House suggests: 'Joe Keeper brought in a Silver Fox this morning for which I offered $80.00. He says the Jews offered him $150.00. It was a medium sized fox, very slightly rubbed in three or four places. I considered my offer of $80.00 quite enough.'[139] In fact, the opposition buyer paid $165, and the difference in price offered might have been the result of a difference in experience with grading furs. Despite the spread of the 'price system,' mercantilism persisted. The annual report for Keewatin recorded in 1928: 'The great bulk of the collection were obtained by barter trade, on which a very substantial margin of profit was also made.'[140] The strength of the HBC rested in its possession of trade goods, and its bargaining strategy was to protect profits by maintaining the markup on trade goods.

The re-emergence of competition after 1900 created conditions similar to trade during the 1763-1821 period because Indians made demands upon traders for more varieties of trade goods. New types of merchandise were introduced, and demand went well beyond the range of goods normally associated with the subsistence production of fur. Again the Hudson's Bay Company had to respond to 'consumer preferences' of Natives that developed as a consequence of merchandise offered by opposition traders. At times the Company ran out of certain types of trade goods. In 1885, McDonald noted that in the Norway House district: 'We are working under a great disadvantage caused by the want of a proper assortment of trading goods as we cannot supply the Indians half their demands – capots, Trousers and assorted Blankets, we have scarcely any at all on hand, as well as sugar, which is a prime article of trade in this quarter.'[141] In 1886, The Pas Indians suggested to the HBC fur buyers that opposition traders had more goods. For the outfit of 1901, the opposition at Lac du Brochet was well supplied and as a result increased its fur collection over the previous year.

In the post-1870 period, flour became an important trade item. As the Cumberland House report for 1875 claimed: 'Flour is now become an indispensable article of trade with us and the more the traders bring out of it the more we will require.'[142] The increased use of flour in this period was designed to direct Native labour towards trapping and away from subsistence. In 1886 at Brochet, it was suggested 'that more Flour be introduced as an article of Trade, but not given away in debt, so as to induce greater activity in Fur-hunting, – the hunters being thereby less occupied in hunting Deer simply as Food.'[143] Lac du Brochet was established to exploit caribou in order to make up for the collapse of plains provisions, but in 1886, the post noted that Indians were complaining about the lack of twine and flour and were considering going to the free trader. The subsistence needs of the HBC and Natives resulted in an increased use of flour, sugar, and bacon to make up for the shortfall in pemmican. These trade items permitted Natives to continue trapping and, in the case of Brochet, the commercial hunting of caribou. Competition actually facilitated the transition from less country food to more imported food. The price system influenced the subsistence sector.

By 1895, flour was no longer a novel import for the Native economy, and Norway House records noted that free traders gave presents: 'Loaves of bread and molasses are the latest inducements used.'[144] As in the period between 1763 and 1821, alcohol was again traded. In 1869, the Reverend H. Budd and The Pas Indians asked the Company not to trade rum. The factor responded with the defence that the opposition traded rum, but he conceded and agreed not to use rum as an article of trade.[145] In fact, one opposition trader was known as Whisky Tom. In 1924, it was noted that 'the usual practice of using liquor as an inducement to the Indian to trade with them was followed to a greater extent than ever.'[146] Alcohol was not the only inducement to trade, and the Cumberland House report for 1885 requested more fancy goods, flour, and bacon, and went on to note: 'Provisions and tea have become absolute necessity.'[147]

In this competitive period, trade goods were not limited to the bare necessities of hunting. In 1873, a York Factory trader was attempting to counter the drift of Indians away from the post and requested 'a number of fancy goods such as I see they have been trading Inland.'[148] In contrast, poor quality trade goods were passed off to the Inuit; Charles J. Griffin wrote from Churchill that 'they, poor creatures [Inuit] have to pay such exorbitant prices for them [trade goods],' and that 'it is a cruel shame to impose a damage [*sic*] article upon them.'[149] The memories of free trader Jan, who operated in the Brochet area, expounded on the category 'fancy goods.' He recalled that after some initial language difficulty, a Cree woman placed an order for a corset, which he eventually filled since 'she was a daughter of one of my best hunters, [so] I had to get it for her.'[150] Clothing made from leather was less important. As Jan explained:

> The Indian women also made their own clothes and those for the children. They liked brilliant colours, but no yellow or white, and this meant that I always had to stock prints and dress materials in colours such as red, cerise, blue and green. They were the fashionable colours and used in society! Some of the young girls and women looked more or less like birds of paradise when they were really dressed up for a dance. In later years, they wanted madeup clothing so I had to stock a certain quantity but the piece goods still sold well, especially for the older women.[151]

Not only was imported cloth replacing country clothing, a trend well established before 1870, but imported made-up clothes began to supplement domestically cloth-tailored clothing. Jan's experiences indicate that traders had to respond to Indian preferences if they wished to be supplied with furs. Incomes during this period provided enough buying power for Natives to select fancy goods.

The shift in the types of trade goods being demanded presented some problems for the HBC, but it availed itself of any chance to protect its own interests. In 1889, the report for Oxford House noted that bulky items burdened the transportation system and consequently: 'Efforts should be made as much as possible to trade on which the largest amount of profit can be obtained. It is impossible to dispense with Capots, Blankets and other heavy goods on which the profit is usually small, but no larger supplies of such goods should be obtained than necessary.'[152] The strategy outlined in the York Factory report for 1890 suggested: 'Great care should be taken to indent as much as possible for goods on which most profit can be obtained and to import as few of those on which the profit is small.'[153] The introduction of light weight, fancy goods offered the Company the chance to recover losses that would have occurred had they stuck to heavy goods. The Company was not always successful in competing on the basis of trade goods. During the outfit of 1927 for Berens River, the annual report complained that 'a Jew' named Trapper carried 'a line of goods purchased in Winnipeg from Fire Sales and Bankrupt Stocks, with the result that the merchandise prices are cut very keenly.'[154]

The decline of a monopoly, albeit with the survival of the Hudson's Bay Company, is central to the economic history of Native peoples. Conventionally, the post-1870 fur trade has been overlooked and frequently it is assumed that after the transfer of Rupertsland, the fur trade stagnated. In fact, the renewal of the fur trade served to retrench Natives in a traditional mercantile economy. Increased incomes from trapping had the effect of pulling Natives out of the new resource industry's labour market. The survival of the Company has been explained by documenting its adjustments and changes to the pricing system, credit policies, new lines of merchandise, relations with competitors, and strategic spatial responses to the spread of competition. Additionally, Innis pointed to the Company's ability to squeeze competitors at isolated points and its extensive communications, capital resources, and selling organization. Furthermore, Innis stressed the quality of the Company's personnel, since 'the Hudson's Bay Company trader meets competitors effectively under the most difficult conditions.'[155] He considered the importance and size and organization of the Company, its reputation in the market, its control over post locations, and, after 1870, 'its connection with other important capital interests in the London market.'[156] Although Innis acknowledged the market situation in 1914, he did not see it in terms of shifting external markets and changing metropolis demands. Moreover, he did not see that the intent of the Company's central authority – in fact, control from London – was designed to maintain a traditional colonial relationship. Ultimately, this centuries-old colonial relationship was undermined because the Company's decisionmakers ignored the growth of North American markets. These new markets entrenched competitive fur buyers in primary markets.

The First World War was felt in the remote subarctic, and the old fur trade was swept away. The erosion of the London market had the effect of transmitting price instability to northern Manitoba. The demise of Company paternalism was eased by a period of prosperity for the Natives. However, in a 'good year,' the Company was able to extract even more surplus value, and of course the extraction of an economic surplus from the region was greatest when prices and demand by external markets were highest. In the buoyant year of 1918, the HBC markup on the cost of furs was 293 per cent at York Factory.[157] While Native trappers could increase their standard of living, the accumulation of wealth from this industry accrued to the advantage of London, New York, St. Louis, Winnipeg, not to York Factory, Split Lake, Nelson House ... Moreover, high fur prices provided enough income to allow white men to live in the bush as commercial trappers. In the end, both the Native trapper and post manager were faced with competitors. The recovery of the fur trade proved to be disruptive, and a return to subsistence was impossible. Industrial capital and the provincial government then filled the void left by the decline of monopoly.[158]

Natives shaped the post-1870 fur trade, but they did not control the system as a whole. They encouraged the spread of the price system and used

HBC competitors in an economic struggle against monopoly. Mercantile exchange procedures did not permit a modern price system. At Lac du Brochet, a rather remote corner of the subarctic, in 1894, an MB in fur was valued at ninety-two cents, but an MB in goods was worth twenty-four cents – a markup of 283 per cent.[159] A competitive price system, using cash, cut into this markup. The HBC system worked best when the Company held a monopoly on supplying trade goods, controlled exchange through a system of debt peonage, and was positioned as sole buyer of furs. The view that the HBC credit system was not debt peonage and could more accurately be categorized as a continuation of communal reciprocity is an important issue for subarctic economic history. The classification of credit as traditional reciprocity negates the commercial dimensions of the fur trade, which, in turn, denies the vital role that Natives played in creating wealth. The argument that the credit system can be equated to traditional reciprocity does not hold with the breakdown of Company paternalism due to the pressure of competitive markets. The credit system operated under certain commercial constraints, which a system of communal reciprocity never did. Debts and subsistence were intertwined, and the system of monopoly credit probably acted as a disincentive to higher levels of production. Because of the overwhelming response to the price system, the economic behaviour of Natives indicates that commodity production was not a minor or sideline activity. To the extent that there was an erosion of the credit system, the highly volatile price system replaced the old paternalism of a mercantile monopoly. To foster the commercial sector of the Native economy, a greater variety of southern manufactures became part of the regional economy of northern Manitoba. Competitive prices made the market a more dominant factor in Native life, and commercial productivity increased as a consequence. Significantly, the price system undermined Company paternalism. Although the encouragement of markets was an economic struggle with monopoly, it did not transform a regional economy based on fur production. If anything, Native responses to competitive markets served to re-enforce a Native role in a revitalized fur trade.

14

'And Now that the Country Has Gone Mining Crazy': Industrial Capital, Native People, and the Regional Economy

Economic indicators in the 1920s and 1930s depicted marked cycles of growth, stagnation, and decline. Although this era is not rich in written documentation, many changes were occurring. Yet at the core, two themes emerge: the shift from mercantile to industrial capital, and the economic problem of the social overhead of the traditional economy. The shift from mercantile to industrial capital was not abrupt. During the early 1880s, when a railway to Hudson Bay was being surveyed, Chief Factor Ross of Norway House wrote to HBC chief commissioner J.A. Graham:

> In some respects it would no doubt be the safest policy to have as little to do as possible with parties engaged in these railway schemes, but when the actual position of affairs in this and the two adjoining districts is considered, it seems to me of paramount importance that such enterprise [surveying] as those carried on here in the past and now at York Factory should be as much as possible under the direct manipulation and control of the Company. The business of this entire section is a close one, carried on after the old debt system of trade and above all things it is essential that as little foreign intercourse or contact be thrown in the way of the Indian as possible.[1]

Ross foresaw that new resource industries would create a labour market, which would disrupt the old system of trade and HBC profits. He suggested that the Company should attempt to control new economic concerns. Ross was trying to reconcile the interests of mercantile capital with new staple industries and transportation enterprises so that some control could be maintained over Native labour. One of the major developments in the post-1870 economy was a disruption of the supply of labour to the fur trade, but industrial capital also made a number of other changes to the regional economy. Ultimately, the HBC was not able to 'manipulate and control' new economic forces. In the 1920s and 1930s, the growth in the influence of industrial capital and government agencies in northern Manitoba is apparent. Its economic authority declined, but the Company survived the impact of industrial capital and the expanding influence of government.

The economic changes in the 1920s and 1930s are apparent in corresponding demographic shifts. A comparison between the 1921 and 1931 census for northern Manitoba indicates significant population growth during the railway building and early mining era.[2] In 1921, the population was 20,402, and this population grew at an average annual growth rate of 5 per cent so that by 1931 there were 30,669 people in northern Manitoba. The portion of the total population residing in mining and major transportation centres rose from 9.1 (1921) to 29.0 per cent (1931). An influx associated with resource development is apparent, since the total male population rose from 53.7 to 59.7 per cent (between 1921 and 1931). Consistent with these changes was a shift in the racial composition of the population: those identified as Native and Indian dropped from 48.2 (1921) to 35.4 per cent (1931).

The railway that crossed northern Manitoba from The Pas to Churchill ushered in a change from a water-based to a land-based transport system. This development modified the settlement system, and railway builder Claude Johnston noted that, in the 1920s: 'Fishermen, trappers and prospectors made The Pas their headquarters and we recall that millions of dollars worth of fur pelts passed through The Pas annually on its way, by rail, to the Winnipeg fur auctions.'[3] The Pas replaced Norway House as the main centre in northern Manitoba. Similarly, railway section divisions became settlements. Johnston described Pikwitonei in the late 1920s: 'There are about thirty families of Metis living in Pickwitonei [sic]. These people exist by trapping, fishing, working for prospectors or working on railway section crews or extra gangs.'[4] Settlement had some of the disorder associated with a capitalist frontier. Johnston noted that at The Pas, 'Natives and prospectors made a practice of squatting on the outskirts of town, along the river bank, where they could catch fish, by net, to feed their sleigh dogs. This went on for many months per year.'[5] Semi-settled surplus labour living off the land served the needs of industrial capital.

By 1930, the land tenure of the province had developed in the manner that had been envisioned by expanding central Canadian capitalism. Figure 14.1 depicts the land tenure of the province in 1930, when arrangements were being made to transfer land and resources to the Province. It shows the distribution of lands that had been granted by the Crown after 1870. Eighty-six per cent (127,484,396 acres) of the province remained as Crown lands. These data are from the Office of the Deputy Minister of the Interior and show the distribution of lands granted by the Crown.[6] Only 2.6

per cent of the land was reserved for Indians. The HBC obtained 1,279,965 acres (6.1 per cent), and railways received 3,553,833 acres or 16.9 per cent of the total. Additionally, 1,453,500 acres were leased for timber, and another 498,496 acres were leased for pulpwood. The total area of Manitoba set aside for Indians was given as 559,301 acres.[7] It was estimated that 36,370 acres still needed to be set aside as Indian reserves but some 89,005 acres had been surrendered.[8] Thus, of the total acreage of Indian reserves, 14.9 per cent had been surrendered and 6.1 per cent had yet to be surveyed by 1930.[9] This was the very outcome that Riel and all the Metis at Red River had tried to prevent during the winter of 1869-70. The current inequality in Manitoba originated when the settler society imposed an unequal land system on the local population. Whether or not the full and honest application of the legal land rights (Aboriginal title) of the Native population would have created a more equal system, land tenure is an essential question.

One of the major changes to the post-1870 regional economy came about with the modernization of transportation. The York boat could not be completely replaced by steam power. Not until 1938 would the Reverend J.W. Niddrie write that canoes were in use 'as the York boat Rejime [*sic*] is now over,' and that 'York boat freighting is now said to be a thing of the past, and has been superseded by canoe, and outboard gasoline engines, or in some cases by airplane. To us it seems strange that the old style of freight lasted so long.'[10] By 1919, most of the inland freighting in the Norway House district was carried out by the manufactured Peterborough canoe. The district report explained: 'The Indians are objecting and in fact refusing to do the strenuous work necessitated by the operating of York Boats, with the result that canoe transportation is being adopted to a greater extent every year.'[11] After 150 years of using the York boat, the Company reverted to the canoe. York boat work had been made more difficult because the portages were not maintained. Furthermore, the imported manufactured canoe would not entail the costs associated with building York boats. On some portages, freight canoes could be moved across on a tramway. The railway established greater access to the hinterland because winter horse freighting extended land transport well beyond the rail line. With the extension of the Hudson Bay Railway, HBC freight for Nelson River and Split Lake posts was no longer brought in by lake steamer. Although horse freighting on winter roads reduced the cost of transportation, Native incomes from boat work, which had been spent in HBC storerooms, were lost. Furthermore, good winter roads made it possible for traders to come in and compete for furs. Presumably, the ultimate displacement of Native transport labour came with the airplane, but initially, Indians were hired to freight gasoline to areas where planes refuelled. The Company's role in subarctic transport was not quickly shunted aside; in 1936, the Norway House journal recorded that mining

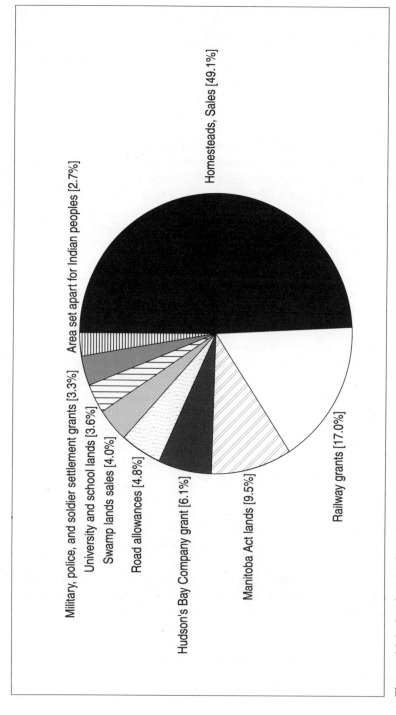

Figure 14.1 Land ownership in Manitoba, 1930

Homesteads, Sales [49.1%]

Area set apart for Indian peoples [2.7%]

Military, police, and soldier settlement grants [3.3%]

University and school lands [3.6%]

Swamp lands sales [4.0%]

Road allowances [4.8%]

Hudson's Bay Company grant [6.1%]

Manitoba Act lands [9.5%]

Railway grants [17.0%]

interests 'still look to the H.B.C. for transportation and advice on the best way to get around the country.'[12]

The construction of the Hudson Bay Railway was carried out in several phases. After the railway reached The Pas in 1908, work on the railway resumed in 1910; and when work stopped in 1917, rails had reached Mile 332. Construction efforts did not resume again until 1926, but in the meantime, a train ran to Mile 214 (Pikwitonei) twice a month. The Churchill extension work was carried out in the late 1920s, and Mile 510 (Churchill) was reached in April 1929. The Churchill extension involved a large influx of non-resident labour. Some 800 men were hired from St. Boniface, and in the winter of 1928-9, some 1,000 men worked out of Mile 350 (Amery) and another 500 men worked on the Churchill port facilities.[13] About seventy Split Lake Indians were hired to rehabilitate the track north of Pikwitonei.[14] The work on the Churchill extension set the precedent for large-scale labour imports. Yet, the railway also served to modernize the fur industry; when the train ran only as far as Pikwitonei, written-bid fur auctions were held in the express cars with buyers from the HBC, The Pas, and Winnipeg. In 1930, Innis correctly predicted that the success of the railway would rest on mining rather than the export of wheat.[15] Overall transport was modernized: the volume of freight was increased, capital replaced labour, and access was increased. The change to a land-based transport system along with the establishment of a mining industry, resulted in a new settlement system. The old water-based transportation system, with fur posts and reserves, became obsolete. By the 1960s, the region would have the appearance of a dual economy (modern and traditional economies).

Exploitation of northern Manitoba's mineral wealth provided an important source of growth for the provincial economy. In 1926, the value added contributed to the economy by the mining industry was $997,000; and during the depression of the 1930s, this grew to $10,969,000 in 1939. Also in 1939, mining accounted for 7.7 per cent of the total value added for Manitoba goods-producing industries. The growth associated with metal mining reinforced an economic legacy based on a sequence of staples. During this period, mining surpassed hunting, trapping, and fishing. Between 1926 and 1939, the value added of hunting, trapping, and fishing totalled $31,245,000, while the value added of mining production was $83,370,000.[16] This value might be compared to the $8,118,138 that the Department of Indian Affairs spent, up to 1929, on carrying out the stipulations for Treaties One, Two, and Five.[17] To the extent that these provincial figures represent production from northern Manitoba, an important shift in export commodities had occurred. This shift in the makeup of the regional economy had implications for Native employment and economic well-being.

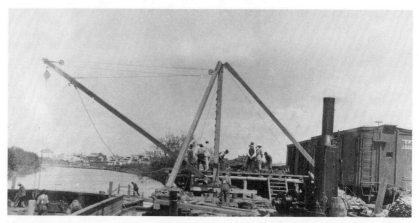

Unloading copper ore from the Mandy mine, ca. 1915. Rich ore was sleighed to
Sturgeon Landing and then barged to The Pas. (PAM, N782)

The start-up of actual mineral production is generally presumed to mark
the time when mining becomes an important activity in the subarctic. Mining activities are assumed to be quite unrelated to Native people. In fact,
mine development was preceded by extensive activities of prospectors. The
lag between prospecting and development is apparent in the case of gold
mining east of Lake Winnipeg. Gold was found at Rice Lake in 1911, but
not until 1927 did this area produce gold. Prospecting in the Snow Lake/
Flin Flon area began in 1896; more than 100 claims had been staked in the
Winter Lake area (Thicket Portage) by 1914; prospectors were active in the
Knee Lake area in 1918; and in the Oxford House area by 1923.[18] The railway facilitated the movements of these mobile prospectors. Native labour
helped with freighting related to prospecting. At the Gods Lake Gold Mine,
Natives were employed at mine-related work. Some seventeen families lived
permanently at the mine site. Indians provided cordwood to the mine but
after a few years expressed a concern about the depletion of timber.[19] Prospectors were in the vanguard of industrial capital, and yet they needed traditional renewable resources to make a living.

The new, more industrial economy of northern Manitoba was quite capable of producing wealth. Indications of the magnitude of this wealth can
be expressed as the net profits after taxes and write-off (not including depletion). Between 1931 and 1942, this form of net profit amounted to
$46,595,380 from metal mining, and between 1932 and 1942, gold net profits
were $6,079,187. A total net profit of $56,674,573 over a twelve-year period
indicates that the creation of surplus in northern Manitoba had been ac-
celerated by industrial capital.[20]

The influence of this new era of modernization was not confined to mining. The extension of the railway encouraged the expansion of commercial fishing. Horse freighting established commercial fishing well beyond the rail line, and thus, many small and distant lakes were brought into production in the 1920s and 1930s. Again, sturgeon was the primary target for the commercialization of this common property. The establishment of a paper mill at Fort Alexander in the 1920s is another example of how industrial capital was invested in the regional economy. Hydro power developments on the Winnipeg and Churchill rivers were a resource development designed to serve industry. The Island Falls (Churchill River) power plant on the Saskatchewan/Manitoba border was built in the late 1920s to provide power to the Flin Flon smelter. Natives were involved in the construction and maintenance of the Island Falls site, and the nearby Native community of Sandy Bay was created.[21]

In the 1920s and 1930s, Natives remained involved in forestry operations. For the Fort Alexander band, the employment and income effects of the demand for cordwood by the Manitoba Paper Company were significant. In this case, industrial capital also affected the subsistence sector. Indian Agent Hamilton reported that 'Indians are somewhat disgruntled with the Manitoba Paper Company because they claim it is as a result of the mill operations and the dumping of filth and dirt in the river that no fish are obtained.'[22] Industrial capital created wealth, gobbled up resources, and spat out waste. Moreover, the investment of industrial capital did not necessarily create the 'pure capitalist mode of production.' The HBC annual report on the fur trade commented on a competitor in 1925:

> This store is run in connection with the Paper Mill, and which Mill now affords the people of Fort Alexander the greater proportion of the work procurable by them. The Paper Mill store, naturally, adopts every means possible so as to necessitate the people of Fort Alexander spending their entire earnings in that store. This is done by handing wage earners books valued at say five or ten dollars, made up of .05c, .10c[,] .25c, and .50c [5, 10, 25 and 50 cents] coupons, which are payable in goods only, at the paper Mill Store.[23]

The HBC report made a guarded comment about the mode of remuneration used by the Manitoba Paper Company. The mill's store had precisely the same motivation as the Company. For decades, the HBC paid its boatmen and other workers in credit at the Company's sale shop in order to earn a markup on the spending of Native workers. Some political economists argue that the mercantile fur trade did not introduce capitalist relations.

However, the use of coupons to pay mill workers defies the *a priori* theoretical assertions that everywhere a clear distinction exists between industrial and mercantile capitalism. In the subarctic hinterland, on the periphery of the world system, this is not so.

The influence of the Hudson's Bay Company upon the regional economy declined markedly in the post-1870 period. In 1862, correspondence from Norway House boasted that 'with exception of the Missionaries & the wandering free traders, the entire white & half breed population is directly or indirectly dependent upon the Company.'[24] The 1909 annual report for the fur trade described the ongoing erosion of the position of mercantile capital: 'Civilizing influences are now invading to a greater or less extent all Fur Trade Districts in the form of Railway developments, Prospecting, Mining, Fishing, Lumbering, Agricultural or other enterprise[s], in many instances created a demand for native labour which to some Indians is more attractive than the uncertainties of the hunt.'[25] The HBC did not recover its position in the 1920s and 1930s. To a limited extent, the HBC attempted to diversify its subarctic operations. In order to maintain its position in merchandising, the Company became involved in commercial fishing in The Pas. The Company also considered acquiring Booth's interests in Manitoba. There were four interlocking dimensions to HBC mercantile control: (1) its own transportation system, which served to reinforce; (2) its trade goods monopoly; (3) its monopoly position as a fur buyer; and (4) its influence over Native labour. This dominance was severely eroded in the post-1870 period. The movement of HBC freight by the railway and the lake steamers of the Northern Fish Company in the 1920s demonstrates the ongoing dismantling of the Company's transportation system. The 1891 report for Grand Rapids indicates how 'civilizing influences' affected the Company's trade goods leverage with Natives: 'The Indians [were] very hard to deal with this past winter. They are getting too knowing and then they were spoiled a great deal last summer by the low prices at which the Fish Company are selling their goods. Thus they have made themselves very troublesome and awkward.'[26] Arthur J. Ray's research shows that by 1941-2 the HBC share of Manitoba's fur output had declined to 27 per cent.[27] The HBC was able to shift its merchandising business; in the 1930s, the demand for goods created by the mining boom in northeastern Manitoba was filled by the Company.

In the post-1870 fur industry, white labour was introduced and competed directly with Natives for resources. The increase in the number of white trappers, however, can be attributed mainly to a revival of the fur trade and as an indirect effect of the expansion of industrial capital. Many white men who came to northern Manitoba to prospect ended up becoming trappers.

Claude Johnston explained the interrelationship between trapping and prospecting: 'Trapping and hunting kept the white transients and natives occupied in a task which did not provide a fortune yet, they were able to make an honest living in the type of work that appealed to them. Prospectors also found this a pretty sure way to pick up a grub stake during winter months so that they could scout around all summer on a full stomach.'[28] Johnston described Herb Lake, an early mining community: 'Here traders, trappers and prospectors were striving to keep the bailiff from the door' and 'fish and fur was the salvation of the settlement.'[29] In 1921, Constable J. Spinnitt of The Pas recorded that 'prospectors and fishermen are preparing to go trapping for the winter.'[30] By the late 1920s, white trappers were well established at Churchill and were outfitted by the HBC; Johnston remembered that 'many white trappers found it convenient to squat along the south bank of the Churchill river.'[31] Thus, by the late 1920s, the railway and mineral exploration had led to an increasing involvement of white labour in fur production.

White trappers and prospectors further disrupted the resource base of the Native economy. In 1928, HBC records reported that 'we saw at least six or more fires in that country during our summer inspection, the country surrounding Reindeer Lake in particular being badly burned ... we have no definite proof, yet we feel a number of these fires are deliberately started by prospectors, in their quest for minerals.'[32] The report went on to state: 'And now that the country has gone mining crazy [it] is not going to help any towards the conservation of fur-bearing animals.'[33] The report anticipated that an influx of whites would hinder resource management. In the following year, the consequence was recorded:

At Lac du Brochet the Rev. Father Egenoff, Roman Catholic Missionary at that point for more than the past twenty years informed us that the last season was the worst he has seen. Caribou, the mainstay of the people at Lac du Brochet in winter, were very, very scarce and the migrating bands did not winter there as in usual years, no doubt due to the fact that much of their feeding grounds have been burned in the past two years, partly due to the quest for mineral[s], and this of course, has also a detrimental effect on fur bearing animals.[34]

Jan, a longtime free trader who had prospected, also attributed forest fires to white encroachment. He recalled: 'There were many prospectors in the country and in travelling you were likely to come across a camp almost anywhere. After the prospectors and more white trappers came in, forest fires were more frequent and miles of the country were destroyed every

Summer. These fires not only destroyed timber but had a lot to do with the gradual decrease in fur-bearing animals. This, of course, made it harder for the Indians to make a living.'[35] These observations indicate that prospecting activity was extensive and that the resources required by the Native economy were disrupted. Work on the railway also led to many forest fires.

Along with the prospectors' forest fires, the influx of whites resulted in direct competition for fur-bearing animals. The white trapper seems to have fallen into two categories: the long-term resident and the itinerant trapper. The itinerant trapper consciously overexploited the resource base. Chief Barker from Hollow Water reserve described the travelling trapper: 'These men used about 500 traps and travelled in groups of as many as eight, with good dog teams and sleds which enabled them to cover a lot of territory. They also moved each winter to new areas where fur was most plentiful.'[36] Acting Indian Agent J.H. Hellofs observed a similar process in northeastern Manitoba: 'The white man and non-resident halfbreeds are so ruthless in their trapping methods, that wherever they trap they kill off every thing completely if possible and leave nothing for future years.'[37] He stated: 'The white and non-resident trappers come into a district, one, two or three years, or as long as the fur lasts, takes and kills all that he can possibly get, and goes somewhere else to do the same thing over again, with never a thought for the poor unfortunate natives who reside in the district, and who must still make their living by hunting and trapping.'[38] These trappers were 'efficient.' By the late 1930s, white trappers had depleted the area around Pukatawagan. H. Halcrow informed the Department of Indian Affairs about the situation at Churchill in 1939: 'They have been, since the opening of Churchill, gradually driven by the white trapper to the coast and around near Churchill and it would seem it is only a matter of time until their hunting grounds are absolutely depleted and they will be forced to become charges of the government.'[39] Higher prices for furs and a mining boom drew white men into the subarctic. Their activities were extensive and penetrating, they occupied areas that until then were familiar only to Indians. The market and the idea of commercial gain drove many of them to exploit fur bearers intensely.

Some pressure was put on the provincial government to do something about white trappers. C. Stewart, superintendent general of Indian Affairs, wrote to Premier John Bracken in 1929: 'During recent years white trappers have invaded Indian hunting grounds in increasing numbers. The Indians are unable to cope with this competition and in consequence many of them are being reduced to destitution.'[40] A 1930 resolution from the Anglican Synod of the Diocese of Keewatin outlined the problem and advocated a solution.

Whereas, since the building of the Hudson Bay Railway through Northern Manitoba, white trappers there, as well as in Southern Manitoba, have penetrated into Indian trapping grounds, and by their ruthless methods of trapping, using not only steel traps, but also poison, have trapped out certain sections of the country, so that the natives find it difficult to eke out an existence and many have suffered from starvation; be it resolved that this Synod recommend that a decided step be taken in reserving certain areas of the country for the maintenance of the Indians only, and that the white trappers be kept out from these areas.[41]

With the advent of the 1930 transfer of natural resources, provincial authorities took a stronger interest in the game and fur-bearing resources of the north. A number of years would pass before registered traplines and fur blocks would be created to protect Native access to fur resources. Nonetheless, the reports of Indian agents and missionaries were confirmed by A.G. Cunningham, director of game and fisheries in a 'Report On Game Conditions' to C.H. Attwood, deputy minister of mines and natural resources. In November 1930, Cunningham wrote: 'At one time the district around Nelson House was consider one of the best fur districts in Manitoba. The white trapper, however, has practically cleaned this district throughout of all game, chiefly through the use of poisoned bait. Forest fires have also depleted the country of considerable fur-bearing animals and big game.'[42] Based on an analysis of the conditions in the districts, he concluded:

It is a well known fact that the wild game in Manitoba is being rapidly depleted and if immediate action is not taken forthwith to control the indiscriminate killing of game, it will mean a practical depletion of all game in Manitoba within a very few years. I would respectfully draw particular attention to fur-bearing animals. During the past five or six years certain districts in the province heretofore noted for large catches of muskrats and mink, are now entirely trapped out. The same may be said of beaver, otter and foxed [sic] including the Artic [sic] fox. This depletion causes a serious loss of revenue to the province in so far as game production is concerned.[43]

By 1930, the fur resources were not in a good state. While Cunningham sought to manage the resource by increased protection, his rationale for managing this resource was not based on securing a viable livelihood for Native peoples. The loss of provincial revenue seemed to be his main concern, although he held white trappers responsible for depletion. Ironically, when fur prices were high, Natives were not in a position to secure incomes to capitalize their communities. The breakdown of the HBC as the decision-making institution for the fur industry and the lack of any government regulations to protect Aboriginal and treaty rights and to counterbalance the wide open pillage, driven by the market, contributed to the marginalization of Native communities.

For the 1920s, the single most valuable archival account on northern Manitoba Natives is Dr. Stone's report on the health of Norway House agency Indians. In addition to documenting the problem of tuberculosis, Stone described the depleted resource base and the impact of white trappers.[44] Stone noted that only Indians in a fair state of health could undertake long-distance trapping. He outlined the situation for the more settled trappers: 'The trapper who undertakes to live at home and operate a fairly local trap line is a hard case. Locally, the country really appears to be trapped out. And in this group fall the people who want to send their children to school.'[45] He also put on record the general standard of living of Natives:

> The fact is that, so long as the earning members of the family are in good health, the family income is, on the whole, sufficient to buy the food and clothing necessary ... And when old age comes their condition is often indeed pitiable. The hardship of the sick and aged would be worse than it is if there did not obtain among them a very admirable community spirit. The successful hunter shares his meat with the poor. The widow, the orphan, the aged are seldom without a home, or at least a refuge. I do not want to give the impression that the economic condition of these Indians is as good as it should be. As matter of fact, judged by modern standards, it is bad. But, in actual fact, there is no starvation, though there is, at times, a certain degree of want.[46]

Stone also compared living standards, stating, 'I think that, in families where there is a fair condition of health, living conditions are as good as among the average working class people of the cities, unskilled labourers, better perhaps than in some foreign sections.'[47] The observation that Indian living standards were comparable to urban wage earners is consistent with the interpretation that economic growth had occurred in the regional economy. In the 1920s, fur prices were still strong. In addition to health problems, which had economic consequences, and the depleted resource base of the 'traditional economy,' Stone concluded that the population exceeded the available resources. He suggested: 'It will become necessary to move many of these Indians especially from Norway House and Cross Lake, out to the reserves where they can set up as farmers. I believe that some of the younger ones would be glad to go now.'[48] Once again, it became obvious that a population surplus to the prevailing economic conditions had become concentrated at Norway House.

No sudden event clearly indicates the point in time when the diversified Native economy ceased to provide growth and security. In 1925, Fort Alexander Indians hunted and worked on power lines. Indians continued to do off-reserve farm labour in the 1920s. Indian Agent C.A. Stevenson explained problems in the game and fish sector in 1928: 'The fur and game is getting practically cleaned out and the only means of a livelihood for these Indians is fishing. Their competitors on Lake Winnipeg are principally Icelanders, who are equipped with large sail boats with auxiliary engines and can go anywhere. The Indians have small skiffs and cannot go far from shore.'[49] In the 1930s, the conversion from sail to gas boats, a recapitalization of commercial fishing, served to further marginalize Natives in this industry. Over time, undercapitalization weakened the presence of the Native in the regional economy. The lumbering industry on Lake Winnipeg did not have the same vitality in the 1920s and 1930s as it had established in previous decades. Reserve timber continued to serve as a source of income when hunting and fishing were inadequate. In 1926, it was reported that Indians were cutting reserve wood on individual permits, but that they 'frequently find themselves at the end of their contract, with no actual advantage in cash and no return for their wood or labour, other than food to support themselves in the winter.'[50] In 1928, the Manitoba Paper Company decided not to obtain wood from Black River and Hollow Water, but Brokenhead and Fort Alexander were receiving good incomes from cordwood and pulpwood. Nonetheless, an Indian Affairs memorandum in 1928 stated that there were only 3,700 cords of wood left on the Fort Alexander reserve and that benefits had been temporary: 'The Indians have been very prodigal in the cutting of this class of material owing to the proximity of the Pulp and Paper Mill at Pine Falls. They have in the past 15 years cut on average 1500 cords annually, but do not seem to have derived much benefit, having earned merely wages, and have received nothing in the way of stumpage, other than the usual dues.'[51] Chief Barker recalled that in 1928 trapping incomes were low: seven months trapping earned him $600, whereas income from his wife's bead and leather work amounted to $800.[52] The staple-based regional economy was not as dynamic as it had been in the 1880-1915 period. Higher fur prices had the effect of drawing labour back into the fur industry, but in the 1920s and 1930s, Natives were facing competition as a fur producer. Competition and high prices in the 1910s and '20s had depleted fur-bearing animals.

By the 1930s, the so-called traditional economy could not provide adequate incomes. During the depression, the volume of relief increased, and government support continued to absorb what had been an HBC responsibility. Chief Barker recalled that the Department of Indian Affairs monthly relief rations amounted to fifteen pounds of flour, five pounds of pork, and half a pound of tea, and that 'there is nobody now living in the present generation who has tasted such hardship.'[53] For northern Manitoba and the Interlake, Indian Affairs relief increased between 1910 and 1936: $20,217 in 1910, $34,424 in 1920, $36,260 in 1930, and $63,910 in 1936.[54] Relief needs were not confined to status Indians. In 1938, Corporal R. Stafford explained:

> The relief situation at Norway House is acute, practically all the Half Breed families receiving relief rations. Their livelihood depends mainly on hunting and trapping, and what few days work they can get during the summer months. During the last trapping season general Fur was very scarce and the prices low. The muskrat hunt was a complete failure. Consequently these men and their families are destitute and there is no prospect in view of any of them getting employment at Norway House this summer.[55]

At Norway House in 1936, the HBC journal made frequent references to 'relief days' and the fact that relief was distributed at frequent intervals indicates that this support was designed for basic subsistence rather than a carry-over measure for periodic shortages. A more general form of relief was now called for due to (1) a contraction of the labour market; (2) a more sedentary residence pattern, which made trapping difficult; and 3) a depleted resource base.

During the 1930s, 'make-work' projects provided some earned income. For example, Norway House Indians worked at road construction near Berens River and Ross Island. An increase in relief led the Department of Indian Affairs to resurrect agricultural policies in order to provide subsistence. Superintendent of Welfare and Training, R.A. Hoey, explained this policy in 1937: 'It would appear, however, that, as the game and fish resources become more restricted, the Indians must turn increasingly to agriculture in an attempt to become more self-supporting and less dependent upon the Government for relief. I find it difficult to justify relief allowances on reserves with land available for cultivation and able-bodied Indians available for such work.'[56] Indian Affairs returned to a policy that had been advocated in the late 1870s: it implemented a practice of issuing vouchers for work on community gardens to reduce relief costs. In northern Manitoba, the Department of Natural Resources was associated with relief. For example, when Corporal Stafford approached commercial operator William Purvis: 'The names of all relief recipients were shown to him and a list made out, whereby the work and wages would be split up more generally, married men with families being given the preference.'[57] In the 1930s, various government agencies became involved as intermediaries between commercial operators and Native peoples so that subsistence level incomes could be achieved and relief costs could be kept at a minimum.

The investment of industrial capital and the production of a variety of staple exports gave the appearance of a more diverse, a more modern economy. In fact, the people of northern Manitoba were more vulnerable to the business cycle. In 1921, mining was at a standstill, wages were decreased at The Pas, and The Pas Lumber Company laid off workers. In 1924-5, business was slow at The Pas because of a lack of mining activity and employment was limited to lumbering. HBC records analyzed the impact of the depression. 'The present period of depression seems to have hit The Pas harder than most places in the country, coming as it did after a period of boom conditions due to intensive mining activities in Northern Manitoba, and, while it is unfortunate that such a heavy loss was incurred in closing out this Post, there is no doubt that its exit as one of our establishments was the wisest move, as had it remained open under present conditions, the loss would have been enormous.'[58] Moreover, the Company 'suffered further heavy declines in Summer Sales due to the lack of summer work for the natives.'[59] In the 1930s, in The Pas area, the HBC encouraged Natives to gather seneca root and berries, to burn lime, and to fish for sturgeon, but it was felt that 'these activities, although small and operated in a small way, served to maintain the sales at these Posts, and also provided the Indians with the means to obtain the necessities of life through what otherwise would have been a very lean season.'[60] In The Pas area, the HBC fortunes had been interlocked with a business cycle associated with finance and industrial capital. Johnston also recorded the impact of this world economic crisis: 'The people living in The Pas seemed to be quite depressed. The world-wide pessimism that hit Canada in the year 1929 was making itself felt in the north country. There was unemployment at every corner and most of the people were pessimistic about the future. Many families were on Manitoba Government relief.'[61] Certainly, this new commercial centre was sensitive to external economic influences. When copper prices dropped in the early 1930s, Sheritt Gordon mines shut down its operations and some of the labour moved off to a new gold venture at Gods Lake. Even marginal sources of income, such as cordwood cutting, were affected; and in 1932 the price of tamarack fell. The era before 1945 was not traditional. The economic security of the Native was related strongly to the responses that capital made to the business cycle.

For the Interlake by the 1930s, the buoyant economy, directed by resource capitalists such as McArthur and Robinson, collapsed. Steamboating lasted until the 1930s, but diesel fuel and the internal combustion engine replaced steam power. During the 1930s, smaller gasoline boats replaced steam tugs in Lake Winnipeg's fishery. The decline of steam power, hastened by the Hudson Bay Railway cutting into the hinterland of Lake Winnipeg, reduced the demand for cordwood and store operations. In the 1930s, McArthur sold his Standard Lumber Company.[62] Perhaps by the 1930s, the life cycle of this staples-oriented economy had run its full course; in 1936 both Robinson and McArthur died.

Conclusion:
A Foreword to a New
Economic Future?

This book challenges the conventional academic view that Native life, prior to 1945, was traditional, unchanging, and stable.[1] The corollary to this romantic view, that Natives were irrelevant to the Canadian economy after the fur trade, can be set aside. It argues that there existed an intricate web of change involving (1) the fur trade (subsistence and commercial dynamics, transportation, and spatial changes), (2) the demise of Aboriginal title (relationships between Native people and the state, settlement patterns, scrip coupons, subsidization of the social cost of the fur industry), and (3) new resource industries (economic and social aspects of the creation of a labour market). This study of the transition from mercantile to industrial capital is the story of the role that Native people played in the regional economy of northern Manitoba. The ever-increasing influence of a variety of external forces on Native communities is at the heart of the matter for understanding the post-1945 economic problems of Native peoples. Thus, the conceptual and methodological problems of the professional twentieth-century ethnographies should be evident. Yet, economic history built upon political economy seems so passé today, a pursuit that is easily denounced as just another logocentric project. In the past, concepts such as mercantilism, industrial capital, social class, and relations of production have been given exaggerated deterministic explanatory powers. Moreover, the cultural geography of the periphery has yet to be synthesized with the method of political economy. For this region, little of the consciousness of human agency can be distilled from written sources; at the best, these sources provide a rough account of experiences of economic history.

In the early 1870s, the regional economy of northern Manitoba was essentially a confederation of a number of local economies, held together by a transport system that moved the products of the subarctic up through a spatial hierarchy of outposts, posts, and district headquarters. Industrial

Europe sent a wide array of manufactured goods that reached the remote corners of the subarctic. The ongoing demand for the products of industrialism, whether essential or frivolous, is the strong thread that connects the periphery with the metropolis. The mix between local and imported provisions, boat building, and the use of human labour to move freight all created direct and indirect demands for resources and labour. The fur trade was an industry; the idea that commercial trapping was some minor sideline activity for Native people is simply wrong. The opening up of Rupertsland after 1870 remade the regional economy, and the local economies of HBC district headquarters were greatly simplified. The community history of York Factory illustrates the vulnerability of Native people to decisions made about transport and organization. Driving Natives back to the bush allowed the HBC to use subsistence resources to reduce the costs of its social obligations. With the adoption of steam power, Native labour was replaced by capital. The economic history of Native people cannot be understood only in racial terms, and Native history cannot be interpreted only from pure legal reasoning.

Yet, influential romantic notions about some sort of original and affluent society persisting until about 1945 hold sway among academics. The tendency for many Natives to seek wage labour with the HBC, to settle near posts, or to work in the new staple industries challenge the portrayal of the Native economy by some recent social science research. Any recognition of the material vulnerability of the traditional life to resource shortages or external agencies lead to questions concerning dependency in the fur industry. Old ethnographies and modern social science share a common lack of appreciation for the economic history of the subarctic; both of these methods downplay the internal and external significance of the market. E.P. Thompson, when considering the industrial revolution in England, observed: 'The exploitative relationship is more than the sum of grievances and mutual antagonisms. It is a relationship which can be seen to take distinct forms in different historical contexts, forms which are related to corresponding forms of ownership and State power.'[2] The intertwining of exploitation, ownership, and state power is relevant to what went on in the subarctic. The successful sabotage of Reverend Stevens's plan to move Natives from northeastern Manitoba to the Interlake is an illustration of the interconnections between exploitation, ownership, and state power. Discussion of political economy of the subarctic has essentially been shut down by ethnohistory. Questions concerning economic exploitation or destitution have been set aside by an incantation that asserts that Natives were not hapless victims but were active participants of history. This seemingly clever locution suffers from the illogic of any false dichotomy. It excludes the possibility that Natives actively participated in historical processes that contributed to the inequality of the present.

Economic history shows that Native people maintained viable economies by incorporating their labour with new resource industries and by responding to new markets. The knowledge of the importance of their labour and resources to the development of northern Manitoba has been all but lost. Indeed, for many communities and for several decades, their material life improved over that of the old fur trade regime, but their lack of control over land and their role as labourers meant that they were not in a position to secure long-term benefits. With respect to historical processes, the ability to make choices is not really a determining issue. For example, although Indians in the Interlake were not in the situation of the Plains Indians following the collapse of the buffalo economy, they were unable to make significant decisions. Yet 'dependence' increased with deeper integration, despite the improvement in material prosperity. The regional economy was largely under the influence of various state agencies and private capital. Economic growth was not self-sustaining, with the result that northern Manitoba developed largely as a response to the needs of the metropolis. And this is precisely the issue that many have missed when attempting to draw conclusions about dependency.

The general usage of the term 'dependency' by ethnohistorians has little to do with the meaning established by political economists studying colonialism. Among those studying the fur trade, 'dependence' has been used extremely loosely and consequently is well suited for arguments based on impressionistic data. The purely inductive use of archival evidence clouds political and economic issues, and the findings tend to collapse into unsound arguments. For example, Laura L. Peers demonstrated that the Saulteaux at Fort Pelly maintained flexible resource use strategies and therefore she argued that 'their bottom lines consist of the ability to make choices about subsistence and resource use. Absolute dependency and loss of autonomy occur when a group runs out of economic alternatives.'[3] Arguably no societies are absolutely dependent, and thus a nonsensical category has been created in place of assessing historical trends. The assumed existence of economic alternatives tells us nothing about deepening integration, racial stratification, unequal trade, or who benefits from economic growth. Moreover, she asserted: 'Such actions as the acceptance of provisions from the trading post may have been seen as proper behaviour and a wise resource-use choice by Native groups.'[4] How can it be that the mere rationalization of a choice on the part of one group is a sufficient condition for proving its autonomy from another group? (Her evidence documented that these provisions were not reluctantly obtained but had been asked for by the Saulteaux.) In essence, Peers's argument challenges the concern by some that the mercantile fur trade created conditions of scarcity. Her challenge is based on two assertions. First, when the Saulteaux received provisions from the post, it was their choice and in no way indicated dependence because such actions by the Saulteaux '*may have* been seen as proper [emphasis added].' Second, because the Saulteaux continued to make free choices, such as 'accepting provisions,' they had not exhausted their alternatives and, therefore, could not be in a state of absolute dependence. If material circumstances lead a group of Natives to consume food from an HBC post, then the simple reclassification of this basic need as some sort of manipulation of traders does not negate the problem of scarcity. Moreover, we are offered no evidence concerning Saulteaux perceptions of post provisions, only that it 'may have been seen as proper.'[5] The inflection of words – 'choice,' 'acceptance of provisions,' 'absolute dependence' – are an important means to convey this argument. These words reveal the missing premises of such arguments. Dependency is set up as a deterministic structure (absolute dependence) and is contrasted with an interpretation based on the primacy of free will in history (choices and alternatives).

It takes little imagination to see the main flaw in Peers's argument. The same reasoning could be used today to argue that 'social assistance' is not a reflection of powerlessness, distress, or dependence but an acquisition of resources through a 'manipulation of relationships' with the 'dominant' society. More than a few eyebrows would be raised were one to argue that 'accepting' welfare was a wise choice that enhanced autonomy. The issue of relative economic power cannot be pursued by restricting research to post-level HBC records. Historical generalizations based largely on an examination of activity at only one level of the fur industry are conceptually flawed. The ability to make some choices within a colonial framework is not a measure of significant power. Over time, the declining ability to keep responding to externally driven changes (to continue to have to make choices, to being forced to respond) is really indicative of the problems of integration. Interestingly, the argument about Native choices concerning subsistence strategies is not juxtaposed with Hudson's Bay Company's choice concerning the running of its enterprise. To argue that autonomy exists until a group runs out of economic alternatives avoids the problem of the accumulation of wealth. The distribution of wealth shapes the available economic alternatives. My investigation of dependency in the mercantile fur trade is not an attempt to skew Native history. It is an effort to seek historical insights into contemporary manifestations of inequality.

The political economy of treaty-making indicates that Indian efforts to secure a viable economic future were largely unrealized. The material circumstances of Indian people at the time of treaty-making informs us of the treaty negotiations as much as the Royal Proclamation of 1763. Thus, any examination of the context of the treaty-making era has to consider the structure of the fur industry; and any long-term assessment of the implementation of Indian treaties has to recognize the major changes going on in the regional economy. If Indians advanced abstract legal rights during the treaty talks, it was simply that the territory wanted by the Dominion of Canada was their tribal property. The Crown did not approach the question of Aboriginal title with the idea of codifying existing Aboriginal conventions of land use and occupancy. Rather, a new European category of property was created and named Indian reserves. Such a legal tradition had implications for treaty-making in Manitoba as well as for the subsequent use and management of the land. Access to game and fish became uncertain; the tribal commons were lost but not completely gone. From that era, a jurisprudence emerged concerning hunting and fishing disputes, but these judgments were not informed by either legal or economic history.[6] Government policies made it difficult for Natives to make long-term adjustments to the post-1870 changes. As a result of the demise of Aboriginal title, many Natives became seasonal labourers; a transitional proletariat. The viability of their incomes indicates that participation was not the result of coercion. The back and forth movement from wage labour to commercial trapping indicates that in the periphery, relations of production were not fixed.

With the re-emergence and persistence of land claims and Aboriginal rights, this book may inspire an interest in reinterpreting political economy. Without some understanding of economic history and political economy, future needs and interests cannot be adequately anticipated. With respect to terms, timing, and accepted procedures, the Treaty Five adhesions were flawed. In this part of Manitoba, Indians could not benefit from a treaty until the government decided to serve the interests of a railway company. Only this necessity, the needs of industrial capital, made the question of Aboriginal title relevant to the Department of Indian Affairs. The ongoing one-sided use of power indicates the failure of Aboriginal rights, in this instance, to create an economy that would compensate for the loss of tribal commons. Ottawa policy-makers knew that 'as their natural resources fail them,' Indians would have to give up the land, to make economic adjustments, and to sell their labour.

Significantly, the stagnation in northeastern Manitoba raises problems regarding the obligations that the Canadian nation state eagerly accepted in the 1869 Address to the Queen concerning the acquisition of Rupertsland. Because of a treaty myopia, most legalists have missed this particular aspect of Indian relations with the Crown. The suffering at York Factory and the starvation documented by Reverend Stevens need not have occurred: 'Adequate provision for the protection of Indian tribes' was not forthcoming in the non-treaty areas. The Department of Indian Affairs chose to wait until their resources failed rather than to act on the obligations acquired by the Rupertsland transfer. Native peoples in this non-treaty area were caught in an economic void: the Canadian state was not acting on its obligations, and the HBC was shedding its paternalism. There may be no remedy for this suffering. Yet, the treaty obligations of the Department of Indian Affairs started shifting the social responsibilities of the fur industry from the HBC to the state. If relations between the Crown and Aboriginal people centre on the question of property, then economic considerations cannot be ignored. The tendency to merely refashion the existing case law on Aboriginal and treaty rights could be bolstered by primary research in the area of economic theory and by exploring the links between law and economy.

Treaties can also be seen as a legal step in the transition from tribal common property to open-access resources, which, in turn, became a form of private property.[7] Mining and timber leases, commercial fishing licences, and registered traplines are certainly indicative of a very different form of land tenure than that which had existed prior to the transfer of Rupertsland. With respect to subsequent resource developments, the 'surrender' of Aboriginal title was not just a matter of facilitating a system of fee simple title for white occupancy – Native property rights were seriously limited. Although treaties alluded to continued resource access for Indians, economic policies did not provide for exclusively Native resource areas (such as fishing reserves). Native economies could have been capitalized if only a small fraction of the value of wealth created through the commercialization of the region's resources had been set aside. The open access to resources was accompanied by the re-encroachment of the market. And the loss of the commons put additional stress on the traditional economy, which, unlike the industrial economy, did not have access to capital. In the case of sturgeon fisheries, high prices led to the overexploitation of the resource. Thus, immediate gain of Native fishermen came at the expense of long-term costs. When fur prices were high, Native incomes increased; but Native trappers also faced competition from white trappers whose reckless overexploitation was not subject to government restrictions. Occasionally, exceptional markets generated strong demand for primary products, but the real income potentials were negated because of resource overexploitation and competition. In other words, when better incomes from the traditional economy were possible, the government failed to protect Native livelihoods.

Halfbreed scrip is the strangest government policy directed at Aboriginal people in this era. Establishing the meaning of scrip was very difficult. Even after detailed research, scrip seems to stand for very little. The relevant sections of the Dominion Lands Act, all the orders in council, numerous claimants' declarations, and corresponding scrip receipt forms do not establish that the Metis, collectively or individually, ever consented to give up their Aboriginal rights. The elaborate claim process only generated a coupon that was of far more interest to a syndicate of buyers dominated by Winnipeg lawyers than it was to the Metis. For the Metis grantees, the source of the value of these coupons could not have been clear, but the keen interest on the part of land scrip speculators gave these coupons a cash value. The issuing of scrip coupons had nothing whatsoever to do with the commitments that Canada had assumed with the transfer of Rupertsland. Today, Metis Aboriginal rights remain a fundamental legal and political problem for the nation. If fiduciary obligations were undertaken by the Crown with the transfer of Rupertsland, then the apparent confusion as to the meaning of scrip can be dispensed with rather easily.

In the first decades following the transfer of Rupertsland, Natives tended to form permanent settlements. The spatial economy was reoriented. Many reserves functioned as small labour pools for the frontier resource industries. The locations selected following treaties were essentially rational, and many fish stations and sawmills located near reserves. In the early reserve transition era, cattle-raising and reserve gardening were an aspect of the Native economy. Indians did not, as envisioned by the Department of Indian Affairs, make a transition from hunters to agriculturists; rather Indian agricultural efforts were appropriate to subsistence needs, land capabilities, available markets, and the possibility of alternate incomes.

In the post-1870 period, staple-related industries – commercial fishing, lumbering, and steamboating – modified the regional economy. Natives played a vital role in 'opening-up' northern Manitoba, especially in the Interlake. A labour market was established and Natives deserted the fur industry. For the Interlake, the diversification of Native economic activities provided more economic security than did the pre-1870 or the post-1945 periods. However, the development of a land-based transport system left many Native communities remote and isolated from labour markets. Overall, the experience with wage labour in northern Manitoba corresponds to Zaslow's generalizations regarding the role of Indians in northern Canada: 'But even when Indians were successful workmen, they were still not masters of their own economic destiny; they worked mainly for wages or sold their produce to middlemen who reaped most of the benefits.'[8] Natives have shared the experience as 'drawers of water and hewers of wood' with other Canadians. In terms of economic history, Natives do not easily fit in the category of the 'other.' And like many Canadian communities based on a single resource industry, the shift away from producing a staple entailed difficult adjustments for Native communities. Future research will assess the relative importance of the problem of lacking some control over economic destiny and the absence of tangible benefits from the government's implementation of treaty and Aboriginal rights.[9]

Numerous changes altered the regional economy after 1870, but by 1930, the preconditions existed for the rapid consolidation of an industrial exploitation of resources. These preconditions included the demise of Aboriginal title, the creation of a labour market, the availability of money for exchange, a more efficient transport system (which could move capital goods and non-resident labour into the region), and the decline of the mercantile HBC. By the 1930s, northern mineral exploration and development showed to policy-makers that the province need not be dependent upon the export of grain. While almost all Indian bands in northern Manitoba were affected by economic changes, Native people did not undergo a steady transition from their role as commercial trappers to permanently employed wage labourers participating in an industrial economy. Many bands that had participated in the new staple resource economy later reverted to commercial trapping. For Native people, economic change was neither constant nor cumulative. Frontier capitalism brought with it a very incomplete form of modernization. Changing transportation modes, the lack of local accumulation of capital, depletion of resources, and the business cycle all had implications for Native communities. Although a market for wage labour was created, self-sustaining development and accumulation of capital in the region did not occur. Consequently, the appearance of modern and traditional economies in northern Manitoba was readily accepted in the post-World War I era of growth.

Swampy Cree wedding at York Factory, 1925 (NAC, C-34155, R.D. Davidson)

The implication of this story is that the economic problems that Native people faced in the post-1945 period are largely the results of preceding underdevelopment. In some respects, it is difficult to assess this era of Native history because of the appearance of material progress, and, moreover, it is difficult to determine why the diffusion of industrial capitalism did not usher in a fully modern society. In this pre-1945 era, which has been labelled as 'contact-traditional' by subarctic ethnologists, Native society experienced increased capitalist penetration following the slow demise of mercantilism. By 1870, the fur trade, with a minimum of fixed investment, had drained a considerable economic surplus. Future research will have to look at the role of the state in the traditional economy. The surrender of Aboriginal title limited Native control over the future regional economy. The importance of subsistence rights have to be weighed against the actual availability of resources; if there are no fish or wildlife to harvest, treaty and Aboriginal rights take on an abstract quality. With the exception of small reserves and hunting and fishing rights, Natives were dispossessed. Because of treaty obligations, this dispossession did not result in a form of absolute destitution that required Natives to sell their labour for low wages. The availability of some subsistence resources and relief meant that Natives could not be pushed into a labour market. But many Natives sold their labour in this era or obtained incomes by producing for markets. With the demise of Aboriginal title, Native property interests in resources were not clear, but Natives were not in a position to collect rents from these resource activities. Consequently, they were largely left with only their labour and some wildlife and fish. The new staple industries were seasonal and shared many of the weaknesses of the fur industry such as a complete dependence upon external markets. For this type of resource economy, Native labour was efficient. Traditional skills and knowledge were relevant, such as the guiding associated with prospecting and railway surveying. Moreover, during slow periods (due to seasonal limitations or weak markets) resource capitalists were not responsible for the social costs of this labour. Indians could return to trapping, fishing, and hunting or draw upon Indian Affairs relief. Because of the availability of seasonal labour, the effects of the stagnation of the fur trade and the consequence of the change in property relations were muted. To the extent that the national priority was to direct human energy to agricultural settlement of the fertile belt, Native labour played an important role by opening up new northern resource lands. White agrarian settlement of the prairie west was neither distracted nor slowed down by the wealth of the North because Native labour was available to build a regional economy.

This book is in accord with Arthur J. Ray's findings concerning the post-1870 fur industry; in particular, he found that increasing costs, dependence on imported goods, competition for fur bearers, and decline in alternative opportunities meant that 'the incomes native people earned from trapping and other activities too often fell short of their requirements and they had to rely on increasing levels of economic assistance.'[10] The compression of Native incomes after 1920, the need for more capital, the problem of who administered growing government relief, and the decline in monopoly are all relevant themes for northern Manitoba. The need for credit in the fur trade, the social overhead of the traditional economy (legally jettisoned by the HBC in 1870 with its surrender of its monopoly charter), the effects of competition from white trappers, and treaty obligations all served to pull the government into an area that had been under the control of the Company. As Ray argued: 'By the end of the 1930s company paternalism was no longer adequate.'[11] He also observed: 'The older paternalistic fur trade, a hybrid of European mercantilism and native reciprocal exchange traditions, was crumbling by 1945, and the groundwork for the modern state welfare system so prevalent in the north today was laid.'[12] Certainly, the legacy of increased government presence in Native communities after 1945 is at the core of much frustration. The simplified view of the traditional Native economy (cash is earned for subsistence) essentially ignores the existence of a social overhead that came into existence with commercialization and scarcity. The state enters into an area that has been vacated by private industry. An historical perspective of the traditional economy is an essential means to understand the expanding role of the state.

During the boom period, the development of social classes within Native communities was possible, but the existence of some prosperous Indian farmers and traders did not lead to the development of a regionally based class that would work towards ongoing capitalist development. And no big white capitalists emerged to replace McArthur and Robinson. Mineral development was in the hands of foreign concerns. The fishing industry did not generate enough local income to accumulate investment for anything other than more fishing gear. This industry did not provide investment for new economic activities.[13] Thus, neither an indigenous Native nor white capitalist class formed in northern Manitoba. After 1930, the provincial government was more involved in managing natural resources. The state – both the provincial government and the federal Department of Indian Affairs – became more interventionist during the depression. Public agencies attempted to maintain incomes from renewable resources. Fur conservation, muskrat blocks, and registered traplines were aimed at rehabilitating the Native economy. In other primary industries, agriculture and fishing, income redistribution through reforms (co-operatives, marketing boards, subsidized credit, and government intervention) occurred. These reforms developed because of the collective actions of producers; co-operatives and commodity pools succeeded at giving producers some power in the market. Trappers did not gain much influence over the marketing of furs, and unlike other primary producers they did not improve their economic livelihood. Instead, the social disruption caused by the market was absorbed by the state, thereby reinforcing dependence and paternalism. Ray has laid out the structure of the international fur industry between 1870 and 1945, but the role of federal and provincial agencies, say between 1945 and 1969, needs to be analyzed more closely. Ron Laliberte's study of the importance of northern migrant Native labour to the southern Alberta sugar beet industry identifies the issues that need to be considered.[14] But the rehabilitated Native economy could not keep up with a growing population. In the post-World War II era, provincial and federal agencies, mindful of increasing welfare costs and a growing disparity in living standards, created urban Natives. By the early 1960s, the surplus Native population of northern Manitoba was being encouraged to move to Winnipeg.[15]

The current interests in Native history cannot readily accommodate economic history. In terms of method, the reinterpretation of qualitative sources without a conceptual framework, and the rejection of all numerical evidence generates a historiography that exculpates colonialism. Indeed, the argument has been made that credit in the fur industry was not an obligation designed to maintain unequal trade, but a concession by HBC management intended to sustain reciprocity.[16] In the dominant paradigm, as long as Indians remain active participants, the problem is reduced to an examination of the imposition of White culture by church and state – thus rendering capitalism invisible as a historical force. This effort to consider Native/white relations while denying or ignoring the question of capitalist exploitation continues to create scholarly clutter. Cultural resistance has provided a powerful theme for the revising of history; however, questions about the transformation and reform of the colonial economy are not asked.[17] Need there be such a thing as a post-colonial economy?

The assimilationist thrust of the White Paper of 1969 was the federal government's approach to the economic insecurity facing Native communities. The desire to preserve self-government in the Constitution stems from decades of political activity, which has reversed the White Paper's plans. Yet, Aboriginal governments will have to face not only the accumulated issues but also the pervasive economic problems inherent within the inequality of the world market. Aboriginal decisions will be framed in the context of ever-increasing competitive global economic forces. While Aboriginal governments will likely seek to facilitate relations with large external agencies, attempts to spread and sustain benefits from economic growth may prove to be as evasive as the treaty obligations of the nineteenth century.

Appendix A
Fur Trade Productivity and Prices: Stagnation and Revival

Figures A.1 to A.9 present statistics on fur production of select species for the Hudson's Bay Company's districts/posts of Cumberland House, Norway House, Island Lake, York Factory, and Churchill. These data are based on records kept at York Factory. Furs produced in a given year (based on a trading year ending in May) were shipped to London and were referred to as the returns of a given outfit. The data for all the posts in the Cumberland House, Norway House, and Island Lake represent district returns, whereas the returns for York Factory and Churchill represent post data. The analysis concentrates on beaver, muskrat, marten, and mink production because, among the dozens of species collected by the Company, these were the most important. One problem with these data is that only the collection of the dominant fur trading company is represented. Other traders obtained some furs during this period. Therefore, it is not clear that trends are entirely the result of ecological limitations. Over time, the leakage of production to a competitor (an economic factor) would result in a decline in HBC yields. The analysis presents the same data by species and by producing area. In the period between 1860 and 1891, competitive opposition to the HBC was strongest in the Cumberland district and weakest at Churchill and York Factory. Given that similar production trends exist for all districts, and despite varying degrees of competition, ecological factors such as population cycles are suggested as the primary explanation for the Company's changing yields. In this way, a spatial comparison helps to separate the ecological determinants from purely economic causes (prices, effort). In this time period, competitive effects were relatively weak and the so-called 'free-traders' had very limited means to transport furs from the subarctic. Since the Company was the dominant and in some cases the exclusive buyer, Figures A.1 to A.9 are useful economic indices for the late nineteenth century fur industry.

Figures A.1 to A.9 display data by species for the five producing areas. For all areas, beaver yields were at a crisis level, given the historical importance of this staple (Figure A.1). Beaver returns are much lower in 1890 than in 1860. Muskrat returns are shown in Figure A.2, and cyclical fluctuations rather than any long-term trends are evident. The trend in marten returns in Figure A.3 are similar to muskrat in that cyclical production trends dominate. Figure A.4 shows mink production. Again, cyclical patterns are paramount. A comparison of Cumberland beaver and muskrat yields suggests that increased muskrat harvesting compensates for the decline in beaver after 1870 (Figures A.1 and A.2).

Fur returns can also be displayed by regions (Figures A.5 to A.9). The Cumberland House returns (Figure A.5) reveal that muskrats made up nearly all of the volume of the district's trade. In 1887, the lower Saskatchewan River was abandoned by some opposition traders because it was 'played out,' but it clearly rebounded shortly afterward.[1] Lower water levels (and the concomitant freezing of muskrats) seemed to have shortened the muskrat cycle in 1891, a year described as one of fur scarcity.[2] In 1891, scarcity at The Pas meant that the 'Indians are consequently more indebted than usual.'[3] In the long run, goods on credit terms maintained Indian labour in the commercialized trapping sector because it provided a way of dealing with year-to-year fluctuations in yields. Norway House returns are shown

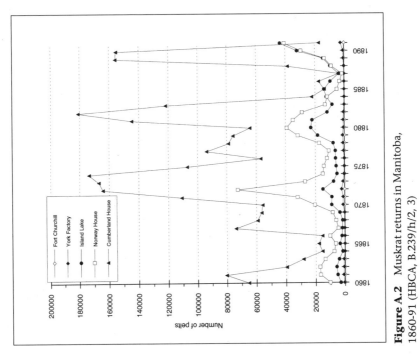

Figure A.1 Beaver returns in Manitoba, 1860-91 (HBCA, B.239/h/2, 3)

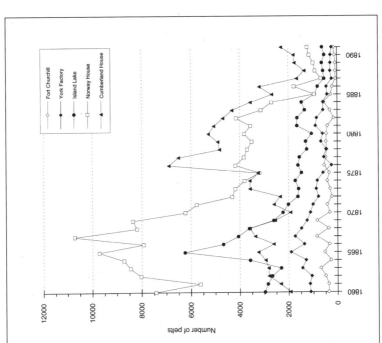

Figure A.2 Muskrat returns in Manitoba, 1860-91 (HBCA, B.239/h/2, 3)

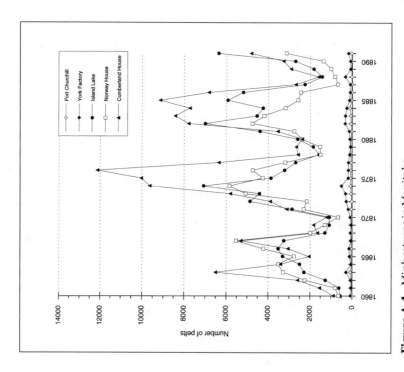

Figure A.3 Marten returns in Manitoba, 1860-91 (HBCA, B.239/h/2, 3)

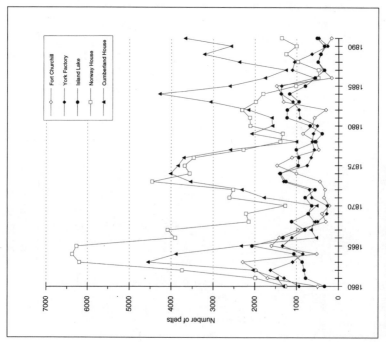

Figure A.4 Mink returns in Manitoba, 1860-91 (HBCA, B.239/h/2, 3)

in Figure A.6 and indicate the increased importance of muskrats after 1869 and the tendency for the Company's other returns to decline between the 1860s and 1891. Island Lake returns (Figure A.7) show an increase in muskrat and mink with a decline in beaver and marten over time. York Factory yields show a significant decline in beaver but no interlocking of cycles for the other species (Figure A.8). Churchill yields (Figure A.9) are without significant trends except for a decline in beaver. In the Norway House and Island Lake districts, declining beaver harvests seem to have forced Natives to direct greater efforts towards trapping muskrats.

Figure A.1 through to Figure A.9 indicate that distinctive regional specialization had taken place as a result of the local environment and the mercantile trade. Clearly, Natives from Cumberland House district had a very different trapping economy from that of the Indians living near York Factory. The former were much more reliant on muskrat than the latter. Cumberland and Norway House districts were the leading producers of marten. At the outset, Norway House was the leading producer, but by 1882 the expansion of the Cumberland House district caused marten yields to surpass Norway House. York Factory and Churchill mink yields were insignificant when compared to those of the other districts (Figure A.4). Specialized commodity production for the market required particular resource strategies and appropriate labour processes. High yields in muskrat trapping can be achieved in an intensive, but short, spring season. Since muskrat harvesting is done after the prime fur season, a shift to beaver, mink, and marten would not occur in the same year. Unanticipated crashes in muskrat populations would be difficult for trappers to absorb.

Price movements for beaver, muskrat, marten, and mink between 1860 and 1910 are shown in Figure A.10. This presentation is based on average prices realized at the Hudson's Bay Company's auction sales. Average fur prices in English currency were converted to a price index; an index of 100 was based on the average of the 1869, 1870, and 1871 prices. Price movements are shown for years before and after the beginning of the study period. In Figure A.10, beaver prices are distinct because, overall, prices tended to increase between 1860 and 1910, peaking in the late 1880s. Beaver prices increased with declining supply (compare Figure A.1 with Figure A.10). In the 1890s, beaver prices declined and stagnated while other fur prices increased. The other furs tended to have a price movement somewhat different from that of beaver. Muskrat prices tended to be higher in the 1860s and early 1870s and, on average, stayed below the 1870 level. A dramatic increase in muskrat prices occurred at the turn of the century. Marten, historically a valuable fur, experienced a significant decline in price in the 1870s. Marten prices remained low until the late 1890s, when prices surpassed the 1870 level. After 1900, marten prices were relatively higher than the nineteenth-century prices. Mink prices corresponded to the general trends established by muskrat and marten – downward price movement in the 1870s, low and stagnant prices in the 1880s, and considerable price increases beginning in the late 1890s. After 1900, price increases were particularly marked. These price changes reflect changing product demand for fur, new markets (U.S. markets), and a diversity of buyers (free traders, new firms, and commissioned sales/auction houses). Fur prices continued to increase after 1900. Very high prices, with marked and rapid fluctuations, are evident in the period 1910-23.[4]

The data on species trends indicate that sporadic information from post journals about fur productivity for any single point in time and space cannot be used to make general conclusions about resource conditions. Unlike the resource base of the plains, subarctic resources were not completely destroyed. Beaver, a mainstay, was scarce, but other commercial resources were available. Essentially, population cycles explain the trends for mink, muskrat, and marten. If anything, low fur prices in the late nineteenth century were a more serious problem than scarcity of fur bearers. More intensive trapping of other fur bearers seems to have compensated for the decreased supply of beaver and the problem of stagnant fur prices. The beaver and muskrat yields infer a switch in effort. Declining prices indicate an era of low incomes, which, in turn, explains the desire for a treaty in the unceded region north of the 1875 boundaries of Treaty Five. Finally, the data serve to highlight the marked regional specialization that existed in the late nineteenth century. Of importance to Native economic history is the fact that these data also indicate that the natural productivity of the commercial sector of the Native economy fluctuated sharply because of the tendency for different species to go through cycles in tandem. This is particularly evident for mink, marten, and muskrat. Between 1860 and 1891, the commercial production

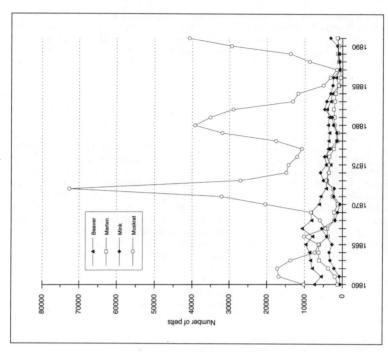

Figure A.5 Cumberland House fur returns, 1860-91 (HBCA, B.239/h/2, 3)

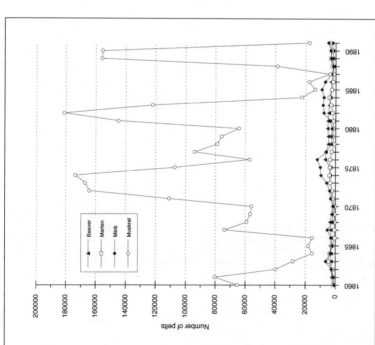

Figure A.6 Norway House fur returns, 1860-91 (HBCA, B.239/h/2, 3)

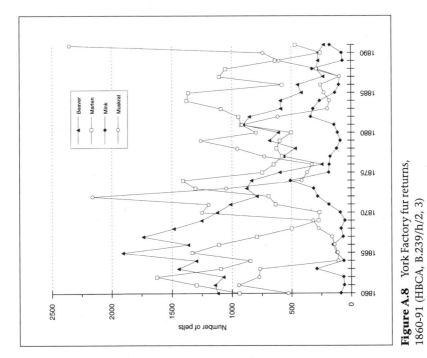

Figure A.7 Island Lake fur returns, 1860-91 (HBCA, B.239/h/2, 3)

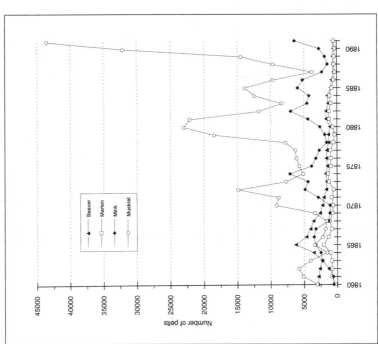

Figure A.8 York Factory fur returns, 1860-91 (HBCA, B.239/h/2, 3)

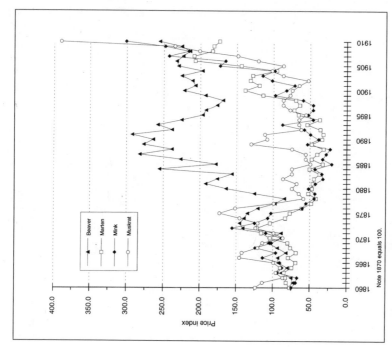

Figure A.10 Fur price indices, 1860-1910 (HBCA, DD. Ga.13)

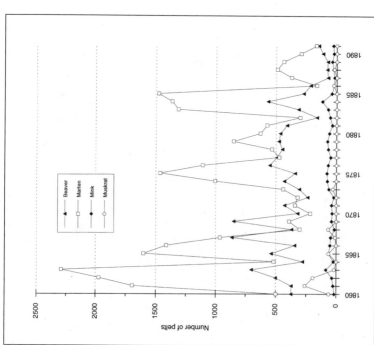

Figure A.9 Fort Churchill fur returns, 1860-91 (HBCA, B.239/h/2, 3)

of the Native economy was acutely influenced by the instability of muskrat, marten, and mink yields and declining beaver harvests.

For Natives dependent upon muskrat, their economy had a 'feast or famine' quality. Clearly, the cycles in fur productivity would reinforce a trapper's need for credit from the Company. Low fur prices suggest that the role of the state must have been important in sustaining the traditional economy. With pronounced swings in productivity, a large company would have advantages over smaller operators. It is also fair to classify the years between 1870 and 1900 as stagnant, but after 1900, due to an upward price movement, the fur industry was revitalized. The higher prices after 1900 have implications for Native incomes. In effect, the period of low prices (ca. 1870 to 1900) is an interlude; the industry was switching from felt fur to fashion fur.

Appendix B
Summary of Treaty Terms
(Written Version)

Treaty One: Indian Obligations
- 'Do hereby cede, release, surrender, and yield up to Her Majesty the Queen, and her successors for ever, all the lands included within the following limits' (see Figure 4.1)
- pledged to observe the treaty
- maintain perpetual peace
- 'not to interfere with the property or in any way molest the persons of Her Majesty's white or other subjects.'

Treaty Two: Indian Obligations
- same land surrender wording as Treaty One
- strictly observe the treaty, conduct and behave as good and loyal subjects
- obey and abide by the law; maintain peace and good order 'between themselves and other tribes of Indians, and between themselves and other of Her Majesty's subjects, whether Indians or whites'
- 'will not molest the person or property of any inhabitants ... or the property of Her Majesty the Queen'
- will not 'interfere with or trouble any person passing or travelling through'
- chiefs 'will aid and assist the officers of Her Majesty in bringing to justice and punishment, any Indian offending against the stipulations of this treaty, or infringing the laws in force.'

Treaty Three: Indian Obligations
- 'Do hereby cede, release, surrender, and yield up to the Government of the Dominion of Canada, for Her Majesty the Queen and her successors forever, all their rights, titles and privileges whatsoever to the lands included within the following limits ...'
- same law and order wording as Treaty Two.

Treaty Four: Indian Obligations
- same land surrender wording as Treaty Three
- similar law and order wordings as Treaty Two.

Revision of Treaties One and Two: Indian Obligations
- 'abandon all claim whatever against the Government in connection with the so called "outside promises" other than those contained in the memorandum attached to the treaty.'

Treaty Five: Indian Obligations
- same land surrender wording as Treaty Three
- same law and order wordings as Treaty Three.

Treaty One: Government Obligations
- reserves of 160 acres per family of five
- location of reserves for particular bands mentioned (see Figure 4.4)
- present of three dollars per person
- school on each reserve
- no intoxicating liquor on reserves
- accurate census of Indians each year
- annuity for each family of five persons of fifteen dollars.

Treaty Two: Government Obligations
- reserves of 160 acres per family of five
- location of reserves for particular bands mentioned (see Figure 4.4)
- present of three dollars per person
- school on each reserve
- no intoxicating liquor on reserves
- accurate census of Indians each year
- annuity for each family of five persons of fifteen dollars.

Treaty Three: Government Obligations
- 'Lay aside reserves for farming lands, due respect being had to lands at present culti-vated by the said Indians, and also to lay aside and reserve for the benefit of the said Indians'
- 'reserves shall be selected and set aside where it shall be deemed most convenient and advantageous for each band or bands of Indians, by the officers of the said Government appointed for that purpose, and such selection shall be so made after conference with the Indians'
- reserves of one square mile per family of five
- present of twelve dollars per family of five
- schools on reserves
- 'Indians, shall have right to pursue their avocations of hunting and fishing throughout the tract surrendered ... subject to such regulations as may from time to time be made by her Government ... saving and excepting such tracts as may from time to time be re-quired or taken up for settlement, mining, lumbering or other purposes'
- sections of reserves can be appropriated by the government
- accurate census of Indians
- annuity of five dollars per person
- $1,500 per year annum for ammunition and twine
- 'Articles to be given once for all for the encouragement of the practice of agriculture': hoes, spades, ploughs, harrows, scythes, axes, saws, files, grindstones, augers, chests of carpenter's tools, wheat, barley, potatoes, and oats, oxen, bulls, cows
- Chief's salary of twenty-five dollars per year; and fifteen dollars per year for subordi-nate's salary; once every three years a suit of clothing for chief and subordinates, and for each chief a flag and medal.

Treaty Four: Government Obligations
- reserves of one square mile per family of five, selected, after a conference with Indians, by officers of the government
- present of twenty-five dollars for each chief, a coat, a Queen's silver medal; for each headman, a present of fifteen dollars, a coat; for each other man, woman, and child a present of twelve dollars, and some powder, shot, blankets, calicoes, and other articles
- annuities for each chief of twenty-five dollars, each headman a suit of clothing every three years
- powder, shot, ball, and twine to the value of $750
- for each chief a flag
- hoes, spades, scythes, and axes; and seed to plant wheat, barley, oats, and potatoes; ploughs, harrow, oxen, bulls, cows, chests of carpenter's tools, saws, augers, saws, files, grindstones once in for all to encourage agriculture

- schools on reserves
- no intoxicating liquor
- 'Indians shall have right to pursue their avocations of hunting, trapping and fishing throughout the tract surrendered, subject to such regulations as may from time to time be made by her Government ... saving and excepting such tracts as may be required or taken up from time to time for settlement, mining, or other purposes
- sections of reserves can be appropriated.

Revisions of Treaties One and Two: Government Obligations
- promises in memorandum attached to Treaty One to be implemented
- annual payments for each Indian raised from three to five dollars; for each chief twenty-five dollars per year, a suit of clothes every three years for each chief and headman.

Treaty Five: Government Obligations
- reserves of 160 acres per family of five; for reserve locations specified for the Berens River, Poplar River, Norway House (including Fisher River fragment), Cross Lake, Grand Rapids, Island bands
- schools on reserves
- no intoxicating liquor on reserves
- 'Indians, shall have right to pursue their avocations of hunting and fishing throughout the tract surrendered' subject to government regulations 'and excepting such tracts as may from time to time be required or taken up for settlement, mining, lumbering or other purposes' by the government or 'by any of the subjects thereof duly authorized ... by the said Government'
- sections of reserves can be appropriated
- accurate census of Indians
- five dollars per Indian
- $500 for the purchase of ammunition and twine
- hoes, spades, ploughs, harrows, scythes, axes, saws, files, grindstones, augers, chests of carpenter's tools; seed to plant wheat, barley, oats, and potatoes; oxen, bulls, cows, once in for all for the encouragement of agriculture
- for each chief twenty-five dollars per year; each subordinate officer fifteen dollars per year; for each chief and subordinate officer a suit of clothing every three years; for each chief a flag and medal.

Source: Alexander Morris, *The Treaties of Canada with the Indians* (Toronto: Coles 1971), 313-50

Appendix C
Some Land Scrip Intricacies

Appendix C recreates the paper trail for a scrip claim. A unique document recording one Metis claimant's experience with scrip buyers is reproduced as a conclusion to this appendix. To fully appreciate the documentation on land scrip, in an effort to come to terms with the legal and historical aspects of Halfbreed scrip, a careful reconstruction of the paper trail is necessary. This information is intended to supplement the findings in Chapter 6. By looking closely at the scrip process for one family, some of the intricacies may be clarified. The documentation supporting claims for scrip is also a rich source of social history. Between the claim for scrip and the achievement of fee simple ownership of 240 acres of land, a chain of written records was created for each Metis application.

The 'ideal' representation of the scrip process typical of the later scrip commissions is simplified in Figure C.1.[1] This model represents the government view of the formal procedures and outcomes. An order-in-council appointed a treaty and scrip commissioner (Phase 1). Other orders-in-council provided specifics as to who qualified for scrip and to the terms of participation in the land grant. A Metis claimant would complete a declaration, which was also witnessed by several individuals who were familiar with him or her (Phase 2). After this, the scrip commissioner would forward the application/declaration to the Land Patents Branch, Department of the Interior in Ottawa. In Phase 3, the information on the application would be checked to determine whether or not the claimant qualified for that particular scrip (date and place of birth were relevant criteria). If the claimant qualified, then his or her name was checked against previous scrip commissions. In the case of Treaty Five Adhesion scrip in northern Manitoba, some eighteen ledgers or indexes were examined. If the claimant had not previously obtained scrip (and in some cases if he had not been disqualified because both his parents received scrip from a previous commission), then the chief clerk would issue an order to the department accountant to have scrip certificates made out for the claimant. Scrip certificates were also referred to as notes, and in this study, the term 'coupons' is used. Orders-in-council authorized the issuing of scrip. (Usually a batch of scrip certificates would be authorized by a separate order-in-council.) Scrip certificates were printed on quality paper, resembled bonds, and had significant serial numbers.

In Phase 4, the scrip certificates were delivered to the Metis grantee. In previous scrip commissions, problems with the delivery of scrip to the grantee had occurred because scrip middlemen had arranged transfers of the scrip property from the grantee to themselves. In these situations, the scrip certificates were not delivered to the Metis grantee but to a representative. For the Treaty Five Adhesions, land scrip had to be delivered to the grantee despite Quit Claim Deeds or powers of attorney. Officials personally delivering the scrip certificates to Metis grantees were instructed: 'That orders, assignments, powers of attorney, agreements of sale or transfers of Half-breed scrip or rights thereto, are not under any circumstances, recognized by the Department.'[2] To ensure delivery, scrip certificates were sent from the Department of the Interior in Ottawa to local Dominion officials. Indian agents or members of the Royal North West Mounted Police were instructed to deliver the scrip certificates personally. The Metis grantee then signed a scrip receipt form acknowledging that he or she had received the scrip.

In Phase 5, the Metis grantee was supposed to use or apply the land scrip certificates, starting another leg of the paper trail, to obtain fee simple title to 240 acres of land. This was the means by which the coupon was converted into 'land.' Procedures and rules governed the conversion of the scrip certificates into a land patent. The scrip certificates could only be applied to lands ordinarily open to homestead entry. This meant that land lying outside the belt of land covered by Dominion Lands Survey or lands that had been set aside for railroad companies or other interests within the surveyed townships were of no use to the grantee. In a Dominion Lands office, the Metis grantee would present the scrip certificates to a Dominion Lands agent and select land parcels of 160 and 80 acres that were open for

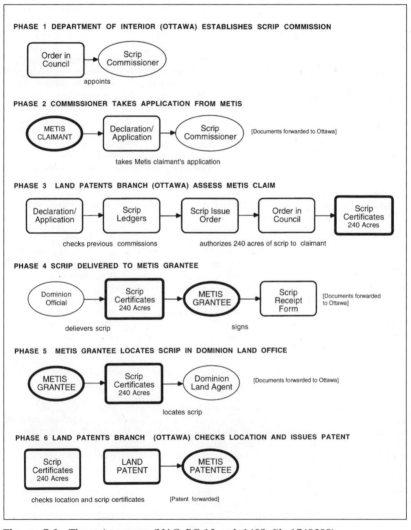

Figure C.1   The scrip process (NAC, RG 15, vol. 1403, file 1748598)

homesteading. The location was then 'entered' or located. The rule concerning the location and entry of scrip stated:

> Land scrip cannot be assigned. Entry for land upon which it is desired to apply the scrip can only be made by the half-breed to whom it has been issued, unless special authority has been endorsed thereon (commonly designated 'red back scrip'), in which case such endorsed land scrip may be located by the holder thereof in the name of the grantee of the scrip. No assignment of right to scrip is recognized, but after the half-breed land scrip has been applied to land, the rights to the land may be transferred. No transfer of such right, however, executed prior to the date of the location of the scrip on the land or executed by a person under twenty-one years of age may be recognized.[3]

The scrip coupons with the locations would be sent to the Land Patents Branch in Ottawa. This documentation would then be processed in the same manner as other applications for patents for Dominion Lands (Phase 6). If there were no complications concerning title, then the Metis grantee would receive a patent for the located land (fee simple title). The ownership would be registered in the local land titles office.

In reality, Metis grantees seldom received patents for land. For 138,320 acres of Treaty Ten and Treaty Five Adhesion land scrip, only one per cent were located and patented by Metis claimants.[4] Scrip middlemen and their agents, who obtained scrip certificates directly and then had the Metis grantee assign the locations to themselves or to others interested in 240 aces of prairie land, greatly modified this ideal model of scrip procedures.

On 10 July 1908, James Swanson, labourer and 'Halfbreed of the Norway House adhesion,' applied for scrip for himself and his family. This reconstruction, displayed by Figures C.2 through C.12, is based largely on Land Patents Branch file 17748598.[5] James Swanson was born at York Factory apparently in 1868; his father was Henry Swanson and his mother was Mary Jane Sinclair. In 1894, scrip was issued to his father's heirs after his father's death, but his mother had not received scrip. James Swanson was one of the Natives of the York Factory region who had vacated that area about fifteen years earlier. At York Factory, he married Maria Bowen in 1890. The application and subsequent notations by officials tell us more about the Swanson family. Their children born at York Factory included: William (born 19 January 1889), Mary Jane (1891), and Fanny (1893). James and Maria's children born at Norway House were Henry (1895), Eliza (1897), David (1899), Emily (1901), and Caroline (1903). According to James Swanson's declaration, one of his children, George, had died at York Factory. His oldest daughter, Mary Jane, was married to Joseph Thomas of Snake Island (Matheson Island) and applied for scrip separately.[6] James Swanson requested scrip for himself, his wife, and eldest son William, but he asked for cash scrip for Fanny, Henry, Eliza, David, Emily, and Caroline. Copies of baptismal records from the register of baptisms, York Factory, made by Reverend R. Faries, tell us that James Swanson was a cooper, but Faries spelled Maria Swanson's maiden name as 'Bone.' William was baptized on 19 February 1888 by G.S. Winter, Mary Jane was baptized in April 1890 by G.S. Winter, and Fanny was baptized on 26 March 1893 by J. Lofthouse. (William's birth date on the scrip application and baptismal record conflict.) In many respects, James Swanson was a typical Native of the fur trade society of this region; he was listed as a labourer, and he had left the York Factory region when the HBC cut back on its operations. He identified both his father and mother as 'Halfbreeds.'

His declaration was taken by John Semmens and was witnessed by William Isbister and James Bagg, and it had been read over to him in English (Figure C.2 portrays the start of their claim). Swanson's application/declaration reached the Department of the Interior in Ottawa on 9 September 1908 (Figure C.3). None of his family's names appeared on other scrip indexes. Chief Clerk Coté's initial assessment was scribbled on a note that indicated that the claim of James Swanson looked good, but that his wife would have to apply separately. The claims of the children born at York Factory (Willie, Mary Jane, and Fanny) also looked good, but the claims of the children born at Norway House (Eliza, David, Emily, and Caroline) after the family had moved from York Factory did not look good. These children, although born before the date of the Split Lake Adhesion, were born in ceded territory.[7] Coté also wanted baptismal certificates to determine the validity of the claim. James Swanson's scrip was approved with a scrip issue order of 12 July 1909, and

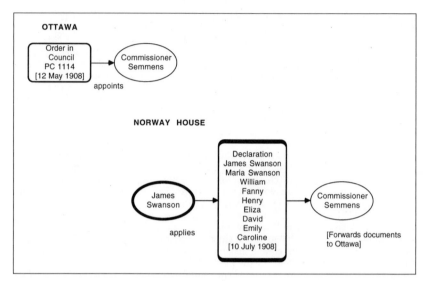

Figure C.2 Establishment of commission (Phase 1) and Swanson's family claim (Phase 2) (NAC, RG 15, vol. 1403, file 1748598)

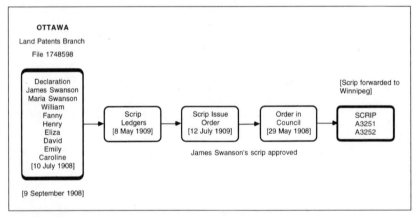

Figure C.3 Approval of James Swanson's claim (Phase 3) (NAC, RG 15, vol. 1403, file 1748598)

scrip certificates A3251 (160 acres) and A3252 (80 acres) were issued under the authority of an order in council dated 29 May 1909. A note in the file indicates that the claims of Willie, Mary Jane, and Fanny were reserved, and the claims of the other children (Henry, Eliza, David, Emily, and Caroline) were disallowed because they were born at Norway House, a territory already ceded. No doubt the geographical peculiarities of this ruling must have been perplexing. Some of the children received scrip, while because of their place of birth, others did not.[8] All were Metis.

In Phase 4 of the scrip process, James Swanson's scrip was delivered to him at Norway House by the Inspector of Indian Agencies John Semmens (Figure C.4). James Swanson

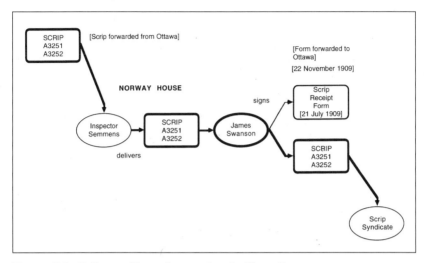

Figure C.4 Delivery of James Swanson's scrip (Phase 4)
(NAC, RG 15, vol. 1403, file 1748598)

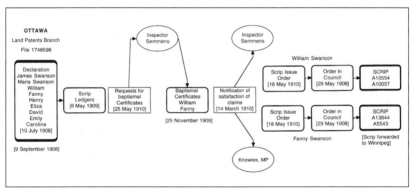

Figure C.5 Approval of William and Fanny Swanson's claim (Phase 3)
(NAC, RG 15, vol. 1403, file 1748598)

signed the scrip receipt form on 21 July 1909, and it reached the Department of the Interior in Ottawa on 22 November 1909.

The rest of the family's claims were stuck in Phase 3, but William and Fanny Swanson's claims were approved (Figure C.5). On 11 November 1909, Semmens forwarded copies of a number of baptismal records, including those of William, Fanny, and Mary Jane Swanson. In February 1910, W.E. Knowles, member of parliament from Moose Jaw, Saskatchewan, provided the Land Patents Branch with a memorandum inquiring about the delays of northern Manitoba scrip, including William and Fanny Swanson claims. On 14 March 1910, the secretary to the Department of the Interior informed Semmens that William and Fanny Swanson's scrip claims had been approved; a copy of this notification was sent to Knowles. On 18 May 1910, Coté issued a scrip order to the department accountant Charles H. Beddoe for 240 acres of land scrip for William Swanson and a separate order (on the same

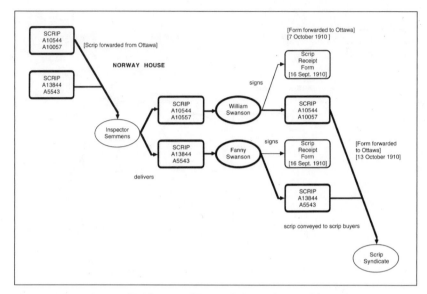

Figure C.6 Delivery of William and Fanny Swanson's scrip (Phase 4)
(NAC, RG 15, vol. 1403, file 1748598)

day) for $240 worth of money scrip for Fanny Swanson. William's land scrip certificates
were numbered A10554 (160 acres) and A10057 (80 acres) and were issued on 19 May 1910.
Fanny's money scrip certificates were numbered A13844 ($160) and A5543 ($80), and were
issued on the same day (Figure C.5). Their scrip was not delivered until the fall of 1910
(Figure C.6).

On 25 May 1910, the land and money scrip of William and Fanny Swanson was forwarded to Inspector Semmens in Winnipeg. With respect to Fanny Swanson, he was instructed to deliver the scrip personally to 'the grantee's father, as Miss Swanson is under
eighteen years of age.'[9] Semmens was not in Winnipeg to receive the scrip, and so it was
returned to Ottawa. Again (9 September 1910), the same scrip certificates with the same
instructions were sent out. The signature of William Swanson appeared on the scrip receipt
form for A10554 and A10057, but the delivery of the scrip was witnessed by P.D. Tyerman
of the well-known scrip syndicate. Fanny Swanson left her mark, an X, and James Swanson's
signature appeared on her receipt. Why a minor's mark would appear on a scrip receipt
form is unclear. The receipt of this money scrip was witnessed by Chester Thompson, a
major coupon collector. Although, with respect to Treaty Five Adhesion scrip, the Land
Patents Branch of the Department of the Interior took pains to make sure the scrip was
delivered to the Metis grantee, scrip middlemen were in place when the scrip was finally
delivered. Information on the delivery of scrip was readily available to the middlemen.
This is apparent because their signatures attest to the fact that they witnessed the personal
delivery of the scrip certificates. The actual scrip certificates or coupons then passed to the
scrip middlemen at the time of delivery. Fanny Swanson's money scrip complicated this
family's claim. Serious efforts were made by the law firm of Richards and Affleck and Member of Parliament Knowles to have her money scrip reissued as land scrip. (Land scrip was
more valuable than money scrip at this time.) After considerable documentation had been
created, the Land Patents Branch decided not to heed this demand from scrip middlemen.

In the case of James Swanson's wife, Maria, her claim took a little longer to assess (Figure
C.7). A note in the file from Coté indicated that she would need to make a separate declaration (19 February 1910). On the same day that Coté wrote that William and Fanny Swanson

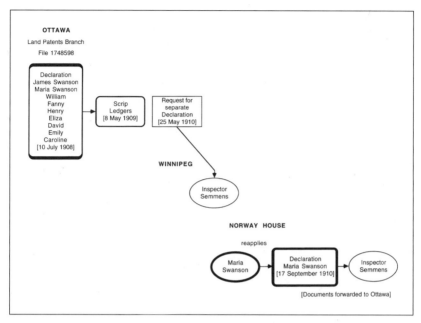

Figure C.7   Maria Swanson's claim (Phase 3 and Phase 2)
(NAC, RG 15, vol. 1403, file 1748598)

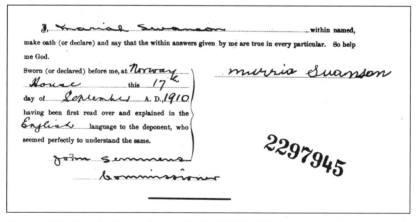

Figure C.8   Detail of Maria Swanson's scrip declaration
(NAC, RG 15, vol. 1403, file 1748598)

would receive scrip (25 May 1910), he instructed Semmens to have Maria 'Bone' (Bowen) 'appear before you with her witness and submit the usual evidence in support of her claim.'[10] As inspector of Indian Agencies, Semmens travelled to northern Manitoba, and in September of 1910 he took a declaration from Maria Swanson (Figure C.7). On the same trip, he delivered scrip certificates to Norway House. Her separate declaration provided additional

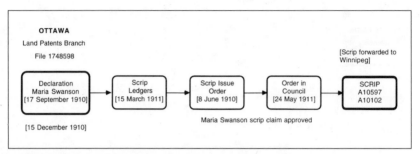

Figure C.9   Approval of Maria Swanson's claim (Phase 3)
(NAC, RG 15, vol. 1403, file 1748598)

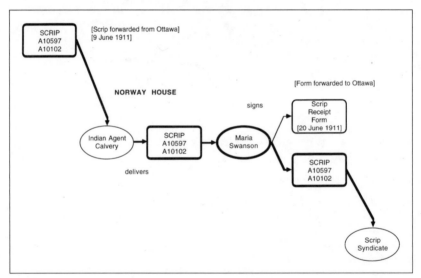

Figure C.10   Delivery of Maria Swanson's scrip (Phase 4)
(NAC, RG 15, vol. 1403, file 1748598)

genealogical information. She was born at York Factory in 1871, both her father (David Bowen) and her mother (Mary Redhead) were 'Halfbreeds.'[11] However, in her declaration, Maria Swanson stated that five of her children had died and that all except George had been unbaptized. She again applied for land scrip. She endorsed the application with her own signature, and her witnesses (Donald McLeod and David Bowen) signed with Xs. (see Figure C.8, but note she spelled her name 'Marria.') Her declaration was not dated when it arrived at the Land Patents Branch.[12] Her claim was checked against the previous scrip indexes, and on 8 June 1911, Coté issued a scrip order for 240 acres of land scrip for Maria Swanson (Figure C.9). The order in council of 24 May 1911 approved the issue of scrip. Her certificates, which were dated 9 June 1911, were numbered A10597 (160 acres) and A10102 (80 acres).

After waiting some thirty-five months, Maria Swanson eventually received her scrip (Figure C.10). She accepted delivery of land scrip certificates A10597 and A10102 in the Indian agent's office at Norway House, and her scrip receipt form was witnessed by W.A.G.

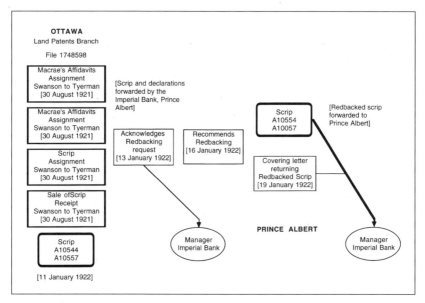

Figure C.11 Redbacking William Swanson's scrip
(NAC, RG 15, vol. 1403, file 1748598)

Crate. She signed the receipt form in a manner similar to her signature on her declaration (Marria Swanson).

The paper trail for scrip did not end with the delivery of the certificates to the Metis grantees. Documentation concerning the transactions and conveyances between Metis claimants and scrip middlemen, and Metis grantees and scrip middlemen, entered the record system of the Land Patents Branch with requests to 'redback' scrip. Figure C.11 demonstrates how scrip certificates were 'redbacked'; that is how those in possession of scrip certificates could begin to convert scrip certificates into land patents. As explained in Chapter 6, redbacking was a way of circumventing the Rule of Location with the approval of the Department of the Interior. On 5 January 1922, the Prince Albert manager of the Imperial Bank of Canada forwarded land scrip totalling 1,120 acres to the Land Patents Branch in Ottawa.[13] This batch of scrip included William and Maria Swanson's scrip. Thus, for ten or eleven years the scrip coupons of William and Maria Swanson had been in possession of the scrip syndicate (Thompson/Richards/Tyerman) and/or the Imperial Bank in Prince Albert.

The scrip claim process was so convoluted, so remote from the daily life of northern Manitoba Metis, that it is easy to see how scrip middlemen, lawyers like Richards and their political front men like MP Knowles and Senator Davis, could keep the paperwork moving. However, once the grantee had passed the coupons on to middlemen, the converting of scrip to land was an issue for the scrip middlemen or small buyers holding coupons. In this sense, the political front men were acting as advocates for the scrip syndicate and not for the Metis grantees. Two days after the scrip coupons and declarations were received, Coté acknowledged the receipt of the scrip and documents. On 16 January 1922, the assistant controller for the Land Patents Branch recommended to W.W. Cory, deputy minister of the interior that 'this evidence be accepted and that the notes in question be endorsed and made available by the holder thereof, in the name of the grantees of the scrip notes, as has been done in connection with other Halfbreed Land Scrip Notes.'[14] The evidence included affidavits and declarations that witnessed the transfer of the scrip notes from William and

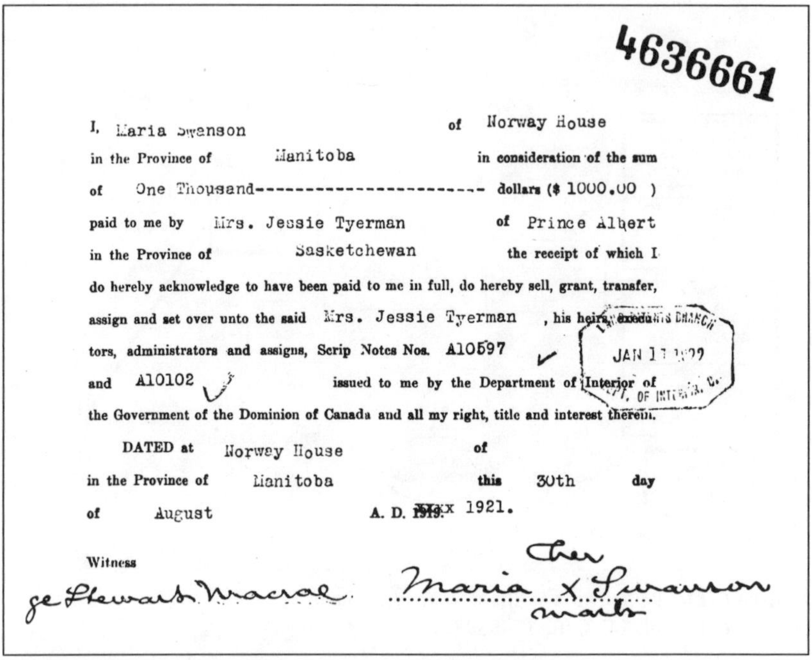

4636661

I, Maria Swanson of Norway House
in the Province of Manitoba in consideration of the sum
of One Thousand------------------------ dollars ($ 1000.00)
paid to me by Mrs. Jessie Tyerman of Prince Albert
in the Province of Saskatchewan the receipt of which I
do hereby acknowledge to have been paid to me in full, do hereby sell, grant, transfer,
assign and set over unto the said Mrs. Jessie Tyerman , his heirs, executors, administrators and assigns, Scrip Notes Nos. A10597
and A10102 issued to me by the Department of Interior of
the Government of the Dominion of Canada and all my right, title and interest therein.

JAN 1 1922

DATED at Norway House of
in the Province of Manitoba this 30th day
of August A. D. 1921.

Witness
ge Stewart Macrae
her
Maria X Swanson
mark

Figure C.12 Detail of Maria Swanson's receipt for the sale of scrip (NAC, RG 15, vol. 1403, file 1748598)

Maria Swanson to Mrs. Jessie Tyerman of Prince Albert. The evidence also purports that the scrip for 240 acres sold for $1,000. Both Maria and William were over twenty-one years of age, and so the scrip could be converted.

The format and content of the declarations and affidavits conveying both Maria and William's scrip to the syndicate were essentially identical. H. Halcrow served as commissioner for all the declarations and oaths, which was rather convenient since Halcrow was the northern front man for the Thompson/Richards/Tyerman syndicate. Halcrow had arranged the claimant's interest in scrip and had purchased scrip on behalf of the syndicate. The declarations were made in Norway House on 30 August 1921, and Mrs. Tyerman received the title of the grantees, William and Maria Swanson. George Steward Macrae of Norway House made all the declarations concerning the transfer of property, and he swore that he was personally acquainted with the Swansons. His affidavit noted that Maria had received the certificates, that the notes were duly sold and assigned to Jessie Tyerman for $1,000, that Maria Swanson was twenty-one years of age, and that 'Maria Swanson has stated to me that she is well satisfied with the said sale' and that 'I have discussed the matter aforesaid ... in the English language.'[15]

Figure C.12 is a reproduction of Maria Swanson's 'receipt' for the sale of her scrip interests to Jessie Tyerman. Apparently, she sold her scrip for $1,000. This receipt is signed with an X, and this is not how she signed her declaration (see Figure C.8) or her scrip receipt form. (On both of these forms she signed her name Marria Swanson.) Several explanations could be advanced to account for the difference between signatures in 1910 and 1921: (1) her signature was forged on two different occasions in 1910 and 1911 in front of government officials, (2) between 1911 and 1921 she forgot how to sign her name, (3) she was directed to sign with an X, or (4) she did not consent to sign or she was not available to sign the documents that purport to transfer her interests some ten years earlier. The redbacking evidence forwarded by law firms does not indicate the date on which the transaction between the grantee and middlemen took place. Dates concerning the transfer or sale of scrip were problematic because such evidence would indicate that the transfer of scrip occurred before the scrip had been located in a Dominion Lands office.

Information concerning the locating and assigning of the Swanson family scrip is compiled in Table C.1. Location registers have been used to present the details for Phase 5 and Phase 6. James Swanson's scrip was located shortly after the scrip had been received. James Swanson's location of land was assigned to Angus McMillan, and the scrip was located on land south of Saskatoon. The reverse side of the face of James Swanson's scrip certificates were signed by Bruno Lundgreen.[16] Apparently, this was done to identify James Swanson at the time the scrip was being located. The land scrip of William and Maria had been redbacked, but it was not located for several years, and their scrip coupons were not converted into land for some seventeen to nineteen years after being issued. The retention of scrip for this length of time suggests that the coupons were regarded as a form of speculative investment. None of this land was assigned to members of the syndicate. Patents were issued by the Land Patents Branch to the assignees some fifty to 146 days after the date of application.

Table C.1

Location and assignment of Swanson family land scrip

James Swanson
A3251
- Issued 15 July 1909
- Located 24 February 1910 on NW 1/4, Section 28, Township 26, Range 21, west of the third meridian
- 160 acres
- Assigned to Angus McMillan, Saskatoon, Saskatchewan
- Patent issued 17 August 1910

A3252
- Issued 15 July 1909
- Located 1 March 1910 on N 1/2 of NE 1/4, Section 10, Township 27, Range 16, west of the third meridian
- 80.5 acres
- Assigned to Angus McMillan, Saskatoon, Saskatchewan
- Patent issued 8 July 1910

William Swanson*
A10554
- Issued 19 May 1910
- Redbacked 19 January 1922
- Located 27 May 1929 on SW 1/4, Section 22, Township 5, Range 30, west of the second meridian
- 160 acres
- Assigned to Joseph Pierre Beauregard, rancher, Scout Lake, Saskatchewan
- Patent issued 16 July 1929

A10057
- Issued 19 May 1910
- Redbacked 19 January 1922
- Located 28 June 1928 on E 1/2 of SE 1/4, Section 3, Township 6, Range 27, west of the second meridian
- 80 acres
- Assigned to Gustave Bouffard, Willow Bunch, Saskatchewan
- Patent issued 21 November 1928

continued on next page

Table C.1 (continued)

Maria Swanson* A10597	• Issued 9 June 1911 • Redbacked 19 January 1922 • Located 14 August 1928 on SW 1/4, Section 7, Township 5, Range 25, west of the second meridian • 160 acres • Assigned to J.O.A. Bonneau, Willow Bunch, Saskatchewan • Patent issued 20 December 1928
A10102	• Issued 9 June 1911 • Redbacked 19 January 1922 • Located 28 June 1928 on W 1/2 of SE 1/4, Section 3, Township 6, Range 27, west of the second meridian • 80 acres • Assigned to Gustave Bouffard, Willow Bunch, Saskatchewan • Patent issued 21 November 1928

Source: NAC, RG 15, vols. 1541, 1549, and 1550, Location Registers of North West Half-Breed Land Scrip
* The location register indicates that assignment was conducted by their attorneys.

One of the problems in understanding the scrip process is the lack of records on the transactions or conveyances of the Metis grantee's scrip interest to the scrip middlemen. While the documents from the Department of the Interior indicate the process for claiming scrip, a statement by Alexander Oman records aspects of the conveyance of scrip from Metis grantee to scrip buyers. Alexander Oman's experience with the front men that obtained scrip was recorded and found its way to the Land Patents Branch. It can be found in file 1578625 pt. 2.[17] Because of the rare nature of this document, it has been reproduced verbatim:

Churchill Sept 12th 1911

[handed in by Supt. Starnes R.N.W.M.P.]

Alexander Oman of Churchill states as follows: – I am a half breed, a married man, my wifes' name is Alice and I have three children. My wife and myself were both entitled to a land scrip and my eldest child Effie Oman was entitled to a minors scrip. Mr Johnson of the Hudson Bay Company came up to Churchill from York with Mr Halcrow on the 1st day of Aug, The first time he saw me he asked me to sign a paper promising him to give him our scrip when we got it, for the Hudson Bay Co that the Company was buying all the scrip. He did not say how much he would give me, he said that he did not know what the scrip was worth, but he would give whatever the scrip was worth. I told him that I did not want to sign the paper because I did not know what was on it. Mr Alston the clerk of the Hudson Bay Company then read the paper to me, but I could not understand what was on it. He told me to sign then. I told him that I did not want to sign. He said why dont you want to sign it, has anybody told you dont sign it. I told him no, nobody has told me not to sign it. He said you are foolish not to sign, I came down to help you people, I will give you as good a price as anybody for your scrip, I did not sign it the first time. Mr Campbell another of the Company came out after me the same evening, told me the best thing I could do was to come up and sign that paper. I told him I did not want to sign it. He told that I was foolish that it was the only chance to sign my scrip, that there were no more buyers coming to buy the scrip. I went up and signed it, I did not know what was on the paper I signed. He gave me $100.00, He said that he did not know what the scrip was worth till the ship came.

When the 'Minto' came after this I got my scrips and two days after I got it, I was up to the Company's, Mr Johnson asked me if I brought up my scrip, I told him no. He told me to come in the office. There were some more papers there that he wanted me to sign. I told him that I was not going to sign any more papers. He asked me why what was my idea. He said that I had already signed one promising to sell him my scrip I told him that when he asked me to sign I did not have my scrip. He asked me about the $100.00, I told him that I would give it back to him. He told me to keep it till I made up my mind. I told him that I was not going to sell my scrip for less than $1000.00 each. He told me that it was not worth that, that it was only worth $450.00 and all the land was flooded and the crops were down or dropping, that I could not make any more if I went out. I told him that Bishop Lofthouse had written Mr Siveir the Missinary to tell us not to sell our scrip under $800.00. He said that it might have been that year, but they are worth only $450.00 this year, I could not give you any more.

The next evening I went up to the post again. He asked me again if I was going to [give?] him my scrip. I told him that I would not give them under $800.00, he repeated that it was not worth it, he then said 'you promised to sell your scrip and if you come to Winnipeg with it I will take it away from you,' I said will you, if you give me the money for it. I went the following evening and gave him my scrip for $1100.00 for the two land and one minor scrip.

Oman's account is interesting because it documents the approaches and tactics of the syndicate front men. Halcrow used the cover of the Hudson's Bay Company to legitimize the buying of scrip. Oman named Johnston, Campbell, and Alston as agents who pressured him to convey his scrip. The facilities of the HBC were used for these purposes. As an individual about to receive scrip, Oman signed a piece of paper that obliged him to sell scrip to the front men (Johnston and Halcrow). He could not read the papers, and even though Ashton Alston read the agreement to him, it did not make sense to him. If an agreement similar to the A.A. Mcdonald contract (Table 6.3) was signed by Alexander Oman, it would be surprising if anyone other than a lawyer could have understood this contract. Considerable pressure was put on Oman to commit to selling his scrip. The agents of the syndicate did not provide a price for the scrip but promised to give him what it was worth. The front men also attempted to determine whether or not Oman's reluctance to part with his scrip was due to advice from another party. The only source of information that Oman had concerning the value of the coupons came from the Church Missionary Society missionaries. The front men countered Oman's price by claiming that the crops had been flooded. Oman's reluctance was his only bargaining tactic, and this succeeded in improving the price slightly. He was informed that there would be no other scrip buyers, and this seems to have been decisive, and he then agreed to sign the papers. The front men's apparent connection with the HBC would only serve to reinforce the monopoly nature of the particular transaction in Oman's mind. The dispute between the grantee and the syndicate's front men in this transaction stemmed from the fact that Oman agreed, in advance of receiving scrip, to sell his coupons without having established a firm price. The front men threatened to take the scrip from him if he attempted to take the scrip to Winnipeg. In the end, he parted with his family's scrip for less than what he thought it was worth. Nothing in Oman's statement suggests that the transferring of scrip had anything to do with the continued use and occupancy of the land. Moreover, the idea that Oman and his family would make use of land scrip to obtain a patent to southern homestead lands is not even a remote possibility and never enters into his statement. This document, Alexander Oman's record of his experiences with scrip buyers, was preserved in a file in the Land Patents Branch, yet no related documents were found indicating any concern, response, or interest on the part of the civil servants that administered this aspect of Aboriginal title.

Notes

Acknowledgments
1 Russell George Rothney, 'Mercantile Capital and the Livelihood of Residents of the Hudson Bay Basin: A Marxist Interpretation' (M.A. thesis, University of Manitoba 1975).
2 Arthur J. Ray, *Indians in the Fur Trade: Their Role as Trappers, Hunters, and Middlemen in the Lands Southwest of Hudson Bay: 1660-1870* (Toronto: University of Toronto Press 1974).
3 See Frank Tough, 'Manitoba Commercial Fisheries: A Study in Development' (M.A. thesis, McGill University 1980); and Tough, 'Native People and the Regional Economy of Northern Manitoba: 1870-1930s' (Ph.D. diss., York University 1987). For inferences drawn from quantitative data, see Tough, '"To Make a Profit without Much Consideration for the Native": The Spatial Aspects of Hudson's Bay Company Profits in Northern Manitoba, 1891-1929,' Geography Discussion Paper, No. 44 (Toronto: Department of Geography, York University 1994); Tough, 'Regional Analysis of Indian Aggregate Income, Northern Manitoba, 1896-1935,' *Canadian Journal of Native Studies* 12, no. 1 (1992):95-146; and Tough, 'Indian Economic Behaviour, Exchange and Profits in Northern Manitoba during the Decline of Monopoly, 1870-1930,' *Journal of Historical Geography* 16, no. 4 (1990):385-401. Also deriving from the dissertation was a discussion of Indian policy, and a revised version has been published as 'Buying Out the Bay: Aboriginal Rights and the Economic Policies of the Department of Indian Affairs after 1870,' in *The First Ones: Readings in Indian/Native Studies*, ed. David R. Miller, Carl Beal, James Demsey, and R. Wesley Heber. (Piapot Reserve: Saskatchewan Indian Federated College Press 1992):399-408.

Introduction
1 W.L. Morton, ed. 'The Proceedings In The Convention, February 3 to February 5, 1870,' *Manitoba: The Birth of a Province* (Manitoba Historical Records Society 1984), 8.
2 Ibid.
3 Ibid., 19.
4 Ibid.
5 Ibid., 20.
6 Ibid., 22.
7 Ibid., 23.
8 Earl Granville, the key Colonial Office official to affect an agreement between Canada and the HBC, wrote on 10 April 1969: 'This question [aboriginal title] had not escaped my notice while framing the proposals which I laid before the Canadian Delegates and the Governor of the Hudson's Bay Company. I did not however then allude to it because I felt the difficulty of insisting on any definite conditions without the possibility of foreseeing the circumstances under which those conditions would be applied.' Canada, *Sessional Papers*, 1869, Report of Delegates Appointed to negotiate the acquisition of Rupert's Land and the North-West Territory, no. 25, p. 38. (Hereafter referred to as CSP, Rupertsland Report.)

9 FrankJ. Tough, 'Aboriginal Rights Versus the Deed of Surrender: The Legal Rights of Native Peoples and Canada's Acquisition of the Hudson's Bay Company Territory,' *Prairie Forum* 17, no. 2 (1992): 245.

10 Arthur J. Ray, *The Canadian Fur Trade in the Industrial Age* (Toronto: University of Toronto Press 1990).

11 The idea of a partnership is developed in Daniel Francis and Toby Morantz, *Partners in Furs: A History of the Fur Trade in Eastern James Bay 1600-1870* (Kingston: McGill-Queen's University Press 1983).

12 Arthur J. Ray, 'The Decline of Paternalism in the Hudson's Bay Company Fur Trade, 1870-1945,' in *Merchant Credit and Labour Strategies in Historical Perspective,* ed. Rosemary E. Ommer (Fredericton: Acadiensis Press 1990), 188-202.

13 This argument is made forcibly by Laura L. Peers, 'Changing Resource-Use Patterns of Saulteaux Trading at Fort Pelly, 1821 to 1870,' in *Aboriginal Resource Use in Canada: Historical and Legal Aspects,* ed. Kerry Abel and Jean Friesen (Winnipeg: University of Manitoba Press 1991), 107-18. Obviously, Indian reports of hardship have to be considered within the conventions of bargaining strategies. I maintain that unequal trade and not cultural relativism is a useful starting point.

14 *Order of Her Majesty in Council Admitting Rupert's Land and the North-Western Territory into the Union* (Court of Windsor, 23 June 1870), Address to Queen, 16 and 17 December 1867, Schedule A. Reproduced in E.H. Oliver, *The Canadian North-West,* vol. 2 (Ottawa: Government Printing Bureau 1915), 946. (Hereafter referred to as *Rupertsland Order.*)

15 Doug Sprague, Metis Land Rights Research Group meeting, Vancouver, May 1993.

16 *Rupertsland Order,* 944.

17 *Rupertsland Order,* Address to the Queen, 29 and 31 May 1969, Schedule B, p. 954.

18 CSP, Rupertsland Report, 38.

19 'Instructions Issued to Lieutenant-Governor Archibald, August 4, 1870,' in Oliver, *The Canadian North-West,* vol. 2, 974.

20 Harold Innis, *The Fur Trade in Canada* (Toronto: University of Toronto Press 1970). (Originally published in 1930.)

Chapter 1: Local Economies – Indian Bands and Company Posts

1 Provincial Archives of Manitoba, Hudson's Bay Company Archives, B.154/a/70 (12 December 1872). (Hereafter referred to as HBCA.)

2 United Church of Canada Archives, personal papers of Frederich George Stevens, 'Autobiography of the Rev. Frederich G. Stevens,' 47. (Hereafter referred to as UCCA, Stevens.)

3 HBCA, B.156/e/12 (1891), fol. 3.

4 Sylvia Van Kirk, *'Many Tender Ties': Women in Fur Trade Society, 1670-1870* (Winnipeg: Watson and Dwyer 1980).

5 Ibid., 53-73.

6 Katherine Pettipas, ed., *The Diary of The Reverend Henry Budd: 1870-1875* (Winnipeg: Manitoba Record Society Publications 1974), 13. (Hereafter referred to as *Budd Diary.*)

7 National Archives of Canada, Church Missionary Society, Microfilm Reel A-114 (6 June 1887). (Hereafter referred to as CMS, A-114.)

8 CMS, A-112 (26 January 1884).

9 HBCA, B.154/a/70 (6 April 1873, 2 April 1874).

10 HBCA, B.42/b/62 (31 July 1869).

11 HBCA, A.11/119a (1 December 1880).

12 Ibid.

13 Ibid.

14 *Budd Diary,* 69.

15 Ibid., 9.

16 Ibid., 76.

17 HBCA, B.154/a/66.

18 HBCA, B.154/a/66 (1868), fol. 144d.

Chapter 2: Reorganizing the Regional System

1 Provincial Archives of Manitoba, F.C. Leach Papers, MG1 A14, no. 10 (Willy Frog Ross, 'York Boats'). (Hereafter referred to as PAM, Leach Papers.)
2 CMS, A-99 (6 September 1890).
3 National Archives of Canada, public records of the Department of Indian Affairs, RG 10, vol. 4009, file 249,461, pt. 1A (24 October 1910). (Hereafter referred to as NAC, RG 10.)
4 UCCA, Stevens, 8.
5 Ibid.
6 Ibid., 10.
7 PAM, Leach Papers, MG1 A14, no. 11 (Ross, 'York Boats').
8 HBCA, B.49/e/12 (1886), ff. 37-8.
9 Canada, *Sessional Papers*, 1898, Annual Report for the Department of the Interior, Report of the Lieutenant-Governor of Keewatin, no. 13, p. 4. (Hereafter referred to as CSP, Keewatin.)
10 Harold A. Innis, *The Fur Trade In Canada* (Toronto: University of Toronto Press 1970), 353.
11 Ibid., 377-8, 341.
12 E.E. Rich, *Hudson's Bay Company, 1670-1870,* vol. 3 (Toronto: McClelland and Stewart 1960), 794.
13 See A.A. den Otter, 'Transportation and Transformation: The Hudson's Bay Company, 1857-1885,' *Great Plains Quarterly* 3, no. 3 (1983): 172-6.
14 HBCA, A.11/51 (1 August 1870), fol. 100.
15 Ibid., fol. 88.
16 Ibid., fol. 89.
17 Ibid., fol. 90. Apparently, the 1869 fur returns were diverted from York Factory to Red River. According to Smith: 'Valuable Fur Returns from the Northern districts, added very much to the power the insurgent halfbreeds last winter over the Company, by placing in their hands the contents of the Fur Store at Fort Garry, and though on our being permitted to resume business, the great bulk of these furs were restored, the amount of petty pillage was unquestionably considerable.'
18 Ibid., fol. 90d.
19 Ibid., fol. 91d.
20 Rich, *Hudson's Bay Company*, 794.
21 den Otter, 'Transportation and Transformation,' 177.
22 This investment was depreciated at 15 per cent per year and the value of the Company steamboating capital was $106,000 (1 June 1879). H. Bowsfield, ed., *The Letters of Charles John Brydges: 1879-1882* (Winnipeg: Hudson's Bay Company Society 1977), 112. (Hereafter referred to as Bowsfield, *Brydges*.)
23 A larger than anticipated profit was earned in 1879 and 1880 as the HBC's steamers had begun to freight for the Department of Indian Affairs and the public. See Bowsfield, *Brydges*, 113.
24 With the steamers the Company still faced the problem of unbalanced cargoes; the *Northcote* carried 600 tons to the Northwest, but only 80 tons of furs returned in 1880. See Bowsfield, *Brydges*, 113.
25 Canada, *Sessional Papers*, 1877, Annual Report for the Department of Indian Affairs, no. 11, p. lii. To move a hundred pounds between Fort Garry and The Pas cost between $5.75 and $6.00 by steamer and $7.00 by York boat.
26 Provincial Archives of Manitoba, John C. Schultz Papers, MG12 B1, reel 2, no. 981, Ruttan to Morris, 6 April 1875. Ruttan estimated that steamboating supplies from Winnipeg would affect 130 to 140 Indians and that tripping to the portage would provide employment for 40 to 50 Natives. R. Ross reported that the summer tripping to York Factory would end. HBCA, B.154/e/11 (1874), fol. 3.
27 HBCA, B.154/e/14 (1875), fol. 3.
28 Ibid., fol. 3d.
29 HBCA, B.154/b/11 (28 December 1885), B.154/e/18 (1888).
30 See den Otter, 'Transportation and Transformation,' 178-80; and Bowsfield, *Brydges*, 112-18.

31 Since they had become unemployed, some of these Indians refused to pay Treaty debts. HBCA, A.74/1 (1891), fol. 185.
32 HBCA, B.154/k/1 (1870-83), fol. 3.
33 HBCA, D.38/1, Rule 90. Smith also outlined the need to add the term 'general services' to the trades contracts. HBCA, A.11/51, fol. 101d.
34 HBCA, B.154/e/11 (1874), fol. 3.
35 HBCA, B.154/e/22 (1890), fol. 4. Wrigley also suggested that lengthy temporary work be paid for with rations instead of with trade.
36 HBCA, B.154/b/11 (30 March 1886).
37 HBCA, B.156/e/12 (1891), fol. 2.
38 HBCA, D.30/6 (1885).
39 HBCA, D.25/19 (1893), fol. 80.
40 Innis, *Fur Trade in Canada*, 354.
41 HBCA, A.11/119a (18 August 1882).
42 Innis, *Fur Trade in Canada*, 356.
43 HBCA, B.154/a/87 (18 July 1919).
44 HBCA, B.156/e/12 (1891), fol. 4.

Chapter 3: The Decline of Kihchiwaskahikanihk (York Factory)
1 HBCA, B.239/a/182 (15 July 1876).
2 For an analysis of York Factory's changes in the first ten years following the Rupertsland transfer, see A.J. Ray, 'York Factory: The Crises of Transition, 1870-1880,' *The Beaver*, outfit 313, no. 2 (Autumn 1982): 29.
3 CMS, A-111 (11 September 1882).
4 Ray, 'York Factory,' 29.
5 See HBCA, A.11/119a (1 December 1880) for details.
6 HBCA, B.239/e/8 (1873), fol. 5.
7 Ibid. Fourteen servants were given notice to retire the next year.
8 HBCA, A.11/119a (1 December 1880).
9 *Proceedings of the Church Missionary Society*, 1869, p. 239; and CMS, A-100 (1 and 11 October 1871).
10 HBCA, A.11/119a (1 December 1880).
11 HBCA, B.239/a/182 (11 June 1875).
12 HBCA, A.11/119a (1 December 1880). Fortescue stated that he gave the boat work to Oxford House men. Thus the profit from the freight brigade was lost and the maintenance of the men was passed on to the post. For the outfit of 1873 he wrote: 'the Indians have shown such a spirit of insubordination this summer, as to warn me that the less I have to do with Indian labor the better.' HBCA, B.239/e/8 (1873), fol. 50.
13 *Proceedings of the Church Missionary Society*, 1869, p. 239.
14 HBCA, A.11/119a (1 December 1880). An epidemic occurred in 1837.
15 Ray, 'York Factory,' 31.
16 CMS, A-100 (24 August 1874), A-101 (21 September 1875).
17 CMS, A-116 (13 December 1889).
18 HBCA, A.11/119a (1 December 1880).
19 HBCA, B.42/e/10 (1885), fol. 1.
20 HBCA, B.239/e/9 (1887), ff. 5-6.
21 Ibid.
22 HBCA, D.25/6 (1889), fol. 309.
23 Provincial Archives of Manitoba, Lieutenant-Governor J. Schultz Papers, MG12 E1, no. 4860, *Bégin Report*. (Hereafter referred to as PAM, Schultz Papers.) In the annual report of 1890 Schultz stated: 'I have also to report a continued decrease of fur bearing animals near the southern shores of Hudson's Bay, with more suffering among the Swampy Crees of the district.' CSP, 1891, Keewatin, no. 17, p. 4.
24 HBCA, B.239/e/16 (1890), fol. 3.
25 HBCA, A.11/119a (26 September 1884).

26 HBCA, B.239/e/9 (1887), fol. 5.
27 Ibid., ff. 5-6.
28 CMS, A-104 (27 April 1880).
29 CMS, A-111 (6 March 1883).
30 HBCA, A.11/119a (2 August 1885).
31 HBCA, B.239/b/135 (12 December 1887), B.239/e/9 (1887) fol. 6.
32 HBCA, B. 239/e/11 (1888), fol. 2.
33 CMS, A-116 (5 August 1889).
34 HBCA, B.239/e/15 (1890), fol. 6.
35 CMS, A-117 (4 June 1891).
36 CMS, A-112 (9 March 1884).
37 HBCA, A.11/119a (7 March 1885). This policy was, in fact, implemented. Reverend Lofthouse noted: 'many who used to live here have been sent off to the bush.' CMS, A-114 (27 September 1886).
38 CMS, A-116 (13 December 1889). Again in 1890 Winter's journal noted: 'Many of them do not intend to come down to the fort, as it would simply be a season of starvation. There is no work for them here, and the country is too poor for them all to exist.' Depopulation of the post continued: 'The first departure took place today. A large number of persons left York Factory never to return. I was sorry to see them sail away: but it is much better than starving here.' CMS, A-116 (20, 25 June 1890).
39 CMS, A-115 (14 December 1888). In 1890 Winter noted a contrast with the preceding summer populations of York: 'I visited the tents of the people from inland; only three, whereas in former years there used to [be] quite a little colony.' CMS, A-116 (3 July 1890).
40 CMS, A-118 (15 April 1892).
41 CMS, A-115 (10 March 1888).
42 CMS, A-116 (19 February 1890).
43 CMS, A-118 (7 March 1893). In 1892 Winter noted that Indians 150 miles inland were well off, but those closer to York suffered scarcity. CMS, A-118 (25 March 1893).
44 CMS, A-114 (1 July 1887).
45 CMS, A-115 (2 April 1888).
46 HBCA, B.154/e/23 (1889), fol. 4.
47 CMS, A-116 (10 March 1891).
48 CMS, A-111 (14 April 1883).
49 CMS, A-117 (28 January 1890).
50 CMS, A-116 (20 February 1890).
51 CMS, A-117 (2 April 1891).
52 CMS, A-115 (29 August 1888).
53 HBCA, B.239/e/9 (1887).
54 Bégin also reported that he had heard about a man with his family while coming to the Post to procure some food from the Company finding it difficult to get anything on his hunting ground, and after eating the Deer skins which he intended selling to the Company, found a dead dog on the trail and eat [sic] it, reached the Post after great suffering and misery. PAM, Schultz Papers, MG12 E1, no. 4863, *Bégin Report*.
55 HBCA, B.239/e/13 (1889), fol. 2.
56 CMS, A-116 (30 April 1890).
57 CMS, A-117 (10 May 1891).
58 CMS, A-114 (27 February 1887).
59 HBCA, B.239/e/9 (1887), fol. 6.
60 CMS, A-116 (6, 20 June 1889).
61 CMS, A-116 (26 August 1890).
62 CMS, A-118 (7 March 1883).
63 CMS, A-116 (10 March 1891).
64 CMS, A-104 (15 February 1890).
65 CMS, A-113 (3 December 1885).

66 HBCA, A.74/2 (1892), fol. 26.
67 HBCA, A.11/119a (1 December 1880).
68 CSP, 1898, Keewatin, no. 13, p. 12.
69 CMS, A-118, (7 August 1893).
70 An argument has been made which dismisses the relevance of accounting records from Native history. See Eleanor M. Blain, 'Dependency: Charles Bishop and the Northern Ojibwa,' in *Aboriginal Resource Use in Canada: Historical and Legal Aspects,* ed. Kerry Abel and Jean Friesen (Winnipeg: University of Manitoba Press 1991), 93-105.

Chapter 4: Geographical and Economic Aspects of Indian Treaties
1 Brian Slattery, 'Understanding Aboriginal Rights,' *Canadian Bar Review* 66 (1987): 727-83.
2 For an overall view of Aboriginal and treaty rights, see Peter J. Usher, Frank J. Tough, and Robert M. Galois, 'Reclaiming the Land: Aboriginal Title, Treaty Rights and Land Claims in Canada,' *Applied Geography* 12 (1992): 109-32.
3 Alexander Morris, *The Treaties of Canada with the Indians* (Toronto: Coles 1971). (Originally published in 1880.) Treaty One, 313-14; Treaty Two, 316-20; Treaty Three, 320-9; Treaty Four, 330-8; Treaty Five, 342-50. (Hereafter referred to as Morris, *Treaties.*)
4 Arthur J. Ray, *The Canadian Fur Trade in the Industrial Age* (Toronto: University of Toronto Press 1990), 3-4.
5 Canada, *Sessional Papers,* 1873, Annual Report of the Department of Indian Affairs, no. 17, p. 5. (Hereafter all annual reports from Indian Affairs published in the *Sessional Papers* will be referred to as CSP, Indian Affairs.)
6 CSP, 1872, Indian Affairs, no. 22, p. 17.
7 Instructions issued to the Honourable William McDougall as Lieutenant-Governor of the North-West Territories, 28 September 1869, as printed in E.H. Oliver, *The Canadian North-West,* vol. 2 (Ottawa: Government Printing Bureau 1914), 879.
8 Instructions issued to Lieutenant-Governor Archibald, 4 August 1879, Oliver, *The Canadian North-West,* vol. 2, 974.
9 Provincial Archives of Manitoba, George Adams Archibald Papers, microfilm, reel 1, no. 153, Dawson Memorandum (19 December 1870). (Hereafter referred to as PAM, Archibald Papers.)
10 CSP, 1872, Indian Affairs, no. 22, p. 6.
11 Morris, *Treaties,* 322.
12 Ibid., 323.
13 Ibid.
14 CSP, 1872, Indian Affairs, no. 22, p. 11.
15 Ibid.
16 Ibid., 6.
17 Morris, *Treaties,* 46.
18 Provincial Archives of Manitoba, Lieutenant-Governor Alexander Morris Papers, MG12 B1, microfilm, reel 5, no. 53, Fort Garry (22 August 1873). (Hereafter referred to as PAM, Morris Papers.)
19 PAM, Morris Papers, MG12 B2, reel 7, no. 108, Morris to the Minister of the Interior (16 April 1874).
20 CSP, 1876, Indian Affairs, no. 9, p. xxxiii.
21 Morris, *Treaties,* 143.
22 PAM, Morris Papers, MG12 B2, reel 5, no. 258, Morris to the Minister of the Interior (31 May 1875).
23 CSP, 1876, Indian Affairs, no. 9, p. xxxiv.
24 PAM, Morris Papers, MG12 B1, reel 2, no. 1003, D. Laird to Morris (7 July 1875).
25 PAM, Morris Papers, MG12 B1, reel 2, no. 668, Reverend E.R. Young to Morris (18 March 1874).
26 CSP, 1872, Indian Affairs, no. 22, p. 12.
27 *The Manitoban* (29 July 1871).

28   CSP, 1872, Indian Affairs, no. 22, p. 13.
29   Ibid., 4.
30   Ibid., 14.
31   Ibid., 16.
32   Ibid., 16-17
33   Ibid., 17.
34   Ibid., 16.
35   Ibid., 31.
36   Ibid., 15.
37   Morris, *Treaties*, 63.
38   Ibid.
39   Ibid., 74.
40   CSP, 1876, Indian Affairs, no. 9, p. xxxii.
41   CSP, 1877, Indian Affairs, no. 11, p. xlii.
42   Duke Redbird, *We Are Metis: A Metis View of the Development of a Native Canadian People* (Willowdale: Ontario Metis and Non Status Indian Association 1980), 39.
43   CMS, A-99 (24 November 1871).
44   PAM, Archibald Papers, reel 1, no. 15, Schultz to Archibald (6 September 1870); and reel 1, no. 22, Notes of an interview with Henry Prince (13 September 1870).
45   PAM, Archibald Papers, reel 1, no. 114, Archibald to J.W. Wright (27 November 1870).
46   PAM, Archibald Papers, reel 1, no. 164, Notice from Fairford Indians, n.d.
47   Richard C. Daniel, 'A History of Native Claims Process in Canada: 1867-1979,' Prepared by Tyler, Wright and Daniel Limited, Research Consultants, for Research Branch, Department of Indian and Northern Affairs, mimeograph, 1980, p. 3.
48   *The Manitoban* (1 July 1871). This notice was signed by Yellow Quill and others and was addressed to John Garriuch. The notice also stated: 'Why we speak to day [*sic*], is because we are poor but we still hold the land for our children that will be born afterwards.'
49   CSP, 1872, Indian Affairs, no. 22, p. 10.
50   Great Britain, *Report from the Select Committee on the Hudson's Bay Company, 1857*, 445. A letter from Peguis, chief of the Saulteaux Tribe at Red River Settlement, to the Aborigines Protection Society, London.
51   Ibid., 445-6.
52   E.E. Rich, *The History of The Hudson's Bay Company, 1670-1870* (London: Hudson's Bay Record Society 1959), 814.
53   CSP, 1872, Indian Affairs, no. 22, p. 27.
54   Morris, *Treaties*, 57.
55   Ibid., 59, 62. Emphasis in original.
56   Ibid., 62.
57   Ibid., 101, 104.
58   Ibid., 106.
59   Tribal concepts about Aboriginal title are also apparent in the records. The Cree had occupied the Red River Valley but were replaced by the Ojibwa when the Cree migrated further west. The Ojibwa had entered the Red River area some seventy to eighty years prior to Treaty One. The reaction to Treaty One by the Saskatchewan Cree was recorded by Archibald: 'The Cree consider the Red River Country theirs, and could not understand what right the Indians here, had except such of them as were Crees, had to treat with for it.' PAM, Archibald Papers, reel 3, dispatch book nos. 3 and 2, Interview with Kas-ish-eway (5 January 1872).
60   Arthur J. Ray, *Indians in the Fur Trade* (Toronto: University of Toronto Press 1974), 228.
61   CSP, 1872, Indian Affairs, no. 22, p. 33.
62   Ibid., 34.
63   Ibid.
64   Ibid., 28.
65   Morris, *Treaties*, 65.
66   CSP, 1872, Indian Affairs, no. 22, p. 31.

67 Morris, *Treaties*, 118.
68 Ibid.
69 On paternalism, see Arthur J. Ray, 'The Decline of Paternalism in the Hudson's Bay Company Fur Trade, 1870-1945,' in *Merchant Credit and Labour Strategies in Historical Perspective*, ed. Rosemary Ommer (Fredericton: Acadiensis Press 1990), 188-202; and Frank Tough, 'Buying Out the Bay: Aboriginal Rights and the Economic Policies of the Department of Interior after 1870,' in *The First Ones: Readings in Indian/Native Studies*, ed. David R. Miller, Carl Beal, James Dempsey, and R. Wesley Heber (Paipot Reserve: Saskatchewan Indian Federated College Press 1992), 399-408.
70 CSP, 1872, Indian Affairs, no. 22, p. 28.
71 Ibid., 14.
73 CSP, 1875, Indian Affairs, no. 8, p. 18.
74 Morris, *Treaties*, 67.
75 Ibid., 95.
76 CSP, 1877, Indian Affairs, no. 11, p. xlviii.
77 See D.J. Hall, '"A Serene Atmosphere?" Treaty 1 Revisited,' *Canadian Journal of Native Studies* 4, no. 2 (1984): 321-58, for copies of the coverage of the treaty talks by *The Manitoban* as well as an analysis. Although the correspondent for this weekly was ethnocentric at times, and treated some issues in a jocular manner, the observations are from a different perspective than government records. Moreover, *The Manitoban* had called for a permanent treaty and considered it to be a serious issue.
78 *The Manitoban* (5 August 1871).
79 Ibid.
80 Ibid. *The Manitoban* reported that Archibald had said on 28 July: 'His Excellency explained that reserves did not mean hunting grounds, but merely portions of land set aside to form a farm for each family. A large portion of the country would remain as much a hunting ground as ever after the Treaty closed.'
81 *The Manitoban* (12 August 1871).
82 Ibid.
83 Ibid.
84 Ibid.
85 Ibid.
86 Ibid.
87 Ibid.
88 Ibid.
89 Ibid.
90 Ibid.
91 Ibid.
92 Ibid.
93 *The Manitoban* (5 August 1871).
94 CSP, 1872, Indian Affairs, no. 22, p. 28.
95 'The Manitoba Indian Treaty,' *Canadian Illustrated News* (9 September 1871): 162.
96 CSP, 1875, Indian Affairs, no. 8, p. 53.
97 Ibid., 61.
98 NAC, RG 10, vol. 3604, file 2553, petition, St Peters (15 October 1873).
99 The revisions of Treaties One and Two are found in Morris, *Treaties*, 338-42. The memorandum of 3 August 1871 can be found in Simpson's report of 3 November 1871 and is printed in CSP, 1872, Indian Affairs, no. 22, p. 28. Morris also discusses Outside Promises (see Morris, *Treaties*, 126-7). Morris met with the Indian commissioners in March 1874. [See NAC, RG 10, vol. 3608, file 3117 (13 March 1874)]. A report to the Privy Council on 30 April 1875 is printed in Canada, *Indian Treaties and Surrender*, vol. 1 (Toronto: Coles 1971), 286 (originally published in 1891).
100 See also Jean Friesen, 'Magnificent Gifts: The Treaties of Canada with the Indians of the Northwest, 1869-76,' *Transactions of the Royal Society of Canada*, ser. 5, vol. 1 (1986): 41-51;

and Jean Friesen, 'Grant Me Wherewith to Make My Living,' in *Aboriginal Resource Use in Canada: Historical and Legal Aspects,* ed. Kerry Abel and Jean Friesen (Winnipeg: University of Manitoba Press 1991), 141-55.

Chapter 5: Treaty Adhesions in Northern Manitoba

1 CSP, 1909, Indian Affairs, no. 27, p. xlvi.
2 Ibid., l.
3 Ibid., xlvi.
4 CSP, 1877, Indian Affairs, no. 11, p. li. In 1878, Island Lake Indians had anticipated a treaty. The daily journal recorded: 'Lots of Indians arrived here last night having a council about starting for Oxford House to hear about the great Money Master'; and 'Two canoes started for Oxford on Sunday about the great Treaty they expect to be made with them.' HBCA, B.93/a/8 (24, 27 August 1878).
5 CMS, A-102 (14 September 1876).
6 PAM, Schultz Papers, MG12 E1, no. 6565, Settee to Schultz (20 September 1894).
7 NAC, RG 10, vol. 3713, file 20626 (ca. 1884).
8 NAC, RG 10, vol. 3658, file 9388 (3 December 1877).
9 PAM, Schultz Papers, MG12 E1, no. 6566 (20 September 1884).
10 CSP, 1884, Indian Affairs, no. 4, p. 97.
11 For examples, see CSP, 1893, Keewatin, no. 13, p. 4; CSP, 1894, Keewatin, no. 13, p. 4; PAM, Schultz Papers, MG12 E1, no. 6565; and CSP, 1898, Keewatin, no. 13, p. 14.
12 CSP, 1880, Indian Affairs, no. 4, p. 75.
13 NAC, RG 10, vol. 3774, file 36924 (17 January 1887).
14 PAM, Schultz Papers, MG12 E1, no. 5926 (14 July 1892).
15 NAC, RG 10, vol. 3722, file 24161 (26 September 1902).
16 Ibid.
17 Ibid.
18 NAC, RG 10, vol. 4009, file 249462, pt. 1 (17 October 1907).
19 NAC, RG 10, vol. 3722, file 24161 (12 November 1880).
20 NAC, RG 10, vol. 3722, file 24161 (26 October 1885).
21 The issue of the treaty boundaries with respect to Split Lake was raised in 1903 concerning commercial fishing operations. NAC, RG 10, vol. 4009, file 249462, pt. 1 (7 September 1903, 5 October 1905).
22 NAC, RG 10, vol. 4009, file 249462, pt. 1 (14 February 1908).
23 NAC, RG 10, vol. 4009, file 249462, pt. 1 (17 October 1907).
24 NAC, RG 10, vol. 4009, file 249462, pt. 1 (14 February 1908, 11 April 1907).
25 NAC, RG 10, vol. 4009, file 249462, pt. 1 (14 May 1908).
26 For example, a copy of the adhesion used in 1910 is found in NAC, RG 10, vol. 4009, file 249462, pt. 1A.
27 Ibid.
28 Semmens was forwarded a copy of Morris's *Treaties of Canada* to use as a version of Treaty Five! Semmens's instructions are found in NAC, RG 10, vol. 4009, file 249462, pt. 1 (29 May 1908).
29 NAC, RG 10, vol. 4009, file 249462, pt. 1 (29 May 1908).
30 NAC, RG 10, vol. 4009, file 249462, pt. 1 (27 April 1907).
31 Ibid.
32 Laird added: 'The letter is mainly useful in showing that the Indians will have to be carefully and wisely dealt with in order to ensure the success of the negotiations.' NAC, RG 10, vol. 4009, file 249462, pt. 1 (30 October 1907).
33 NAC, RG 10, vol. 4009, file 249462, pt. 1 (17 October 1907).
34 A.V. Thomas, 'Bringing into Treaty the Indians of the Far Northern Wilds of Canada,' *Toronto Star Weekly* (26 November 1910): 13.
35 Ibid.
36 NAC, RG 10, vol. 4009, file 249462, pt. 1 (21 October 1909).
37 NAC, RG 10, vol. 4009, file 249462, pt. 1 (9 December 1908).

38 NAC, RG 10, vol. 4009, file 249462, pt. 1A (Report on 1910 treaty party, n.d.).
39 Ibid.
40 NAC, RG 10, vol. 4009, file 249462, pt. 1 (30 August 1908).
41 NAC, RG 10, vol. 4009, file 249462, pt. 1 (4 September 1909).
42 Thomas, 'Bringing into Treaty,' 13. Semmens was a little prone to paternalism, he declared: 'It is equally pleasant to be able to bear testimony of the faithful determination of the Indian Department to keep faith with the Indians, to fulfill all promises made, to meet the wants of the sick and helpless poor, to correct all possible wrong, and save the wards of the government from both themselves and their enemies.' CSP, 1912, Indian Affairs, no. 27, p. 119.
43 NAC, RG 10, vol. 4009, file 249462, pt. 1A (Report on 1910 treaty party, n.d.).
44 NAC, RG 10, vol. 4009, file 249462, pt. 1 (4 September 1909).
45 Thomas, 'Bringing into Treaty,' 13.
46 Semmens's commission involved three tasks: take adhesions of Non-Treaty Indians, negotiate adhesions with bands, and take scrip applications. This was performed during several months of summer travel by a man who was sixty years old in 1910. With respect to this incorrect adhesion, the main file of Treaty Five adhesions does not include a copy of the Split Lake adhesion, but it is unlikely that the department actually corrected the mistake by having it resigned. While the senior department official's criticism was harsh, the department did not write to him until 12 May 1909 – long after the adhesion had been approved by Privy Council Order 2662 (5 December 1908). See NAC, RG 10, vol. 4009, file 249462, pt. 1 (12, 17 May 1909).
47 In fact, Semmens's diary sometimes suggests that the treaty was signed before the election; but then, who signed the treaty? For details of the procedures see Semmens's reports and diaries of the adhesions. For example, Island Lake: negotiations open at 10:00 AM, treaty signed at 1:00 PM, and elected Chief at 1:30 PM. See NAC, RG 10, vol. 4009, file 249462, pt. 1 (Report on 1909 treaty party, n.d.). Clearly, the talks did not begin with the election of a Chief to represent the band. On some occasions the choice of a chief was difficult. Thomas recorded: 'The Commissioner announced at length that the treaty party would take dinner, and that he expected them to make their choice by the time dinner was over. This they did, for I think they were anxious to receive the free meal from the King.' Thomas, 'Bringing into Treaty,' 13.
48 It is hard to understand what Semmens was attempting to achieve with the smaller annuity for the very group that had accepted him as a missionary in the mid-1870s. Another one of Semmens's errors was failing to change the wording in the adhesion from three to five dollars with respect to the gratuity. The next year Nelson House Indians were given the difference in gratuity since Scott noted 'friction and misunderstanding might arise.' NAC, RG 10, vol. 4009, file 249462, pt. 1 (20 October 1909).
49 Leonard Mason, *The Swampy Cree: A Study in Acculturation* (Ottawa: National Museums of Canada 1967), 43.
50 NAC, RG 10, vol. 4009, file 249462, pt. 1 (21 October 1909).
51 Ibid.
52 NAC, RG 10, vol. 4009, file 249462, pt. 1A (22 May 1914).
53 NAC, RG 10, vol. 4009, file 249462, pt. 1A (5 July 1916).
54 NAC, RG 10, vol. 4009, file 249462, pt. 1 (4 September 1909).
55 United Church of Canada Archives, John Semmens, 'Under the Northern Lights: Notes on Personal History,' 79. (Hereafter referred to as UCAA, Semmens.)
56 This editorial was probably written by A.V. Thomas for the *Manitoba Free Press* (26 October 1910).

Chapter 6: Metis Aboriginal Title

1 The Manitoba Act, 1870, 33 Victoria, chap. 3. See E.H. Oliver, *The Canadian North-West*, vol. 2 (Ottawa: Government Printing Bureau 1914), 970.
2 N.O. Coté, 'Grants to the Half-Breeds of the Province of Manitoba and the Northwest Territories, Comprising the Provinces of Saskatchewan and Alberta in Extinguishment of Indian Title 1870-1925.' Ottawa: Department of the Interior, 1929, mimeographed, p. 7.

This copy was found in the National Archives of Canada, public records of the Department of the Interior, RG 15, vol. 227. (Hereafter referred to as the *Coté Report*.)

3 The means and procedures for dispossessing the Metis are complex. See D.N. Sprague, 'The Manitoba Land Question, 1870-1882,' *Journal of Canadian Studies* 15, no. 3 (1980): 74-84; and D.N. Sprague 'Government Lawlessness in The Administration of Manitoba Land Claims, 1870-1887,' *Manitoba Law Journal* 10, no. 4 (1980): 415-41. Recent literature includes: Gerhard Ens, 'Dispossession or Adaptation? Migration and Persistence of the Red River Metis, 1835-1890,' *Canadian Historical Association Papers,* 1988, 120-44; Thomas Flanagan, 'The Market for Metis Lands in Manitoba: An Exploratory Study,' *Prairie Forum* 16, no. 1 (1991): 1-20; and D.N. Sprague, 'Dispossession vs. Accommodation in Plaintiff vs. Defendant Accounts of Metis Dispersal from Manitoba, 1870-1881,' *Prairie Forum* 16 no. 2 (1991): 137-55. For an explanation of the paper trail for individual Metis applicants, see Frank Tough and Leah Dorion, '"The Claims of the Half-Breeds ... Have Been Finally Closed": A Study of Treaty Ten and Treaty Five Adhesion Scrip,' unpublished research report, Royal Commission on Aboriginal Peoples, October 1993.

4 Sprague, 'Manitoba Land,' 77.

5 Speculators would suggest to the Metis that, because the land would not be granted, the scrip was worthless; but they would offer twenty-five dollars for the claim. Sprague noted that when the money scrip reached the Dominion Lands Office in 1876 it was picked up by assignees and attorneys. Sprague, 'Manitoba Land,' 79.

6 Ibid., 78.

7 Ibid., 83. Sprague argued that the use of powers of attorney to obtain scrip meant that 'the goal of dispossessing was more important than scrupulously safeguarding the rights of illiterates.' Sprague, 'Manitoba Land,' 79.

8 However, this does not suggest that Metis are not 'constitutional Indians,' or that they do not come under Section 91 (24) of the Constitution Act, 1982, or that the Metis are not covered by the resource rights of the Natural Resources Transfer Agreement. Moreover, after 1930, provincial resource policies in northern Manitoba recognized the Aboriginal distinctiveness of the Metis.

9 'To satisfy any claims existing in connection with the extinguishment of the Indian title, preferred by half-breeds resident in the North-West Territories outside the limits of Manitoba, on the fifteenth day of July, one thousand eight hundred and seventy, by granting land to such persons, to such extent and on such terms and conditions as may be deemed expedient.' Dominion Lands Act, 1879, 42 Victoria, chap. 31, sec. 125 (e).

10 Scrip commissions were the main means for dealing with Metis title: however, Dominion Lands agents were allowed to take applications and Orders in Council approved scrip applications. Ken Hatt, 'The Northwest Scrip Commissions as Federal Policy – Some Initial Findings,' *Canadian Journal of Native Studies* 3, no. 1 (1983): 119.

11 John Leonard Taylor, 'An Historical Introduction to Metis Claims in Canada,' *Canadian Journal of Native Studies* 3, no.1 (1983): 165.

12 In 1885, $240 scrip went for $165, and $160 scrip went for $110. D.J. Hall, 'The Half-Breed Claims Commission,' *Alberta History* 25, no. 2 (1977): 5.

13 Provencher was faced with expanding treaty lists in the early 1870s and indicated that all Halfbreeds who wanted to participate in the land grant would be removed from treaty lists. CSP, 1875, Indian Affairs, no. 8, p. 54.

14 CSP, 1872, Indian Affairs, no. 22, p. 30.

15 Taylor, 'Metis Claims,' 163. The scrip claim then raised the problem of past annuities and repayment.

16 CMS, A-118 (7 February 1893).

17 National Archives of Canada, public records of the Department of the Interior, RG 15, vol. 554, file 166507, R. Goulet and N.O. Coté, 'Report of the Northwest Half-breed Claims Commission,' 1888. (Hereafter referred to as NAC, RG 15.)

18 McColl wrote to the deputy superintendent that Indian Agent Reader (The Pas) had told Indians in 1885 and 1886 that they would get scrip. McColl explained the situation with respect to children to Grand Rapids Metis. NAC, RG 10, vol. 3856, file 80513 (5 April 1892).

A. Flett, former chief at Cumberland House, requested re-entry to treaty and left because children were promised scrip. NAC, RG 10, vol. 3775, file 37267-1 (27 January 1887).

19 For examples, see NAC, RG 10, vol. 3856, file 80513 (5 April 1892), and vol. 3747, file 29701 (6 June 1886).

20 The problems centred on payment: Metis who received commutation could not get scrip (1886). In 1886, Treaty payments were deducted from scrip, but 1888 Metis were not required to return commutation payments. See NAC, RG 15, vol. 554, file 166507 (27 October 1891); see also Taylor, 'Metis Claims.' The Department of Indian Affairs seems to have had a flexible policy on residence since most of those who had withdrawn were still living on the Sandy Bay reserve in 1895. See NAC, RG 10, vol. 3828, file 60717 (18 September 1895).

21 NAC, RG 15, vol. 554, file 166507, Goulet and Coté, report, 1888.

22 NAC, RG 10, vol. 3828, file 60717 (13 March 1895).

23 McColl was willing to readmit the sick to treaty on the recommendation of the Indian agent. See NAC, RG 10, vol. 3856, file 80513 (5 April 1892).

24 NAC, RG 10, vol. 3775, file 37267-1 (2 May 1887).

25 Applications for scrip were taken at Brochet in 1907 (Treaty Ten). See NAC, RG 15, vol. 991, file 1247280.

26 *Coté Report*, 27-8.

27 NAC, public records of the Privy Council, RG 2, vol. 973, PC 1060 (29 May 1909); and RG 2, vol. 1015, PC 1193 (24 May 1911). (Hereafter referred to as RG 2.) The Order in Council of 29 May 1909 also permitted scrip to be issued to claimants who did not come under the scope of the Treaty Five adhesion scrip, provided, however, that their claims were in accordance with the terms of the relevant commission.

28 NAC, RG 15, vol. 1016, file 1578625, pt. 1.

29 NAC, RG 10, vol. 4009, file 249462, pt. 1 (28 February 1908). Lowes would later write that information concerning the pending surrender of Aboriginal title had been leaked by an assistant commissioner. UCCA, Alexander Sutherland Papers, Indian Missions 1905-10, box 7, H1 29 2, Lowes to Sutherland (31 March 1909).

30 NAC, RG 10, vol. 4009, file 249462, pt. 1 (7 May 1980). McLean also passed on Lowes's letter of 28 February 1908.

31 NAC, RG 10, vol. 4009, file 249462, pt. 1 (30 August 1908).

32 NAC, RG 15, vol. 1016, file 1578625, pt. 1 (16 January 1909).

33 NAC, RG 10, vol. 4009, file 249462, pt. 1 (10 October 1908). Some years later Semmens would recall that scrip buyers followed him on the 1908 trip. UCCA, Semmens, 75. In 1909, Lowes wrote: 'Through the HBC stores they (scrip buyers) have already made advances to some on their scrip.' Lowes felt that the scrip buyers in 1908 and 1909 were fronting for the same interests. UCCA, Sutherland Papers, Lowes to Sutherland (29 March 1909).

34 NAC, RG 10, vol. 4009, file 249462, pt. 1 (10 October 1908). No Halfbreeds were identified at either Island Lake or Gods Lake.

35 NAC, RG 10, vol. 4009, file 249462, pt. 1A (24 October 1910).

36 Ibid.

37 Ibid.

38 Ingrams added: 'Much ill-feeling has been engendered, by this action, against the Company, whom the Natives have always been taught to respect and honour because of its strict integrity in its dealing with them.' HBCA, A.12/FT MISC/273, ff. 41, 43.

39 For the details of Hall and the Treaty Ten scrip, see Tough and Dorion, 'A Study of Treaty Ten and Treaty Five Adhesion Script,' 41-6.

40 W.P. Fillmore, 'Half-breed Scrip,' *Manitoba Bar News* (1968): 126.

41 Ibid., 127.

42 HBCA, A.12/FT MISC/273, ff. 41, 43.

43 PAM, RG 17, box 89, B1, file 17.2.1 (22 September 1947).

44 HBCA, A.12/FT MISC/273, fol. 47. A number of names are associated with scrip buying. In 1908, Reverend Lowes mentioned a D. Flett, a Mixedblood from Norway House; a Mr

Anderson, clerk; and C.C. Sinclair, assistant paymaster at Norway House (and acting chief factor, Norway House District); a Mr Laing, clerk; (all with the HBC); and an A.A. McDonald. R.H. Hall and H.S. Johnson both worked for the HBC. Similarly, Ashton Alston worked for the HBC, his wife and children received scrip; but he also pressured Oman into selling. Tremayne's role is unclear since he appears to have alerted the London office of the HBC about Hall, although he also accompanied C.C. Sinclair and H. Halcrow. Dr Tyerman (Prince Albert), C. Thompson, and Halcrow were tied in with the Richards and Affleck law firm, although Richards's correspondence is on the letterhead of S.E. Richards, W.A.J. Sweatman, A.L. Kemp, and W.P. Fillmore. Richards was the son of Mr Justice Richards. Fillmore had been involved in scrip buying in the early 1900s. Kemp was involved in scrip buying in northwestern Saskatchewan and acted as Thompson's secretary during the 1908 adhesion in Keewatin. A Mr Rosseau purchased scrip claims at York Factory for Thompson in 1909. Nanton wrote several letters on behalf of Hall in his capacity as a member of the HBC's Canadian Committee, but used stationary from the law firm of Osler, Hammond, and Nanton. Osler had been involved in purchasing scrip during the earlier scrip commissions. However, as late as 1940, representatives from Osler, Hammond, and Nanton attempted to locate scrip. PAM, RG 17, box 89, B1, file 17.2.1. Clearly, the Treaty Five adhesion scrip buying represented an interlocking of lawyers, financiers, and HBC personnel. Hall was said to have a one-ninth share in the syndicate.

45 PAM, RG 17, box 89, B1, file 17.2.1 (3 May 1946).
46 An analysis of location registers for the Treaty Ten and Treaty Five adhesion scrip indicates that less than 1 per cent of 138,320 acres recorded the Metis grantee as patentee of the land. NAC, RG 15, vols. 1547-50; see also Tough and Dorion, 'A Study of Treaty Ten and Treaty Five Adhesion Scrip,' 57-8.
47 Typescript copy of a section of bulletin no. 21 (2 January 1930), Department of the Interior, copy found in PAM, RG 17, box 89, B1, file 17.2.1 (19 November 1931).
48 Fillmore, 'Half-Breed Scrip,' 128.
49 Ibid.
50 NAC, RG 15, vol. 1016, file 1578625, pts. 1, 2.
51 PAM, RG 17, box 89, B1, file 17.2.1, statutory declaration by S.E. Richards, forwarded 3 May 1946.
52 PAM, RG 17, B1, box 89, file 17.2.1 (17 June 1946). Cowan was willing to accept Richards's claim because he was in possession of the scrip and because of an affidavit bolstering the Quit Claim Deed.
53 PAM, RG 17, B1, box 89, file 17.2.1.B (8 October 1928).
54 PAM, RG 17, B1, box 89, file 17.2.1. The chain of title executing the transfer of Jessie Campbell's interests in scrip coupons is rather interesting. Records indicate that a letter of guardianship appointed William Campbell legal guardian over his children. William Campbell agreed to sell Jessie Campbell's scrip to Chester Thompson; Chester Thompson's interest in Jessie Campbell's scrip transferred to Richards through Thompson's will after various assignments between John Spurr, Maud Spur, Mary Margaret Beachell, and Richards. There is no indication that Jessie McIvor (née Campbell) signed over power of attorney after she reached the age of majority. Jessie Campbell was interested in her scrip and soon after reaching the age of majority wrote to the Department of the Interior in Ottawa to inquire about it. The Manitoba government redeemed a total of 560 acres of scrip for $3,360 from Richards. Richards owed a considerable amount of back taxes to the Manitoba government, and he was able to use Metis scrip to pay his tax bill.
55 The affidavit of execution indicates that the contract would have been read over, interpreted, and explained to the Halfbreed before signing. However, for such a one-sided agreement to be upheld by the courts in today's legal climate, it would probably be necessary to prove that the Halfbreeds had received independent legal advice on the agreement. I wish to acknowledge the assistance rendered by the legal analysis of Lesley C. Tough.
56 NAC, RG 15, vol. 1043, file 1748625 (6 July 1921, 7 June 1924).
57 NAC, RG 15, vol. 1080, file 2253692 (7 March 1939). Both of these claimants had been born after the date of the Split Lake adhesion.

58 NAC, RG 15, vol. 1080, file 2253678 (24 February 1919).

59 Ibid.

60 NAC, RG 15, vol. 1016, file 1578625, pt. 2 (12 September 1911).

61 Fillmore, 'Half-breed Script,' 127.

62 NAC, RG 15, vol. 1043, file 1748598 (10 November 1910).

63 HBCA, A.12/FT MISC/273, fol. 36.

64 Ibid., fol. 48.

65 Ibid.

66 Ibid., fol. 25.

67 Most of the scrip issued from 1906 to 1912 was located on Alberta and Saskatchewan land. During this period, 1,573,737.18 acres of school lands sold for $22,631,365.25, thus indicating a gross sale price of $14.38 per acre. In Saskatchewan, 2,466,302.6 acres sold for $42,576,677.71, indicating an average price of $17.27 per acre. NAC, public records of royal commissions, RG 33-51, vol. 3, exhibit 4-D.

68 The best reconstruction of land scrip issued in northern Manitoba indicates that 126 claims amounting to 30,240 acres were issued. By 1935, some 3,800 acres had not been redeemed. Thus, some 26,440 acres is an estimate of the scrip located and entering the market. Based on the Alberta school lands prices ($14.38 per acre) this scrip had a market value of $380,207.20. With the highest, if somewhat doubtful, price of scrip ($4.17 per acre), all the scrip (30,240 acres) would have been purchased for no more than $126,100.80. A conservative estimate of the surplus gained by scrip middlemen or other purchasers of scrip would be $254,106.40. If Alexander Oman's scrip price more accurately indicates the purchase price of scrip from Metis grantees ($1.53 per acre), then the surplus to landowners and middlemen is in the order of $333,940.00.

69 NAC, RG 10, vol. 4009, file 249462, pt. 1A (24 October 1910).

71 NAC, RG 15, vol. 1016, file 1578625, pt. 2 (11 May 1914).

72 UCCA, Alexander Sutherland Papers, box 7, H129, Pedley to Sutherland (2 June 1909).

Chapter 7: Native Settlement Patterns and Indian Agriculture

1 Report by Charles Stringfellow on Norway House, Rossville, *41st Annual Report of the Missionary Society of the Wesleyan Methodist Church in Canada*, 1865-6.

2 Great Britain, *Report from the Select Committee on the Hudson's Bay Company, 1857*, 445.

3 HBCA, B.51/e/1 (1820), fol. 14.

4 CSP, 1889, Indian Affairs, no. 16, p. 47.

5 Report by Edward Eves on Norway House, *67th Annual Report of the Missionary Society of the Wesleyan Methodist Church in Canada*, 1890-1, xxxix.

6 Katherine Pettipas, ed., *The Diary of the Reverend Henry Budd: 1870-1875* (Winnipeg: Manitoba Record Society Publications 1974), xxxvii.

7 Report by Egerton R. Young on Berens River, *51st Annual Report of the Missionary Society of the Wesleyan Methodist Church in Canada*, 1874-5, xxix.

8 PAM, Schultz Papers, MG12 E1, no. 6461A, Semmens to Schultz, (24 April 1894).

9 UCCA, Stevens, 12.

10 CSP, 1877, Indian Affairs, no. 11, p. xlvi.

11 Ibid., li.

12 Ibid., xlii. Almost all members of this band perished as a result of smallpox in 1876.

13 See CSP, 1884, Indian Affairs, no. 4, p. 137; and NAC, RG 10, vol. 3677, file 11528 (13 July 1881).

14 PAM, Morris Papers, MG12 B1, reel 8, no. 175 (25 February 1876).

15 NAC, RG 10, vol. 4019, file 279393-6 (18 December 1910).

16 CSP, 1880, Indian Affairs, no. 4, p. 60.

17 Provincial Archives of Manitoba, Reverend John Semmens Papers, MG7 F1, p. 40. (Hereafter referred to as PAM, Semmens Papers.)

18 CSP, 1875, Indian Affairs, no. 8, p. 58.

19 NAC, RG 10, vol. 4009, file 249462, pt. 1A (7 February 1911).

20 NAC, RG 10, vol. 4065, file 412786-1 (22 May 1914).

21 NAC, RG 10, vol. 3638, file 7305 (17 November 1876). Emphasis in original.
22 NAC, RG 10, vol. 3685, file 13033 (21 May 1884; 9 March 1885).
23 NAC, RG 10, vol. 3945, file 121968-58 (21 January 1895).
24 CSP, 1912, Indian Affairs, no. 27, p. 120.
25 NAC, RG 10, vol. 3693, file 14421 (29 June 1879).
26 The Duck Bay/Pine Creek settlement changes were complicated by the desires of the Catholic clergy. See NAC, RG 10, vol. 3649, file 8293, and vol. 3727, file 25276; CSP, 1881, Indian Affairs, no. 6, p. 109; CSP, 1883, Indian Affairs, no. 5, pp. 40, 148; CSP, 1887, Indian Affairs, no. 6, pp. 59, 167; and CSP, 1888, Indian Affairs, no. 15, pp. 60, 63.
27 CSP, 1880, Indian Affairs, no. 4, p. 65.
28 CSP, 1908, Indian Affairs, no. 27, p. 89.
29 CSP, 1878, Indian Affairs, no. 10, p. 42.
30 CSP, 1879, Indian Affairs, no. 7, p. 51.
31 CSP, 1881, Indian Affairs, no. 14, p. 59.
32 CSP, 1886, Indian Affairs, no. 4, p. 48.
33 Ibid., 49.
34 CSP, 1884, Indian Affairs, no. 4, p. 138.
35 CSP, 1900, Indian Affairs, no. 14, p. 104.
36 CSP, 1880, Indian Affairs, no. 4, p. 66.
37 *Proceedings of the Church Missionary Society,* 1879-1880, 146.
38 CSP, 1903, Indian Affairs, no. 27, p. 84.
39 CSP, 1888, Indian Affairs, no. 16, p. 51.
40 CSP, 1902, Indian Affairs, no. 27, p. 99.
41 CSP, 1901, Indian Affairs, no. 27, p. 81.
42 For example, CSP, 1903, Indian Affairs, no. 27, pp. 91, 100.
43 CSP, 1887, Indian Affairs, no. 6, p. 76.
44 CMS, A-118 (7 February 1893).
45 NAC, RG 10, vol. 3581, file 808 (30 January 1895).
46 CSP, 1903, Indian Affairs, no. 27, p. 78.
47 CSP, 1893, Indian Affairs, no. 14, p. 55.
48 CMS, A-99 (24 November 1871).
49 CMS, A-100 (13 August 1872).
50 CSP, 1875, Indian Affairs, no. 8, p. 57.
51 CSP, 1872, Indian Affairs, no. 22, p. 31.
52 CSP, 1876, Indian Affairs, no. 9, p. 32.
53 CSP, 1892, Indian Affairs, no. 14, p. 178.
54 CSP, 1879, Indian Affairs, no. 7, p. 54.
55 CSP, 1880, Indian Affairs, no. 4, p. 68.
56 CSP, 1882, Indian Affairs, no. 6, p. 108.
57 CSP, 1893, Indian Affairs, no. 14, p. 56.
58 CSP, 1887, Indian Affairs, no. 6, p. 155.
59 CSP, 1881, Indian Affairs, no. 8, p. 1.
60 PAM, Schultz Papers, MG12 E1, no. 5924, Eves to Schultz (14 July 1892).
61 CSP, 1901, Indian Affairs, no. 27, p. 73.
62 CSP, 1904, Indian Affairs, no. 27, pp. 84, 117.
63 CSP, 1888, Indian Affairs, no. 15, p. 53.
64 CSP, 1894, Indian Affairs, no. 14, p. 46.
66 HBCA, B.324/e/1 (1890), fol. 2.
67 NAC, RG 10, vol. 3581, file 808 (30 January 1895).
68 For a study of reserve agriculture and Department of Indian Affairs policy, see Sarah Carter, *Lost Harvests: Prairie Indian Reserve Farmers and Government Policy* (Montreal: McGill-Queen's University Press 1990).
69 CSP, 1884, Indian Affairs, no. 4, p. 141.
70 Ibid., 138.
71 CSP, 1889, Indian Affairs, no. 16, p. 48.

72 CSP, 1894, Indian Affairs, no. 14, p. 49.
73 CSP, 1888, Indian Affairs, no. 15, p. 62.
74 CSP, 1901, Indian Affairs, no. 27, p. 79.
75 Similarly, at Berens River, Swinford was told by one Indian 'that it did not pay him to stay home and bother with a garden, as he could make so much so much more money in other ways, and he could buy his potatoes in the fall.' A member of the Hollow Water Band explained that 'he and the family were always away during the growing season and he could buy potatoes cheaper than he could raise them.' CSP, 1905, Indian Affairs, no. 27, pp. 114, 115, 118.
76 CSP, 1889, Indian Affairs, no. 16, pp. 78-80.
77 UCCA, Stevens, 3, 34.
78 CSP, 1901, Indian Affairs, no. 27, p. 111.
79 CSP, 1903, Indian Affairs, no. 27, p. 97; and CSP, 1905, Indian Affairs, no. 27, p. 109.
80 CSP, 1905, Indian Affairs, no. 27, p. 109.
81 CSP, 1893, Indian Affairs, no, 14, p. 145.
82 CSP, 1905, Indian Affairs, no. 27, pp. 94-5.
83 Data up to 1935 show that agriculture was the dominant form of income for Manitowapah bands from 1910 to 1935. See Frank Tough, 'Regional Analysis of Indian Aggregate Income, Northern Manitoba: 1896-1935,' *Canadian Journal of Native Studies* 12 no. 1 (1992): 95-146.
84 CSP, 1887, Indian Affairs, no. 6, p. 164.
85 CSP, 1904, Indian Affairs, no. 27, p. 99.
86 CSP, 1916, Indian Affairs, no. 27, p. 50; and CSP, 1917, Indian Affairs, no. 27, p. 48.
87 CSP, 1916, Indian Affairs, no. 27, p. 50.
88 See CSP, 1909, Indian Affairs, no. 27, pp. 79-81; and CSP, 1910, Indian Affairs, no. 27, pp. 84, 114. Department of Indian Affairs records claimed that Indians relocated at Peguis had built houses, cleared land, and were pleased with the change from St Peters. NAC, RG 10, vol. 4019, file 279393-6 (5 March 1913). For an Indian viewpoint on this surrender, see Chief Albert Edward Thompson, *Chief Peguis and His Descendants* (Winnipeg: Peguis 1973), 38-52. A good outline of this surrender and the extensive documentation see Richard C. Daniels, 'A History of Native Claims Process in Canada: 1867-1979,' prepared by Tyler, Wright, and Daniel Limited, Research Consultants, for Research Branch, Department of Indian and Northern Affairs, mimeograph, 1980, pp. 104-211.
89 See NAC, RG 10, vol. 8047, file 501/32-4-3-4, pt. 1.
90 CSP, 1915, Indian Affairs, no. 27, p. 47.
91 *The Manitoban* (5 August 1871).
92 CSP, 1913, Indian Affairs, no. 27, p. 114.
93 PAM, Schultz Papers, MG12 E3, box 19 (August 1890).

Chapter 8: Resource Conflicts over Common-Property Fisheries
1 This chapter has benefited from my master's thesis: 'Manitoba Commercial Fisheries: A Study in Development' (McGill University, Montreal, 1980). Consequently, some of the interesting aspects of the political economy of this industry's development (the structure of the industry, foreign ownership) have not been repeated. However, additional archival research has refined the analysis of this period. In particular, the papers of Lieutenant-Governor John C. Schultz, Provincial Archives of Manitoba, MG12 E1, E2, E3, and the public records of the Department of Indian Affairs, RG 10, National Archives of Canada, have reinforced my original findings. See F. Tough, 'The Establishment of a Commercial Fishing Industry and the Demise of Native Fisheries in Northern Manitoba,' *Canadian Journal of Native Studies* 4, no. 2 (1984): 303-19.
2 Important literature on Native freshwater fisheries include: Tim E. Holzkamm, Victor P. Lytwyn, and Leo G. Waisberg, 'Rainy River Sturgeon: An Ojibway Resource in the Fur-Trade Economy,' *Canadian Geographer* 32, no. 3 (1988): 194-205; Victor P. Lytwyn, 'Ojibwa and Ottawa Fisheries around Manitoulin Island: Historical and Geographical Perspectives on Aboriginal and Treaty Rights,' *Native Studies Review* 6, no. 1 (1990): 1-30; John V. West,

'Ojibwa Fisheries, Commercial Fisheries Development and Fisheries Administration, 1873-1915: An Examination of Conflicting Interests and the Collapse of the Sturgeon Fisheries of the Lake of the Woods,' *Native Studies Review* 6, no. 1 (1990): 31-65; and Lise C. Hansen, 'Treaty Fishing Rights and the Development of Fisheries Legislation in Ontario: A Primer,' *Native Studies Review* 7, no. 1 (1991): 1-21.

3 W.B. Scott and E.J. Crossman, *Freshwater Fishes of Canada* (Ottawa: Fisheries Research Board of Canada 1973), 83; and HBCA, B.51/e/1 (1820), fol. 6.

4 Jack Steinbring, 'The Sturgeon Skin "Jar,"' *Manitoba Archaeological Newsletter* 11, no. 3 (1965): 4-5.

5 John Franklin, *Narrative of a Journey to the Shores of the Polar Sea, in the Years 1819-20-21 and 22* (Edmonton: Hurtig 1969), 711 (originally published in 1823).

6 Canada, *Sessional Papers*, 1886, 'To an Address of the House of Commons, dated 29th March; For a copy of Report of the Minister of Marine and Fisheries to the Privy Council under date 15th of December, 1869,' no. 77b, pp. 3-4. Interestingly, this 1869 statement was an argument against making concessions to the Americans on fisheries issues.

7 Canada, *Sessional Papers*, 1873, Annual Report for the Department of Marine and Fisheries, no. 8, p. 194. (Hereafter referred to as CSP, Fisheries.)

8 Ibid.

9 CSP, 1879, Indian Affairs, no. 7, p. x.

10 CSP, 1883, Indian Affairs, no. 5, p. 48.

11 CSP, 1876, Fisheries, no. 8, p. 225; CSP, 1873, Fisheries, no. 8, p. 194.

12 CSP, 1877, Fisheries, no. 5, pp. 350-1; CSP, 1878, Fisheries, no. 1, p. 311.

13 CSP, 1882, Indian Affairs, no. 6, p. 88.

14 CSP, 1887, Fisheries, no. 16, p. 312.

15 CSP, 1885, Fisheries, no. 9, p. 298; CSP, 1889, Fisheries, no. 8, p. 221.

16 CSP, 1886, Fisheries, no. 11, pp. 331-2.

17 PAM, Schultz Papers, MG12 E3, box 19, F.L. Hunt to Schultz, (20 December 1889).

18 CSP, 1888, Fisheries, no. 6, p. 307.

19 PAM, Schultz Papers, MG13, E3, box 19, J. Stewart to Schultz, (1 October 1888).

20 CSP, 1884, Indian Affairs, no. 4, p. 144.

21 CSP, 1885, Indian Affairs, no. 3, p. 129.

22 CSP, 1887, Indian Affairs, no. 6, p. 59.

23 CSP, 1887, Indian Affairs, no. 6, p. 79.

24 CSP, 1887, Fisheries, no. 16, p. 318.

25 CSP, 1886, Indian Affairs, no. 4, p. 50.

26 CSP, 1885, Indian Affairs, no. 3, p. 54.

27 CSP, 1891, Fisheries, no. 8, p. 58 (Samuel Wilmot, 'Special Report on the Preservation of Whitefish Fisheries of Lake Winnipeg').

28 Ibid.

29 CSP, 1889, Indian Affairs, no. 16, p. liii.

30 CSP, 1890, Indian Affairs, no. 12, p. 310.

31 CSP, 1891, Indian Affairs, no. 18, p. 33.

32 CSP, 1890, Indian Affairs, no. 12, pp. 177-8.

33 CSP, 1889, Indian Affairs, no. 16, p. 51.

34 PAM, Schultz Papers, MG12 E3, box 19, Butler to Schultz (8 September 1889).

35 CSP, 1890, Indian Affairs, no. 12, p. 177.

36 PAM, Schultz Papers, MG12 E3, box 19, Phair to Schultz (n.d., 1888).

37 PAM, Schultz Papers, MG12 E3, box 19 (2 October 1888, 6 August 1889).

38 PAM, Schultz Papers, MG12 E3, box 19 (6 September 1889).

39 PAM, Schultz Papers, MG12 E3, box 19, (8 December 1889).

40 PAM, Schultz Papers, MG12 E3, box 19, La Touche Tupper to Schultz (10 October 1889).

41 PAM, Schultz Papers, MG12 E3, box 19, Phair to Schultz (1888).

42 Ibid.

43 PAM, Schultz Papers, MG12 E3, box 19, Butler to Schultz (26 December 1889).

44 Ibid.
45 PAM, Schultz Papers, MG12 E3, box 19, petition, Norway House (28 January 1890).
46 PAM, Schultz Papers, MG12 E3, box 19, notes of an Indian council at Treaty Rock, Berens River (12 July 1890). For a published version of this document, see Document One, 'Notes on Indian Council at Treaty Rock, Beren's River, Lake Winnipeg, Man. 12th July 1890,' *Native Studies Review* 3, no. 1 (1987): 117-27.
47 Ibid.
48 Ibid.
49 Ibid.
50 CSP, 1891, Fisheries, no. 8, p. 56.
51 CSP, 1890, Fisheries, no. 17, pp. 233-4.
52 CSP, 1891, Fisheries, no. 8, p. 61.
53 Ibid., 60.
54 Ibid., 56.
55 Ibid., 62.
56 Ibid.
57 CSP, 1873, Fisheries, no. 8, p. 194.

Chapter 9: Economic Boom and Native Labour

1 *The Manitoba Daily Press* (8 October 1888).
2 Ibid.
3 Ibid.
4 Ibid.
5 A.A. den Otter, 'Transportation and Transformation: The Hudson's Bay Company, 1857-1885,' *Great Plains Quarterly* 3, no. 3 (Summer 1983): 178-89; H. Bowsfield, ed., *The Letters of Charles John Brydges: 1879-1882* (Winnipeg: Hudson's Bay Record Society 1977), 112.
6 T. Barris, *Fire Canoe: Prairie Steamboat Days Revisited* (Toronto: McClelland and Stewart 1977), 62-3.
7 Using data from the Hudson's Bay Company Archives, the annual reports for the Department of Fisheries, and Crown Timber Agency reports from the Department of the Interior, I calculate that for the Lake Winnipeg/Interlake region in 1885 the value of fur production was $35,756 and the value of fish and lumber production was $93,618. In 1886, fur production was worth $31,923 and fish and lumber production was worth $61,495.
8 Barris, *Fire Canoe*, 230-2.
9 Ibid., 253. The reports of the Crown Timber agents do not indicate the same degree of concentration of sawmill operations on Lake Winnipeg as implied by Barris. Canada, *Sessional Papers*, 1902, Reports of the Crown Timber agents, annual reports of the Department of the Interior, no. 25, p. 98. (Hereafter referred to as CSP, Timber.)
10 Barris, *Fire Canoe*, 208-14.
11 Ibid., 197.
12 Provincial Archives of Manitoba, H.A. Bayfield, 'Diary and Photographs of a trip from Winnipeg to Port Nelson,' 27 May to 22 June 1915, MG1 B24, p. 7. (Hereafter referred to as PAM, Bayfield, MG1 B24.)
13 CSP, 1906, Indian Affairs, no. 27, p. 81. Baker mentions a Cree steamboat captain on Lake Winnipeg. See George Barker, *Forty Years a Chief* (Winnipeg: Peguis 1979), 33.
14 Barris, *Fire Canoe*, 92-3.
15 CSP, 1896, Interior, no. 13, pp. 45, 49.
16 NAC, RG 10, vol. 7056, file 501/20-7-17 (6 May 1917).
17 NAC, RG 10, vol. 3677, file 11528 (18 April 1882).
18 CSP, 1884, Indian Affairs, no. 4, p. 137.
19 CSP, 1889, Indian Affairs, no. 16, p. 80.
20 UCCA, Stevens, 3.
21 CMS, A-110 (8 April 1882).
22 Ibid.

23 CSP, 1883, Indian Affairs, no. 5, p. 141.
24 CSP, 1905, Indian Affairs, no. 27, pp. 113-14.
25 Provincial Archives of Manitoba, H.A. Bayfield, 'Lake Winnipeg Trip,' 1899, MG1 B25, p. 3. (Hereafter referred to as PAM, Bayfield, MG1 B25.)
26 CSP, 1905, Indian Affairs, no. 27, p. 115.
27 CSP, 1910, Indian Affairs, no. 27, p. 115.
28 CSP, 1884, Indian Affairs, no. 4, pp. 57, 59.
29 CSP, 1905, Indian Affairs, no. 27, p. 117.
30 CSP, 1885, Indian Affairs, no. 3, p. 54.
31 NAC, RG 10, vol. 7461, file 18, 125-5(1) (17 October 1894).
32 CSP, 1887, Indian Affairs, no. 6, p. 161.
33 CSP, 1891, Indian Affairs, no. 18, p. 130.
34 NAC, RG 10, vol. 7844, file 30125-3 (30 January 1914).
36 In fact the first sawmill at The Pas was purchased by the band with its annuities. This sawmill was used to improve housing. CSP, 1905, Indian Affairs, no. 27, p. 110. Barris noted that in one year 1,400 men and 400 horses were put to work at The Pas lumbering operations. Barris, *Fire Canoe*, 195, 198, and 204. For more details on the lumber industry in Manitoba, see J.P. Mochoruk, 'The Political Economy of Northern Development: Government and Capital along Manitoba's Resource Frontier, 1870 to 1930' (Ph.D. diss., University of Manitoba 1992), 113-33.
37 PAM, Bayfield, MG1 B25, p. 5.
38 CSP, 1901, Keewatin, no. 25, p. 3.
39 CSP, 1893, Indian Affairs, no. 14, p. 166.
40 CMS, A-118 (4 July 1893).
41 CSP, 1910, Indian Affairs, no. 27, p. 103.

Chapter 10: Economic Change and Incomes
1 CSP, 1901, Indian Affairs, no. 27, p. 88.
2 CSP, 1897, Indian Affairs, no. 14, p. 115.
3 CSP, 1899, Indian Affairs, no. 14, p. 72.
4 CSP, 1901, Indian Affairs, no. 27, p. 79.
5 CSP, 1906, Indian Affairs, no. 27, p. 99.
6 CSP, 1883, Indian Affairs, no. 5, p. 37.
7 CSP, 1886, Indian Affairs, no. 4, p. 45.
8 CSP, 1888, Indian Affairs, no. 15, p. 54.
9 CSP, 1887, Indian Affairs, no. 6, p. 47.
10 CSP, 1893, Indian Affairs, no. 14, p. 143.
11 CSP, 1900, Indian Affairs, no. 14, p. 77.
12 CSP, 1872, Indian Affairs, no. 22, p. 31.
13 CSP, 1901, Indian Affairs, no. 27, p. 98.
14 CSP, 1914, Indian Affairs, no. 27, p. 112. For example, with the Ebb and Flow reserve in 1913, Inspector S.J. Jackson reported: 'This band is making very little progress, and the gardens show that very little attention is being given to them. No vegetables were visible in the garden at the date of my visit, though the chief said that the various seeds and potatoes were sown. The members of this band go out to work with the farmers a good deal and neglect their own places.' CSP, 1914, Indian Affairs, no. 27, p. 114.
15 CSP, 1903, Indian Affairs, no. 27, p. 88.
16 Canada, *Sessional Papers*, 1901, Dominion Lands Office, Annual Report of the Department of the Interior, no. 25, p. 19.
17 CSP, 1905, Indian Affairs, no. 27, p. 94.
18 CSP, 1917, Indian Affairs, no. 27, pp. 40-1.
19 NAC, RG 10, vol. 4019, file 279393-6 (5 March 1913).
20 CSP, 1908, Indian Affairs, no. 27, p. 135.
21 CSP, 1913, Indian Affairs, no. 27, p. 117.
22 CSP, 1915, Indian Affairs, no. 27, p. 47.

23 CSP, 1912, Indian Affairs, no. 12, p. 102.
24 See NAC, RG 10, vol. 4009, file 249462, pt. 1 (21 October 1909); CSP, 1910, Indian Affairs, no. 27, p. 104; CSP, 1913, Indian Affairs, no. 27, pp. 104, 122; CSP, 1916, Indian Affairs, no. 27, pp. 54-5.
25 CSP, 1882, Indian Affairs, no. 6, p. xxxviii.
26 CSP, 1914, Indian Affairs, no. 27, p. 88.
27 CSP, 1915, Indian Affairs, no. 27, p. 46.
28 CSP, 1889, Indian Affairs, no. 16, p. 47.
29 CSP, 1906, Indian Affairs, no. 27, p. 95.
30 CSP, 1905, Indian Affairs, no. 27, p. 81.
31 PAM, Bayfield, MG1 B24, p. 5.
32 HBCA, B.154/b/11 (3 January 1883).
33 Ibid.
34 HBCA, D.25/2 (1887), fol. 69.
35 HBCA, D.25/6 (1889), fol. 173.
36 HBCA, A.74/1 (1891), ff. 140-1.
37 HBCA, D.25/13 (1891), fol. 236. Similarly, it was reported for Berens River: 'The Indians are comparatively well off. Many of them do not hunt furs in winter, but are employed in fishing. Said to be lazy as hunters.' HBCA, D.25/13 (1891), fol. 297.
38 HBCA, A.12/FT 322/1 (a) (1905), fol. 173.
39 HBCA, B.49/e/13 (1887), fol. 1.
40 HBCA, B.285/e/1 (1891), fol. 1.
41 HBCA, D.25/19 (1893), fol. 17.
42 The first written references by Indian agents to women selling tanned hide articles was made in 1915. See CSP, 1915, Indian Affairs, no. 27, p. 46; and CSP, 1917, Indian Affairs, no. 27, p. 41.
43 CSP, 1900, Indian Affairs, no. 14, p. 106.
44 CSP, 1902, Indian Affairs, no. 27, p. 73.
45 NAC, RG 10, vol. 8046, file 501/32-3-4-3 (21 April 1899); see also CSP, 1900, Indian Affairs, no. 14, p. 107.
46 CSP, 1902, Indian Affairs, no. 27, p. 91.
47 CSP, 1883, Indian Affairs, no. 5, p. 34; CSP, 1904, Indian Affairs, no. 27, p. 115; and NAC, RG 10, vol. 4009, file 249462, pt. 1A (24 October 1910). Jim Mochoruk documented a lower wage rate in frontier lumbering areas than in cities. See Mochoruk, 'The Political Economy of Northern Development: Government and Capital along Manitoba's Resource Frontier, 1870 to 1930' (Ph.D. diss., University of Manitoba 1992), 119-20.
48 CSP, 1904, Indian Affairs, no. 27, p. 82.
49 CSP, 1903, Indian Affairs, no. 27, p. 96.
50 CSP, 1888, Indian Affairs, no. 15, p. 54.
51 CSP, 1894, Indian Affairs, no. 14, p. 47.
52 CSP, 1901, Indian Affairs, no. 27, p. 109.
53 CSP, 1902, Indian Affairs, no. 27, p. 77.
54 CSP, 1904, Indian Affairs, no. 27, pp. 98-9.
55 CSP, 1885, Indian Affairs, no. 3, p. 53.
56 CSP, 1901, Indian Affairs, no. 27, p. 80.
57 CSP, 1886, Indian Affairs, no. 4, p. 46.
58 CSP, 1905, Keewatin, no. 25, p. 4. During the HBC monopoly, the Company's paternalistic system dealt with wills and pensions.
59 CSP, 1902, Indian Affairs, no. 27, p. 77.
60 CSP, 1897, Indian Affairs, no. 14, p. 112.
61 CSP, 1901, Indian Affairs, no. 27, p. 79.
62 CSP, 1917, Indian Affairs, no. 27, p. 43.
63 CSP, 1903, Indian Affairs, no. 27, p. 96.
64 CSP, 1906, Indian Affairs, no. 27, p. 95; and CSP, 1904, Indian Affairs, no. 27, p. 99.
65 CSP, 1897, Indian Affairs, no. 14, p. 112.

66 CSP, 1904, Indian Affairs, no. 27, p. 130.
67 CSP, 1888, Indian Affairs, no. 27, p. 58.
68 CSP, 1897, Indian Affairs, no. 14, p. 112.
69 CSP, 1884, Indian Affairs, no. 4, p. 56.
70 CSP, 1905, Indian Affairs, no. 27, p. 116.
71 Ibid., 120.
72 CSP, 1889, Indian Affairs, no. 16, p. 51.
73 CSP, 1904, Indian Affairs, no. 27, p. 116.
74 CSP, 1908, Indian Affairs, no. 27, p. 75.
75 Baker, *Forty Years a Chief,* 33.
76 CSP, 1886, Indian Affairs, no. 4, p. 67.
77 CSP, 1908, Indian Affairs, no. 27, p. 76.
78 CSP, 1905, Indian Affairs, no. 27, p. 116.
79 CSP, 1915, Indian Affairs, no. 27, p. 41.
80 UCCA, Stevens, 44.
81 CSP, 1910, Indian Affairs, no. 27, p. 85.
82 See CSP, 1913, Indian Affairs, no. 27, p. 114; and CSP, 1914, Indian Affairs, no. 27, p. 88.
83 CSP, 1910, Indian Affairs, no. 27, p. 84.
84 CSP, 1901, Indian Affairs, no. 27, p. 79.
85 CSP, 1888, Indian Affairs, no. 15, p. 54.
86 E.P. Thompson, *The Making of the English Working Class* (Harmondsworth: Penguin Books 1968), 230, 231 (originally published in 1963).

Chapter 11: Surplus Labour, Migrations, and Stagnation
1 CMS, A-113 (24 September 1885).
2 Ibid.
3 HBCA, B.154/e/14 (1875), fol. 2d.
4 Ibid., fol. 3. Ross's statement here implies that some of the Norway House Village Indians were originally Red River Halfbreeds. This is possible, since the recruitment of Portage La Loche brigades shifted from Red River to Norway House in about 1871.
5 Ibid., fol. 3.
6 UCCA, Semmens, 30.
7 HBCA, B.154/b/11 (14 August 1880).
8 PAM, Schultz Papers, MG12 E1, no. 4651, McDonald to Schultz (September 1890).
9 PAM, Schultz Papers, MG12 E1, no. 6331, McLean to Schultz (14 September 1893).
10 HBCA, A.74/9 (1900), fol. 22.
11 PAM, Schultz Papers, MG12 E1, no. 4863, *Bégin Report.*
12 UCCA, Stevens, 15; see also NAC, RG 10, vol. 3722, file 24161 (18 February and 20 July 1897).
13 UCCA, Stevens, 15.
14 Ibid., 32. Stevens brought some of the Sandy Lake Crane Indians out to tell their story. See also NAC, RG 10, vol. 3722, file 24161, Chipman to Indian Commissioner (6 June 1901); *Manitoba Free Press* (29 May, 14 August, and 29 August 1901). Between 15 and 20 Indians died of starvation. For more information on the starvation in the Sandy Lake area, see Chief Thomas Fiddler and James R. Stevens, *Killing the Shamen* (Moonbeam: Penumbra Press 1985), 61-8. Fiddler and Stevens suggest that between 20 and 35 people died.
15 *Manitoba Free Press* (28 August 1901); see also PAM, Schultz Papers, MG12 E1, no. 6332, McLean to Schultz (14 September 1893); and NAC, RG 10, vol. 3722, file 24161 (3 October 1901).
16 See NAC, RG 10, vol. 3722, file 24161 (8 February 1898, 14 October 1901, 9 January 1902).
17 NAC, RG 10, vol. 3722, file 24161 (8 February 1898, 14 October 1901).
18 NAC, RG 10, vol. 3722, file 24161 (9 January 1902).
19 Ibid. Emphasis added.
20 NAC, RG 10, vol. 3722, file 24161, Semmens to Laird (15 October 1901).

21 Annuity Paylists, Genealogical Research Unit, Indian and Northern Affairs Canada, Ottawa.
22 CSP, 1913, Indian Affairs, no. 27, p. 88.
23 NAC, RG 10, vol. 4009, file 249462, pt. 1A (24 October 1910).
24 Ibid.
25 Ibid.
26 Ibid.
27 Ibid.
28 Ibid.
29 CSP, 1916, Indian Affairs, no. 27, p. 56.
30 CSP, 1898, Keewatin, no. 13, p. 6.
31 The address of the House of Commons and Senate (29 and 31 May 1869) to the Queen stated: 'That upon the transference of the territories in question to the Canadian Government it will be our duty to make adequate provision for the protection of the Indian tribes whose interests and well-being are involved in the transfer, and we authorize and empower the Governor in Council to arrange any details that may be necessary to carry out the terms and conditions of the above agreement.' Oliver, *Canadian North-West*, 954.
32 CSP, 1897, Indian Affairs, no. 14, p. 127.
33 CSP, 1904, Keewatin, no. 25, p. 4.
34 CSP, 1900, Indian Affairs, no. 14, p. 107.
35 CSP, 1907, Indian Affairs, no. 27, p. 81.
36 HBCA A.12/FT MISC/227 (1914-15).
37 CSP, 1910, Indian Affairs, no. 27, p. 85.

Chapter 12: The Demise of Native Fisheries
1 CSP, 1876, Indian Affairs, no. 9, article of a treaty concluded at Berens River (20 September 1875) and Norway House (24 September 1875), xxxvii.
2 NAC, RG 10, vol. 3581, file 878, pt. A, included a copy of *Regulations Relating to Fishing in Manitoba and the North-West Territories* (8 May 1894) from *Canada Gazette* (26 May 1894). (Hereafter referred to as *Fisheries Regulations, 1894*.)
3 PAM, Schultz Papers, MG12 E3, box 19, notes of an Indian council at Treaty Rock, Berens River (12 July 1890).
4 CSP, 1876, Indian Affairs, no. 9, p. xxxvi, Treaty Five.
5 Ibid.
6 NAC, RG 10, vol. 3788, file 43850 (12 March 1888). S. Stewart noted in a memo: 'There is little reason for doubt that the Indians believed that they would be allowed to fish and hunt for all time without being compelled to pay a license fee. This view is confirmed by statements made by Commissioners who took part in the conferences when the Treaties were made.' NAC, RG 10, vol. 3908, file 107297-1, memorandum signed by S. Stewart (ca. 1895).
7 NAC, RG 10, vol. 3788, file 43856.
8 NAC, RG 10, vol. 3788, file 43856 (letter received 12 January 1889).
9 NAC, RG 10, vol. 3788, file 43856 (20 December 1889).
10 CSP, 1882, Indian Affairs, no. 6, p. 67.
11 CSP, 1884, Indian Affairs, no. 4, p. 144.
12 Ibid.
13 PAM, Schultz Papers, MG12 E3, box 19, Butler to Schultz (8 September 1889). The depositing of spawn by fish caught in nets would not necessarily ensure fertilization, survival, and propagation. Whitefish generally spawn on a hard, stony, or sandy bottom in depths of water less than twenty-five feet. W.B. Scott and E.J. Crossman, *Freshwater Fishes of Canada* (Ottawa: Fisheries Research Board of Canada 1973), 271.
14 PAM, Schultz Papers, MG12 E3, box 19, Tupper to Schultz (10 October 1889).
15 PAM, Schultz Papers, MG12 E3, box 19, notes of an Indian council at Treaty Rock (12 July 1890).
16 Ibid.

17 *Fisheries Regulations, 1894.*
18 NAC, RG 10, vol. 3573, file 149, pt. 1 (21 July 1881).
19 NAC, RG 10, vol. 3908, file 107297.1, memo on fishing privileges claimed by Indians (18 November 1895), including an extract of a letter by S. Dawson (28 April 1895).
20 PAM, Schultz Papers, MG12 E3, box 19, Phair to Schultz (1888).
21 NAC, RG 10, vol. 3865, file 84823, Fisheries Inspector Gilchrist's report on a meeting with The Pas Indians (4 July 1893).
22 Ibid.
23 For a more detailed analysis of fish yields, see Frank Tough, 'Native People and the Regional Economy of Northern Manitoba' (Ph.D diss., York University 1987), 252-4.
24 CSP, 1892, Fisheries, no. 11, p. 161.
25 This ratio is based on the observation of J. Bégin (North-West Mounted Police) at Grand Rapids. See Thomas Andrew Judson, 'The Freshwater Fishing Industry of Western Canada' (Ph.D diss., University of Toronto 1961), 32.
26 NAC, public records of the Department of Marine and Fisheries, RG 23, vol. 366, file 3216 (3). Minutes of the Royal Commission 1909-10. (Hereafter RG 23.)
27 Scott and Crossman, *Freshwater Fishes*, 86.
28 CSP, 1899, Fisheries, no. 11A, p. 208.
29 CSP, 1904, Fisheries, no. 22, p. 205.
30 CSP, 1899, Fisheries, no. 11A, p. 208.
31 CSP, 1901, Fisheries, no. 22, p. 153; and CSP, 1904, Fisheries, no. 22, p. 202.
32 CSP, 1906, Fisheries, no. 22, p. 196.
33 CSP, 1904, Fisheries, no. 22, p. 202.
34 CSP, 1906, Fisheries, no. 22, p. 196; and CSP, 1905, Fisheries, no. 22, p. 207.
35 Local fisheries inspectors commented on the importance of sturgeon for domestic fisheries. Professor E.E. Prince, Dominion Commissioner of Fisheries, was aware of the many aspects of sturgeon fisheries. See Prince, 'The Canadian Sturgeon and Caviar Industry,' in CSP, Fisheries, no. 22, Special Appended Reports, pp. liii-lxx.
36 CSP, 1901, Indian Affairs, no. 27, p. 104.
37 CSP, 1903, Fisheries, no. 22, p. 117; CSP, 1903, Fisheries, p. 123; and CSP, 1904, Fisheries, no. 22, p. 205. Fish in the round refers to a complete fish. Sometimes fish were purchased headless or with the offal removed. There is no evidence that Indians were paid for caviar at the Nelson River fishery. Records suggest that after 1900 an oligopolistic situation existed, where Ewing and Fryer and the Dominion Fish Company reduced the price of sturgeon products by purchasing sturgeon in the round. Prior to the merger, sturgeon eggs were purchased from fishermen at one dollar per pail and were sold by the companies for fifteen dollars. NAC, RG 23, vol. 112, file 110 (2) (2 May 1899). In the 1890s, when prices were lower (flesh at five cents per pound and eggs at fifty cents per pound), a 50 pound sturgeon with 20 pounds of roe would be worth $12.50. CSP, 1905, Fisheries, no. 22, p. lxii.
38 CSP, 1904, Fisheries, no. 22, p. 205; and CSP, 1909, no. 22, Fisheries, p. 205.
39 CSP, 1905, Fisheries, no. 22, p. 208.
40 CSP, 1906, Fisheries, no. 22, p. 193.
41 CSP, 1912, Fisheries, no. 22, p. 283.
42 CSP, 1899, Fisheries, no. 11A, p. 215.
43 See Tough, 'Native People and the Regional Economy,' 261.
44 NAC, RG 23, vol. 112, file 110 (2) (2 May 1899).
45 NAC, RG 23, vol. 112, file 110 (2), Statement made before Prof. Prince and Mr. Wilmot re: application for a commercial licence for 1894 (12 May 1894).
46 NAC, RG 23, vol. 112, file 110 (2), petition (19 April 1900).
47 NAC, RG 23, vol. 365, file 3216 (1) (16 March 1908).
48 See NAC, RG 23, vol. 112, file 110 (2), petitions (3 May 1899 and 19 April 1900); and NAC, RG 23, vol. 365, file 3216 (1).
49 NAC, RG 23, vol. 366, file 3216 (3), minutes of the commission of 1909-10.
50 Ibid.
51 Ibid.

52 Ibid.
53 Canada, Dominion Fisheries Commission for Manitoba and the North West: 1909-10, *Interim Report and Recommendations* (Ottawa: Government Printing Bureau 1909), 5.
54 Ibid., 5-6.
55 Ibid., 6.
56 *Report of the Manitoba Fisheries Commission, 1909-1910* is found in the National Library of Canada under Canadian Federal Royal Commission Reports, microfiche 51, no. 148, 1911.
57 *Moody's Manual of Railroad and Corporation Securities, 1916* (New York: Moody's Manual Company 1916), 3971.
58 Until the creation of the Freshwater Fish Marketing Corporation, Manitoba fish producers received a small portion of the market value of the fish.

Chapter 13: The Demise of the Hudson's Bay Company and the Re-Emergence of Competition

1 Harold A. Innis, *The Fur Trade in Canada* (Toronto: University of Toronto Press 1956), 378. Innis's earlier work, *The Fur-Trade of Canada* (Toronto: University of Toronto Library 1927), is an important study of the post-1870 period.
2 HBCA, B.154/e/11 (3 April 1880); B.154/e/19 (1889); and B.156/e/5 (1885).
3 HBCA, A.74/5 (1896), fol. 31.
4 HBCA, D.FTR/11 (1919), fol. 51.
5 CMS, A-112 (25 July 1884).
6 HBCA, D.25/6 (1889), fol. 219.
7 HBCA, A.74/5 (1895), fol. 31.
8 HBCA, A.74/7 (1897), fol. 28.
9 HBCA, B.53/e/2 (1888), fol. 7.
10 HBCA, A.74/20 (1910), fol. 19.
11 HBCA, A.74/17 (1907), fol. 21.
12 HBCA, A.74/7 (1897), ff. 20-1.
13 HBCA, A.12/FT 322/1(c) (1908), fol. 85.
14 HBCA, A.74/21 (1911), fol. 13.
15 HBCA, D.FTR/11 (1919), fol. 69.
16 HBCA, A.74/42 (1927), fol. 15.
17 HBCA, D.FTR/27 (1934), fol. 5.
18 HBCA, D.FTR/19 (1918), fol. 62.
19 HBCA, A.74/43 (1928), fol. 2.
20 HBCA, B.154/e/15 (1885), fol. 1.
21 CMS, A-117 (ca. January 1890).
22 HBCA, A.74/42 (1927), fol. 5.
23 HBCA, B.154/a/78, fol. 7d.
24 HBCA, B.154/b/11 (20 July 1878).
25 HBCA, B.239/b/135 (12 December 1887).
26 HBCA, D.FTR/25 (1932), fol. 4.
27 HBCA, A.74/18 (1908), fol. 20.
28 HBCA, A.74/1 (1891), fol. 184.
29 HBCA, A.74/40 (1925), fol. 40.
30 HBCA, A.74/39 (1924), fol. 9. There was also an agreement between the HBC and Revillon Fréres to exchange information. A.74/41 (1920), fol. 4.
31 HBCA, D.FTR/23 (1930), fol. 7.
32 HBCA, B.154/e/23 (1889), fol. 1.
33 HBCA, B.154/e/9 (1889), fol. 7.
34 HBCA, D.FTR/13 (1920), fol. 93.
35 Innis, *Fur-Trade of Canada*, 132.
36 HBCA, A.74/34 (1923), fol. 219.
37 Ibid., 214.
38 HBCA, A.74/35 (1924), fol. 10.

39   HBCA, A.74/35 (1924). The Northern Trading Company operated in the Mackenzie District. Max Finklestein bought it out in 1925 and reorganized as Northern Traders Limited. Innis, *Fur Trade In Canada*, 366. In 1926 Northern Traders Limited operated in the Saskatchewan District. HBCA, A.74/41 (1926), fol. 9. A concern which may have been related to Finkelstein, Northern Trading Company began to operate at Berens River in 1927 and at Norway House in 1928. HBCA, A.74/42 (1927), fol. 13; and A.74./43 (1928), fol. 9.
40   HBCA, A.74/39 (1925), fol. 9.
41   Innis, *Fur-Trade of Canada*, 137.
42   J. Melven, *The Fur Industry of Manitoba* (Manitoba Economic Survey Board 1938), 8.
43   HBCA, A.74/12 (1902), fol. 17.
44   There appear to be at least eight different white trappers in the Churchill area. One of these trappers had previously operated at Great Slave Lake. HBCA, B.42/a/208 (August 1929). See also D.FTR/23 (1930-1), fol. 5.
45   Innis, *Fur Trade in Canada*, 375.
46   For example, in the Setting Lake area 'cash goes out of the country entirely, the majority of the trappers in that vicinity being whitemen, who have interests elsewhere on which they spend their money.' See HBCA, A.74/38 (1924), fol. 155.
47   HBCA, B.296/e/4 (1900-01), fol. 2.
48   HBCA, B.154/e/18 (1888), fol. 5.
49   HBCA, A.74/7 (1898), fol. 25.
50   HBCA, A.74/32 (1923), fol. 11.
51   HBCA, D.FTR/23 (1930), fol. 4.
52   Ibid.
53   HBCA, D.FTR/127 (1934), fol. 5.
54   HBCA, A.74/42 (1927), fol. 9.
55   Tom Boulanger, *An Indian Remembers: My Life as a Trapper in Northern Manitoba* (Winnipeg: Peguis 1971), 2.
56   Ibid., 10.
57   HBCA, D.FTR/17 (1922), fol. 126.
58   Provincial Archives of Manitoba, Arthur J. Jan, 'Memoirs of 56 Years in Canada,' MG8 B41 (1960), 46. (Hereafter referred to as PAM, Jan, MG8 B41.)
59   Ibid., 45-6.
60   Ibid., 46.
61   Ibid., 47. Boulanger recalled that with the right prices he would ship to George Soudack. Boulanger, *An Indian Remembers*, 11.
62   Innis, *Fur-Trade of Canada*, 119.
63   Melven added: 'So from generation to generation, the fur trade in northern Manitoba took its even way, returning handsome profits to investors in London ... and playing the beneficent despot to the Indian.' Melven, *Fur Industry of Manitoba*, 4-5.
64   Ibid., 5.
65   HBCA, A.74/23a (1914), fol. 3.
66   Ibid.
67   HBCA, A.74/24 (1915), fol. 5. The overall decline in the Company's volume was 53 per cent. HBCA, A.74/23a (1914), fol. 4.
68   HBCA, A.74/24 (1915), fol. 6; and A.74/25 (1916), ff. 3-4.
69   HBCA, A.74/25 (1916), ff. 5-6.
70   Ibid. fol. 5.
71   HBCA, A.74/24 (1915), fol. 4.
72   HBCA, A.74/25 (1916), fol. 5.
73   HBCA, A.74/22 (1913), fol. 3.
74   Melven, *Fur Industry of Manitoba*, 6.
75   HBCA, D.FTR/13 (1920), fol. 63.
76   Ibid.
77   PAM, Jan, MG8 B41, p. 47.
78   Ibid.

79 Ibid. Jan also suggested that Funsten Bothers took several banks with them when they went down.
80 HBCA, A.74/32 (1923), fol. 12.
81 HBCA, RG 2/106, fur purchase tariff (uncatalogued material).
82 HBCA, D.FTR/26 (1933), fol. 8. The amounts paid for fur were $3,408,00 (1930); $2,601,000 (1931); $2,015,000 (1932); and $1,617,000 (1933).
83 Ibid., fol. 14. The Company's profits were +$14,311 (1930); -$37,514 (1931); -$19,421 (1932); and +$9,144 (1933).
84 Melven, *Fur Industry of Manitoba*, 6.
85 Innis, *Fur Trade in Canada*, 374-5.
86 HBCA, B.154/k/1, fol. 145.
87 HBCA, D.38/1, rule 33.
88 HBCA, B.154/k/1, fol. 36.
89 Ibid., fol. 178.
90 CMS, A-99 (12 December 1868).
91 CMS, A-114 (11 June 1886).
92 CMS, A-117 (30 November 1890).
93 HBCA, B.49/e/8 (1875), fol. 3d.
94 HBCA, B.154/a/70 (11 January 1873).
95 HBCA, B.154/e/23 (1890), fol. 4.
96 HBCA, A.74/11 (1901), fol. 19.
97 HBCA, B.42/e/11 (1889), ff. 7-8.
98 For the problem of intra-post rivalry, see HBCA, B.42/b/62, B.42/e/11, B.239/b/135, B.239/e/11, B.239/e/13, B.239/e/16, and D.25/6.
99 HBCA, A.11/119a (1 December 1880).
100 HBCA, B.285/e/4 (1901), fol. 1.
101 HBCA, D.FTR/15 (1921), fol. 93.
102 HBCA, D.FTR/17 (1922), fol. 134.
103 HBCA, D.FTR/23 (1930), fol. 11.
104 HBCA, A.11/119a (1 December 1880).
105 HBCA, D.FTR/11 (1919), fol. 57.
106 Ibid., fol. 36.
107 HBCA, B.154/a/94 (8 April 1937). This observation is verified by Norway House Indian Agent Lasenby: 'I find that a number of Indians are selling only a portion of their catch to the traders and holding the rest, hoping for a better price later on.' NAC, RG 10, vol. 6737, file 420-4-3 (April 1937).
108 HBCA, B.239/e/8 (1873), fol. 4d.
109 HBCA, B.154/e/19 (1889), fol. 4.
110 HBCA, B.156/e/9 (1889), ff. 2-3.
111 HBCA, B.16/a/10 (17 April 1888).
112 HBCA, B.156/e/12 (1891), fol. 2.
113 HBCA, B.154/e/23 (1889), fol. 4.
114 CMS, A-118 (7 February 1893).
115 CMS, A-111 (15 March 1883), and A-115, (24 December 1888).
116 HBCA, B.154/b/11 (14 October 1885).
117 HBCA, A.74/1 (1891), fol. 144.
118 HBCA, B.154/e/22 (1890), fol. 4; see also B.49/e/16, B.239/e/14, and B.156/e/11.
119 HBCA, D.25/19 (1891-4), fol. 90.
120 HBCA, B.156/e/11 (1890), fol. 2.
121 HBCA, B.154/e/17, fol. 2.
122 Ibid., fol. 3; and A.74/1 (1891), fol. 187.
123 HBCA, B.16/a/11 (7 October 1900).
124 HBCA, B.16/a/11 (9 November 1901).
125 HBCA, A.74/1 (1891), fol. 208.
126 HBCA, B.154/b/11 (22 December 1883).

127   HBCA, D.FTR/9 (1918), fol. 62.
128   HBCA, D.FTR/3 (1914), fol. 69.
129   HBCA, B.154/a/70 (9 June 1873).
130   HBCA, B.154/a/94 (31 May 1937).
131   HBCA, B.49/e/8 (1875).
132   HBCA, B.49/e/10 (1886), ff. 4d-5.
133   HBCA, B.42/b/62; A.11/119a (1 December 1880), and B.154/b/11.
134   HBCA, D.FTR/8 (1917), fol. 47.
135   HBCA, B.156/e/10 (1890), fol. 2.
136   HBCA, D.25/6 (1889), fol. 434.
137   HBCA, D.FTR/3 (1914), fol. 64.
138   HBCA, B.154/k/1 (1892), fol. 145.
139   HBCA, B.154/a/87 (7 February 1919).
140   HBCA, A.74/42 (1927), fol. 7.
141   HBCA, B.154/b/11 (5 January 1885).
142   HBCA, B.49/e/8 (1875), fol. 3d. In another instance, Donald A. Smith noted: 'Five parties of Free Traders have wintered in it, some being well supplied with flour have collected more Furs than they would have done in the absence of this useful article of trade.' HBCA, A.11/51 (1 August 1870), fol. 94.
143   HBCA, D.25/1 (1886), fol. 30.
144   HBCA, B.154/a/78 (21 December 1895).
145   CMS, A-99 (21 March 1869).
146   HBCA, A.74/32 (1923), fol. 11.
147   HBCA, B.49/e/9 (1885), fol. 1d.
148   HBCA, B.239/e/8 (1873-4), fol. 6.
149   HBCA, B.42/b/62 (19 July 1871).
150   PAM, Jan Papers, MG8 B41, p. 20.
151   Ibid.
152   HBCA, B.156/e/9 (1889), fol. 8.
153   HBCA, B.239/e/15 (1890), fol. 3.
154   HBCA, A.74/42 (1927), fol. 13.
155   Innis, *Fur Trade in Canada*, 376; see also Arthur J. Ray, *The Canadian Fur Trade in the Industrial Age* (Toronto: University of Toronto Press 1990).
156   Innis, *Fur Trade in Canada*, 376.
157   See HBCA, A.76/35, district and post balances (1918).
158   Ray, *The Canadian Fur Trade*.
159   HBCA, D.25/19 (1894), fol. 156.

Chapter 14: Industrial Capital, Native People, and the Regional Economy
1   HBCA, B.154/b/11 (3 January 1883).
2   Canada, *Census of Canada 1921*, vol. 1, and *Census of Canada 1931*, vol. 2. Northern Manitoba may be defined as Census Division 16.
3   Provincial Archives of Manitoba, Claude Johnston, Reminiscences of Northern Manitoba – the Bay Railway, MG11 A22, p. 29. (Hereafter referred to as PAM, Johnston, MG11 A22.)
4   Ibid., 41.
5   Ibid., 30.
6   NAC, public records for Royal Commissions, RG 33/52, vol. 1, file 7. (Hereafter RG 33.)
7   NAC, RG 33/52, vol. 2, file 36. Another figure gave 573,521 as the acreage, but this included 89,005 acres that had been surrendered.
8   Ibid.
9   If the lower estimate of total reserve acreage is used, then 15.5 per cent of the reserves had been surrendered and 6.3 per cent had yet to be surveyed.
10   Glenbow-Alberta Institute, A.N664, Reverend John W. Niddrie, 'Familiar Places and Names or, Manitoba Hinterland,' 3, 6.
11   HBCA, D.FTR/15 (1921-2), fol. 88.

12 HBCA, B.154/a/94 (12 August 1936).
13 PAM, Johnston, MG11 A22, pp. 61, 70, and 5.
14 Ibid., 32.
15 Harold A. Innis, 'The Hudson Bay Railway,' *Geographical Review* 20, no. 1 (January 1930): 28.
16 Canada, Statistics Canada, *Survey of Production, 1976,* vol. 55 (November 1978), catalogue 61-292, annual, pp. 38, 41-3.
17 NAC, RG 33/52, vol. 2, file 36. The annual expernditure for these treaties, according to Duncan Campbell Scott, was $326,000.
18 See R.G. Zahalan, *Mining in Manitoba* (Winnipeg: Manitoba Department of Energy and Mines, Mineral Resources Division 1980), 16, 19.
19 NAC, RG 10, vol. 6817, file 486-6-9 (1939-43).
20 Provincial Archives of Manitoba, public records of the Department of Natural Resources, RG 17B1, box 74, file 44.4.1A. (Hereafter referred to as PAM, RG 17 B1.)
21 HBCA, A.74/43 (1928-9), fol. 3.
22 NAC, RG 10, vol. 8047, file 501/32-4-4, pt. 2 (20 December 1937).
23 HBCA, A.74/40 (1925-6), fol. 64.
24 HBCA, A.11/51 (25 June 1862).
25 HBCA, A.74/18 (1908-9), fol. 55.
26 HBCA, B.285/e/1 (1891), fol. 2.
27 Arthur J. Ray, *The Canadian Fur Trade in the Industrial Age* (Toronto: University of Toronto Press 1990).
28 PAM, Johnston, MG11 A22, p. 17.
29 Ibid., 35.
30 National Archives of Canada, public records of the Royal Canadian Mounted Police, RG 18, vol. 3156, file G.846-4-21 (22 August 1921).
31 HBCA, B.42/a/208 (1929-30); PAM, Johnston, MG11 A22, p. 139.
32 HBCA, A.74/42 (1927), fol. 2.
33 Ibid.
34 HBCA, A.74/43 (1928), fol. 3.
35 PAM, Jan, MG8 B41, p. 45.
36 George Barker, *Forty Years a Chief* (Winnipeg: Peguis 1979), 61.
37 NAC, RG 10, vol. 6737, file 420-4-2 (9 January 1928).
38 Ibid.
39 Document collection (Churchill file, 478/30-54), Treaties and Historic Research Centre, Indian and Northern Affairs Canada.
40 NAC, RG 10, vol. 6731, file 420-1 (2 February 1929).
41 PAM, RG 17 B1, box 35, file 38.1.1. This resolution is not dated; possibly it passed on 2 July 1930.
42 Provincial Archives of Manitoba, John Bracken, Premier's Office Papers, MG13 I2, box 37, file 423, A.G. Cunningham, Report on Game Conditions (20 November 1930), p. 8.
43 Ibid., 1.
44 HBCA, A.92/Can 251/1. This document has been published in 'Health and Disease at the Norway House Indian Agency, 1926, by Dr. E.L. Stone,' *Native Studies Review* 5, no. 1 (1989): 237-56.
45 Ibid.
46 Ibid.
47 Ibid.
48 Ibid.
49 PAM, RG 17 B1, box 45, file 13.9.1 (11 April 1928).
50 NAC, RG 10, vol. 7844, file 30125-4 (5 February 1926).
51 NAC, RG 10, vol. 7844, file 30125-4 (2 August 1928).
52 Barker, *Forty Years a Chief,* 50.
53 Ibid., 9.
54 NAC, RG 10, vol. 6731, file 420-1.

55 PAM, RG 17 B1, box 51, file 46.1.1 (6 June 1938).
56 NAC, RG 10, vol. 7599, file 10125-3 (4 October 1937).
57 PAM, RG 17 B1, box 51, file 46.1.1 (6 June 1938).
58 HBCA, D.FTR/23 (1930-1), fol. 16.
59 Ibid.
60 HBCA, D.FTR/25 (1932-3), fol. 7.
61 PAM, Johnston, MG11 A22, p. 133.
62 Theodore Barris, *Fire Canoe: Prairie Steamboat Days Revisited* (Toronto: McClelland and Stewart 1977), 228.

Conclusion

1   The findings of this study are similar to Elias's work on the economic history of the Dakota of Manitoba and Saskatchewan. See Peter Douglas Elias, *The Dakota of the Canadian Northwest: Lessons for Survival* (Winnipeg: University of Manitoba Press 1988). For British Columbia, see Percy Gladstone, 'Native Indians and the Fishing Industry of British Columbia,' *Canadian Journal of Economics and Political Science* 19, no. 1 (1953): 20-34; and James K. Burrows, '"A Much-Needed Class of Labour": The Economy and Income of the Interior Southern Plateau Indians, 1897-1910,' *BC Studies* no. 71 (1986): 27-46. A pioneering, but most influential work in the area of Indian economic history is Rolf Knight's *Indians at Work: An Informal History of Native Labour in British Columbia, 1858-1930* (Vancouver: New Star Books 1978).
2   E.P. Thompson, *The Making of the English Working Class* (Harmondsworth: Penguin Books 1968), 222.
3   Laura L. Peers, 'Changing Resource-Use Patterns of Saulteaux Trading at Fort Pelly, 1821 to 1870,' in *Aboriginal Resource Use in Canada: Historical and Legal Aspects,* ed. Kerry Abel and Jean Friesen (Winnipeg: University of Manitoba Press 1991), 116.
4   Ibid.
5   In fact, any Indian reports suggesting difficulties with material production are classified as trade rhetoric. This evidence is then reclassified as Indian manipulation of traders because Indians received assistance from the post.
6   On this topic, see Sidney L. Harring, 'The Rich Men of the Country: Canadian Law in the Land of the Copper Inuit, 1914-1930,' *Ottawa Law Review* 21, no. 1 (1989): 1-64.
7   See the seminal piece by Irene M. Spry, 'The Tragedy of the Loss of the Commons in Western Canada,' in *As Long as the Sun Shines and Water Flows,* ed. I.A.C. Getty and A.S. Lussier (Vancouver: University of British Columbia Press 1983), 203-28.
8   Morris Zaslow, *The Opening of the Canadian North: 1870-1914* (Toronto: McClelland and Stewart 1971), 234.
9   For a very crucial analysis of economic history and Aboriginal rights, see Dianne Newell, *Tangled Webs of History: Indians and the Law in Canada's Pacific Coast Fisheries* (Toronto: University of Toronto Press 1993).
10 Arthur J. Ray, *The Canadian Fur Trade in the Industrial Age* (Toronto: University of Toronto Press 1990), 201.
11 Ibid., 220-1.
12 Ibid., 221.
13 Frank Tough, 'Manitoba Commercial Fisheries: A Study In Development' (M.A. thesis, McGill University 1980).
14 Ronald F. Laliberte, 'The Canadian State and Native Migrant Labour in Southern Alberta's Sugar Beet Industry' (M.A. thesis, University of Saskatchewan 1994).
15 See, for example, Stuart Jamieson and Harry Hawthorn, 'The Role of Native People in Industrial Development in Northern Manitoba, 1960-1975,' working paper prepared for the Committee on Manitoba's Economic Future, 1962.
16 Toby Morantz, '"So Evil a Practice": A Look at the Debt System in the James Bay Fur Trade,' in *Merchant Credit and Labour Strategies in Historical Perspective,* ed. Rosemary E. Ommer (Fredericton: Acadiensis Press 1990), 202-32. This is an interesting compilation of information on HBC credit.

17 Ronald L. Trosper, 'That Other Discipline: Economics and American Indian History,' in *New Directions in American Indian History*, ed. Colin. G. Calloway (Norman: University of Oklahoma Press 1988), 199-222.

Appendix A

1 HBCA, B.49/e/13 (1887), fol. 2.
2 HBCA, A.74/1 (1891), ff. 56, 52.
3 HBCA, B.49/e/17 (1891), fol. 4.
4 For an account of the changing organization of the industry and the movement of prices, see Arthur J. Ray, *The Canadian Fur Trade in the Industrial Age* (Toronto: University of Toronto Press 1990).

Appendix C

1 This model is based on the later northern scrip commissions. The scrip issued under the Manitoba Act, 1870, and in the scrip commissions in the late 1880s would only approximate this particular representation.
2 NAC, RG 15, vol. 1043, file 1748598 (9 September 1910), Secretary P.G. Keyes to John Semmens.
3 Typescript copy of a section of bulletin no. 21 (2 January 1930), Department of the Interior, copy found in PAM, RG 17, box 89, B1, file 17.2.1 (19 November 1931).
4 Frank Tough and Leah Dorion, '"The Claims of the Half-Breeds ... Have Been Finally Closed": A Study of Treaty Ten and Treaty Five Adhesion Scrip,' unpublished research report for the Royal Commission on Aboriginal Peoples, Saskatoon, 1993, p. 57.
5 There are other Department of the Interior files on this family's claims, but already the presentation is complicated.
6 Their scrip information is in file 1748629.
7 Norway House had been ceded in 1875. However, in this sense the Dominion government was treating Indians and Metis very differently. In the adhesion to Treaty Five, Indians that had moved from the unceded territory were added to the Norway House and Cross Lake bands, as were any of their children who had been born after moving to the ceded territory. In effect they were placed in a large class of potential claimants who had been born after 1885 in ceded territory.
8 In this sense, scrip rules did not treat all living Metis claimants equally.
9 NAC, RG 15, vol. 1043, file 1748598 (25 May 1910), Secretary P.G. Keyes to John Semmens.
10 Ibid.
11 Her declaration indicates that the family had left Norway House in 1892 and that she had married James Swanson in 1889 at York Factory. (James Swanson's declaration reported that they had married in 1890.) Another child was born in April 1910. This application indicates that five children had died, but the other four had not been baptized. This would explain why only George Swanson was identified as a child who had died. Note that G.S. Winter had spelt Maria Swanson's maiden name (Bowen) as Bone.
12 It probably arrived with some correspondence from Semmens (9 November 1910) as he mentions a baptismal certificate for 'Mariah' Swanson.
13 Along with William and Maria Swanson, land scrip granted to Jessie Sanders, William Sanders, and George Oman, all of northern Manitoba, was forwarded for redbacking.
14 NAC, RG 15, vol. 1043, file 1748598 (16 January 1922).
15 NAC, RG 15, vol. 1043, file 1748598, affidavit of George Stewart Macrae (30 August 1921).
16 NAC, RG 15, vols. 1406 and 1410. Bruno Lundgreen must have known a number of Metis, since he endorsed the backs of some thirty-three scrip certificates from the Treaty Five adhesion scrip.
17 NAC, RG 15, vol. 1016, file 1578625, pt. 2.

Index

Migration, 219-24, *224*; economic influences on, 219-20; effect of treaty process on, 103; to Fisher River, 57, 224, 228, 231, 232; from Gods Lake, 226; to Interlake, 220, 224, 227, 300; Methodist scheme for, 224-8; missionary influence on, 220; from Norway House, 171, 220, 224, 231; to Norway House, 103; from Oxford House, 224, 226, 231; policies of Department of Indian Affairs, 219, 226, 231, 233; policies of HBC, 220, 223, 226; problems with, 228-31; to Split Lake, 103, 222; to Winnipeg, 309; from York Factory, 66, 68, 70, 72, 103, 171, 219, 220, 222, 224, 226-8, 231-3, 270, 300
Miller, E. (Fisheries Inspector), 241, 242, 243
Mining, 192, 202, 203, 287, 288, 306-8
Mink. *See* Fur bearers
Mission settlements, 144-6
Molson Lake, 215
Moodie, E.D. (RNWMP), 111-12
Moody's Manual of Railroads and Corporation Securities, 247
Moore, Willie, 214
Moose. *See* Game
Moose Island, 196
Moose Lake, 4; agriculture at, 166; fisheries, 176, 241; reserve, 156, 157; seasonal economy, 27, 31, *33*
Moose Lake Indians, 151, 203-4, 242
Morris, Alexander (Lieutenant-Governor), 80, 81, 83, 84, 88, 90, 91, 101, 110, 151, 165
Muckle A.M. (Indian Agent), 169, 200, 201, 205, 211, 212, 214, 218, 235

Nanton, Augustus (HBC), 137, 138, 140
Natural Resources, transfer of, 141, 293, 344 n. 8
Nelson House: credit/debt at, 274; fur trade at, 256; fur trade competition at, 254; HBC fur trade profits at, 250; Native labour at, 58; reserve survey, 156, *158*; settlement at, 146; sketch plan of, *40*; and Treaty 5 adhesions, 106, 343 n. 48; treaty problems, 111
Nelson River, 3, 26, 27; introduction of commercial fishing to, 239; steamboating on, 192; sturgeon fishing in, 240-2
Nelson River Indians: Aboriginal title of, 102; migration to Norway House, 103; request for treaty, 102; trade, 270
Nesbitt Liquidators, 267
New York, 258, 281
Niddrie, Rev. J.W. (missionary), 285

Nolin, Charles, 7, 8, 84
North West Company, 231, 258
North West Navigation Co. (NWN Co.), 188, 189
Northern Department. *See* Hudson's Bay Company
Northern Fish Company, 207, 290
Northern Trading Company, 260, 267, 358 n. 39
Northwest Territories Council, and Indian treaties, 78
Northwestern Territory, 228
Norway House, 3, 15, 23, 27, 31, 35, *38*, 54, 56, 60, 66, 67, 70; adhesions to, *225*; agriculture at, 166, 214; credit/debt at, 274, 275; decline of fur trade at, 251; district returns from, 310; economy of, *22*, 290; fisheries, 175, 200, 240-1; freighting at, 285; fur trade, 257-8, 273, 277, 278, 310, 313, *314*; Metis/Halfbreeds at, 119, 148, 162, 354 n. 4; migration of surplus population, 171, 220, 224, 231; moving of provisions to, 48; Native labour at, 58, 216; overpopulation at, 294; payment of annuities at, 101; relief at, 296; resource use, *21*; scrip, 136, 327, 363 n. 7; seasonal economy, 20, *24*, 35; settlement at, 146, 160; sketch plan of, *38*, 39-40; trade goods at, 279; as a trans-shipping centre, 48, 53; and Treaty 5 adhesions, 106
Norway House Indians: railway employment, 204; and forestry, 192; relocation to Fisher River, 222; reserve, 148-9, 222; trade, 270

Ojibwa: and agriculture, 144; importance of fish to, 175; movement of, 231, 340 n. 59; and sturgeon fisheries, 248; and Treaty 3, 84, 89, 91, 93
Oji-Cree, 3
Oman, Alexander, 129, 136, 332-3, 346 n. 44, 347 n. 68, 363 n. 13
Order-in-Council. *See* Scrip
'Original affluent society,' 52, 300
Osler, Hammond, and Nanton (law firm), 346 n. 44
Outside Promises, 97-8, 108
Oxford House, 3, 40, 56, 60, 66, 273; concluding of treaty at, 110; credit/debt at, 274, 275; dependency on wage labour, 62; fisheries, 27; government reasons for rejecting treaty, 104-5; impact of treaty, 112; living standards at, 222; migration from, 224, 226, 231; mining at, 288; prices at, 277; scrip at, 125; seasonal cycle at, 27, *30*; settlement